ROUTLEDGE LIBRARY EDITIONS: INTERNATIONAL TRADE POLICY

Volume 7

THE CONTRIBUTIONS OF JOHN MAYNARD KEYNES TO FOREIGN TRADE THEORY AND POLICY

THE CONTRIBUTIONS OF JOHN MAYNARD KEYNES TO FOREIGN TRADE THEORY AND POLICY

1909–1946

JOSEPH R. CAMMAROSANO

LONDON AND NEW YORK

First published in 1987 by Garland Publishing, Inc.

This edition first published in 2018
by Routledge
2 Park Square, Milton Park, Abingdon, Oxon OX14 4RN

and by Routledge
711 Third Avenue, New York, NY 10017

Routledge is an imprint of the Taylor & Francis Group, an informa business

© 1987 Joseph R. Cammarosano

All rights reserved. No part of this book may be reprinted or reproduced or utilised in any form or by any electronic, mechanical, or other means, now known or hereafter invented, including photocopying and recording, or in any information storage or retrieval system, without permission in writing from the publishers.

Trademark notice: Product or corporate names may be trademarks or registered trademarks, and are used only for identification and explanation without intent to infringe.

British Library Cataloguing in Publication Data
A catalogue record for this book is available from the British Library

ISBN: 978-1-138-06323-5 (Set)
ISBN: 978-1-315-14339-2 (Set) (ebk)
ISBN: 978-1-138-29516-2 (Volume 7) (hbk)
ISBN: 978-1-138-29519-3 (Volume 7) (pbk)
ISBN: 978-1-315-10075-3 (Volume 7) (ebk)

Publisher's Note
The publisher has gone to great lengths to ensure the quality of this reprint but points out that some imperfections in the original copies may be apparent.

Disclaimer
The publisher has made every effort to trace copyright holders and would welcome correspondence from those they have been unable to trace.

FOREIGN ECONOMIC POLICY OF THE UNITED STATES

The Contributions of John Maynard Keynes to Foreign Trade Theory and Policy
1909–1946

JOSEPH R. CAMMAROSANO
Fordham University

GARLAND PUBLISHING, INC.
NEW YORK & LONDON • 1987

Copyright © 1987 Joseph R. Cammarosano
All rights reserved

For a complete list of the titles in this series,
see the final pages of this volume.

Library of Congress Cataloging-in-Publication Data

Cammarosano, Joseph R.
  The contributions of John Maynard Keynes to foreign
trade theory and policy, 1909-1946.

  (Foreign economic policy of the United States)
  Originally presented as the author's thesis (Ph.D.--
Fordham University, 1956)
  Bibliography: p.
  1. Commercial policy. 2. International economic
relations. 3. Keynes, John Maynard, 1883-1946--
Contributions in commercial policy. I. Title.
II. Series.
HF1411.C323   1987   382.1'04   87-23775
ISBN 0-8240-8076-9

All volumes in this series are printed on acid-free,
250-year-life paper.

Printed in the United States of America

TABLE OF CONTENTS

PART I: KEYNES' NATIONALISM AS EVIDENCED BY HIS OPPOSITION TO THE INTERNATIONAL GOLD STANDARD

Chapter   Page

I. INTRODUCTION.................................... 1

II. KEYNES WAS OPPOSED TO THE PRE-WORLD WAR I GOLD STANDARD, BECAUSE, BY FAILING TO EFFECT AN ECONOMY IN THE USE AND A CENTRALIZATION OF GOLD RESERVES IN THE VAULTS OF THE CENTRAL BANK, IT HAMPERED THE MONETARY AUTHORITY IN ITS ATTEMPT TO PROTECT THE ECONOMY FROM INTERNAL AND EXTERNAL DISEQUILIBRIA........................... 22

III. KEYNES WAS OPPOSED TO THE TRADITIONAL GOLD STANDARD, BECAUSE IT DID NOT PERMIT THE PURSUANCE OF AUTONOMOUS MONETARY POLICIES........... 36

IV. KEYNES WAS OPPOSED TO THE PRE-WORLD WAR I GOLD STANDARD, BECAUSE ITS RIGID EXCHANGE RATE SYSTEM WAS DISRUPTIVE OF INTERNAL PRICE STABILITY AND FACILITATED THE INTERNATIONAL TRANSMISSION OF ECONOMIC FLUCTUATIONS THROUGH CHANGES IN NATIONAL PRICE LEVELS.............................. 47

V. KEYNES' PRIOR CONCERN WITH THE PROMOTION AND MAINTENANCE OF DOMESTIC EQUILIBRIUM AS EVIDENCED BY HIS OPPOSITION TO GREAT BRITAIN'S RETURN TO THE GOLD STANDARD AT THE PRE-WAR PARITY OF EXCHANGE... 64

VI. KEYNES' QUEST FOR NATIONAL AUTONOMY AS EVIDENCED BY HIS PREFERENCE FOR A MANAGED MONETARY STANDARD... 90

PART II: THE EVOLUTION OF KEYNES' THINKING ON FOREIGN TRADE THEORY AND POLICY

VII. KEYNES' EARLY FREE TRADE VIEWS...................... 124

VIII. THE TREATISE ON MONEY............................... 132

IX. ADDENDUM I TO THE MACMILLAN REPORT.................. 152

X. THE REVENUE TARIFF EPISODE......................... 170

XI. GREAT BRITAIN'S ABANDONMENT OF THE GOLD STANDARD.... 197

XII.	THE MEANS TO PROSPERITY	207
XIII.	NATIONAL SELF-SUFFICIENCY	223

PART III: KEYNES' FOREIGN TRADE VIEWS DURING THE ERA OF THE GENERAL THEORY

XIV.	THE THEORY OF EMPLOYMENT AND ITS IMPLICATIONS FOR INTERNATIONAL ECONOMICS	241
XV.	THE NATURE OF INVESTMENT AND ITS IMPLICATIONS FOR INTERNATIONAL ECONOMICS	265
XVI.	KEYNES IS SYMPATHETIC TOWARDS A PROTECTIONIST POLICY IN HIS TREATMENT OF MERCANTILISM	287
XVII.	KEYNES' FOREIGN TRADE VIEWS IN THE PERIOD PRIOR TO WORLD WAR II	297

PART IV: KEYNES OF THE WORLD WAR II ERA

XVIII.	THE INTERNATIONAL CURRENCY PROPOSALS	307
XVIX.	KEYNES' FORMULATION OF THE CLEARING UNION AND HIS SUBSEQUENT ENDORSEMENT OF THE INTERNATIONAL MONETARY FUND AGREEMENT DID NOT CAUSE HIM TO RESCIND THE HIGH PRIORITY WHICH HE HAD ATTACHED TO NATIONAL ECONOMIC CONSIDERATIONS DURING THE INTER-WAR PERIOD, BECAUSE BOTH SCHEMES UPHOLD THE RIGHT OF EACH MEMBER STATE TO DETERMINE ITS OWN POLICIES	339
XX.	THE ANGLO-AMERICAN FINANCIAL ARRANGEMENTS	367
XXI.	CONCLUSION	393
	BIBLIOGRAPHY	404

CHAPTER I

INTRODUCTION

Over the course of his life, Keynes often abandoned ideas previously developed and at times assumed positions which were contradictory to his earlier thought.[1] This inconsistency, it is charged, is especially true of his thinking in the field of international economics where he alternated between free trade

---

1. That Keynes was inconsistent in certain areas of thought cannot be questioned, but this was only because the views of Keynes the economist reflected those of Keynes the administrator, the adviser, the business man, the statesman and the diplomat (Cf. "The Law and the Prophet," The London Economist, CLV, 5492, Nov. 27, 1948, p. 879) and if ideas previously developed were unable to stand the test of practicability, he was quick to discard them and set to thinking along different channels. Keynes was essentially practical, and when convinced that the best solution to a problem was unattainable, he was willing to seek another. He had "no vested interest in his own past thoughts" and never permitted them to impede further intellectual progress. (Cf. "John M. Keynes," The London Economist, CLV, 5492, April 27, 1946, p. 658.)

For some, consistency involves pressing the same solution through thick and thin just because it is the best solution. Whether there is any hope of its being adopted does not enter into their consideration. To these people, going over to a less satisfactory, though more practical, solution seems to constitute an inconsistency. But so far as Keynes was concerned, "no one ever better demonstrated that a foolish consistency is the hobgoblin of little minds." (Vide R. F. Harrod, The Life of John Maynard Keynes, New York, Harcourt, Brace and Company, 1951, p. 469 and "John M. Keynes," The London Economist, op. cit., p. 658.)

and protection.[1]

That Keynes did so vacilate between "internationalism" and "nationalism" cannot be denied. Keynes was, as we shall have occasion to see more fully in the development of this thesis, a free trader at least up to 1923.[2] After this date, his views on the efficacy of free trade underwent change with the consequence that in the spring of 1931 he openly came out in favor of protection for Great Britain.[3] After the Treasury's abandonment of the gold standard in September, 1931, Keynes modified his views somewhat respecting the need for protection.[4] He thought that the advantage to be gained by British industry from a devalued pound now made the question of restricted trade obsolete; however, his new position did not reinstate him as a free trader, for during the remainder of the 'thirties he largely favored a policy of national autarky.[5] It was not until he began his thinking on the Clearing Union proposal in late 1941

---

1. R. Hinshaw, "Keynesian Commercial Policy," The New Economics, ed. S. Harris, New York, Alfred A. Knopf, 1947, p. 315.
2. J. M. Keynes, "Free Trade," The Nation and Athenaeum, XXIV, 8, Nov. 24, 1923, pp. 302-303.
3. J. M. Keynes, "Proposals for a Revenue Tariff," The New Statesman and Nation, I N.S. 2, Mar. 7, 1931, pp. 53-54.
4. J. M. Keynes, "The Tariff Question" (Letter to the Editor), The London Times, Sept. 29, 1931, p. 15.
5. J. M. Keynes, "National Self-Sufficiency I," The New Statesman and Nation, VI, N.S. 124, July 8, 1933, pp. 65-67.

that he gave any indication of moderating his views on the question of international economic cooperation.[1] But despite this change of attitude, it is questionable whether Keynes did completely revert to the free trade doctrine espoused by the classical school of thought, or whether his new position still left him outside the pale of orthodoxy.

In view of the variable and uncertain nature of Keynes' position on this question of free versus restricted trade, it is impossible to find any common agreement as to what his ultimate status was on this issue. For example, L. R. Klein believes that Keynes' break with classical thinking on free trade was of short duration. He asserts that, although Keynes broke with the free traders in 1931, he "made a complete turn-about on the question of free trade" in 1933 with his publication of *The Means to Prosperity*, wherein he suggested a simultaneous expansion of trade through the abolition of trade restrictions.[2] Dr. Seymour Harris is also of the conviction that Keynes' break with free trade was short-lived. He maintains that Keynes broke with the protectionists as soon as more effective tools than tariffs were fashioned for the attainment of international equilibrium.[3] Presumably, he is referring to the devaluation of the British pound in September, 1931, following Great Britain's abandonment of the gold standard.

---

1. R. F. Harrod, op. cit., pp. 525-526.
2. L. R. Klein, *The Keynesian Revolution*, New York, Macmillan Co., 1947, pp. 41-42.
3. S. Harris, "International Economic Relations: Introduction," *The New Economics*, op. cit., p. 245.

There is another body of opinion which feels that, although Keynes did return to the free trade camp, it was not until a much later period. Professor Alvin H. Hansen, the foremost Keynesian economist in this country, contends that Keynes had a change of heart respecting free trade sometime towards the end of 1941.[1] Others, like R. F. Harrod[2] and H. R. Burrows,[3] claim that Keynes reverted to his position of free trader only towards the close of his life.

There is a third school of thought which claims that Keynes was never able to resolve the conflict between "nationalism" and "internationalism". This is the contention of A. E. Robinson who was one of Keynes' students at Cambridge and at present is co-editor of The Economic Journal.[4] The London Economist similarly questions whether Keynes effectively resolved this question. According to it, Keynes, through the greater part of his career, had tried to insulate the domestic economy from the disturbances of the outer world; and yet, as chief architect of the Bretton Woods system, accepted many provisions from the Americans which

---

1. A. H. Hansen, A Guide to Keynes, New York, McGraw-Hill Co., 1954, pp. 225-227.
2. R. F. Harrod, op. cit., pp. 469-470, p. 531 and pp. 609-610.
3. H. R. Burrows, "J. M. Keynes - Part I - His Life and Thought," The South African Journal of Economics, XX, 2, June, 1952, p. 164.
4. A. E. Robinson, "John M. Keynes," Economic Journal, LVII, 225, March, 1947, p. 46.

contravened his traditional position. His untimely death, which "caught him in one of his major inconsistencies," cheated him of the opportunity to resolve this difficulty one way or another.[1]

In the face of this conflicting testimony, how must historians of economic doctrine ultimately interpret Keynes' stand on the question of free versus restricted international trade? Did Keynes, in modifying his protectionist position of the 'thirties, revert unequivocally to the principles of classical free trade towards the end of his life or did he fail to close the breach completely? How must he be classified? This, in effect, is the question to be answered by this dissertation.

The position of this thesis is that, after he divorced himself from the tenets of classical free trade in the early 'thirties, Keynes never again returned to them, as such. Instead, he subscribed to those principles of international trade and finance, developed by him from the Tract on Monetary Reform to the General Theory, which placed considerations of internal equilibrium above those of a purely external character.

In this paper, the answer to the question whether or not Keynes was a free trader or protectionist is not predicated on his advocacy or rejection of tariffs. If this were the criterion for judging Keynes' international trade position, he would, of necessity, have to be classified as a free trade, for he openly favored tariffs only for a matter of a few months in 1931.

---

1. "John M. Keynes," The London Economist, op. cit., p. 658.

The fact that Keynes may not have consistently favored the imposition of tariffs does not of itself make him a member of the classical free trade school, for many of the objectives obtainable through a restrictive trade program can be just as readily secured by other protective devices such as regulation of foreign investment, exchange control, quotas, adjustment of exchange rates, exhortations to buy at home, etc.

The issue involved here is far more subtle than whether or not Keynes favored the imposition of tariff barriers on the flow of international trade. The problem in this thesis deals not so much with Keynes' commercial policy, as such, as it does with the broader question of determining whether his economic philosophy was based on national or on international considerations. Only by first resolving this question will it be possible to determine whether or not Keynes was, in the final analysis, an orthodox free trader.

An important clue to this question respecting Keynes' "nationalism" or "internationalism" may be had by examining his attitude towards the so-called automatic international monetary adjustments. The difficulty confronting Keynes in the international sphere was not unlike the one he had to countenance in the domestic sector, namely, could the most intimate relations of our economic system be left to the operation of the so-called automatic forces or should they be subjected to some form of conscious guidance and control? A brief examination of Keynes' General Theory of Employment, Interest and Money reveals that he was emphatically in favor of the latter course of action.[1] And his attitude was no different so far as the conduct of a nation's external affairs is concerned. Truly, Keynes was "no more sympathetic to the old orthodoxy that prevailed in external economic policy than to that which obtained in internal policy."[2]

Insofar as the free traders of the classical and neo-classical schools of economic thought are concerned, they would leave the adjustments required for the restoration or maintenance of external equilibrium, i.e. balance in the foreign account, to be made by purely "automatic" forces such as gold flows, fluctuations in income and prices, changes in interest rate policy etc.[3] Often, these devices succeeded in obtaining the desired equilibrium only by sacrificing domestic well-being through the dissemination of internal deflation and unemployment.

Keynes, however, rejected the utilization of such "automatic" forces which depended upon the disruption of internal equilibrium

---

1. That this was Keynes' attitude may be demonstrated by his recommendation that national monetary authorities pursue cheap money policies in an effort to reduce the level of interest, so that it might better equate with the marginal efficiency of capital and thereby encourage investment. Failing this, he argued, governments should then institute public works programs to help restore the level of employment.
2. A. L. Rowse, Mr. Keynes and the Labor Movement, London, Macmillan and Co., Ltd., 1936, p. 41.
3. We are referring here, of course, to the period in which the international gold standard enjoyed universal acceptance.

for their efficacy. Instead, he recommended the employment of devices which would consciously effect the necessary correction in the external sector, while leaving the internal economy unaffected. In place of an automatic gold standard Keynes would substitute a managed standard; in lieu of a stable exchange rate and a fluctuating domestic price level, he recommended a variable exchange rate and a stable domestic price level; instead of inflating and deflating the currency and credit system, as a means of satisfying the requirements of the gold flows, he would establish an autonomous monetary policy geared to meet the purely internal needs of the economy; and in place of exchange appreciation he favored exchange stabilization. The fact that Keynes was opposed to having adjustments which are required for the maintenance or restoration of external equilibrium adversely effect the domestic economy and that he sought to have their incidence fall on the external sector, instead, clearly indicates the priority which he accorded to national over international economic considerations.

Another factor which helps to establish Keynes' primary concern with internal problems and thus further distinguishes him from the more internationally-minded neo-classicists is his preoccupation with the problem of unemployment. In Keynes' view, a condition of full employment is the exception rather than the rule, for the economy has a tendency to equilibrate at a level of less than full employment. In consequence of this condition, Keynes is vitally concerned with seeking measures whereby the volume of consumption and particularly the amount of investment may be increased, so that national income and employment may be sustained at a high level. Thus, by the very nature of the objective which he sought to achieve, viz. full employment of manpower and resources, it is clear that Keynes had to accord prior preference to national over international requirements.

The classicists and neo-classicists, on the other hand, start with the assumption that full employment already exists; hence, their main concern is with the optimum allocation and most efficient use of economic resources. Their thinking is largely constructed in terms of the opportunity cost analysis which naturally presages the validity of the comparative cost argument.[1] In their system, free international trade is the logical answer to their quest for the optimum allocation and maximum efficiency of the productive factors. Thus, by virtue of the objectives which they seek, the classical and neo-classical economists are of necessity more inclined towards "internationalism".

Keynes was keenly aware of the advantages to be derived from a system of free international trade when combined with

---

1. In formulating their theory of comparative advantage and the derived theory of comparative cost, the classicists of the early nineteenth century and even the neo-classicists of this century did so in terms of the long rather than the short run period; hence, they assumed away the problem of unemployment. (Cf. N. S. Buchanan, N.S., *International Investment and Domestic Welfare*, New York, Henry Holt and Co., p. 57.)

the full utilization of manpower and resources. Under such an ideal condition of full employment and free trade among nations, wages and other forms of real income would be maximized, for productivity would be at its highest possible level. In this type environment, each country would produce those items in which it enjoyed the greatest comparative advantage and exchange them with other countries for commodities in which they enjoyed the highest comparative advantage. Given a condition of full employment, Keynes found it difficult to deny the economic advantages of free trade, as the following passage from the General Theory will bear out.

> If nations can learn to provide themselves with full employment by their domestic policy, there need be no important economic forces calculated to set the interest of one country against that of its neighbors.
>
> International trade would cease to be what it is, namely, a desperate expedient to maintain employment at home by forcing sales on foreign markets and restricting purchases, which, if successful, will merely shift the problem of unemployment to the neighbor which is worsted in the struggle, but a willing and unimpeded exchange of goods and services in conditions of mutual advantage.[1]

However, Keynes was not equally convinced of the virtues of free trade under conditions of less than full employment. If it be admitted that the self-restorative powers of the modern economy are sufficiently strong to guarantee a reasonably high

---

1. J. M. Keynes, The General Theory of Employment, Interest and Money, New York, Harcourt, Brace and Company, 1935, pp. 382-383.

level of employment and income, the arguments in favor of free trade cannot be refuted. But if the international specialization of labor be carried on between economies that are experiencing less than full employment of their manpower and resources, then it does not necessarily follow that these nations will be better off in pursuing a policy aimed at increasing productivity and expanding trade, for what is gained through the international division of labor may be more than offset by the displacement of workers in the home market.[1] A second argument which may be presented against the free trade doctrine in conditions of depressed activity is that adherence by a nation to a liberal commercial policy and the promotion of full employment policies, e.g. monetary expansion, are often times incompatible in such circumstances.[2] Thus, just as Keynes was forced to question classical theory, generally, because of its illicit assumption of full employment, so, too, it was this postulate which caused him, specifically, to take exception with the doctrine of free trade.

Essentially, the problem for free traders and Keynesians alike is to find measures whereby domestic policies do not restrain international cooperation and whereby international

---

1. N. S. Buchanan, op. cit., p. 150. Also Cf. D. Dillard, The Economics of John M. Keynes, New York, Prentice-Hall, Inc., 1948, p. 283.
2. J. E. Meade, Public Works in their International Aspect, London, The New Fabian Research Bureau, 1933, pp. 17-20.

policies do not introduce instability into domestic employment.[1] Ideally, each country should enjoy simultaneously the high productivity of labor resulting from free trade and the maximum national output resulting from the full utilization of its productive capacity.[2] Unfortunately, it is not always possible for a nation to enjoy both of these advantages, because of the conflict which often emerges between its membership in an open free trade system and its promotion of full employment policies. Professor G. Haberler pinpoints this issue and indicates the difficulty of resolving it in the following very lucid terms.

> One of the most challenging tasks of rational economic policy and one of the most intriguing and controversial problems to economic science is how to avoid or eliminate conflicts between domestic prosperity and maximum gain from international trade and international division of labor. Maximization of national output and income depends on both, full employment of resources at home and full utilization of the opportunities of international trade.
>
> Conflicts between the two conditions in the sphere of monetary and fiscal policy are quite frequent, because measures appropriate for maintaining full employment are not always conducive to promoting stability of foreign exchange and of international trade and vice versa. These conflicts are rarely, if ever, irreconcilable, but there is no simple formula or easy automatic device which would permit satisfactory conciliation in every single case.[3]

Now, the specific difference between Keynes and the classical free traders is that should the conflict between the promotion of domestic

---

1. J.B. Condliffe, "Exchange Stabilization and International Trade," The Review of Economic Statistics, XXVI, 4, November, 1944, p. 166.
2. T. Scitovszky, "Trade of Nations - A Review," Journal of Political Economy, LV, 5, October, 1947, p. 475.
3. G. Haberler, "Comments on National Central Banking and the International Economy," (n.d.), p. 82.

prosperity and the stability of international trade be irreconcilable, Keynes would support the former, while the classical free traders would go along with the latter alternative. Keynes was basically a "nationalist," for unlike the classicists who were concerned with the development of principles applicable to an open or world economic system, he was largely engrossed with the formulation of principles for a closed economic system.[1] As a result of his deep appreciation of the problem of unemployment, an understanding which the neo-classicists did not possess, Keynes was more acutely aware of the needs of the domestic economy, and, so, more inclined to placing them above purely external considerations. Add to this the fact that he was primarily a Briton, and one has the essential reasons why Keynes cannot be classified as a free trader in the tradition of the neo-classical school.

Keynes was at all times and above all else a Briton. Although he was intensely concerned with the interwar problems as they affected the community of nations, he was particularly concerned with the way in which they influenced the position of Great Britain.[2] Keynes' writings were always concerned with the formulation of policies to meet the changing status of English economic life.[3] His theories were fundamentally the product of the post-World War I depressions, especially the long period of deflation existing in Great Britain during the 'twenties and the world-wide holocaust of the 'thirties, which was in a

---

1. J.H. Williams, *Postwar Monetary Plans*, Oxford, Basil Blackwell, 1949, p. 160.
2. J.H. Williams, "An Appraisal of Keynesian Economics," *American Economic Review*, XXXVIII, 2, May, 1948, p. 275.
3. B. Banerjii, *A Guide to the Study of Keynesian Economics*, Calcutta, N.N. Dey, 1951, p. 62.

way superimposed on the continuing British depression.[1]

In tracing the development of Keynes' thought during this era it is well to bear in mind that the Great Britain which emerged from World War I was a seriously weakened nation. British foreign trade and investment was decreasing in importance. London was steadily losing her international supremacy. Taxes were heavy. British industry was plagued by obsolescence. The formerly well disciplined English laborers were now well organized. British costs relative to the rest of the world were too high. Tastes and technology were changing rapidly. Many of Britain's former customers were able to take care of needs formerly supplied by her, e.g. cotton goods. In addition to these ominous developments, Great Britain had to face in her foreign markets the increasing competition of the United States, which was rapidly becoming the dominant world power in wealth and productive capacity.[2]

Schumpeter aptly summarizes the British situation after World War I in the following way.

> She (Great Britain) had not emerged from the war of the Napoleonic era. She had emerged impoverished; she had lost many of her opportunities for the moment and some of them for good. Not only this, but her social fabric had been weakened and had become rigid. Her taxes and wage rates were incompatible with vigorous development, yet there was nothing that could be done about it.[3]

---

1. C.B. Hoover, "Keynes and the Economic System," The Journal of Political Economy, LVI, 5, Oct., 1948.
2. G.A. Elliott, "The Significance of the General Theory of Employment, Interest and Money," Canadian Journal of Economic and Political Science, XIII, 3, August, 1947, p. 372.
3. J.A. Schumpeter, Ten Great Economists from Marx to Keynes, New York, Oxford University Press, 1951, p. 274.

Keynes was conscious of these new conditions. He was especially aware of the impact which these changes would exert on the international sphere. And it was out of his desire to cope with these changes that he was forced to alter his position, in consequence of which, he was accused of inconsistency. However, one should not make the mistake of identifying Keynes' practical inconsistency, if such it should be called, with an inconsistency of the Keynesian mind.[1]

That Keynes' economic thinking was always colored by British considerations may be elicited from the following excerpt of an article written by the Canadian economist, W. A. Mackintosh.

> The most steadfast of his (Keynes') roots was his passionate belief in and concern for England. This is often not explicit in his writings but is imbedded in the fabric and is an essential clue to the pattern. From the "Economic Consequences of the Peace" to his last article in the Economic Journal, whether he was concerned with the dismemberment of Europe, the flexibility of the exchange rates, the relation between investment and income, or buffer stocks of food and raw materials, the pattern of his problem was English.[2]

The essentially nationalistic and particularly British character of Keynes thinking may be further substantiated by Schumpeter's excellent testimony.

---

1. R. F. Harrod, op. cit., p. 470.
2. W. A. Mackintosh, "Keynes as a Public Servant," Canadian Journal of Economics and Political Science, XIII, 3, August, 1947, p. 380.

> It cannot be emphasized too strongly that
> Keynes' advice was in the first instance
> always English advice, born of English
> problems even where addressed to other
> nations. Barring some of his artistic
> tastes, he was surprisingly insular,
> even in philosophy, but nowhere so much
> as in economics. And he was fervently
> patriotic - of a patriotism which was
> indeed quite untinged by vulgarity but
> was so genuine as to be subconscious and
> therefore all the more powerful to impart
> a bias to his thought and to exclude full
> understanding of foreign viewpoints,
> conditions, interests, and especially
> creeds. Like the old free-traders, he
> always exalted what was at any moment
> truth and wisdom for England into truth
> and wisdom for all times and places.[1]

It now remains for this thesis to show that, because of the priority which he assigned to the realization of internal equilibrium, as reflected by stable prices and high levels of employment, Keynes could not accept unequivocally and without reservation the traditional tenets of unrestricted multilateral trade. More specifically, the task of this paper is two-fold: first, to establish Keynes' bias towards "nationalism"; and second, to indicate how this prior concern for the attainment of domestic equilibrium conditioned his views on the question of foreign trade.

On account of the many varied meanings associated with the term, "nationalism,"[2] it is well at the very outset of this work

---

1. J. A. Schumpeter, op. cit., p. 274.
2. Webster defines nationalism as "Devotion to or advocacy of national interests or national unity and independence." (N. Webster, Webster's New International Dictionary of the English Language, Springfield, Mass., G. & G. Merriam Co., 1939, p. 1629.)

to cite the specific sense in which it will be employed in this paper. The concept, as used in this thesis, is not to be interpreted in its narrow sense.[1] Rather, it should be construed as a propensity to prefer those economic policies which seek to promote internal equilibrium with a minimum of disruption and interference from external forces. It is an attitude which accords preference to national over international economic requirements. In this sense, nationalism is completely opposite to the international gold standard, for the latter sought to promote external equilibrium by subordinating domestic to international considerations. Viewed from the standpoint of its objectives, nationalism seeks to achieve for the home economy full development and employment of manpower and resources, even if this should entail higher costs and prices than would prevail under free trade, and the maintenance of a stable price level. To realize these ideals, nationalism would depend upon the following policies: the attainment of external equilibrium by means that will not upset domestic equilibrium; a system of flexible instead of rigid exchange rates which will make possible independent national wage and price levels; the encouragement of domestic over foreign investment, the pursuance of autonomous monetary policies attuned to domestic requirements; conscious

---

1. Cf. F. A. von Hayek, *Monetary Nationalism and International Stability*, London, Longmans, Green and Co., 1937, p. 2.

control of the balance of payments, v.g. regulation of capital movements; independence from external forces which depress the domestic economy, e.g. cyclical fluctuations originating abroad; and freedom of the home economy from external controls.

In view of the fact that the international gold standard is antithetical to the realization of these ideals, it may be said that it is inversely related to economic nationalism. Therefore, we can substantiate our contention that Keynes' economic thinking was of a nationalistic character by demonstrating his opposition to the traditional gold standard system. This we shall endeavor to do in Part I of this thesis.

Following our confirmation of the above proposition, we shall undertake a comprehensive treatment of Keynes' views respecting international trade theory and policy. This investigation will cover Keynes' contributions to foreign trade theory and policy from the earliest phase of his career to his untimely passing in 1946. This portion of the thesis will consist of three parts (II, III and IV). The first will consider Keynes' foreign trade views from the beginning of his career to the early 'thirties; the second will deal with his foreign trade convictions as expressed during the period of the General Theory; and the third will investigate his trade position of the Clearing Union-World War II era.

In these sections, it will be shown that, because of his strong desire to promote the national economic welfare, Keynes was not disposed to have foreign trade relations supersede or interfere with the pursuit of those domestic policies which were intended to promote high levels of employment and income. Unlike the orthodox economists, Keynes was primarily concerned with the question of full employment and ultimately it was this consideration which precluded his complete reversion to the ideals of doctrinaire free trade.

But though Keynes cannot, in the final analysis, be classified as a free trader, neither can he be categorized as a confirmed protectionist. In short, no categorical statement can be made respecting his ultimate foreign trade position. Essentially, our conclusion will be that Keynes was primarily interested in the promotion of internal equilibrium and the protection of that equilibrium from external interference; hence, his attitude on the question of participation by a country, particularly his own, in international trade was conditioned by what was required to promote the national advantage. At times, this might be accomplished by free trade, while at other times nothing would succeed short of protection. In effect, Keynes' foreign trade thinking was reduced to a function of the domestic well-being. Truly, he made it the handmaid of domestic prosperity.

PART I

KEYNES' NATIONALISM AS EVIDENCED BY HIS OPPOSITION TO THE INTERNATIONAL GOLD STANDARD

SCOPE OF PART I

To prove Keynes' nationalism, exhaustive reference will be made in this section to his views on the pre-World War I international gold standard. For his opposition to the traditional gold standard reflects, in practically every instance, his strong preoccupation with the national welfare.

Although there is enough material available on this particular subject to warrant a thesis of its own, perhaps, we may best summarize Keynes' hostility to this type monetary system by centering our attention on the following arguments. First, the orthodox gold coin standard, by failing to effect an economy in the use and a centralization of gold reserves in the vaults of the Central Bank, did not enable the monetary authority to protect the economy from internal and external disequilibria. Secondly, the traditional gold standard did not permit the pursuance of an autonomous monetary policy. And lastly, the fixed exchange rates, which are an essential property of the gold standard system, were disruptive of internal price stability and facilitated the international transmission of economic fluctuations via changes in national price levels. Each of these arguments will be treated in the next three chapters of this section.

In Chapter 5, we shall try to indicate further the precedence which Keynes customarily accorded to domestic over international considerations by directing attention to his opposition to the restoration of the gold standard in Great Britain at the pre-war parity of exchange. And in Chapter 6, which is the concluding one of Part I, we shall endeavor to establish even more conclusively the nationalistic bias of Keynes' economic thinking by analyzing his proposals for a managed monetary standard. Keynes' purpose in advancing such a monetary standard was that, unlike the gold standard, it would safeguard a nation's monetary autonomy and thus enable it to achieve both internal and external equilibrium with a minimum of disruption.

In establishing Keynes' opposition to the international gold standard in the ensuing chapters of this section, our main purpose for doing so will be to show that his rejection of the gold system was simply a manifestation of his abiding desire to seek first the welfare of the national economy, which he spelled in terms of "stability of prices, credit and employment."[1]

---

1. J. M. Keynes, A Tract on Monetary Reform, London, Macmillan and Company, Ltd., 1923, p. 176.

CHAPTER II

KEYNES WAS OPPOSED TO THE PRE-WORLD WAR I GOLD STANDARD, BECAUSE, BY FAILING TO EFFECT AN ECONOMY IN THE USE AND A CENTRALIZATION OF GOLD RESERVES IN THE VAULTS OF THE CENTRAL BANK, IT HAMPERED THE MONETARY AUTHORITY IN ITS ATTEMPT TO PROTECT THE ECONOMY FROM INTERNAL AND EXTERNAL DISEQUILIBRIA.

Keynes' opposition to the gold coin standard was voiced as early as 1913 in his first major work,[1] Indian Currency and Finance.[2,3] Keynes pointed out that, although a gold coin standard worked successfully in a creditor country,[4] it did not work equally well in a debtor country such as India. The reason for this is that the bank rate instrument cannot, of itself, be relied upon to produce the desired results with sufficient

---

1. Herein Keynes gives an indication of the nature of his later monetary thinking. Schumpeter believes that there are certain elements in this work which appear in his later writings. In his view, much of Keynes' general attitude towards monetary phenomena and monetary policy expressed in his work of 1913 foreshadowed many of the ideas expressed by him in his Treatise on Money which appeared in 1930. Accordingly, he states, "add the theoretical implications of the English experience of the 'twenties to the theory of Indian Currency and Finance and you will get the substance of the Keynesian ideas of 1930." Vide J. A. Schumpeter, op. cit., pp. 264-5.
2. J. M. Keynes, Indian Currency and Finance, London, Macmillan and Co., Ltd., 1913.
3. Keynes was appointed to the Royal Commission inquiring into the problem of Indian currency and finance in April, 1913, largely as a result of this publication. His apprenticeship in the India Office, doubtless, was also of consideration in his attainment of this assignment.
4. One of the principal reasons why the gold standard achieved the success that it did in Great Britain is the unique power and prestige which the London Money Market enjoyed in the world at this time. (Vide J. M. Keynes, Indian Currency and Finance, op. cit., p. 18.)

rapidity.[1]

As a consequence, Keynes recommended for India and all other such debtor countries, which did not have highly developed nor self-supporting money markets, a modified gold standard. In place of the so-called automatic or gold coin standard Keynes recommended that there be substituted the gold exchange standard[2] which had been gradually evolving in India.[3]

---

1. The bank rate policy of a creditor country is quite effective in bringing about a balance in its foreign account, for all its Central Bank has to do is reduce its short-period loans to foreign countries. In a debtor country, however, the solution is not quite so simple, for the country is already a borrower in the international market. The problem here is to increase further its borrowing -- a task not always readily accomplished.
2. Vide Chapter II of *Indian Currency and Finance* for a complete treatment of the gold exchange standard. Schumpeter believes that this is the foremost work in the field. He says, "I think it fair to call this book the best English work on the gold exchange standard." (Vide J. A. Schumpeter, op. cit., p. 265.) Also, vide the excellent article prepared by J. S. Nicholson on the same subject, "The Report on Indian Finance and Currency in Relation to the Gold Exchange Standard," *Economic Journal*, XXIV, 94, June, 1914, pp. 236-247.
3. Indian currency had been a perplexing question ever since 1873, the date which marks the abandonment by the world of the bimetallic standard. India went off the silver standard in 1893 and in 1899 the Fowler Commission, the second of its kind within a period of ten years, recommended that India adopt a gold coin standard of the British type. The recommendation was never carried out and, instead, the monetary system which was ultimately established was one developed out of ad hoc administrative measures adapted to meet particular exigencies as they occurred. The net resultant of these actions was a gold exchange system. (Vide R. F. Harrod, op. cit., p. 165.)

Keynes likens the principle underlying this type standard to that of ordinary commercial banking. He points out that just as individuals have learned that it is cheaper and safer to keep their funds on deposit in the local bank, so, too, some nations have come to recognize that it is cheaper and safer for them to keep a part of the cash reserves of their banks on deposit in a foreign money center.[1]

The difference between the gold coin and gold exchange standard rests in the partial suspension by the latter of free payments in gold. Briefly, the essentials of the gold exchange standard, as conceived by Keynes, are the utilization of a non-gold medium of circulation at home,[2] an unwillingness to exchange that local currency for gold, but a willingness to sell foreign exchange for payment in local currency at a specified rate, and the use of foreign credits with which to accomplish this.[3] With respect to the local medium of exchange, Keynes points out that so long as it may be converted into gold for payments of international indebtedness at an approximately fixed ratio, it makes little difference whether or not gold actually circulates internally.[4] In actual practice, "the government would redeem the local currency (rupees) in bills

---

1. J.M. Keynes, Indian Currency and Finance, op. cit., p. 25.
2. By his own admission, Keynes recognizes that this point of view had been maintained by economists of earlier periods. David Ricardo, for example, had similarly based his proposals for a sound and economical currency on the principle of keeping gold out of actual circulation. John S. Mill also argued along the same lines, asserting that "gold wanted for exportation is almost invariably drawn from the reserves of banks, and is never likely to be taken from the outside circulation while the banks remain solvent." (Vide J. S. Mill, Political Economy, London, Longmans, Green and Co., 1891 edition, Book III, Ch. XXII.)
3. J.S. Nicholson, op. cit., p. 241.
4. J.M. Keynes, Indian Currency and Finance, op. cit., p. 30.

payable in international currency (gold) at a foreign center (London) than to redeem it outright locally."[1] The Government would also assume responsibility for providing local currency in exchange for international currency; hence, it would have to keep two types of reserves, one for each of these purposes.

To sum up, it may be said that a gold exchange standard obtains,

> when gold does not circulate in a country to an appreciable extent, when the local currency is not necessarily redeemable in gold, but when the Government or Central Bank makes arrangements for the provision of foreign remittances in gold at a fixed maximum rate in terms of the local currency, the reserves necessary to provide these remittances being kept to a considerable extent abroad.[2]

Keynes favored a gold exchange standard for India, because he thought that such a plan would accord greater stability to the Indian currency and price systems.[3] Wide fluctuations in the Indian price level, caused largely by movements of gold in and out of the country,[4] could be better controlled were the monetary authority in possession of an adequate gold reserve. The gold exchange standard, by substituting a cheaper domestic medium of exchange, would make possible a release of gold to the monetary authority.[5] Fortified with such centralized gold

---

1. Ibid., p. 11.
2. Ibid., p. 20.
3. L.R. Klein, op. cit., p. 2.
4. During this time India served as the sink for the world's excess gold supply, thus giving the western nations a cushion against inflationary price movements. But while this diversion of the metal to Asia may have been beneficial to these nations, it led directly to price fluctuations and undesirable currency speculation in India.
5. India did not have a Central Bank at this time. Keynes strongly recommended the establishment of such an institution, but without success. (Vide J. M. Keynes, Indian Currency and Finance, op. cit., pp. 232-239.)

reserves, the authority would be in a superior position to meet extraordinary foreign monetary drains and thus be better equipped to combat price and currency gyrations. Under the gold standard system, on the other hand, the Government's ability to cope with such crises would be far more limited, for its immediate gold reserve is but a fraction of the actual gold circulation.[1] And to withdraw the necessary gold from circulation is out of the question, for "gold in the pockets of the people is not in the least available at a time of crisis or to meet a foreign drain."[2]

For these reasons Keynes considered gold circulation much too burdensome for the internal economy of a country such as India. Although he recognized the value of the gold standard to the conduct of a nation's foreign commerce, he felt that the price which would have to be paid by the internal economy for such an advantage was much too high. Thus, it was this innate desire, which manifested itself even at this early date, to service first the needs of the domestic economy that motivated Keynes' recommendation of a gold exchange standard.[3] Such a standard, by effecting an economy in the use of gold, would permit nations not possessing large stocks of it to enjoy the external advantages associated with the international gold standard, without at the same time having to experience the internal disruptions attending it, v. g. the wide fluctuations in the domestic price level caused by the influx and efflux of the precious metal from

---

1. Ibid., p. 92.
2. Ibid., p. 71.
3. M. A. Heilperin, *International Monetary Economics*, London, Longmans, Green and Co., 1939, p. 215.

the monetary system.

Keynes further crystallized his objections to the international gold standard in the period following World War I. In a major article written for the April 20, 1922 issue of the Manchester Guardian Commercial Supplements on European reconstruction,[1] Keynes made an important pronouncement on the restoration of the gold standard.

In view of the need to restore trade among the nations of Europe, Keynes suggested an immediate resumption of the gold standard. The reason for his making such a recommendation is that restoration of the gold standard would, by eliminating wide variations in the rates of exchange, facilitate the international flow of goods and services.[2] Moreover, such a return to the gold standard would promote "a tremendous revival not only of trade and production but of international credit and the movement of capital to those areas where needed most."[3]

---

1. Over the period, April, 1922 to January, 1923, the Manchester Guardian Commercial sponsored a series of twelve supplements on the problem of European reconstruction. These installments contained articles written by leading authorities on finance, industry, trade, labor and other such subjects bearing upon the rehabilitation of Europe. In addition to being the editor of these works, Keynes was himself an active contributor.
2. Dudley Dillard summarizes well the advantage of the gold standard to international trade when he says, "A gold standard insures the stability of the exchange rate among countries on such a standard. Such stability is desirable for it eliminates much of the risk attending transactions of an international character. Stable foreign exchange rates promote this stability by enabling those who buy from foreigners and those who sell to foreigners to know how much they will have to pay and how much they will receive in terms of their own currency." (D. Dillard, op. cit., p. 288.)
3. J. M. Keynes, "The Stabilization of the European Exchanges: A Plan for Genoa," Reconstruction in Europe, The Manchester Guardian Commercial, p. 3.

Although Keynes was in favor of returning to the gold standard at the earliest possible date, he made it clear that he was not disposed to returning to the gold coin standard of the pre-World War I era. Instead, he proposed the institution of a gold bullion standard and, in doing so, took the same position as he did in recommending a gold exchange standard for India in 1913. For the gold bullion standard, like the gold exchange standard, keeps the precious metal out of the public's pockets and uses it, instead, to insulate the domestic economy from foreign-induced price and currency fluctuations.[1]

The reason why Keynes suggested that gold be withdrawn from active circulation is that the nations of Europe would need all the gold they could muster to combat fluctuations in their rates of exchange. Under these circumstances, it would be much wiser for each monetary authority to keep its gold centralized for immediate use than to have it "dissipated in the pockets or hoards of the public."[2] By so concentrating gold reserves in the vaults of the Central Bank, the bullion standard recommended by Keynes would better protect the national economy from the oscillations of its exchange and therefore keep at a minimum the number of resultant internal price corrections.[3]

---

1. Ibid., pp. 3-4.
2. Ibid., p. 4.
3. Keynes was so convinced of the merits of this type of monetary standard that he suggested its adoption as one of the proposals to be considered by the Genoa Conference

Keynes regarded the utilization of gold reserves for purposes of sheltering the home economy from outward disturbances so important that in the period following the restoration of the gold standard he recommended that the Bank of England determine its reserve requirements not in accordance with the note issue, but with respect to the international account.[1] His argument was as follows:

> The Bank of England's gold reserve is exclusively required to meet the fluctuations in our international account, which depend partly on the balance of trade, but mainly on our huge international banking and investment business. In these changed circumstances it is no longer reasonable to provide that the amount of gold available for the latter purpose should depend on the amount of notes required for the former.[2] For there is very little direct connection between the two.[3]

---

3. which convened in 1922. Specifically, the standard urged by Keynes would have the banks of each country exchange legal tender for gold; however, they would not mint this metal nor permit it to circulate as legal tender. Gold would be available on demand in exchange for notes at a fixed ratio; however, the gold so obtained would be used exclusively for international transactions. To restrict the use of gold in this manner, Keynes suggested that notes be exchanged for gold bullion only in large amounts, v.g. £50,000 or more. (Vide J. M. Keynes, "The Stabilization of the European Exchanges: A Plan for Genoa," op. cit., p. 4.)
1. This recommendation constitutes a very important feature of Keynes' managed currency proposal. We shall have occasion to examine it at much greater length in Chapter 6 of this thesis.
2. Under the existing system, the amount of gold available for foreign requirements was equal to the excess above the legal reserve required for the note issue; hence, it was determined by the size of the note circulation. (Vide J.M. Keynes, "Is there enough Gold?" The Nation and Athenaeum, XLIV, 16, Jan. 19, 1929, pp. 545-546.)
3. J.M. Keynes, "The Amalgamation of the British Note Issues," The Economic Journal, XXXVIII, 150, June, 1928, p. 322.

Keynes argued that the proper size of a nation's gold reserves should be calculated on the basis of what the maximum probable strain of a temporary disequilibrium in the balance of payments is likely to be on the economy.[1] The appropriate function of gold reserves is not to enable a country to meet the gold claims against its currency liabilities, but to satisfy the deficits it incurs in its international balance of payments.

This requirement clearly indicates a preference for the gold bullion standard. Under this type standard, the Central Bank's obligation to exchange gold coin for paper money is done away with. Gold can be obtained in bullion form, of course, but only in large amounts, thereby discouraging would-be holders of gold from converting their money assets into the yellow metal. To the extent that these claims against the Central Bank to redeem gold for notes are minimized, the need to keep immobilized reserves against these note liabilities is lessened. In this way, a much lower gold reserve against the note issue will suffice and the freed portion of the gold reserves can be employed to greater advantage in meeting balance of payments contingencies.

By withdrawing gold from active circulation and at the same time reducing the amount of gold to be kept as a reserve against the note issue, the gold bullion standard places a larger volume of resources at the disposal of the Central Bank. The larger this reserve, the longer will the monetary authority be able to

---

1. *Ibid.*, p. 322.

withstand external disruptions without having to transmit their effects to the internal sector of the economy. Thus, if the gold bullion standard were to be substituted for the gold coin standard of pre-war vintage and a conscious effort were made to gear reserve requirements to the needs of international trade and finance, the Central Bank could better combat the external imbalances, without having to transmit their harmful effects to the internal sector, as Keynes contends below.

> Therefore if the Bank of England had this volume of gold reserves available for foreign trade considerations, then at any moment the expansion of production and employment at home would not have to be interfered with by irrelevant consideration arising out of our international banking business. In this way the threat of enforcing a contraction of credit injurious to home industry would be greatly reduced.[1]

This passage illustrates well Keynes' desire to shield the home economy from the upsetting forces of the external sector.

As an adjunct to this topic, it may be indicated that Keynes was opposed to the gold coin standard not only because it hampered the monetary authority's efforts to ward off disequilibrating movements from without, but also because it did not accord the Central Bank sufficient latitude in pursuing a money policy intended to satisfy the domestic requirements. Basically, the problem created by a gold coin standard is that, by permitting the actual circulation of the metal in the form of coin and providing for the gold redemption of notes, it reduces the

---

1. J. M. Keynes, "The Amalgamation of the British Note Issues," op. cit., p. 325.

potential reserves of the Central Bank.[1] As a consequence of this efflux of gold into active circulation, the capacity of the Central Bank to increase the volume of credit is severely restricted.[2] For the smaller the value of the gold base which the monetary authority has at its disposal, the smaller will be the amount of credit that it will be able to generate.

If the gold coin standard could be replaced by a gold bullion standard, there would no longer be any obligation on the Central Bank to issue gold coin or to convert its notes into that medium.[3] It would be required to surrender only gold bullion or foreign gold exchange in large denominations, v.g. ₤50,000, for its note liabilities.[4] With its obligations to redeem notes lessened and to issue gold coins terminated, the amount of gold outside the Central Bank's vaults would be reduced and the amount of such gold inside its vaults correspondingly increased. The increase in the

---

1. J. M. Keynes, "Is there enough Gold?" op. cit., p. 545.
2. Committee on Finance and Industry; Report of the Committee on Finance and Industry, (The Macmillan Report), cmd. 3897, London, H.M. Stationery Office, June, 1931, p. 121.
3. Keynes was of the conviction that the responsibility of the Central Bank is not to exchange its notes into gold coin, but solely to maintain the value of its note liabilities on par with gold. This the Central Bank could accomplish by standing ready to ship gold bullion or sell foreign gold balances. This view was also accepted and incorporated into its Report by the Macmillan Committee. (Vide Report of the Committee on Finance and Industry, op. cit., p. 121.)
4. J. M. Keynes, "The Stabilization of the European Exchanges: A Plan for Genoa," op. cit., p. 4.

Bank's gold reserves together with the weakening of the public's prerogative to acquire gold would appreciably lessen the threat of an internal drain of the precious metal. And as a result, the Central Bank would be in a position to pursue a far more liberal money policy – one, perhaps, that might better conform to the economy's needs.

Compare this money mechanism to that prevailing under the old gold coin standard. Under the latter system, a nation could not exercise mastery over its own fate, for, if it were to create a volume of credit as dictated by its internal needs, the amount might be too burdensome for the Central Bank to honor in terms of gold. That is to say, the amount of credit required might force the Bank's ratio of gold to liabilities well below the level at which it could honor claims for gold.[1] Therefore, it would have to restrict the volume of credit as soon as the gold reserves reached their minimum legal requirements, notwithstanding the financial and economic needs of the country.

It was inconceivable to Keynes that a purely mechanical requirement of the gold standard, such as this convertibility privilege, should be given consideration prior to the real and present monetary and credit needs of the domestic economy. In view of this stricture which the gold coin standard placed on the promotion of an expansive domestic money and credit policy, Keynes refused to sanction it. If gold had to remain as the bulwark of the monetary system, he insisted that, at least, it

---

1. Committee on Finance and Industry, *Macmillan Report*, op. cit., p. 121.

be a bullion standard which, by taking gold out of the public purse and placing it at the disposal of the Central Bank, might accord the domestic economy some measure of discretion in the promotion of a more liberal money policy.

Summary

To summarize the findings of this chapter, it may be said that from the earliest phase of his career as a professional economist Keynes was opposed to the traditional gold standard, because it operated against the best interests of the national economy. The pre-war gold standard transmitted external disturbances to the home economy in the form of unstable currency and price systems and at the same time did not accord the monetary authority the necessary measures wherewith to combat these disruptions.

Keynes was more favorably disposed towards a gold exchange or a gold bullion standard, since both these monetary systems made possible an economy in the use and a centralization of gold reserves, which could be employed to overcome purely external frictions and to promote a more liberal domestic monetary policy.

Whether Keynes was diagnosing the pre-war economic maladies of India or those of the war-weary nations of Europe, his prescription was characteristically national. Although he was cognizant of the advantages associated with an international monetary system like that of the pre-1914 period, he understood far better the havoc and disorder visited by such a standard on the internal sector. Thus, it was out of this desire to shield the home economy from these disturbances that Keynes rejected the traditional, so-called automatic gold coin standard and urged in its place a modified bullion version, which would accord it a greater degree of protection and at the same time permit it to pursue a more expansive monetary policy.

CHAPTER III

KEYNES WAS OPPOSED TO THE TRADITIONAL GOLD STANDARD, BECAUSE IT DID NOT PERMIT THE PURSUANCE OF AUTONOMOUS MONETARY POLICIES.

The primary reason why Keynes was opposed to the international gold standard is that it makes independent national action impossible.[1] It circumscribes national autonomy by denying to governments freedom of internal action, especially in monetary management.

The reason why the gold standard does not permit such autonomous action is that it seeks to establish a uniform standard of currency throughout the world without regard to particular national needs.[2]

In an international gold standard system, the primary duty of each Central Bank is to keep gold movements at a minimum through manipulation of the interest rate. However, by regulating its credit policy in a way that gold will flow neither into nor out of its vaults, the Central Bank is, in effect, surrendering its right of independent action. For the monetary authority is constrained to promote a money and credit policy not in keeping with the needs of the domestic economic situation, but in accordance with the average behavior of all other Central Banks. For example, if the more powerful monetary authorities are pursuing a

---

1. A. Smithies, "Reflections on the Work and Influence of John M. Keynes," *The Quarterly Journal of Economics*, LXV, 4, Nov., 1951, p. 595.
2. J. M. Keynes, "The Problems of the Gold Standard," *The Nation and Athenaeum*, XXXVI, 25, March 21, 1925, p. 866.

restrictive money policy, then all others will have to follow suit. Even a small and temporary divergence in the local rate of interest from the international rate may prove to be upsetting of their external balance,[1] because, as the interest rate is raised in the more powerful financial countries, gold will start to flow there in quest of the higher interest return. To halt this loss of gold, the Central Banks which are experiencing the outflow will raise their bank rate to a level more proximate to that prevailing in the higher paying centers. In this way, the behavior of each Central Bank will be made to conform with the average behavior of all the other banks in the system, i.e. the level of pure interest is now approximately the same throughout the world, and so, there will no longer be any inducement to transfer funds from one country to another.

Although this uniformity of behavior will insure the attainment of external equilibrium, it cannot be obtained without sacrificing a nation's monetary autonomy.[2] This was especially true in the post-World War I era. Keynes argued that, if Great Britain were to return to the gold standard at this time, she would have to surrender her economic independence to the United States, for the gold standard is simply a device tying up the economy of a weaker nation with that of a stronger country.[3] With the Federal

---

1. J. M. Keynes, <u>A Treatise on Money</u>, New York, Harcourt, Brace and Co., 1930, vol. II, p. 309.
2. <u>Ibid</u>., p. 285.
3. J. M. Keynes, "The Return towards Gold," <u>The Nation and Athenaeum</u>, XXXVI, 21, Feb. 21, 1925, p. 708.

Reserve Banks in control of the major share of the world's gold supply,[1] monetary policy in Great Britain would be placed largely at the mercy of decisions made by the Federal Reserve Board of the United States.[2] Keynes aptly summarizes this situation as follows.

> With the existing distribution of the world's gold, the reinstatement of the gold standard means, inevitably, that we surrender the regulation of our price level and the handling of the credit cycle to the Federal Reserve Board of the United States. Even if the most intimate and cordial cooperation is established between the Board and the Bank of England, the preponderance of power will still belong to the former. The Board will be in a position to disregard the Bank. But if the Bank disregards the Board it will render itself liable to be flooded with or depleted of, gold, as the case may be.[3]

Keynes was opposed to this gearing of internal monetary policy to the average behavior of all other Central Banks,[4] because he felt that the primary function of money and credit policy was to service the internal, not the external, equilibrium needs of the economy.[5] The prevailing economic situation in

---

1. R. G. Hawtrey, *The Art of Central Banking*, London, Longmans, Green and Co., 1932, p. 228.
2. P. Cortney, *The Economic Munich*, New York, Philosophical Library, 1949, p. 212.
3. J. M. Keynes, *A Tract on Monetary Reform*, op. cit., p. 174.
4. This average was biased towards the particular behavior of the Federal Reserve Banks, since their policies carried the greatest weight at this time.
5. J. M. Keynes, "The Problem of the Gold Standard," op. cit., p. 866.

Great Britain made the retention of national monetary autonomy all the more important - a fact which caused Keynes to be even less sympathetic to any imminent restoration of the gold standard, as witness his following statement.

> With our industries in their present struggling condition and employment at its present level, I reckon it of the first importance that we should keep the control of our internal credit system in our own hands. We are not in a condition to stand shocks or storms. I think that we shall make a big mistake if we expose ourselves to them, merely for the convenience of a fixed rate of exchange with the dollar....
>
> Adoption of the gold standard would mean.... losing the control of our credit system, which we might have used, if only we had paused to think, for the mitigation of the curses of unemployment and trade instability.[1]

Keynes was further opposed to the uniform pattern of behavior which obtains under the international gold standard, because the resulting level of prices, though suited for the maintenance of external equilibrium, might prove to be disruptive of internal equilibrium.[2] Keynes points out that under the operation of the gold standard the price level must be everywhere the same. In the economic environment of the 'twenties, it more properly meant that it had to be the same as that of the United States. But to have the British price level conform to that of the United States, argued Keynes, meant that the British economy would have to share in all of the fluctuations experienced by

---

1. *Ibid.*, p. 870.
2. J. M. Keynes, "The Return Towards Gold," *op. cit.*, p. 707.

the United States. Although these changes would not be too serious for the United States, they would have serious repercussions on the British economy, as Keynes indicates below.

> The United States live in a vast and increasing crescendo. Wide fluctuations, which spell unemployment and misery for us, are swamped for them in the general upward movement. A country, the whole of whose economic activities are expanding, year in, year out, by several per cent per annum, cannot avoid, and at the same time can afford temporary maladjustments.[1]

In view of the fact that the British are not equally equipped to withstand these fluctuations, this is all the more reason why they should be permitted an autonomous money policy. Given such independence in the management of their own internal money affairs, they would be better able to insulate themselves from the disturbances attending the gyrations of the American price level.

In addition to prescribing a uniform price level, the international gold standard further stipulates, as indicated above, that the level of interest be the same throughout the entire system. This further encroachment on a nation's monetary autonomy has serious implications for the volume of domestic investment activity. For if a country's rate of interest be fixed for it by outside circumstances, this level may be too high to enable it to achieve investment equilibrium at home.[2]

In the light of the above considerations, it is plain to see why "adherence to an international standard limits unduly the

---

1. *Ibid.*, p. 709.
2. J. M. Keynes, *A Treatise on Money*, op. cit., vol. II, pp. 303-304.

power of a Central Bank to deal with its own domestic situation so as to maintain internal stability and the optimum of employment."[1]

The underlying reason why participation in an international system by national monetary authorities causes them such difficulty in resolving their own internal problems is that the mean behavior which evolves from the policies and practices of all the members in the system may be inadequate for the solution of unique national problems,[2] other than those, perhaps, of the strongest participants.[3] Thus, one of the principal reasons why Keynes was opposed to the maintenance of a single monetary standard is that, by stipulating the same prescription throughout the world, the

---

1. Ibid., p. 309.
2. Ibid., vol. I, p. 285.
3. In the pre-World War I era, there was no opposition between external and internal monetary policy so far as Great Britain was concerned. The reason for this is that during this time the strength of the Bank of England was so great that it succeeded in making the average behavior of all the Central Banks conform with the best domestic interests of Great Britain. This is indicated rather artistically by Keynes in the following passage. "During the latter half of the 19th century the influence of London was so prominent that the Bank of England could almost have claimed to be the conductor of the international orchestra. By modifying the terms on which she was prepared to lend, aided by her readiness to vary the volume of her gold reserves and the unreadiness of other Central Banks to vary the volume of theirs, she could to a large extent determine the credit conditions prevailing elsewhere." (Vide J. M. Keynes, A Treatise on Money, op. cit., vol. II, pp. 306-307. Also Cf. J. M. Keynes, "The Return towards Gold," op. cit., p. 709.)

gold standard failed to take cognizance of the varied and divergent policies required to promote the domestic well being of particular nations.[1]

In the above, it was demonstrated how financial developments in other parts of the world prevent a nation which has membership in an international monetary system from enjoying an autonomous monetary policy. The traditional gold standard further impedes the attainment of such independence over purely domestic monetary matters by virtue of the fact that, when a country experiences a balance of payments disequilibrium, its bank rate policy cannot be set autonomously, i.e. with respect to domestic needs and objectives, but must be established with reference to restoring equilibrium in the external sector. Keynes expresses this very well when he says,

> With an international currency system, such as gold, the primary duty of a Central Bank is to preserve 'external' equilibrium. Internal equilibrium must take its chances or, rather, the internal situation must be forced sooner or later into equilibrium with the external situation.[2]

Keynes believed that, in committing itself to the international gold standard, a country could no longer exercise mastery over its own economic fate. In effect, a country subscribing to this type standard loses its autonomy, for it must make its domestic economic considerations subservient to those of the external sector.

---

1. R. F. Harrod, op. cit., p. 410.
2. J. M. Keynes, A Treatise on Money, op. cit., vol. I, p. 164.

The bank rate mechanism has two separate sets of consequences. One is its effect on the international flow of capital, as already noted above, and the second is its effect on the internal credit situation.[1] Although this instrument is quite effective in maintaining or restoring external equilibrium, its utilization in this capacity takes away from the monetary authority the liberty to employ it to achieve the equilibrium of the internal economy.

To cite the case of a country experiencing a trade deficit, the proper technique for it to employ to restore equilibrium in the external sector would be to raise the bank rate. If the rate of interest were thus raised above the level prevailing elsewhere, that country would experience an influx of foreign capital and a slowing down in the efflux of its own capital to abroad.

Insofar as the internal sector is concerned, such an increase in the rate of interest would bring about a contraction of credit and a falling off in capital outlay. This would, in turn, lead to a diminution of purchasing power and a reduction in the general level of prices. As a result of this contraction, unemployment would start to increase and, when it became sufficiently widespread, employers could then obtain a general reduction in wages which would be in keeping with the reduction in prices. When costs and prices were thus sufficiently reduced, the products of the country experiencing the readjustment would again become competitive in world markets. This would stimulate an increase

---

1. J. M. Keynes, "The Committee on the Currency," *The Economic Journal*, XXXV, 138, June, 1925, pp. 302-303.

in the volume of its exports and a contraction of its imports, thereby correcting the adverse trade balance. The adjustment of the trade balance in this manner would then reverse the outflow of gold into an inflow and equilibrium would be thus restored.[1]

If these tendencies are sufficiently strong, the balancing of the foreign account is quickly achieved and the parity of the

---

1. Keynes of the <u>Treatise</u> defined external equilibrium as an equality between the net amount of lending to foreigners and the foreign balance (the excess of exports over imports). The following is his account of the manner in which this equilibrium would be achieved. "Raising the Bank Rate obviously has the effect of diminishing L, the net amount of lending to foreigners. But it has no direct influence in the direction of increasing B, the foreign balance. On the other hand, just as the dearer money discourages foreign borrowers, so also it discourages borrowers for the purpose of home investment - with the result that the higher Bank Rate diminishes the volume of home investment. Consequently, total investment falls below current savings* (assuming that there was previously equilibrium) so that prices and profits, and ultimately earnings fall, which has the effect of increasing B, (the foreign balance) because it reduces the costs of production in terms of money relatively to the corresponding costs abroad. On both accounts, therefore, B and L are brought nearer together, until in the new position of equilibrium they are again equal." (Vide J. M. Keynes, <u>A Treatise on Money</u>, <u>op. cit.</u>, vol. I, pp. 214-215.)

*In his thinking of the <u>Treatise</u>, Keynes, through a peculiarity of the definitions he assigned, conceived it possible for savings and investment to be unequal at times. In the <u>General Theory</u>, of course, these terms were modified, so that they would, of necessity, always be equal. A further refinement introduced by Keynes in the latter work was that the equality between savings and investment was not insured by variations in the interest rate, but by changes in the level of income.

exchange is thus safeguarded.[1] But while the bank rate mechanism restores equilibrium in the external sector, it destroys it in the internal sector, as witness the contraction and unemployment which it induces. According to Keynes, the greater the success realized by the rank rate in promoting the first objective, the less successful will it be in producing those credit conditions which are conducive to the maintenance of equilibrium in the home sector. The monetary authority cannot employ the bank rate for combatting a decline in capital outlay and unemployment, for a solution of these problems would require just the opposite prescription, i.e. a reduction of the interest rate. Consequently, to achieve balance in the external sector, a Central Bank which has membership in an international monetary system must relinquish its right of local autonomy and independent action.[2]

Summary

Keynes was very much opposed to the monetary authority's loss of independence in directing the credit system towards the realization of domestic objectives such as price stability, high levels of investment, and full employment. In his estimate, the bank rate

---

1. That this adjustment is quickly achieved is very much doubted by Keynes as witness his contention that "The instrument of Bank Rate and Credit Contraction can only be successful as a means of remedying a fundamental international maladjustment, so far as it diminishes employment and, if the unemployment thus caused is sufficiently intense and prolonged, eventually forces a reduction of money wages." (Vide J. M. Keynes, "The Future of the Foreign Exchanges," Lloyd's Bank Ltd. Monthly Review, N.S. VI, 68, Oct., 1935, p. 533.)
2. J. M. Keynes, A Treatise on Money, op. cit., vol. II, p. 304.

should be manipulated solely for the benefit of domestic considerations[1] and not to neutralize financial developments in other countries or to restore balance in a nation's foreign account, as is the case under the international gold standard. Thus, Keynes' dislike of the gold standard stemmed largely from the fact that, by tying the bank rate to external considerations, it does not permit an autonomous monetary policy for the attainment of domestic equilibrium. Under the gold standard system, each Central Bank must keep in step with the policies of every other Bank, regardless of whether its own domestic situation warrants such action or not. This disregard of purely local considerations is just one more reason why Keynes was forced to reject the so-called automatic international gold standard.

---

1. J. M. Keynes, "The Bank Rate," The Nation and Athenaeum, XXXVI, 23, March 7, 1925, pp. 790-792.

CHAPTER IV

<u>KEYNES WAS OPPOSED TO THE PRE-WORLD WAR I GOLD STANDARD, BECAUSE ITS RIGID EXCHANGE RATE SYSTEM WAS DISRUPTIVE OF INTERNAL PRICE STABILITY AND FACILITATED THE INTERNATIONAL TRANSMISSION OF ECONOMIC FLUCTUATIONS THROUGH CHANGES IN NATIONAL PRICE LEVELS.</u>

Keynes' opposition to the gold standard may be further evidenced by his aversion to a system of fixed exchange rates, such as was provided by that monetary standard, and his preference, instead, for a system of flexible exchange rates.[1] He objected to a fixed exchange rate system, because it could be obtained only at the expense of a stable internal price level. Keynes felt that the proper object of monetary policy is not to maintain the fixity of a particular exchange value, but to keep the price level stable,[2] and in this conviction is to be found further demonstration of his

---

1. For a consideration of the arguments on both sides of this question of Stable Prices vs. Stable Exchange Rates consult the following sources:
M. A. Heilperin, <u>International Monetary Organization</u>, Geneva, International Institute of Intellectual Cooperation, League of Nations, 1939, passim.
B. Ohlin, <u>Report in International Economic Reconstruction</u>, Paris, Carnegie Endowment and International Chamber of Commerce, 1936, pp. 78 et seq.
C. R. Whittlesey, <u>International Monetary Issues</u>, New York, McGraw-Hill, Inc., 1937, passim.
R. F. Harrod, <u>International Economics</u> (Second Edition), London, Cambridge University Press, 1939, Ch. 7.
P. B. Whale, "The Theory of International Trade in the Absence of an International Standard," <u>Economica</u>, III, 9, February, 1936, pp. 24-38.
2. J. M. Keynes, "Bank Rate and Stability of Prices - a Reply to Critics," <u>The Nation and Athenaeum</u>, XXXIII, 15, July 21, 1923, p. 530.

48

disposition to place matters of a domestic nature above those of a purely external character.

Although Keynes recognizes the advantage of the exchange stability associated with a system of fixed exchange rates, especially for those nations which conduct a sizable volume of foreign trade, he explains that at times it is difficult to achieve simultaneously both this objective and a stable price level. In fact, one may be realized only at the sacrifice of the other. The reason for this is that the value of a nation's exchange rate depends largely on the relation between the internal and external price levels; hence, unless both these price levels remain stable, the exchange rate will vary.

Such stability of both price levels is unusual. For, although a nation may succeed in stabilizing its own price level, there is not much likelihood that it can similarly influence the external price level. Therefore, if the external price level fluctuates, as it often does, the economy is faced with two courses of action. It may keep its internal price level the same and vary its exchange rate, or it may vary the internal price level and keep its exchange rate constant.[1] Given the existence of such external price fluctuations, each nation is compelled to determine whether it desires a stable price level or a constant rate of exchange for its currency.

The choice will largely be determined by the relative

---

1. J. M. Keynes, A Tract on Monetary Reform, op. cit., p. 154.

importance of foreign trade and investment in each country's economy;[1] however, even in those countries wherein the volume of international trade is of sizable import, Keynes feels that the stability of prices is of greater domestic benefit, because it avoids the evils of both inflation and deflation.[2] Though there be advantage in both types of stability, he concludes that "there does seem to be in almost every case a presumption in favor of the stability of prices, if only it can be achieved."[3]

Prior to World War I, gold served the double function of according the nations of the world a stable exchange rate system and a stable price level. But even during this time, Keynes feels that the gold standard owed its popularity more to its success in realizing a stable level of prices than in attaining a stable exchange rate, as note his following assertion.

> The convenience of traders and the primitive passion for solid metal might not, I think, have been adequate to preserve the dynasty of gold, if it had not been for another, half-accidental circumstance; namely, that for many years past gold had afforded not only a stable exchange but, on the whole, a stable price level also.[4] In fact, the choice between stable exchanges and stable prices had not presented itself as an acute dilemma.[5]

---

1. A.D. Gayer, *Monetary Policy and Economic Stabilization*, London, A. and C. Black, Ltd., 1935, pp. 191-192.
2. For a consideration of the evils associated with monetary instability vide J.M. Keynes, *A Tract on Monetary Reform*, op. cit., Ch. I.
3. J.M. Keynes, *A Tract on Monetary Reform*, op. cit., p. 155.
4. An important reason why the gold standard provided a stable price level as well as a stable exchange rate during the pre-war era is that, during the 19th century, the expansion of gold output from the mines kept pace with the expansion in general production. (Vide A. Johnson, "Keynes on Monetary Reform," *The New Republic*, XXXVII, 479, Feb. 6, 1924, p. 288.)
5. J.M. Keynes, *A Tract on Monetary Reform*, op. cit., p. 158.

Under the pre-war system of monetary arrangements, the internal price level adjusted itself to the external value of a nation's currency, but the required adjustments[1] were of a minor nature. Moreover, they were slow and insensitive; hence, they were not too disruptive of internal price stability.

Although the gold standard was able to provide moderate price stability in the pre-war period, because of the relatively minor adjustments that had to be made between a nation's internal price level and that prevailing internationally, Keynes felt that it would not be equally successful in the post-war environment. In this new economic setting, he averred, it is extremely doubtful whether the gold standard can cope with the large and sudden divergences which take place between a nation's internal price level and that prevailing abroad.[2] One of the reasons why such disparities occurred between internal and external price levels is that the domestic level of prices was no longer being geared to the value of the fixed exchange, as was the case prior to the war. Instead, it was now being largely determined by internal currency

---

1. The necessary adjustments were effected through the familiar gold flow mechanism. For example, as gold flowed out of the country in response to lower prices elsewhere, this loss of gold would bring about a tightening of credit, thereby affecting the prices of those classes of goods most sensitive to easy credit terms. Gradually, the prices of these goods would spread their influence to the prices of all goods generally, including those entering into foreign trade. In time, the nation's general level of prices would be reduced sufficiently to conform to the external value of its currency. At this juncture, its internal price level would be in equilibrium with the external price level and the value of its exchange rate would again be justified. (Vide J. M. Keynes, *A Tract on Monetary Reform*, op. cit., pp. 159-160.)
2. Ibid., p. 159.

and credit policy,[1] and insofar as these policies varied between countries, it was natural that disparities should emerge between their respective price levels.

Keynes' contention is that, while it is theoretically possible for the pre-war method to bring about the necessary adjustments, it is likely to break down in practice, because it cannot effect the readjustment of prices quickly enough. The pre-war process of adjustment, as already indicated, was slow and insensitive. It might take months to work itself out. But in the post-war environment the gold reserves might just about be depleted before the corrective factors had time to operate. Moreover, the amount of inflation or deflation required to bring the two price levels into balance with one another might be of such magnitude as to perpetrate intolerable inconveniences on the economy.[2] The penalty that a nation must suffer for the restoration of balance between its own price level and that prevailing abroad, in order that its exchange rate may remain stable, is, indeed, a heavy one. This is especially so in the case of deflation, when the price it has to pay is exacted in terms of contraction and unemployment. In view of the high cost attending a stable exchange rate, it is no wonder that Keynes wanted to foresake the gold standard in favor of flexible exchange rates and stable internal

---

1. The monetary system which emerged after the war in place of the gold standard was favorably accepted by the general public, due to the growing awareness of the value of a stable price level and an economy insulated from outside disturbances, especially those of a deflationary character. This sentiment led to increasing opposition to fixed exchange rates and a movement towards exchange rate adjustments as a means of correcting imbalances in the foreign account. (Vide A.I. Bloomfield, op. cit., p. 297. Also Cf. J.M. Keynes, A Treatise on Money, op. cit., vol. I, p. 166.)
2. J.M. Keynes, A Tract on Monetary Reform, op. cit., pp. 160-162.

prices.

Another reason, apart from the increased disparity between internal and external price levels, why the gold standard could not operate effectively in the post-war period is the fact that price and cost structures were becoming increasingly rigid.[1] But the gold standard mechanism cannot restore equilibrium between external and internal prices unless the latter be flexible. Therefore, if the gold standard is made to operate under such conditions, it will either force the brunt of the adjustment on the internal sector in the form of business losses and unemployment or break down completely.[2]

Being especially concerned with the national advantage, it would be inconsistent for Keynes to favor the attainment of exchange rate stability, for this could be attained only by engendering instability of prices, employment and output within the economies of individual countries. This meant, therefore, that if an adjustment had to be made between internal and external prices, Keynes preferred that the onus of the correction be placed not on the domestic economy in the form of an unstable price level, but on the external sector in the form of a fluctuating

---

1. That price adjustments, especially downward, are difficult to effect is admitted even by members of the orthodox school who are partial to the gold standard. In this regard, Dr. Heilperin asserts, "It is quite true that the price and cost structure has become increasingly rigid through the action of trade unions and cartels. This makes it impossible, or at least difficult to bring about downward price adjustments of considerable size." (Vide M. A. Heilperin, International Monetary Economics, op. cit., p. 200.)
2. These rigidities, especially in wages, were largely the cause of Great Britain's difficulties in the period after her return to the gold standard. The ultimate consequences of this ill-advised policy were severe deflation and widespread unemployment. (Vide Chapter 4 of this thesis.)

exchange rate, as the following contention will testify.

> Our conclusions up to this point are, therefore, that, when stability of the internal price level and stability of the external exchanges are incompatible, the former is generally preferable; and that on occasions when the dilemma is acute, the preservation of the former at the expense of the latter is, fortunately perhaps, the line of least resistance.[1]

In place of the system of fixed exchange rates, as provided by the gold standard, Keynes favored a mechanism of fluctuating exchange rates such as emerged in the absence of the gold standard in the immediate post-war period. Under this system, adjustments between a nation's internal price level and that obtaining abroad are achieved instantaneously[2] and without need of inflating or deflating the currency, as was the case under the gold flow mechanism.[3]

In a system of fluctuating exchange rates, the brunt of the adjustment between national and external price levels falls on the rate of exchange. The following illustration will bear this out. If, at the prevailing exchange rate, the amount of sterling offered in the market exceeds the supply of dollars available, due to the more favorable prices obtaining in the United States, there is no way of procuring the added dollars except by paying

---

1. J. M. Keynes, A Tract on Monetary Reform, op. cit., pp. 163-4.
2. Ibid., p. 160.
3. The process of adjustment under the gold flow mechanism is time consuming, because the credit policy which it sets in motion requires time to exert its full effect on the level of internal prices.

a higher price for them. The pressure of the British demand will force the dollar exchange up to a point where the offerings of both currencies are in balance with one another. At this new level of exchange, more sterling must be surrendered for the same dollar value, or, too, fewer dollars need be surrendered for the same amount of sterling. As a result of this new exchange relationship existing between sterling and dollars, the relative prices of those commodities entering into British and American trade, v.g. cotton, copper and wheat, will adjust themselves to the new rate of exchange within the hour.[1] At this point, the heretofore lower American prices will appear higher to British buyers, because of the higher cost of American dollars, while, on the other hand, the higher British prices, which obtained under the former rate of exchange, will now appear cheaper to the American buyer, because of the lower cost of sterling. In this way, the British and American price levels are effectively brought into balance with one another without reference to either inflationary or deflationary processes. These major monetary corrections are largely dispensed with, for under a system of fluctuating exchange rates there is no need to regulate domestic currency and credit policy, so as to conform with the gold movements, since these are non-existent under this type exchange mechanism.

Thus, the advantage of a system of fluctuating over a

---

1. J. M. Keynes, *A Tract on Monetary Reform*, op. cit., p. 161.

system of fixed exchange rates is that the adjustments in the former are effected immediately and without recourse to fostering internal price instability by inflating or deflating the currency. In effect, equilibrium may be restored in the external sector by a mere modification of the exchange value. And in this way, the stability of domestic prices, output and employment may be preserved.[1]

The one disadvantage of a fluctuating system of exchange rates, when compared to the fixed system which prevails under the gold standard, according to Keynes, is that it is extremely sensitive; consequently, relative prices may be altered by any purely transitory development. But despite this shortcoming, he believes that when fluctuations are large and sudden, a quick reaction, as accorded by a system of flexible exchange rates, is needed for the maintenance or restoration of equilibrium; hence, he considered it an indispensable mechanism for the monetary climate of the post-war period.

It is claimed that this preference on Keynes' part for a system of flexible exchange rates and stable internal prices implies "a choice in favor of nationalism over internationalism."[2] But more specifically, how does Keynes' partiality towards flexible exchange rates and stable domestic price levels constitute such a disposition in favor of nationalism? Why is their

---

[1]. J. M. Keynes, *A Treatise on Money*, op. cit., vol. I, pp. 357-363.
[2]. P. Cortney, op. cit., p. 209.

attainment so advantageous for the home economy?

There are many reasons for identifying a fluctuating exchange rate and a stable internal price level with the national advantage. First of all, a system of fluctuating exchange rates makes possible a high degree of national monetary autonomy. In such a system, the interest rate need not be used for bringing the internal price level back into line with the fixed exchange rate, for, in this case, the correction is simply made by having the exchange rate adjust itself to the prevailing price level.[1] There is now no longer any need to adjust internal credit policy to the exchange rate; rather, the adjustment is made the other way round. The exchange rate must adapt itself to whatever credit policy is required at home.[2] Thus freed from the necessity of synchronizing its credit policy with external requirements, the monetary authority is now at liberty to set its monetary policy in

---

1. Keynes cites the different roles played by the interest rate under fixed and flexible exchange rate systems in the following terms: "With the pre-war method discount policy is a vital part of the process for restoring equilibrium between internal and external prices. With the post-war method it is not equally indispensable, since fluctuations of the exchanges can bring about equilibrium without its aid; -- though it remains, of course, as an instrument for influencing the internal price level and through this the exchanges, if we desire to establish either the one or the other at a different level from that which would have prevailed otherwise." (Vide J. M. Keynes, A Tract on Monetary Reform, op. cit., p. 163.)
2. In this regard, R. F. Harrod points out that, if a country is determined to combat cyclical disturbances, especially depression, it must be prepared to experience a sizable alteration of its exchange rate. (Vide R. F. Harrod, The Trade Cycle, Oxford, The Oxford University Press, 1936, p. 188.)

accordance with the internal needs of the economy.[1]

Compare this to a system of fixed exchange rates such as obtains under the gold standard. In such a system, no autonomy is possible, for all the members of the monetary system must keep in step with one another or experience the disequilibrating effects of the gold flows. For example, if a particular Central Bank is pursuing a deflationary policy in keeping with its domestic needs, while no similar effort is being made elsewhere, it will be subjected to a drain of monetary reserves. To halt this outflow, it will have to raise its interest rate structure to a level conforming with that obtaining in other countries and thus terminate its monetary expansion program, notwithstanding the requirements of the domestic economy.[2] Thus, a nation on the gold standard is forced to surrender control over its own economic destiny. And it is this loss of national monetary autonomy which explains quite pointedly why Keynes, who was so intent on utilizing monetary policy for the promotion of domestic equilibrium, should be so opposed to the gold standard and its rigid exchange rates.

A system of flexible exchange rates further promotes the national welfare by protecting the internal economy from disturbances originating in the foreign sector.[3] This type exchange mechanism would help the monetary authority to insulate a country against the influence of cyclical disturbances[4] and undesirable price movements which are so

---

1. P.B. Whale, op. cit., p. 26.
2. M.A. Heilperin, International Monetary Economics, op. cit., p. 233.
3. F.C. James, "Some Practical Effects of the Doctrines Suggested by John M. Keynes Prior to 1930," The Economic Doctrines of John M. Keynes, New York, National Industrial Conference Board, 1938, p. 3.
4. C.R. Whittlesey, op. cit., p. 233.

disruptive of domestic equilibrium.[1] Such a possibility would, of course, be precluded by the monetary authority under the gold standard.

In the pre-war monetary system the currencies of all countries participating in it were placed on a common basis. As a consequence of the fixed exchange relationships obtaining in this system, all national price structures had to be in approximate balance with one another.[2] Changes in the price level of one country were necessarily transmitted to other countries; hence, the deflation or inflation which occurred at different stages of the business cycle would be passed on from one gold standard country to another via changes in their internal price levels.[3]

From this it is clear that, if a nation wishes to protect itself from price and cyclical disturbances originating abroad, it must isolate its price level from those of other countries,[4] for this is the channel through which these disturbances are transmitted.[5] To accomplish this a

---

1. Keynes' desire to insulate the home economy from outward cyclical disturbances constitutes one of the more impelling reasons why he urged Great Britain to abandon the traditional gold standard with its rigid exchange rates, and institute in its place a monetary system with flexible exchange rates. (Vide G. Haberler, The Theory of International Trade, London, William Hodge and Co., Ltd., 1936, p. 46. Also Cf. M.A. Heilperin, International Monetary Economics, London, Longmans, Green and Co., 1946, p. 228.)
2. M.A. Heilperin, International Monetary Economics, op. cit., p. 223.
3. C.R. Whittlesey, op. cit., p. 230. Also vide L. Fisher, "Are Booms and Depressions Transmitted Internationally through Monetary Standards?" The Hague, Bulletin de L'institut International de statistique, 1935, pp. 1-32.
4. M.A. Heilperin, International Monetary Economics, op. cit., p. 223.
5. It should be understood that a system of fluctuating exchange rates does not preclude all changes in the internal price level arising out of foreign trade activity. A flexible exchange rate mechanism can eliminate only the general shifts in incomes and domestic prices such as occur under the gold standard; however, relative price changes are another matter. Under any monetary system, relative changes are also required in the domestic price structure. These are made necessary by the redistribution of demands in the process

nation must subscribe to a monetary system with variable exchange rates.[1] In this way, should there occur unfavorable price developments abroad, their effect would be exercised on the value of the exchange rate and not on the internal price level.[2]

Insofar as a stable price level is concerned, this, too, has significant advantages for the home economy. In fact, this stability is so vital to the functioning of free economic systems that they cannot survive without it. It is Keynes contention that,

> Modern individualistic society, organized on lines of capitalistic industry, cannot support a violently fluctuating standard of value, whether the movement is upwards or downwards. The arrangements presume and absolutely require a reasonably stable standard. Unless we can give it such a standard, this society will be stricken with a mortal disease and will not survive.[3]

One of the most important arguments in favor of price stability is that it is conducive to capital formation. A high level of national income cannot be achieved unless there be an immense and ever increasing volume of capital. But capital formation rests on saving and saving depends upon the confidence which people have in

---

5. of international adjustment and by factors not directly related to the balance of payments. Therefore to effect these changes in relative price relationships, absolute changes in prices, defined in terms of the national currency, will be required. Thus, some price adjustment is required even in this type of monetary arrangement; however, the amplitude of the total price fluctuation required herein is much less than that necessitated by a system of rigid exchange rates. (P.B. Whale, op. cit., pp. 24-25.)
1. C. R. Whittlesey, op. cit., p. 231.
2. Cf. J. M. Keynes, "The Objective of International Price Stability," The Economic Journal, LIII, 210-211, June - September, 1943, pp. 185-187.
3. J. M. Keynes, "Currency Policy and Unemployment," The Nation and Athenaeum, XXXIII, 19, Aug. 11, 1923, p. 612.

the value of the monetary unit.[1] Thus, by encouraging investment, which in turn stimulates a higher level of national income, a stable price level serves to promote national prosperity.

A stable price level is beneficial to domestic business not only in its long term capital undertakings, but in its short term operations as well.[2] Price instability, especially deflation, worsens business expectations and so leads to cutbacks in productive activity. Consequently, to the extent that falling prices or the prospects of same can be replaced by stable price expectations, the business situation can be substantially stabilized.[3]

The stability of internal prices is further promotive of the national welfare, because it lessens the possibility of economic crisis. Keynes believed that the evils of unemployment, industrial disputes and business bankruptcy owed their existence in large measure to the instability of prices.[4] Therefore, if prices could be stabilized, these ills, especially widespread unemployment, could be substantially eradicated.[5] So confident

---

1. A. Johnson, op. cit., p. 288.
2. Schumpeter declares that one of Keynes' principal aims in stabilizing the standard of value was the stabilization of the domestic business situation. (Vide J. A. Schumpeter, Ten Great Economists from Marx to Keynes, op. cit., p. 273.)
3. J. M. Keynes, "Currency Policy and Unemployment," op. cit., p. 611.
4. R. C. Hawtrey, "A Tract on Monetary Reform - A Review," The Economic Journal, XXXIV, 134, June, 1924, p. 234.
5. J. S. G. Wilson, Lord Keynes and the Development of Modern Economic Theory, Sidney, The Economic Society of Australia and New Zealand, 1946, p. 19.

was Keynes of the efficacy of a stable domestic price level and the means whereby it could be attained, viz. a fluctuating exchange rate, that in later years he came to defend "exchange instability and disparity in national price levels in the name of Full Employment dogma."[1]

An additional reason why a fluctuating exchange rate and stable internal price level better serve the interests of the domestic economy than do a fixed exchange rate and a fluctuating price level is that only a part of national output is affected by the value of the exchange, whereas the whole of the national product is affected by the internal value of money. Because of this preponderance of purely domestic transactions, the nation, as a whole, will stand to gain far more from a stable price level than from a fixed rate of exchange.[2] In fact, Keynes questions whether it might not be more advantageous even for a country with a large volume of foreign trade to pursue a stable internal purchasing power of its currency, instead of a stable external value.[3] This is a view which he entertained not only in the early 'twenties, but also in 1930, as will be borne out by the following quotation from the *Treatise on Money*.

---

1. P. Cortney, op. cit., p. 205.
2. J. M. Keynes, "The Bank Rate," op. cit., p. 790 and p. 792.
3. A. D. Gayer, op. cit., p. 146.

> So far as foreign trade is concerned, I think that the advantage of fixing the maximum fluctuations of the foreign exchanges within quite narrow limits is usually much overstated. It is, indeed, little more than a convenience. It is important for anyone engaged in foreign trade that he should know for certain, at the time that he enters into a transaction, the rate of forward exchange at which he can cover himself....It is not important that the rate of exchange at which he covers himself this year should be exactly the same as the rate at which he covered himself for a similar transaction last year.[1]

Summary

To summarize the findings of this chapter, it may be said that Keynes was further opposed to the traditional gold standard, because the fixed exchange mechanism associated with it was disruptive of domestic stability. A fixed exchange rate can be maintained only by sacrificing domestic price stability. For as the external price level is altered, the domestic price level must be adjusted accordingly, in order to warrant the given value of exchange. Such instability of the internal price level has dire consequences for national prosperity, especially when the adjustments are downward. In these circumstances, the fixed value of the exchange may be realized only by fostering general contraction with its accompanying unemployment, industrial strife and business bankruptcy.

Among other reasons for Keynes' opposition to the fixity of exchange and the gold standard are that such a money system

---

1. J. M. Keynes, *A Treatise on Money*, op. cit., vol. II, p. 333.

prohibits an autonomous monetary policy attuned to domestic needs and leaves the home economy open to cyclical fluctuations which originate abroad.

To remove these unstabilizing influences, Keynes recommended that the gold standard be replaced with a system of flexible exchange rates. In this way, any adjustment between internal and external price levels could be accomplished via an alteration of the exchange rate and would, thereby, leave the domestic economy unaffected.

This opposition to the gold standard and the disequilibrating effects of the fixed exchange mechanism associated with it and preference, instead, for a substitute system which would eliminate these distortions reveals once again Keynes' lasting desire to keep external considerations from impinging upon the national prosperity.

To illustrate further Keynes' prior concern with the attainment and preservation of internal economic well-being, a brief account of his opposition to the restoration of the British pound to its pre-war parity of exchange will be presented in the subsequent chapter.

CHAPTER V

KEYNES' PRIOR CONCERN WITH THE PROMOTION AND MAINTENANCE OF DOMESTIC EQUILIBRIUM AS EVIDENCED BY HIS OPPOSITION TO GREAT BRITAIN'S RETURN TO THE GOLD STANDARD AT THE PRE-WAR PARITY OF EXCHANGE.

Keynes' concern for the national welfare is further exhibited by his opposition to the restoration of the gold standard in Great Britain at the pre-war parity of exchange. Keynes was against returning to the gold standard on such terms, because he felt that this could be accomplished only by fostering a widespread deflation - a prospect he faced with disquiet, because of the disequilibrating effects which such a policy would have on the domestic economy.[1]

To appreciate fully Keynes' opposition to a resumption of the gold standard on pre-war terms, it is first necessary to understand why the process of deflation operates counter to the best interests of the domestic economy, and why, therefore, he was opposed to it.

Keynes argues that, whereas rising prices constitute an injustice to rentiers and therefore discourage saving, falling prices inhibit production and therefore lead to unemployment.[2] Although both species of instability have their characteristic disadvantage, Keynes regards deflation as having the more serious

---

1. L. R. Klein, op. cit., p. 11.
2. J. M. Keynes, *A Tract on Monetary Reform*, op. cit., p. 39.

consequence for the domestic economy,¹ as witness his following contention.

> Thus Inflation is unjust and Deflation is inexpedient. Of the two perhaps Deflation is, if we rule out exaggerated inflations such as that of Germany, the worse; because it is worse, in an impoverished world to provoke unemployment than to disappoint the rentier.²

Deflation promotes unemployment largely by discouraging business investment.³ Modern business is largely conducted with borrowed capital, but if entrepeneurs are faced with the prospect that their investments will in time be worth only a fraction of their current value, this means that lengthy productive processes

---

1. Keynes first expressed this sentiment in an article he prepared late in 1922* for the eleventh installment of the Manchester Guardian Commercial Supplements on European Reconstruction. (Vide J. M. Keynes, "The Stabilization of the European Exchanges - II," Reconstruction in Europe, op. cit., Dec. 7, 1922, pp. 658-661.)

   This view is somewhat surprising if one considers that only three years prior to this time it was inflation which gave Keynes greater cause for concern. In his Economic Consequences of the Peace, published in 1919, Keynes argued that the great injustice of inflation is that it confiscates arbitrarily, and in the process of redistributing the wealth of the community, impoverishes some and enriches others. (Vide J. M. Keynes, The Economic Consequences of the Peace.)

   * Harrod believes that it was at this juncture that Keynes began the reformulation of his economic thinking. He contends that Keynes' warning against the evils of deflation may be considered as heralding the work which was to absorb his interests for the next fifteen years and lead him far from his original starting point. (Cf. R. F. Harrod, op. cit., p. 314.)
2. J. M. Keynes, A Tract on Monetary Reform, op. cit., p. 40.
3. L. R. Klein, op. cit., p. 5.

involving large money outlays cannot be undertaken, whereupon there ensues unemployment.[1]

Paradoxically, during such deflationary periods, there is a greater possibility of reward in not producing and undertaking risk than in producing and incurring all species of uncertainty. Under these circumstances, it is more profitable for the entrepeneur to withdraw from "the risks and exertions of activity" by converting his assets into cash, and to await "in country retirement the steady appreciation promised him in the value of his cash."[2] Thus, the curtailment of output and employment is actually encouraged by a program of deflation.

In the second place, Keynes was opposed to a policy of deflation because of the existence at that time of large internal debts in most European capitals.[3] Should deflation occur under such circumstances, money incomes would be appreciably reduced. But owing to the fixed nature of the service charges on the Public Debt, taxes could not be reduced accordingly; hence, such a policy would place an intolerable strain on the productive classes of society.[4] In effect, the fixed income groups, v.g. rentiers and government bond holders, would profit at the

---

1. J. M. Keynes, "Currency Policy and Unemployment," op. cit., p. 611.
2. J. M. Keynes, A Tract on Monetary Reform, op. cit., pp. 156-157.
3. J. M. Keynes, "The Stabilization of the European Exchanges-II," op. cit., p. 659.
4. D. Dillard, op. cit., p. 304.

expense of the working classes, for they would now receive a larger share of the real national income.[1] By so changing the real value of the existing monetary standard, the process of deflation redistributes wealth in a manner detrimental both to business and social stability.[2] Deflation involves a transfer of wealth from the borrowing to the lending classes. This is particularly lamentable, asserts Keynes, because the transfer is effected from the active to the inactive classes of society. But such a situation is not likely to exist for any extended period, for "the active and working elements in no community, ancient or modern, will consent to hand over to the rentier or bond holding class more than a certain proportion of the fruits of their work."[3]

Therefore, concludes Keynes, downward price adjustments are bad enough, but a deliberate policy of deflation, v.g. as would be required by the restoration of the gold standard at the pre-war par of exchange, is even worse. For insofar as the business world believes that the monetary authority really intends to carry out a declared deflationary policy they are more likely to lose confidence in the existing level of prices and are therefore more certain to restrict output and employment.[4]

---

1. J. M. Keynes, "The Stabilization of the European Exchanges-II," op. cit., p. 658.
2. J. M. Keynes, A Tract on Monetary Reform, op. cit., p. 155.
3. J. M. Keynes, "The Stabilization of the European Exchanges-II," op. cit., p. 658.
4. J. M. Keynes, "Currency Policy and Unemployment," op. cit., p. 611.

This, in fact, is the chief reason why Keynes favored a devaluation of the European currencies rather than a restoration to their pre-war parity.[1] To increase the external value of the currency, it is imperative that its internal purchasing power be first augmented. Obviously, this necessitates internal deflation. But because of the serious implications which such a policy has for the home economy, viz. falling prices, output and employment, Keynes was forced to reject outright any plan for appreciating the value of the currency. No one so vitally concerned with the welfare of one's country as Keynes was could possibly look forward to a return to the gold standard at the old parity of exchange.[2] Thus, he favored, instead, a program of immediate stabilization, as suggested in the following passage.

> It would be better to return to more modest values in order that the risk of a fiasco and a breakdown may be as little as possible. Furthermore, an appreciating currency by lowering home prices, may have a depressing effect on trade, and by constantly increasing the real burden of the National Debt will aggravate the already nearly insoluble problem of the National Budget.[3]

In the section that follows a summary will be given of the events leading up to the restoration of the gold standard in Great Britain in 1925. In it an attempt will be made to show that Keynes' opposition to such restoration stemmed largely from his desire to protect the home

---

1. The issue between devaluation and the appreciation of the exchange rate was fundamentally an aspect of the broader question of inflation versus deflation. The question at hand was whether a country should fix the value of its currency at the prevailing post-war level or whether it should return to the pre-war parity. The former would mean an immediate stabilization of the currency, whereas the latter alternative would spell deflation.
2. P. Cortney, op. cit., p. 212.
3. J.M. Keynes, "The Stabilization of the European Exchanges- A Plan

economy from the distressing consequences of deflation.

The first clash between Keynes and the advocates of restoring the gold standard at its pre-war value occurred in the summer of 1923. The outbreak was precipitated by the Bank of England's action on July 7 in raising the bank rate from 3 to 4 per cent.

This action did not appear to be at all consistent with the prevailing economic situation, for at this time Great Britain was in the midst of a severe depression.[1] When unemployment is increasing, enterprise disheartened, and prices are declining, this is hardly the moment to raise the bank rate.[2] Thus, Keynes took the bank authorities to task, charging that "the raising of the Bank Rate to 4 per cent is one of the most misguided movements of that indicator which have ever occurred."[3]

If raising the interest rate structure could hardly be construed as a move calculated to encourage business recovery, what, then, was the Bank's justification for taking this action? The authorities gave no answer, but Keynes asserted that it was to be found in the decline of the dollar exchange by about 2 per cent.[4] This action, he charged, constituted just one more step in the deflationary policy initiated by the Bank of England some 18 months previously[5] for the purpose of

---

3. for Genoa," op. cit., pp. 4-5.
1. H. R. Burrows, op. cit., p. 156.
2. J. M. Keynes, "Bank Rate and Stability of Prices," The Nation and Athenaeum, XXXIII, 16, July 21, 1923, p. 530.
3. J. M. Keynes, "Bank Rate at 4 Per Cent," The Nation and Athenaeum, XXXIII, 15, July 14, 1923, p. 502.
4. Ibid.
5. Keynes estimates that the actual deflation during this period amounted to circa 10 per cent.

restoring sterling to its pre-war dollar value.[1]

Although raising the general level of British interest rates would, in time, enhance the value of the dollar exchange, it would do so only at the expense of the home economy. For any improvement in the British exchange position could be accomplished only by fostering internal deflation with its attending business depression and unemployment. In fact, Keynes attributes to this deliberate deflationary policy much of the blame for Great Britain's failure to keep pace with the economic revival in the United States during the first half of 1923.[2] Nonetheless, it seems that the Bank authorities deemed it "more important to raise the dollar exchange a few points than to encourage flagging trade."[3] In so choosing this course of action, avers Keynes, "the Bank of England, acting under the influence of a narrow and obsolete doctrine[4] has made a grave mistake."[5]

As Great Britain continued to move irresistibly towards restoration of the gold standard at the pre-1914 parity, Keynes became more vehement in his protest against such a prospect.[6] The reason

---

1. J. M. Keynes, "Is Credit Abundant?" The Nation and Athenaeum, XXXIII, 14, July 7, 1923, p. 470.
2. J. M. Keynes, "The Measure of Deflation," The Nation and Athenaeum, XXXIII, 17, July 28, 1923, p. 558.
3. J. M. Keynes, "Bank Rate at 4 Per Cent," op. cit., p. 502.
4. The "narrow and obsolete doctrine" to which Keynes refers is the manipulation of the interest rate for the purpose of effecting adjustments in a country's external affairs rather than for the promotion of stable prices and high levels of output and employment.
5. J. M. Keynes, "Bank Rate at 4 Per Cent," op. cit., p. 502.
6. J. M. Keynes, "The Policy of the Bank of England," The Nation and Athenaeum, XXXV, 16, July 19, 1924, pp. 500-501.

for his antagonism was the same now as in 1922,[1] viz. the current level of British domestic prices relative to that prevailing in other countries was inordinately high; hence, a return of the pound to its pre-war value would necessitate a substantial deflation.[2] Keynes indicates this in the following statement.

> I believe that our price level is too high, if it is converted into gold at the par of exchange, in relation to gold prices elsewhere, and if we consider the prices of those articles only which are not the subject of international trade and of services, i.e. wages,[3] we shall find these

---

1. Vide Keynes' two articles in the <u>Manchester Guardian Commercial Supplements</u> on the question of exchange stabilization for his arguments against restoration of the gold standard at the pre-war parity: "The Stabilization of the European Exchanges - A Plan for Genoa," <u>Reconstruction in Europe</u>, <u>op. cit.</u>, pp. 3-5, and "The Stabilization of the European Exchanges - II," <u>Reconstruction in Europe</u>, <u>op. cit.</u>, pp. 658-661.
2. A deflationary policy is not absolutely required. For restoration could be accomplished without it, provided that gold would depreciate abroad while prices at home remained constant. Such an eventuality, however, was quite unlikely at this time. Cf. J. M. Keynes, "Is Sterling Over-valued - II," <u>The Nation and Athenaeum</u>, XXXVII, 3, April 18, 1925, p. 86.
3. To give some indication of the disproportion existing between British wages and those prevailing elsewhere, Keynes cites the following comparison of wages received by steel workers in Great Britain and various European countries. In early 1925, skilled iron and steel workers were receiving the equivalent of ₤ 1 18 s per week in Belgium, ₤ 1 13 s in France and ₤ 2 2 s 6 d in Germany; whereas, in Great Britain the weekly pay for shorter hours and for the average of both skilled and non-skilled workers amounted to ₤ 3 3 s.

Further evidence of this disparity between British and other European wage levels may be had by referring to the average daily wages paid by an American overseas firm to factory workers engaged by it in a number of European countries. These wages which prevailed in the latter part of 1924 were converted into gold at the then current rates of exchange. The relationship compares favorably with the one cited above. In Great Britain, the daily wage was equal to $2.28; whereas,

are materially too high – not less than 5 per cent and probably 10 per cent. Thus, unless the situation is saved by a rise of prices elsewhere, the Chancellor is committing us to a policy of forcing down money wages by perhaps two shillings to the pound.[1]

Keynes was opposed to this deflationary policy, because it could be accomplished only at great cost to the domestic economy. First of all, it would mean that the real burden of the national debt would be increased by 10 per cent. This is so, for, although money incomes would be reduced, the cost of servicing the debt would remain the same.[2]

---

3. in Germany, France, Belgium and Italy, it amounted to $1.55, $1.24, $1.14 and $.96 respectively. (Vide J. M. Keynes, "Is Sterling Over-valued – II," op. cit., p. 86.)

Although gold wages in Great Britain were considerably higher than in these other countries, the level of real wages was not commensurately higher. The reason for this is that the prevailing British rate of exchange overstated the internal value of sterling in terms of purchasing power. In short, gold bought much less in Great Britain than elsewhere. The British price level (cost of living index) in 1925 showed a far greater increase over the pre-war period than did the price levels of the other European countries under consideration. For whereas the British cost of living had increased by 79 per cent over the pre-war era (1913), in Germany, France, and Italy, the advance amounted to only 25, 3, and 21 per cent, respectively. Therefore, the British difficulty rested not so much in higher real wages* as in the fact that relatively, the gold cost of living rose much more in England than in other countries. (Vide J. M. Keynes, "Is Sterling Over-valued?" op. cit., passim.)

* The orthodox explanation of Great Britain's inability to compete in overseas markets at this time was the existence of high real wages at home. (Vide W. Beveridge et al., Tariffs: The Case Examined, London, Longmans, Green and Co., 1932, pp. 68-69.)

1. J. M. Keynes, "The Gold Standard," The New Republic, XLII, 546, May 20, 1925.
2. J. M. Keynes, "The Policy of the Bank of England," op. cit., p. 500.

Secondly, money wages would similarly be reduced by 10 per cent. This in itself would be of no real consequence, provided the reduction in costs and prices were carried out uniformly.[1] Such, though, was not likely, because of the many rigidities associated with the internal cost and price structure. Any attempt, then, to reduce the level of money wages would certainly lead to industrial strife.[2] Interestingly enough, Keynes uttered in this regard the following prophecy which later came to pass.[3]

> The working classes...attacked first are faced with a depression of their standard of living, because the cost of living will not fall until all the others have been successfully attacked too, and therefore, they are justified in defending themselves.... Therefore, they are bound to resist as long as they can; and it must be war, until those who are economically weakest are beaten to the ground.[4]

Thirdly, Keynes argued that unless the adjustment of internal prices and costs kept pace with the improvement in the exchange rate, the cost-price relationship of British exports, v.g.

---

1. J. M. Keynes, "The First Fruits of the Gold Standard," The Nation and Athenaeum, XXXIX, 12, June 26, 1926, p. 345.
2. J. M. Keynes, "The Gold Standard," The Nation and Athenaeum, XXXVII, 5, May 2, 1925, p. 129.
3. Keynes' prophecy was verified in 1926 when the resistance by the coal miners to the wage reductions urged upon them led not only to a strike in that industry but to a General Strike which encompassed the entire nation.
4. J. M. Keynes, The Economic Consequences of Mr. Churchill, London, The Hogarth Press, 1925, p. 9.

coal[1] and textiles, would be distorted. Given a higher exchange value for sterling, British export prices would have to be lowered. But unless the internal costs associated with the production of these goods were correspondingly reduced, the British export industries would be unable to compete in foreign markets.[2] Only when sufficient depression and unemployment had been propagated in these industries to bring internal costs, v.g. wages, into line with prices, could the competitive status of the British export industries be restored.[3]

Lastly, the mere declaration of a deflationary policy would be enough to inhibit many industrialists engaged in purely domestic production and trade. Faced with the certainty of declining prices, many producers would curtail their current

---

1. Among those export activities hardest hit by this cost-price distortion, following the restoration of the gold standard, was the coal industry. This activity experienced extraordinary difficulty, because wages, its most important cost, could not be altered downward to conform to the lower price being received for its product in foreign markets. (Vide J. M. Keynes, "The First Fruits of the Gold Standard," op. cit., p. 345.)

   For a more exhaustive consideration of the plight facing the British export industries after the return to the gold standard vide J. M. Keynes, "Back to the Coal Problem," The Nation and Athenaeum, XXXIX, 16, May 15, 1926; J. M. Keynes, "Coal: A Suggestion," The Nation and Athenaeum, XXXIX, 4, April 24, 1926; J. M. Keynes, The Economic Consequences of Mr. Churchill, op. cit., Ch. IV; J. M. Keynes, "The Position of the Lancashire Cotton Trade," The Nation and Athenaeum, XL, 6, Nov. 13, 1926, pp. 209-210.

2. J. M. Keynes, The Economic Consequences of Mr. Churchill, op. cit., p. 6.
3. J. M. Keynes, "Great Britain's Cross of Gold," The New Republic, XLIV, 563, Sept. 16, 1925, p. 88.

operations as well as put off any capital improvements they may have contemplated. On the demand side, prospective buyers would postpone the acquisition of commodities and services in anticipation of still lower prices. Therefore, concludes Keynes, the threat of falling prices is bad enough, but the certainty of such deflation must surely aggravate unemployment and retard productive activity. It is this depressing effect on output and employment that causes Keynes to quip,

> A cheerful programme! Would the public fall down and worship the gold standard with gratitude and awe?[1]

Clearly, Keynes was averse to a restoration of the gold standard at the pre-war parity of exchange because of the havoc which the required policy of deflation would visit on the domestic economy. As noted in the foregoing, the restoration of the gold standard at the pre-war value would require a drastic alteration of domestic economic relationships, so that they might conform to the accretion in the external value of sterling. This prospect was extremely repugnant to Keynes, for it was inconceivable to him that domestic prosperity should be sacrificed solely for the implementing of a monetary device designed to gain a purely external advantage.

Being primarily concerned with the domestic welfare, Keynes preferred that, instead of forcing the internal situation into balance with the external, the adjustment be effected the other

---

1. J. M. Keynes, "The Policy of the Bank of England," op. cit., p. 501.

way round. That is why he suggested that the British forego a restoration of the gold standard at the old par of exchange and permit, instead, the external value of the currency to seek its own level, as note his following remarks.

> I believe that it would be much better for us, as well as much easier, to let our exchange adjust itself to the present level of our prices and wages, which have now been fairly steady for some time....[1]

> It seems to me wiser and simpler and saner to leave the currency to find its own level for some time longer than to force a situation where employers are faced with the alternative of closing down or of lowering wages, cost what the struggle may.[2]

Despite Keynes' admonition that the time was not propitious for a return to the gold standard, because of the distortions between British prices and those prevailing abroad, the City and the British public made up their minds that Great Britain should return to the gold standard at the pre-war exchange value.[3] Let

---

1. J. M. Keynes, "Is Sterling Over-valued - I," The Nation and Athenaeum, XXXVII, 1, April 4, 1925, p. 28.
2. J. M. Keynes, "The Gold Standard," The New Republic, op. cit., p. 339.
3. That such determination should be so widespread is strange, because most Britishers were not unmindful of the dangers associated with such restoration. In fact, they even expressed a certain hesitancy about returning to gold, as attested to by the following observation made by Keynes. "Nevertheless most people now appreciate the dangers and the complexities of the case, and sincerely wish that they had not talked so much about the blessings of hurrying back to par. It is in this chastened mood that the British public will submit their necks to the golden yoke, - as a prelude, perhaps, to throwing it off forever at not a distant date." (Vide J. M. Keynes, "Is Sterling Over-valued - II," op. cit., p. 86.)

us review briefly some of the more immediate developments that led to this resumption of the gold standard.

Throughout most of 1924, the Federal Reserve Banks pursued a cheap money policy.[1] During this same period, the Bank of England had the opportunity of similarly easing credit to bolster employment or keep credit restricted and induce thereby an appreciation of the sterling exchange. The authorities selected the second course of action.[2]

As a result of the easy money policy pursued by the Federal Reserve Banks between May, 1924 and February, 1925, dollar prices in this period rose by about 10 per cent. During the same interval, the Bank of England's Bank Rate remained at 4 per cent with the consequence that there occurred little change in the volume of outstanding credit. Although British prices rose somewhat in sympathy with the American advance, the increase during this period amounted to only 4 per cent. This differential caused the dollar sterling exchange to appreciate by 8 per cent in favor of sterling.[3] Another factor leading to the appreciation of the exchange rate in the closing months of 1924 was the element of speculation present in the market. Due to the dealings of the bulls, who were

---

1. The rediscount rate of the New York Federal Reserve Bank was reduced from $4\frac{1}{2}$ per cent in May, 1924 to 3 per cent in August of that same year. It remained at that level until February 26, 1925 at which time it was raised to $3\frac{1}{2}$ per cent.
2. R. G. Hawtrey, Currency and Credit, (Fourth Edition), London, Longmans, Green and Co., 1950, p. 395.
3. J. M. Keynes, "The Bank Rate," The Nation and Athenaeum, XXXVI, 23, March 7, 1925, p. 790.

anticipating Great Britain's return to the gold standard at the pre-war parity, sterling was given an additional stimulus.[1]

In January, 1925, the exchange touched 1 £ = $4.78;[2] however, subsequent action by the Federal Reserve Banks was to make further appreciation difficult. In February, 1925, the New York Federal Reserve Bank raised its rediscount rate from 3 to $3\frac{1}{2}$ per cent. The Bank of England, intent on completing the task it had set out for itself, raised its Bank Rate to 5 per cent.[3] Although this was not a popular consequence of the Bank's policy to return to the gold standard, public clamor for a resumption of the gold standard at the pre-war parity continued unabated.[4] In the early months of 1925, there occurred a mounting pressure on the part of the financial community and the general public to implement the recommendations of the Cunliffe Committee of 1918 and of the Currency Committee[5] of 1924 that Great Britain return to the gold standard at the pre-war parity.[6]

---

1. R. F. Harrod, op. cit., p. 357.
2. Keynes was heartened by this appreciation in the value of the sterling exchange, because it was realized without reference to any deflationary action on the part of the Bank of England. He reasoned that, if British prices could be stabilized while American prices continued to rise somewhat more, the pound could be restored to its pre-war parity without any positive deflation and with a minimum of disruption to the domestic economy. (Vide J. M. Keynes, "The Return Towards Gold," The Nation and Athenaeum, XXXVI, 21, Feb. 21, 1925, p. 707.)
3. R. G. Hawtrey, The Gold Standard in Theory and Practice, London, Longmans, Green and Co., 1939, p. 125.
4. R. G. Hawtrey, Currency and Credit, op. cit., p. 395.
5. A. E. Robinson, op. cit., p. 34.
6. The members of the Committee on the Currency were Lord Bradbury, Mr. Gaspard Ferrer, Sir Otto Niemeyer and Professor A. E. Pigou.

The ultimate consequence of all this was the acceptance of the gold standard by the Chancellor of the Exchequeur in April, 1925. Winston Churchill, who was the Chanellor at this time, announced in his Budget Speech on April 27, 1925, that the Bank of England would resume the sale of gold for export without hindrance at the old parity price of £ 3.17 s 10½ d per standard ounce.[1] Churchill's announcement that Great Britain would return to the gold standard at the pre-war parity meant, in effect, that the official value of the pound would be raised from the then prevailing rate of 1 £ = $4.40 to 1 £ = $4.86, an increase of about 10 per cent in the external value of sterling.[2]

Although the restoration of the pound to its pre-war parity was thus officially realized, there was still a very serious obstacle to be overcome before such a resumption could be made truly effective. This was the problem of reducing British internal prices and costs by at least 10 per cent, so as to warrant the higher external value of sterling. Keynes blamed the existence of this problem on the failure of the Committee on the Currency to distinguish between the index of wholesale prices and the index of internal purchasing power.

---

1. A. W. Crawford, _International Monetary Developments between the First and Second World Wars_, Finance Department Chamber of Commerce of the United States, 1944, p. 3.
2. D. Dillard, _op. cit._, p. 304.

In urging the restoration of the gold standard at the pre-war parity, the Committee based its recommendation on the fact that the wholesale price index was adjusting itself to the improvement which had been taking place in the exchange value of sterling. It reasoned that, since the prices of commodities entering into wholesale trade were adapting themselves to an improvement in the exchange, all other prices would similarly adjust themselves to this appreciation in the external value of sterling.[1] On these grounds, an immediate return to the gold standard at the pre-war parity could be effected without difficulty.

The fact that the British wholesale price index compared favorably with the corresponding measure of the United States and other countries did not warrant, argued Keynes, the conclusion that the internal purchasing power of their respective currencies bore the same relationship to one another as in the pre-war period and that therefore a return to the pre-World War I exchange rate between the dollar and the pound was justified. The reason for this is that such a comparison of these indices does not give a proper indication of the relative purchasing power associated with different currencies.

As a matter of fact, the level of wholesale prices throughout the world should be approximately the same. Keynes reasoned that nearly two-thirds of all the commodities which enter into the calculation of these wholesale price indices are traded in highly

---

1. J. M. Keynes, The Economic Consequences of Mr. Churchill, op. cit., p. 11.

organized international markets;[1] therefore, after allowance for tariffs and transportation costs, the prices of these goods must be the same for all countries when defined in terms of a common currency.[2] In effect, the prices of these internationally-traded commodities cannot differ materially from one center to another.[3] And because wholesale indices are largely made up of these commodities which move in international trade, it follows that these, too, must be approximately equal.

If there do occur fluctuations in the ratio of one country's wholesale price index to that of another, these changes must correspond closely to the fluctuations in the exchange rates between their currencies and conversely.[4] For example, if the external value of sterling is increased, British wholesale prices would have to be reduced. If British quotations for wholesale goods remain the same under these circumstances, sterling prices

---

1. Ibid.
2. J. M. Keynes, A Treatise on Money, op. cit., vol. I, pp. 69-70.
3. J. M. Keynes, "The Gold Standard - A Correction," The Nation and Athenaeum, XXXVII, 6, May 9, 1925, p. 170.
4. The Purchasing Power Parity Theory of the Foreign Exchanges is basically a restatement of the proposition stated above to the effect that the rates of foreign exchange between two currencies move in the same way as the ratio of their respective international or wholesale index numbers. This is nothing more than a truism and no one can take exception with it. The difficulty with Cassel's formulation is that it extended illigitimately to the Purchasing Power of Money itself, i.e. it claimed that the rate of exchange between two currencies moves in the same fashion as the ratio of their respective purchasing power indices. For a fuller treatment of this subject vide J. M. Keynes, A Tract on Monetary Reform, op. cit., pp. 87 et seq. Also see J. M. Keynes, A Treatise on Money, op. cit., vol. I, pp. 69-74.

will exceed world prices because of the higher cost entailed in the purchase of sterling exchange. Consequently, if a nation exacts a higher price for its currency, then the prices at which it sells in international markets will have to be correspondingly reduced, assuming, of course, that there occur no price increases in other countries. In short, if a nation alters the value of its exchange, its wholesale price level will have to be correspondingly adjusted and conversely.

In view of this tendency to adjust themselves quickly between different countries, the prices of those goods which enter into the compilation of the wholesale price index are not likely to state properly any existing over or under-valuation of the currency.[1] Therefore, the claim that the British pound was moving towards parity with the American dollar, because the British wholesale index was adjusting itself to the higher sterling exchange, could not be accepted.

If the prices of all goods were to adjust themselves to a new rate of exchange, as do those goods and services which enter into wholesale trade, v.g. cotton, copper and other raw materials, there would be no difficulty in moving to a new level of exchange; however, not all commodity prices are quite so sensitive to such exchange variations. For example, there are certain costs, v.g. housing, taxes, interest, railway charges, and wages, which respond

---

1. G. Haberler, "The Choice of Exchange Rates After the War," American Economic Review, XXXV, 3, June, 1945, pp. 311-312.

slowly, if at all, to an improvement or deterioration of the exchange rate.[1] These costs do not enter directly into international trade and for this reason may differ from their counterparts in other countries.[2]

Although these services are largely exchanged within the economy, they have an important bearing on the export industries. Unless their prices are adjusted to a higher exchange value, they will have serious implications for the export industries. For while their production costs will be high, the prices they obtain for their commodities in foreign markets will be low, due to the appreciated exchange. Keynes indicates the dilemma very succinctly in the following comment.

> An improvement in the sterling exchange necessarily lowers all the 'unsheltered' prices, and if this is unaccompanied by forces tending to depress the 'sheltered' prices to an equal extent, those who produce in the 'unsheltered' industries are in obvious difficulties, because they are selling at the 'unsheltered' price level and, in part at least, buying and consuming at the 'sheltered' price level.[3]

This is precisely the difficulty which Keynes foresaw in the Treasury's decision to return to the gold standard at the pre-war

---

1. According to the Purchasing Power Parity Theory of the Foreign Exchanges, in the long run, all prices must adjust themselves to the exchange rate; otherwise, the repercussion of the domestic wage level and the cost of goods and services, produced domestically, but utilized in the unsheltered or export trades, will so impair the country's ability to compete in foreign markets that either the exchange rate must be adjusted or gold will flow out until such time as the domestic price level is reduced. (Vide J. M. Keynes, "The Gold Standard - A Correction," op. cit., p. 170.)
2. J. M. Keynes, "Monetary Policy - Relation of Price Levels," The London Times, Sept. 4, 1925, p. 20. Also vide J. M. Keynes, "The First Fruits of the British Gold Standard," The New Republic, XLVII, 600, June 2, 1926, p. 54.
3. J. M. Keynes, "The Committee on the Currency," op. cit., p. 301.

parity. Although the exchange rate was being increased, the internal level of prices was not sufficiently low to warrant this higher external value. Keynes argued that, only when domestic costs are sufficiently reduced to enable exporters to sell at a lower price level, would such a return to parity be justified. The question of parity, opined Keynes, entails not only a consideration of the prices of those commodities which enter into international trade, but also those which do not or which do so only indirectly. Therefore, he thought it far more realistic to consult the cost of living index, in which the latter type of good plays a more important role, than the wholesale price index for determining whether or not the time was propitious for a return to the gold standard at the pre-war parity.[1]

Had the Committee on the Currency recognized this distinction between goods which enter directly into international trade, v.g. raw materials, and those which do not, v.g. goods and services associated with the non-export or sheltered industries, it is unlikely that they would have made the mistake they did. Unfortunately, they reasoned that all prices behaved in the same fashion as those on the wholesale level; hence, if these prices were adjusting themselves to the higher exchange value, so would all other prices.[2] Specifically, the source of the Committee's error rested in its illicit extension of the Purchasing Power Parity Theory of the Foreign Exchanges to the purchasing power

---

1. J. M. Keynes, "The Gold Standard - A Correction," op. cit., p. 170.
2. J. M. Keynes, A Treatise on Money, op. cit., vol. I, p. 74.

of money itself, as Keynes indicates in the following passage.

> At the time of Great Britain's return to the gold standard the Treasury and the Bank of England were led to the false conclusion that, because the Wholesale Index, which was almost the same thing as the British International Index, was moving rapidly into adjustment - as an International Index must necessarily do - with the movement of the gold exchanges, therefore, the same thing was true of 'prices generally'.[1]

Had it not been for this confusion of identifying the wholesale price index with that of general purchasing power, Keynes feels that Great Britain would not have returned to the gold standard at the pre-war parity.

> I do not believe that Great Britain would have returned in 1925 to the Gold Standard at the pre-war parity if it had not been for the habit of regarding the Wholesale Standard as a satisfactory indicator of general purchasing power.[2]

Keynes took further exception with the Committee on grounds that, although it fully recognized the over-valuation of the pound and the need for further deflation,[3] it failed to disclose, specifically, how much deflation[4] was required and just how the whole range of British prices and wages was to be reduced, in order to make the internal value of the currency conform to its enhanced external value.[5]

Keynes suspected that the Committee hoped to effect the

---

1. *Ibid.*, pp. 74-75.
2. *Ibid.*, p. 89.
3. J. H. Williams, *op. cit.*, p. 301.
4. Unofficial estimates of the required deflation ranged from 5 per cent on up. (Vide G. Cassel, *The Downfall of the Gold Standard*, London, Oxford University Press, 1926, p. 36.)
5. R. F. Harrod, *op. cit.*, p. 359.

necessary reduction of internal prices and costs by raising the bank rate. The intermediate steps of the correction would then work out in the following manner. An increase in the bank rate will immediately lead to a curtailment of credit which, if sufficiently widespread, will lead to a reduction of employment. If enough unemployment can be generated, wages can be forced downward under the pressure of hard facts even in the "unsheltered" industries.[1] Accorded these lower wage costs, British exporters will again be in a position to sell their goods at the lower prices prevailing in foreign markets. At this stage, the British internal price and cost structure would be in equilibrium with that prevailing abroad and the higher exchange value for sterling would now be justified.[2]

This process of adjustment sounds entirely plausible, if one be unmindful of its social ramifications on the labor force. But even apart from this, it is found wanting, for it fails to take into account the highly inelastic conditions of the British industrial system. The mobility of labor and the competitiveness of the wage level, assumed by this adjustment mechanism, were simply non-existent in Great Britain of the post-war world, as Keynes' statement testifies.

> I suspect that their conclusions may be based on theories, developed 50 years ago, which assumed a mobility of labor and a competitive

---

1. J. M. Keynes, The Economic Consequences of Mr. Churchill, op. cit., p. 17.
2. J. M. Keynes, "The Committee on the Currency," The Economic Journal, XXXV, 138, June, 1925, p. 302.

> wage level which no longer exist; and that
> they have not thought the problem through
> over again in the light of the deplorably
> inelastic conditions of our industrial
> organism today.[1]

In previous periods, asserts Keynes, the pressure exerted by the loss of profits and the unemployment of the productive factors operated more quickly than they do now to bring about a desired income deflation. Even in this environment, the resistance to a downward revision of wage rates was substantial; but, avers Keynes, in the present economy, wherein trade unions and a proletarian electorate are extremely strong, this resistance[2] is even stronger.[3]

Thus, Keynes understood well the consequences attending a return to the gold standard at the pre-war parity. If the value of all transactions expressed in money terms could be lowered simultaneously to correspond with the appreciation of the exchange, there would be no problem. However, such was not the case, for not all prices could adjust themselves in the same way to changes in the external value of the currency.[4] The basic source of the difficulty, then, rested in the varying rates at which prices and costs would orient themselves to the new exchange rate.[5] As a

---

1. Ibid.
2. The resistance of British wages and other internal costs to adjustment served only to intensify rather than correct the existing imbalances. The net resultant of all this was a highly unstable economic situation and a chronic condition of unemployment and semi-depression which ultimately led to Great Britain's divorce from the gold standard in 1931. (Vide J.H. Williams, *Postwar Monetary Plans*, op. cit., pp. 301-302.)
3. J. M. Keynes, *A Tract on Monetary Reform*, op. cit., p. 183.
4. J. M. Keynes, *The Economic Consequences of Mr. Churchill*, op. cit., p. 11.
5. J. M. Keynes, "The First Fruits of the Gold Standard," op. cit., p. 345.

consequence of this lack of flexibility in the internal cost and price structure, the deflation required for the restoration of the gold standard at its pre-war value would create many frictions which would, in turn, lead to a discouragement of production and employment.[1]

This curtailment of production and employment, says Keynes, is the result of

> the so-called 'sound' policy, which is demanded as a result of the rash act of pegging sterling at a gold value, which it did not - measured in its purchasing power over British labor - possess as yet. It is a policy, nevertheless, from which any humane or judicious person must shrink.[2]

Summary

The foregoing account of Keynes' opposition to the restoration of the gold standard at the pre-war parity of exchange gives further substance to our claim that he was primarily concerned with the promotion of domestic as opposed to the furtherance of purely external objectives. Although the return of Great Britain to the gold standard at the pre-war value of sterling would be a great boon to an international financial center such as London, Keynes felt that the price which the internal economy would have to pay in terms of deflation and unemployment would more than offset that external advantage. To obviate such internal disequilibrium, he

---

1. Keynes estimates that the restoration of the gold standard may have reduced the national wealth, as compared with an alternative monetary system, by ₤ 150,000,000 a year.
2. J. M. Keynes, The Economic Consequences of Mr. Churchill, op. cit., p. 17.

urged that the external value of sterling be made to conform to its internal value and not the other way round. In this way, the level of domestic activity would not be impaired unduly, for the incidence of any adjustment between the internal and external sectors would largely fall on the latter.

The fact that Keynes made external considerations subservient to those of a purely domestic nature is of critical importance to the determination of his ultimate position on the question of free versus restricted foreign trade. For just as it was this concern for the domestic welfare which caused him to take exception with the international gold standard, so, too, it was this same consideration which caused him, in the final analysis, to part company with the doctrinaire free traders.

In view of the crucial importance of our contention that Keynes geared his economic thinking primarily to the internal requirements of the economy, it is well to substantiate further this proposition, by showing how he tried to protect the domestic welfare from external disruptions through his proposals for a managed standard. This will be our objective in the next chapter.

CHAPTER VI

KEYNES' QUEST FOR NATIONAL AUTONOMY AS EVIDENCED BY HIS PREFERENCE FOR A MANAGED MONETARY STANDARD

Concerned as he was with the inability of the traditional gold standard to advance the well-being of the domestic economy, Keynes suggested in its place a type standard that would make possible the realization of many of the objectives cited in the earlier chapters of this section. He thought that these could be best achieved through the instrumentality of a managed currency.[1] Conscious control of the monetary standard is imperative, he argued, for

> We can no longer afford to leave it in the category of which the disturbing characteristics are possessed in different degrees by the weather, the birth rate, and the Constitution, - matters which are settled by natural causes or are the resultant of separate action of many individuals acting independently, or require a Revolution to change them.[2]

---

1. It should be noted that, although Keynes' managed currency schemes were opposed to the so-called automatic gold standard of the pre-war period, they did not exclude gold completely. Keynes did, in fact, retain an important reserve function for gold in his monetary system, as he indicates in the following passage. "I retain for gold an important role in our system. As an ultimate safeguard and as a reserve for sudden requirements, no superior medium is yet available. But I urge that it is possible to get the benefit of the advantages of gold, without irrevocably binding our legal tender money to follow blindly all the vagaries of gold and future unforeseeable fluctuations in its real purchasing power." (J. M. Keynes, A Tract on Monetary Reform, op. cit., p. 197.) Thus, although Keynes would favor some role for gold in his system, he would do so only on condition that it serve as "a constitutional monarch, shorn of his ancient despotic powers and compelled to accept the advice of a Parliament of Banks." (J. M. Keynes, A Tract on Monetary Reform, op. cit., p. 173.)
2. J. M. Keynes, A Tract on Monetary Reform, op. cit., p. 40.

Keynes' interest in a managed standard does not have its genesis in the post-World War I era, for this was one of his prime preoccupations even in the earliest phase of his career. This is evidenced by the very first work written by him while a young instructor at Cambridge.[1] This effort, entitled, "Recent Economic Events in India,"[2] deals with the monetary disturbances which took place in that country in 1907-1908 and their relation to the management of the rupee.[3]

During the course of 1908, India experienced an unfavorable balance of trade. This imbalance was caused principally by a harvest failure in that year and a large increase in the coinage which had taken place in the previous year.[4] The former development served to increase the volume of imports and the latter led to an inflation of prices which quite naturally discouraged the level of exports. Unfortunately, India had no sizable gold reserve with which to meet this external debt; hence, the exchange value of the rupee headed towards a serious depreciation.

---

1. Keynes was made a fellow at King's College in 1908 largely through the efforts of his former professor and benefactor, Alfred Marshall, who occupied the Chair of Economics at Cambridge University.
2. J. M. Keynes, "Recent Economic Events in India," The Economic Journal, XIX, 73, March, 1909, pp. 51-67.
3. R. F. Harrod, The Life of John M. Keynes, op. cit., p. 146.
4. In 1907, India enjoyed a prosperous export trade and an influx of foreign capital. These factors stimulated the sale of Council bills which, when encashed by Indian nationals, swelled the volume of currency in circulation. (Vide J. M. Keynes, "Recent Economic Events in India," op. cit., p. 66.)

Such a prospect, however, was averted by the unprecedented action of the Secretary of State in making available sufficient resources for the support of the rupee exchange.[1]

Keynes commended this action of the Secretary in not permitting the free market forces to run their natural course, which, in this instance, would have led to a severe depreciation of the external value of the rupee. Thus, even at this early date, Keynes' attitude towards monetary management was clear. He regarded the currency system not as a mechanism that should be automatic and free from any type of tampering, but as a device which should admit of management for the purpose of obtaining a desired result.[2]

Keynes' early preference for a managed currency is further exhibited in an article he prepared for the *Economic Journal* in late 1914 on monetary problems of the early war period. In it he argued that it was needless for civilized countries to expose themselves "to sudden and arbitrary disturbances of their social and economic system by leaving fluctuations of the monetary standard outside their control, when they might be within it."[3] Such control is entirely possible for "it is easy to invent modes of regulating the value of the standard which, however far from perfection, are at least better than what we have at present."[4] Only the public will to accept this conscious direction remains to be attained and

---

1. J. M. Keynes, "Recent Economic Events in India," op. cit., pp. 66-67.
2. R. F. Harrod, *The Life of John M. Keynes*, op. cit., p. 146.
3. J. M. Keynes, "The Prospects of Money, November, 1914," *The Economic Journal*, XXIV, 96, Dec. 1914, pp. 626-627.
4. Ibid., p. 627.

this, he asserted, is not in the too distant future.

> It is...a possible consequence of the present war...that some international standard will be forced on the principal countries of the world. If it prove one of the after-effects of the present struggle, that gold is at last deposed from its despotic control over us and reduced to the position of a constitutional monarch, a new chapter of history will be opened. Man will have made another step forward in the attainment of self-government in the power to control his fortunes according to his own wishes.... A new dragon will have been set up at a new Colchis to guard the Golden Fleece from adventurers.[1]

Keynes had made a similar prognastication concerning the acceptance of a managed monetary standard at an even earlier date. This may be found in his *Indian Currency and Finance* wherein he states,

> The time may not be far distant when Europe, having perfected her mechanism of exchange on the basis of a gold standard, will find it possible to regulate her standard of value on a more rational and stable basis. It is not likely that we shall leave permanently the most intimate adjustments of our economic organism at the mercy of a lucky prospector, a new chemical process, or a change of ideas in Asia.[2]

Despite Keynes' earlier anticipation of a struggle in the post-World War I period between a managed and a so-called automatic gold standard, none came to pass, because the former was already a "fait accompli". There could be no question of an issue between these two money systems at this time, for the

---

1. Ibid.
2. J. M. Keynes, *Indian Currency and Finance*, op. cit., pp. 100-101.

existing monetary and banking systems dealt largely in paper money and credit, the volume of which was, in fact, consciously controlled. As Keynes pointed out, "In the modern world of paper currency and bank credit there is no escape from a 'managed' currency, whether we wish it or not."[1]

The so-called automatic gold standard could not exist in this period, because the value of gold was no longer determined by a variety of independent forces, as was the case prior to the war. During the pre-war period, the intrinsic value of gold was largely determined by the demand of the Arts and the hoards of Asia. The value of gold did not depend upon the policy decisions of any single institution. However, all this was changed in the post-war era with the rise of the United States as the major gold-holding power. With most nations off the gold standard, the supply of gold would have been redundant, if the United States had chosen to restrict her gold holdings to her real needs. This, of course, the United States did not do, for if she were to restrict the amount of gold held, and thereby permit its value to fall to its proper level, her own standard would be seriously depreciated. Therefore, in order to maintain the value of gold at an artificial value, the Federal Reserve Banks were constrained to bottle up a sizable portion of the world's supply, but, in so doing, they divorced the gold standard from its automatic nature. Thus, concludes Keynes, because

---

1. J. M. Keynes, *A Tract on Monetary Reform*, op. cit., p. 170.

the future value of gold depends upon the policy of the Federal Reserve Board, or, at most, the policies of the three or four most powerful Central Banks, gold has de facto become a managed standard.[1]

Another reason cited by Keynes for the passing of the automatic nature of the gold standard at this time was the impounding of gold by the Federal Reserve Banks. This action resulted from their practice of sterilizing the inflow of gold into the United States. Instead of regulating their discount rates according to the inflow and outflow of gold and the proportion of gold reserves to their liabilities, the Banks ignored this ratio and accepted gold without permitting it to effect an inflation of credit and prices.[2] In so preventing gold movements from exerting their full influence on credit and prices, the Federal Reserve Board destroyed the automatism of the gold standard.[3]

Monetary and credit policy in the United States was not determined by reference to the above criteria, as would be expected under the "automatic" gold standard, but by the requirements of stable prices, trade and employment, as Keynes points out below.

---

1. Ibid., pp. 166-168.
2. Ibid., p. 198.
3. This impounding of gold by the Federal Reserve Board to keep it from exercising its full natural effects on credit and prices is tantamount to demonitization. (Vide A. Johnson, "Keynes on Monetary Reform," op. cit., p. 288.)

> In practice the Federal Reserve Board often
> ignores the proportion of its gold reserve
> to its liabilities and is influenced, in
> determining its discount policy, by the
> object of maintaining stability in prices,
> trade, and employment. Out of convention
> and conservatism it accepts gold. Out of
> prudence and understanding it buries it.[1]

This policy was not peculiar to the United States alone, for even in Great Britain strides were being made at this time towards the ideal of regulating bank rate and credit policy by reference to the internal price level rather than by reference to the pre-war criteria of the amount of money in circulation, the status of the gold reserves or the value of the dollar exchange.[2]

In the light of these conditions obtaining in the post-war world, particularly in the United States, Keynes concluded that there could be no issue between a managed and an automatic standard, for the former had already supplanted the latter, as he indicates in the following assertion.

> In truth, the gold standard is already a
> barbarous relic. All of us, from the Governor
> of the Bank of England downwards, are now
> primarily interested in preserving the stabi-
> lity of business, prices and employment, and
> are not likely, when the choice is forced upon
> us, deliberately to sacrifice these to the
> outworn dogma, which had its value once, of
> £ 3:17:10½ per ounce. Advocates of the ancient
> standard do not observe how remote it now is
> from the spirit and the requirements of the age.
> A regulated non-metallic standard has slipped
> in unnoticed. It exists.[3]

---

1. J. M. Keynes, *A Tract on Monetary Reform, op. cit.*, p. 197.
2. *Ibid.*, p. 185.
3. *Ibid.*, pp. 172-173.

The real issue in Keynes' mind was not whether the monetary standard should be managed, but for what purpose it should be managed. Should it be managed with the objective of securing a stable internal price level or a stable exchange rate?[1] Keynes' concept of a managed standard took into account both objectives. It was to be

> I. A method for regulating the supply of currency and credit with a view to maintaining, as far as possible, the stability of the internal price level; and
>
> II. A method for regulating the supply of foreign exchange so as to avoid purely temporary fluctuations, caused by seasonal or other influences and not due to a lasting disturbance in the relation between the internal and the external price level.[2]

Although Keynes includes the stabilization of the exchange rate as one of the objectives to be achieved by a managed currency, this in no way contradicts his earlier position on the primacy of a stable internal price level,[3] as note his following statement.

> At any rate, my scheme would require that they (Treasury and Bank of England) should adopt the stability of sterling prices as their 'primary' objective - though this would not prevent their aiming at exchange stability also as a secondary objective by cooperating with the Federal Reserve Board in a common policy.[4]

Keynes points out that his advocacy of exchange stability as a secondary objective would in no way impair the realization of

---

1. H. R. Burrows, op. cit., p. 156.
2. J. M. Keynes, A Tract on Monetary Reform, op. cit., p. 177.
3. A. F. Smithies, op. cit., p. 588.
4. J. M. Keynes, A Tract on Monetary Reform, op. cit., p. 186.

the first objective. It would simply be a by-product of stable prices in both Great Britain and the United States. His contention is that "so long as the Federal Reserve Board was successful in keeping dollar prices steady the objective of keeping sterling prices steady would be identical with the objective of keeping the dollar sterling exchange steady."[1] However, Keynes is emphatic in warning that should the Federal Reserve Board fail to keep dollar prices stable, sterling prices should not be made to follow them simply for the sake of maintaining a fixed parity of exchange.[2]

Further proof that Keynes was entirely consistent in his advocacy of both a stable internal price level and a stable exchange rate may be gathered from a consideration of the type exchange stability sought by him. The kind of stability favored by Keynes was unlike the long period stability accorded by the international gold standard. All he desired to accomplish was the elimination of seasonal and other passing influences not caused by a lasting disturbance between the internal and external price levels.[3] In effect, Keynes favored a stabilization of the exchange only for a short period. In the long run, the exchange should be left free to conform to the relation existing between the internal and external price levels.[4]

The next consideration of Keynes' managed currency scheme deals with the criteria to be utilized by the Treasury and the banking

---

1. Ibid.
2. Ibid., p. 186.
3. J. S. G. Wilson, op. cit., p. 19.
4. A. E. Robinson, op. cit., p. 33.

system for judging whether fiscal and monetary policies are being properly directed towards the attainment of these objectives.

The first norm suggested by Keynes is an index number of prices compiled in a way to register the price of a standard composite commodity. The authorities should adopt this composite commodity as their standard of value in the sense that they would try to prevent a movement of its price by more than a certain percentage either above or below a certain normal, just as prior to the war they utilized all their resources in keeping the price of gold from varying by more than a certain amount.[1]

Keynes does not rely exclusively on this price index, because the action resulting from this indicator might be unduly delayed.[2] As Hawtrey points out, "It is not the past rise in prices but the future rise that has to be counteracted" and the same would be true of a price decline.[3] In addition to actual price movements, Keynes suggests the following standards: the state of employment, the volume of production, the effective demand for bank credit, the structure of interest rates, the volume of new issues, the amount of cash in circulation, the volume of foreign trade and the level of the exchanges. All these statistics, says Keynes, should be studied for the purpose of achieving stability of domestic prices.[4]

---

1. J. M. Keynes, *A Tract on Monetary Reform*, op. cit., pp. 187-8.
2. R. F. Harrod, *The Life of John M. Keynes*, op. cit., p. 344.
3. R. G. Hawtrey, *Monetary Reconstruction*, New York, Longmans, Green and Co., 1923, p. 105.
4. J. M. Keynes, *A Tract on Monetary Reform*, op. cit., pp. 188-9.

Given its assignment and the requisite statistical tools, the next problem facing the monetary authority is how to combine the stability of domestic prices with a maximum stability of the exchanges. The crux of the problem is to obtain stability of prices over long periods and stability of exchange over short periods; or to put it in other terms, the object is to dampen the excessive sensitivity of the exchanges to temporary influences, as was the case under the old gold standard, without at the same time leaving the internal economy open to all the vagaries associated with movements in the value of gold.[1]

Keynes believes that it is possible to stabilize the exchange rate and at the same time not to subject the internal economy to the disequilibrating effects of the gold and capital movements, provided a number of innovations be introduced into the money and banking system which emerged after the war. These are regulation of the gold buying and selling prices, forward exchange dealings, spreading the gold points, control over the rate of long-term foreign lending, divorce of gold reserves from the note circulation, and increasing the size of Central Bank reserves. These monetary instruments were largely developed by Keynes in the period 1920-1930 and are treated principally in his A Tract on Monetary Reform (1923) and A Treatise on Money (1930).

Just as the Bank of England stipulates the rate of discount every Thursday morning, Keynes would have it quote buying and

---

1. Ibid., pp. 189-190.

selling prices for gold at the same time. These prices might remain unchanged for a considerable period; however, unlike the pre-war era, they would not be pegged for all time. In determining these gold prices, Keynes at first recommended that a spread of 1/2 to 1 per cent be established between the buying and selling quotations.[1] Later on, he suggested a range of at least 2 per cent. The significance of having the Bank of England stand ready to exchange gold for sterling at stipulated prices is that the range of fluctuations in the rate of exchange over the short run would be minimized. For example, if the exchange rate of sterling for dollars had a tendency to soften, this depreciation of sterling could not go beyond a certain point, viz. the gold export point for sterling, for then it would be cheaper to convert sterling notes for gold at the Bank of England and remit the metal to the United States. By so having the Bank of England guarantee the gold value of its currency over short intervals, the exchange rate would be kept from falling below a certain level, and in this way would not have to be subjected to the pressures of every minor movement.

Although the exchange rate would be stabilized over the short run, it would not be so stabilized over the long run, for this would be tantamount to surrendering the stability of the internal price level. This means, therefore, that in order

---

1. Prior to World War I the spread between these quotations, ₤3:17s:10½d and ₤3:17s:9d, amounted to 1½d.

to keep the domestic price level steady, the Central Bank would either have to adjust the exchange rate, by altering its gold buying and selling prices, or it would have to alter its discount rate.[1]

For example, if at the prevailing bank rate and level of gold prices there occurs an influx or efflux of gold, which is disruptive of domestic prices, the monetary authority will have to determine whether this gold movement is due to the operation of internal or external forces. Suppose that there occurs an efflux of gold from the country, how may the outflow be stopped and prices stabilized? If this loss of gold appears to be caused by a tendency of sterling to depreciate in terms of commodities, i.e. by internal inflationary pressures, the proper remedy would be to raise the bank rate. If, on the other hand, this gold outflow can be explained by a tendency of gold to appreciate abroad in terms of goods and services, i.e. by lower foreign prices, the correct procedure would be to raise the buying price for gold.

By raising the value of gold in terms of sterling, more pounds would be surrendered to the foreign customer for the same amount of gold as heretofore.[2] This action would have the effect of bringing the higher British prices into balance with those prevailing internationally without affecting their value internally. In short, a devalued pound would permit the British

---

1. J. M. Keynes, *A Tract on Monetary Reform*, op. cit., p. 190.
2. This amounts, of course, to a devaluation of sterling.

103

to compete in foreign markets without having to subject their economy to serious deflation. Once this balance between local and world prices is achieved, the gold outflow will come to a halt and may, in fact, be reversed.[1]

Under the orthodox gold standard, when gold appreciated in terms of foreign commodities and therefore started to flow abroad, the only way this outflow could be checked was for domestic prices to fall into line with those prevailing abroad; hence, deflation. In the monetary mechanism proposed by Keynes, however, such a disruption of the domestic price level would be unnecessary, for the Central Bank would effectively bring it into balance with the price levels obtaining abroad by simply surrendering more of its cheapened currency for the same quantity of gold.

The second recommendation made by Keynes for managing the currency dealt with forward exchange dealings. In addition to its quotations for the purchase and sale of gold, Keynes urged that the Bank of England quote rates at which it would be prepared to sell three months forward exchange on one or two selected financial centers.[2] These prices would be established

---

1. J. M. Keynes, *A* *Tract* *on* *Monetary* *Reform*, op. cit., p. 191.
2. Keynes deals extensively with this question of the forward exchanges in one of his contributions to the *Manchester* *Guardian* *Commercial* *Supplements*. Vide J. M. Keynes, "The Forward Market in the Foreign Exchanges," *Reconstruction* *in* *Europe*, op. cit., April 20, 1922, pp. 11-15. Keynes also treats this topic in *A* *Tract* *on* *Monetary* *Reform*, op. cit., Ch. III, Section IV; *A* *Treatise* *on* *Money*, op. cit., pp. 323-327; and in his article, "The Future of the Foreign Exchanges," *Lloyd's* *Bank* *Monthly*, op. cit., pp. 527-535.

at a reasonable discount or premium on the spot quotation, depending upon the relative standing of the interest rates in the two centers.[1]

For example, if the rate of interest in New York is 3 per cent higher than in London, the price of dollars purchased forward should be 3 per cent per annum cheaper than spot dollars in terms of sterling. This means that an individual who is desirous of converting sterling into forward dollars under these conditions should be able to obtain them at a discount on the spot price, whereas a person wishing to exchange dollars for forward sterling would have to pay a premium on the spot price, in order to make up for the lower interest return obtainable in London.

According to Keynes, given two money markets in which unlike rates of interest prevail, "forward quotations for the purchase of the currency of the dearer money market tend to be cheaper than spot quotations by a percentage per month equal to the excess of the interest which can be earned in a month in the dearer market over what can be earned in the cheaper"[2] and the forward quotations for the purchase of the currency of the cheaper money market will tend to be higher by this amount.

To eliminate as much risk as possible from the Bank's forward exchange operations, Keynes suggests that it deal in both the spot

---

1. Although the margin between the spot and forward quotations is basically caused by differences in the interest rates, there are also a number of other influences at work. These are financial and political risk, the demand and supply of forward exchange, and the size and competitive nature of the various foreign money markets.
2. J. M. Keynes, A Tract on Monetary Reform, op. cit., p. 124.

and forward markets. Every sale of forward exchange should be accompanied by a corresponding spot purchase of the currency being traded. In this way, the Central Bank can earn interest on the spot purchase and thus escape the risk of loss. Similarly, every purchase of forward exchange should be matched by a corresponding spot sale of the currency being exchanged.[1] However, not every forward transaction need be covered by a corresponding spot purchase of sale, provided that a forward sale of exchange on a particular center may be matched with a forward purchase on that same center. By so offsetting these forward contracts one against the other, it will not be necessary for the Bank to assume a speculative position.[2] Moreover, such a matching of contracts will obviate the need to transfer funds in either direction,[3] which is, of course, one of the important objectives of such forward dealings.

To handle such forward operations, the Central Bank would have to maintain a certain amount of cash resources or adequate borrowing facilities in the financial centers on which it bought and sold exchange. This fund should be large enough to sustain any possible loss incurred by the Bank in its operations. Losses are to be contemplated, in fact, because very often the Central Bank may have to set an arbitrary rate on these exchange ratios

---

1. R. G. Hawtrey, *The Art of Central Banking*, London, Longmans, Green and Co., 1932, p. 415.
2. R. F. Mikesell, *Foreign Exchange in the Postwar World*, New York, The Twentieth Century Fund, 1954, p. 163.
3. R. G. Hawtrey, *Currency and Credit*, (Fourth Edition), London, Longmans, Green and Co., 1950, pp. 141-143.

which is moving against the market forces.[1] But even allowing for these losses, the fund would not have to be quite so large as one set up for the purpose of maintaining the exchange value of a currency, for it would be a revolving one, in that it would be automatically replenished at the maturity of the forward contracts.[2] So much for the mechanics of forward exchange operations. Let us now consider their value to the attainment of domestic economic stability.

Keynes' motives in urging the establishment of such a forward exchange market were to support the stability of the exchange, to insulate further the home economy from outward disturbances and to permit the Central Bank to pursue a monetary policy in consonance with its own domestic needs, rather than with purely external requirements.

Under the pre-war gold standard system, domestic equilibrium was often disrupted from the outside by the existence of different interest rate structures in the various international financial centers. As a result of these variations, short term balances would move from those centers offering a relatively low rate of interest to those financial capitals offering a higher return. In order to control these inward and outward capital migrations, the level of bank rate, though corresponding to domestic needs, would have to be altered. The Central Bank would have to set

---

1. C. R. Whittlesey, op. cit., pp. 221-222.
2. J. M. Keynes, A Tract on Monetary Reform, op. cit., p. 134.

aside its own domestic monetary objectives and adjust its interest rate to the world level.[1] This meant, therefore, that a nation's domestic rate of interest would be dictated by external forces - a prospect much opposed to by Keynes, for if a nation's interest rate is determined for it by outside forces, it may be impossible for it to achieve domestic investment equilibrium.[2]

It is quite clear, therefore, that if a nation was to achieve some degree of autonomy in the determination of its interest rate policy, it would have to exercise control over short term capital movements. This Keynes hoped to accomplish, in part, via the forward exchange mechanism.[3] The plan envisioned by him would have the Central Bank regulate (within limits) the movement of capital funds by entering into forward exchange operations. Through its purchase and sale quotations for forward exchange, the Central Bank could act upon the gain or loss which attends the exchanging of one currency for another, and thereby control the movement of funds between different financial centers.[4] Thus freed from the necessity of employing its bank rate to satisfy external requirements, the Central Bank could then utilize this device for the promotion of stable prices, full employment and

---

1. A. I. Bloomfield, op. cit., pp. 298-299.
2. "This will happen," says Keynes, "if its foreign balance is inelastic, and if, at the same time, it is unable to absorb the whole of its savings in new investment at the world rate of interest." (J. M. Keynes, A Treatise on Money, vol. II, op. cit., p. 304.)
3. J. M. Keynes, Monetary Reform (British Edition), op. cit., p. 208.
4. C. R. Whittlesey, op. cit., p. 220.

other purely domestic objectives.¹ The following is an account of the fashion in which the plan would work out in practice.

Suppose that the Central Bank lowers its bank rate to a level below that prevailing in foreign financial centers. To take advantage of the higher interest rate obtainable there, bankers and other holders of balances, which are available for short-term investment, will be inclined to place them in foreign bills or to deposit them abroad.² This type of investment involves considerable risk, because of the possibility of an unfavorable exchange fluctuation. Therefore, to protect himself from such an eventuality, the holder of these foreign investments enters into a contract to sell foreign exchange 30 or 90 days forward, depending upon the maturity of his investment.³ If, however, an adjustment could be made on the rate of exchange adopted for forward exchange dealings by the Central Bank,⁴ the rate charged might be such as to offset any gain in interest realized from the foreign investment of funds. In short, should the discount on the forward exchange be sufficiently large to delete the gain in interest, no one could gain from the higher interest rate abroad by transfering funds there, except by incurring an exchange risk.⁵ And since no one would be likely to remit funds

---

1. A. I. Bloomfield, op. cit., p. 298.
2. R. G. Hawtrey, The Art of Central Banking, op. cit., p. 407.
3. R. G. Hawtrey, Currency and Credit, op. cit., p. 142.
4. The Central Bank would not deal directly with the public in its forward exchange operations; rather, it would deal only with approved banks and financial houses. (Vide J. M. Keynes, Monetary Reform (British Edition), op. cit., p. 145.)
5. R. G. Hawtrey, The Art of Central Banking, op. cit., p. 414.

temporarily from one money market to another on any large scale simply to take advantage of a $\frac{1}{2}$ to 1 per cent per annum differential in the interest rate, while leaving himself open to a possible exchange loss, the migration of short term balances would be greatly restricted.[1]

In effect, by adjusting the buying or selling rate on forward exchange, the Central Bank could make short period interest rates at home stand temporarily in such relation (within limits) to similar rates abroad as it might deem advisable.[2] By neutralizing the differential in foreign and domestic interest rates, the Central Bank would inhibit any movement of funds between international financial centers.[3] And by so separating the domestic from the foreign money markets, it could maintain different short term interest rates for foreign and domestic funds.[4]

Thus relieved of the need to employ bank rate as a means of preserving equilibrium in its balance of payments and stability of its exchange, the monetary authority could then utilize this device exclusively for satisfying internal economic requirements, especially the maintenance of a high level of employment. That the main function of bank rate should be the promotion of purely domestic objectives is clearly indicated by Keynes in his following statement.

---

1. J. M. Keynes, Monetary Reform, op. cit., p. 148.
2. J. M. Keynes, A Treatise on Money, vol. II, op. cit., pp. 325-326.
3. C. R. Whittlesey, op. cit., p. 221.
4. J. M. Keynes, A Treatise on Money, vol. II, op. cit., p. 327. (Also vide J. M. Keynes, "The Future of the Foreign Exchanges," op. cit., pp. 530-531.)

> I have expressly excluded from my devices changes
> in bank rate and in the volume of domestic credit,
> which were the main instruments of pre-war policy.
> It is the outstanding lesson of our post-war ex-
> perience that these methods must be entirely
> discarded as a means of regulating the exchanges.
> They required for their success certain special
> conditions which no longer obtain, and may have
> been responsible even in pre-war days for much
> damage. It is essential that they should be
> employed in future with exclusive regard to
> internal conditions and, in particular, the state
> of employment.[1]

Although the forward exchange mechanism was effective in discouraging the movement of funds when the exchange rate was at a level somewhere between the gold points, it was not equally effective when the value of the exchange reached one of these extremes. So long as the exchange rested at some intermediate point, there was a strong possibility that it might move up or down. This meant that if the owner of international balances transferred his funds to abroad at such a rate of exchange, he would run the risk of not being able to repatriate them at the same rate.[2] Thus, in contemplating whether or not he should avail himself of the higher interest return obtainable abroad, the holder of these balances would have to offset this advantage by the possibility of an exchange loss. Often, this risk was sufficient to inhibit any outward flow of short-term capital.

The situation was altogether different, however, when the

---

1. J. M. Keynes, "The Future of the Foreign Exchanges," op. cit., p. 531.
2. R. G. Hawtrey, The Art of Central Banking, op. cit., p. 407.

exchange rate stood at either the gold export or import point. For example, if the dollar-sterling rate of exchange is anchored at the gold-export point for sterling, an interest rate in London higher than the one prevailing in New York will induce a flow of funds from New York to London. The reason for this is that, as the exchange reaches this point, there is no threat that the value of sterling will drop below this level; hence, the owners of dollar balances are certain that they may return their capital home without incurring any exchange loss.[1] In fact, there is a strong possibility that during the period of the loan, the value of sterling will appreciate in terms of dollars; hence, the owners of these funds stand to make an exchange profit in addition to the higher interest return. The same situation, of course, would obtain in the opposite direction. Clearly, if the movement of short term capital is to be discouraged, this element of certitude attending these transactions must be removed. This may be done by permitting a wider fluctuation of the exchange rate than was possible under the existing spread of the gold points.[2] In short, a widening of the gold points is indicated. Let us examine briefly Keynes' arguments for such a proposal.[3]

---

1. J. M. Keynes, *A Treatise on Money*, op. cit., vol. I, p. 324.
2. M. A. Heilperin, *International Monetary Economics*, op. cit., p. 228.
3. This notion of spreading the gold points was not novel to Keynes of the *Treatise* period, for he had dealt with this mechanism as early as the publication of *Indian Currency and Finance* as a means of coping with floating balances. In this work, he indicated that differences in interest rates between financial centers will not lead to short term capital movements when their costs of remittance are high. Specifically, he points out that, although the interest rate may go to 7 or 8 per cent on excellent security, fully 3 per cent more than can be obtained in London, the cost of

When the exchange rate is fixed or set within very narrow limits, as is the case in the international gold system, loans in different national currencies are virtually identical, because the two currencies are interchangeable without cost and at a rate of exchange known in advance. In view of the fact that there is no risk attending the making of such loans, bank balances migrate freely.[1]

Keynes reasons that to discourage the movement of short term capital in response to interest rate differentials, it is necessary to destroy the identity between loans expressed in different currencies. This may be done by introducing some element of doubt or expense in the conditions attending the exchange of one currency for another. If this be done, then the rate of interest on loans

---

3. transferring funds between London and India works out higher than would be anticipated. Keynes calculates that the cost of remittance on a rupee amounts to 3/32 d or .6 per cent. Now, in order to recoup this amount in three months, the rate of interest in India must be circa 2½ per cent per annum higher than in London; hence, there is little incentive to transfer British funds to India under these circumstances. $F_u$nds may be further inhibited from moving, if there be danger of an exchange fluctuation or if gold cannot be freely obtained.

These cost and risk factors determine the gold point spread, which may be defined as the maximum variation between the best and worst terms on which two currencies may be exchanged. It is the existence of this variation, between the terms on which one currency is exchanged for another and the terms on which this transaction may be later reversed, that serves to repress the sensitivity of capital flows to interest rate differentials, and thereby permits unlike interest rate structures to obtain in different money markets. (Vide J. M. Keynes, Indian Currency and Finance, op. cit., pp. 243-251. Also Cf. J. M. Keynes, "Stabilization of the European Exchanges - A Plan for Genoa," op. cit., p. 4.)

1. J. M. Keynes, A Treatise on Money, op. cit., vol. II, p. 319.

in terms of one currency may fluctuate within a range set by the amount of cost and degree of doubt, without regard to the rate of interest on loans stated in terms of the second currency. The range between the terms on which a currency can be exchanged for another, and the terms on which it may be exchanged again for the original currency at a later date is determined by the distance between the gold points.[1] The farther apart these points are set, the less sensitive to external variations in the interest rate[2] a country's foreign lending activity will be.[3]

---

1. The margin between the gold points is a function of two factors - doubt and cost. The first element consists of the uncertainty attending the future terms of exchange between currencies. Such a condition obtains when the Central Bank fails to guarantee the parity value of its currency. The cost factor is made up of two components. The first is the difference between the Central Bank's buying and selling prices for gold. In the case of the Bank of England, this amounted to 1 1/2 d, the difference between ₤ 3:17:10½ and ₤ 3:17:9 per ounce. The second cost element comprises those expenses associated with transferring gold from one locale to another, v.g. freight charges, insurance and loss of interest while in transit. In general, the maximum cost range for different pairs of countries varies from 1/2 to 1 1/2 per cent. (Vide J. M. Keynes, A Treatise on Money, op. cit., vol. II, pp. 320-322.)
2. J. M. Keynes, A Treatise on Money, op. cit., vol. II, p. 320.
3. The importance of the gold spread in discouraging capital movements is brought out by the following illustration. If the gold points between sterling and dollars are 3/4 per cent apart, the interest rate in New York can enjoy a maximum differential of 3 per cent over the rate prevailing in London when the exchange reaches the gold export point for sterling. The reasoning is as follows. The cost of transferring British funds amounts to 3/4 per cent of the principal. But in 90 days this sum can earn only one-fourth of the amount that could be earned by the annual rate, or 3/4 per cent. Thus, although the

This may be substantiated by the following reasoning. The wider the margin between the gold points, the greater will be the range of fluctuation permitted the exchange rate. But the greater the amplitude of the possible exchange fluctuation, the greater will be the possibility of exchange loss; hence, the less certain is the owner of foreign balances that he may repatriate his money on the same terms at which he lent it.[1] Confronted with this greater exchange risk, the holders of international balances will be more hesitant to send their money abroad in quest of a higher interest return. Moreover, a widening of the gold points will further lessen the possibility of capital movements, because the farther apart they are set, the fewer will be the occasions on which the exchange will reach either of these limits. The less frequently this happens, the less often can a prospective lender of international funds be certain that he can make a loan with the certainty that he may subsequently reverse this transaction without danger

---

3. British owner of capital would earn 3/4 per cent more interest in New York than in London for a three month period, it would cost him 3/4 per cent to do so; hence, there would be no advantage in entering into this transaction. From this it may be inferred that the farther apart these gold points are set, and the maximum cost of transferring funds accordingly increased, the greater can be the disparity in the interest rates prevailing in different financial centers. (Vide J.M. Keynes, A Treatise on Money, op. cit., vol. II, pp. 323-324.)

1. W. Egle, "The Spreading of the Gold Points as a Means of Controlling the Movement of Foreign Short Term Balances," The Journal of Political Economy, XLVII, 6, Dec. 1939, p. 859.

of an exchange loss.[1] As a result of the operation of these two forces, viz. the increase in the amplitude of the possible exchange fluctuation and the reduced probability of the exchange's reaching either gold point, which are made possible by a widening of the gold points, bank balances are certain to be less sensitive to variations in the level of interest prevailing abroad than they would be under a system of more narrow gold points. It is this margin between the gold points, avers Keynes, "which protects the money market of one country from being upset by every puff of wind which blows in the money markets of other countries."[2] The magnitude of

---

1. C. R. Whittlesey is of the opinion that a widening of the gold points, as suggested by Keynes, would not resolve completely the problem of disequilibrating short-term capital movements. According to him, if the gold points are widened, then whenever the exchange approaches either one of the gold limits, there will occur an even stronger tendency than heretofore to convert funds into the weaker currency, because the possible movement of the exchange in the opposite direction is much greater now than it was under a narrower spread of the gold points. Whittlesey's contention is that, given a wider spread of the gold points, the frequency with which balances are transferred will be reduced; however, the amount of money involved in these transfers will be increased, because of the possibility of a greater exchange profit.

   Whittlesey's own preference is for a system of freely fluctuating exchange rates. For under such a system the fact that there is no guarantee as to how far the value of the exchange may fall will interpose a greater risk for holders of international balances, and thus more severely restrict them in transferring funds from one center to another. (Vide C. R. Whittlesey, *International Monetary Issues*, op. cit., pp. 115-121.) R. G. Hawtrey is also of the opinion that a widening of the gold points will not be a completely effective way of dealing with this problem. (Vide R. G. Hawtrey, *The Art of Central Banking*, op. cit., pp. 419.)
2. J. M. Keynes, *A Treatise on Money*, op. cit., vol. II, p. 325.

this difference is of extreme importance to the domestic economy, for, so far as it protects the Central Bank from the disequilibrating effects of floating balances, it enables it to pursue an autonomous monetary policy aimed at the attainment of domestic stability - the primary objective of Keynes' managed currency proposal. Therefore, Keynes urged that "the difference between a Central Bank's obligatory buying and selling prices of gold should be made somewhat greater than hitherto, say 2 per cent, so that there would be at least this difference between the gold points irrespective of the actual costs of transporting gold."[1]

As a further means of protecting the home economy from the movement of international funds, Keynes suggested that the monetary authority control the rate of long term foreign lending, i.e. the rate at which purchases of foreign securities are made. To accomplish this, he recommended that the Bank of England place an embargo on new issues floated in London whenever the situation so dictated and the Treasury impose a punitive tax on the income derived from securities purchased on foreign exchanges.[2]

The last feature of Keynes' managed currency scheme deals with the size of Central Bank reserves and measures whereby they may be augmented. Keynes was opposed to setting aside a minimum

---

1. Ibid.
2. Ibid., pp. 311-319.

reserve of gold against the note issue,[1] for the effect of such a requirement is to sterilize a like amount of the precious metal which the monetary authority might use to meet temporary or sudden deficits in its balance of payments.[2] The effect of relating the gold reserve to the note issue is to make the amount of gold available to meet international emergencies and indebtedness dependent upon the amount of paper money in circulation despite the

---

1. Keynes made this suggestion prior to the time that Great Britain restored the gold standard. He had hoped that, by establishing a gold bullion instead of a gold coin standard, the convertibility issue would be eliminated and the gold reserve could be divorced from the note circulation. But despite his exhortation, the Bank of England continued to relate the note issue to the size of its gold stocks even after the establishment of the bullion standard. (Vide J. M. Keynes, "The Amalgamation of the British Note Issue," *The Economic Journal*, XXXVIII, 150, June, 1928, pp. 321-328.)
2. Keynes further disagreed with the theory of tying up the note issue with the gold reserve on grounds that this practice did not promote national economic objectives. The real purpose of stipulating the amount of gold to be held against the volume of notes was to indicate to the Central Bank that, as the minimum reserve of gold to notes was reached, a curtailment of credit and purchasing power was in order, if it was to maintain the value of its legal tender money at lawful parity. Although adherence to this ratio would preserve convertibility, it did not equally guarantee the stability of prices. As Keynes points out, "This method belongs indeed to a period when the preservation of convertibility was all that one thought about, and before the idea of utilizing bank-rate as a means of keeping prices and employment steady had become practical politics." In keeping with his desire to promote the real welfare of the domestic economy, instead of the efficient operation of the gold standard, Keynes argued that the amount of paper money in circulation should not be determined by the gold reserve, but should depend upon the state of trade, prices and employment. (Vide J. M. Keynes, *A Tract on Monetary Reform*, op. cit., p. 210.)

fact that there is no direct nexus between the two. Keynes believed that gold should be used exclusively as a reserve for correcting the influences of a temporarily adverse balance of payments and in this fashion insure the day to day stability of the exchange.[1] Given more substantial gold reserves, Keynes feels that the Central Bank could afford to vary their amount on a larger scale and thus better offset unfavorable developments in the balance of payments.

Although Keynes' exhortation to divorce the gold reserve from the note issue was rejected, he continued to agitate for increased Central Bank reserves. He argued that too much gold was being needlessly locked up by legal restriction,[2] thereby circumscribing the Central Bank's ability to cope with balance of payments contingencies. Therefore, to increase the size of the Central Bank's effective gold reserves to a more comfortable figure, Keynes urged a general reduction in the size of its legal reserve ratio.[3]

In addition to increasing the Central Bank's free or excess reserves, Keynes urged that large liquid balances be held in foreign centers and that these balances be permitted to experience wide fluctuations. He also suggested that over-draft facilities[4] be arranged among Central Banks and that borrowing and lending arrangements be established between Central Banks and a

---

1. J. M. Keynes, *A Treatise on Money*, op. cit., vol. II, pp. 209-213.
2. Ibid., p. 272.
3. Ibid., p. 310.
4. This notion was later incorporated in Keynes' Clearing Union proposal.

Supernational Bank.[1]

Summary

To sum up, we may say that the principal feature of Keynes' managed currency scheme of the interwar years was that it sought to achieve external equilibrium without at the same time upsetting equilibrium in the internal sector. Under the traditional gold standard system, external balance could be realized only by forcing the domestic economy into line with the external sector. In effect, a nation would have to sacrifice its internal equilibrium for the sake of maintaining the value of its exchange at parity or to preserve balance in its foreign account. To accomplish this, it would often have to pursue a deflationary policy by raising interest rates and contracting the volume of money and credit.

Being primarily concerned with the attainment of full employment and other purely domestic objectives, Keynes was opposed to the notion that these goals should be sacrificed simply to insure the maintenance of external equilibrium. Not only was he opposed to this outside interference with the promotion of domestic well-being, but also to the employment of bank rate for the purpose of effecting these internal adjustments. For, in his estimate, the bank rate should be used exclusively for the satisfaction of domestic and not international requirements.

---

1. J. M. Keynes, *A Treatise on Money*, op. cit., vol. II, p. 311.

Certainly, Keynes recognized that external equilibrium would have to be achieved; however, he felt that it should not be accomplished at the expense of domestic well-being. If adjustments between the international and external sectors had to be made, these should be effected in the latter, as witness his suggestions that the Central Bank alter its gold buying and selling prices, quote buying and selling prices for forward exchange, widen the spread between the gold points, and increase the size of its gold reserves. In so causing the external sector to be brought into balance with the domestic economy, instead of the other way round, the Central Bank could then pursue its monetary policies independently and without fear of interference or pressure from without. Not only would the monetary authority be relieved of any anxieties respecting the transmission of external disturbances into the internal sector, but it would also be in a position to utilize the bank rate instrument exclusively for the advancement of purely domestic policies.

Keynes' quest for national monetary independence and insulation of the domestic economy from disruptive external forces, through a managed monetary standard, illustrates once again his abiding desire to promote above all else the welfare of the domestic economy. Ultimately, it was this involvement with the problem of attaining domestic equilibrium, particularly in terms of high levels of employment, that caused him to part company with the classicists on the question of free trade - a proposition which we shall seek to establish in the subsequent sections of this work.

PART II

THE EVOLUTION OF KEYNES' THINKING ON FOREIGN TRADE THEORY AND POLICY

Scope of Part II

The purpose of this section will be to examine the development of Keynes' foreign trade views from the earliest phase of his career down to his publication of the *General Theory of Employment, Interest and Money*. In the course of this investigation it will be demonstrated how Keynes altered his position from that of a classical free trader to that of an outright protectionist. Further, it will be shown that this transformation of ideas was motivated by a deep desire to promote first the national welfare, an attitude already established in the preceding section.

CHAPTER VII

KEYNES' EARLY FREE TRADE VIEWS

Although Keynes was opposed to the traditional gold standard even at the very outset of his career,[1] his early views on the question of free trade were entirely orthodox. The first confirmation of this proposition is to be found in the pages of his early post-war contribution, The Economic Consequences of the Peace.[2] According to the terms of the Peace Treaty, Germany was required to cede to France the region of Alsace-Lorraine – a territory which accounted for approximately 75 per cent of the iron ore mined in Germany. Keynes conceded that the Germans should so lose this rich territory; however, he was of the conviction that a sizable quantity of this ore should be freely exported to Germany for processing in view of her existing steel

---

1. H. C. O'Neil, "Men of Today. (1) J. M. Keynes," Today and Tomorrow, I, 2, January, 1931, p. 130.
2. This work, published in 1920, was widely acclaimed by the public, because it disclosed to a far greater extent than anything up to that time the proceedings at the Versailles Conference where the Treaty with Germany was being drafted. Keynes, who attended these meetings as a member of the British Treasury delegation, showed himself to be no meek author, but a brilliant writer who was determined to deliver his message to the world and be heard. The gospel he sought to preach, according to Harrod, was that the Treaty was "an act of wickedness and folly." It was hypocritic and against the principles enunciated in the Armistice. (Vide H. C. O'Neil, "Men of Today. (1) J. M. Keynes," op. cit., pp. 130 ff. Also Cf. R. F. Harrod, The Life of John M. Keynes, op. cit., p. 255.)

making capacity.¹ Certainly, this appeared to be the most economical course to take, since France did not possess adequate facilities. That France would agree to such a proposal was doubtful, for having recovered the deposits of Lorraine, she would now surely aim at supplanting the German steel making facilities by new ones within her own frontier.²

This contravention of free trade principles (in this case the principle of comparative advantage) was condemned by Keynes, for such a policy would reduce the amount of steel forthcoming and thus retard European reconstruction. If only political considerations could remain subservient to economics, he asserted, the principles of free trade could be made to operate and thus achieve the greatest advantage for all nations concerned.³ This sentiment, as found expressed in the following argument, gives us the earliest indication of Keynes' free trade philosophy.

> In fact, here, as elsewhere, political considerations cut disastrously across economics. In a regime of Free Trade and free economic intercourse it would be of little consequence that iron lay on one side of a political frontier, and labor, coal, and blast furnaces on the other. But as it is, men have devised ways to impoverish themselves and one another, and prefer collective animosities to individual happiness. It seems certain, calculating on the present passions and impulses of European capitalistic society, that the effective iron output of Europe will be diminished by a new political frontier (which sentiment and historic justice require), because nationalism and private

---

1. Although Germany was required to surrender her rich iron ore fields in the Alsace-Lorraine region, she was not similarly forced to give up her blast furnaces and steel foundaries, for these were largely located within Germany proper.
2. J. M. Keynes, The Economic Consequences of the Peace, op. cit., pp. 97-99.
3. Ibid., p. 99.

interest are thus allowed to impose a new economic frontier along the same lines. These latter considerations are allowed, in the present governance of Europe, to prevail over the intense need of the Continent for the most sustained and efficient production to repair the destructions of war, and to satisfy the insistence of labor for a larger reward.[1]

The most conclusive evidence of Keynes' early free trade convictions available in <u>The Economic Consequences of the Peace</u> is to be found in its closing pages wherein he recommends the formation of a Free Trade Union under the auspices of the League of Nations. The nucleus of this alliance would be comprised of Germany, Poland, the new States which were formerly included in the Austro-Hungarian and Turkish Empires and the Mandated States. Membership by these states in the union would be compulsory for a period of ten years; however, all other nations would be left free to join on a voluntary basis. Although Keynes anticipated some reluctance on the part of certain nations to participate in this organization, he hoped "that the United Kingdom, at any rate, would become an original member."[2] All countries adhering to this union would agree to impose no protectionist tariffs whatever against the goods and services produced by any other member of the association.[3]

Keynes proposed such an organization, for he felt that, by promoting a system of freer trade, at least some part of the organization and efficiency which was lost by the creation of new but economically incomplete national states could be restored. In accordance with the

---

1. <u>Ibid</u>., pp. 99-100.
2. <u>Ibid</u>., p. 265.
3. <u>Ibid</u>.

orthodox view that national self-sufficiency is possible only for those countries with vast diversified areas, Keynes argued that the partition of the Empires of Germany, Austria-Hungary, Russia and Turkey into some twenty sovereign powers made such national autarky no longer possible. If these newly formed states were to survive, economic cooperation was essential. Moreover, a Free Trade Union, as conceived by Keynes, comprising the whole of Central, Eastern, and South-Eastern Europe, Siberia, Turkey and the United Kingdom might do just as much for the peace and prosperity of the world as the newly formed League of Nations.[1]

On the basis of his advocacy of a multilateral free trade system, Keynes' early foreign trade position may be unequivocally established. In fact, so convinced was he of the benefits to be enjoyed from such a free trading system, that he even urged membership for his own country. Such adherence to an international organization would appear to be quite advantageous for Great Britain, since she had enjoyed unique success in the past as a free trader. Thus, in urging his country to continue in the free trade tradition, Keynes did not in any way jeopardize the internal economic welfare of his country.

Keynes continued to hold steadfast to his free trade convictions throughout the early 'twenties. As in the Economic Consequences of the Peace, he adhered to the view that free trade was essential for European recovery. Writing on this question in the Manchester Guardian Supplements, he asserted,

---

1. Ibid., p. 268.

> We must hold to Free Trade, in its widest interpretations, as inflexible dogma, to which no exception is admitted, wherever the decision rests with us. We must hold to this even where we receive no reciprocity of treatment and even in those rare cases where by infringing it we could in fact obtain a direct economic advantage. We should hold to Free Trade as a principle of international morals and not merely as a doctrine of economic advantage.[1]

Further evidence of Keynes' preference for free trade at this time may be obtained from two contributions he made in behalf of the Liberal Party campaign for the General Election of November, 1923. It is claimed that the classical influence is nowhere better exhibited in Keynes' writings than in these contributions in defense of free trade.[2]

During the campaign, Mr. Stanley Baldwin, the Conservative Party candidate, came out in favor of protection as a means of combatting the existing unemployment in Great Britain. In defending free trade against the charge made by Mr. Baldwin, Keynes cited two fundamental truths upon which its validity is based.

The first is the familiar Law of Comparative Advantage which he states in the following terms.

> It is better to employ our capital and our labour in trade where we are relatively more efficient than other people are, and to exchange the products of these trades for goods in the production of which we are relatively less efficient.[3]

Keynes contends that this principle is readily understandable, for every sane person abides by it. In his economic life he performs

---

1. J. M. Keynes, "The Underlying Principles," _Reconstruction in Europe_, op. cit., Jan. 4, 1923, p. 717.
2. L. R. Klein, op. cit., p. 10.
3. J. M. Keynes, "Free Trade," _The Nation and Athenaeum_, XXXIV, 8, Nov. 24, 1923, p. 302.

those functions for which he is best qualified and leaves to others those operations which they are capable of doing better than he can. There are, of course, certain exceptions to this principle which Keynes clearly recognized. Like most free traders, he agreed that protection might be justified on non-economic grounds, e.g. national defense. He also concurred in the view that it might be warranted for supporting vital infant industries, and for contending with the problem of dumping. Ever mindful of national requirements, he indicated that protection might also be used for dealing with "the competition from imports from countries with depreciating currency."[1] In the main, however, Keynes' defense of the Law of Comparative Advantage was much like that of any student nurtured on the principles of classical economics.

The other important truth on which the efficacy of free trade is based is that imports are beneficial to a country's economy. Keynes summarizes this as follows.

> The second great principle is that there can be no disadvantage in receiving useful objects from abroad. If we have to pay at once, we can only pay with the export of goods and services, and the exchange would not take place unless there was an advantage in it. Every import, which is not paid for by an import, represents a decrease in the capital available within the country.[2]

Keynes' view in the above is anti-mercantilistic, which is quite in keeping, of course, with the classical tradition. He was opposed to the imposition of any restriction on the volume of imports for

---

1. *Ibid.*
2. *Ibid.*

the purpose of obtaining a favorable balance of trade, since this was tantamount to sending goods to the rest of the world without receiving payment for them. Keynes considered imports as a payment for exports and "to put obstacles in their way is to be as crazy as a businessman would be who tried to prevent his customers and his debtors from paying their bills."[1]

In arguing along these strictly orthodox lines, Keynes, strangely enough, gave expression to his own nationalism. When a nation exports more than it imports, the difference is equal to its foreign investment. But, argued Keynes, such a deflection of capital to abroad was detrimental to the national well-being at this time, as his following contention will testify.

> With our shortage of housing and the need of factories and equipment to render efficient our growing supply of labour, we need to keep more capital at home, and so to arrange matters that our surplus resources are occupied in increasing our own equipment for future production and for the shelter of our population. There is already, in my opinion, too much encouragement to the export of our capital. With our diminished savings and our increasing needs, we are not in the position in which we used to be for sending out goods to the rest of the world and getting back, for the time being, nothing whatever in return.[2]

Thus, it may be seen that, although Keynes was a free trader at this point, this position did not in any way contravene his basic desire to secure first the national welfare. In fact, it is entirely

---

1. Ibid.
2. J. M. Keynes, "Free Trade for England," The New Republic, XXXVII, 472, Dec. 19, 1923, p. 86.

possible that the reason why he did subscribe to the tenets of free trade at this time is that he may have deemed them the most promotive of the national prosperity.

Having established the efficacy of free trade on the basis of these two principles, viz. the Law of Comparative Advantage and the necessary equality between imports and exports, Keynes then meets Mr. Baldwin's argument head on. He reasons that if tariff barriers be raised, as advocated by the Conservatives, this action will contract the volume of trade.[1] For protection simply constitutes an effort to extract from foreign customers a money price in excess of the competitive price. Such an attempt to charge a higher price, argues Keynes, can only serve to reduce the volume of imports. But, the argument continues, if imports are reduced, exports will be similarly reduced because the two are always equal; unless of course, these exports be given to foreigners gratuitously.[2] Instead of expanding activity a protectionist policy contracts it and thereby aggravates further the problem of unemployment.[3] Thus Keynes concludes,

---

1. J. M. Keynes, "Free Trade," op. cit., p. 302.
2. J. M. Keynes, "Free Trade and Unemployment," The Nation and Athenaeum, XXIV, 9, Dec. 1, 1923, p. 335.
3. Keynes does admit, however, the possibility that a protectionist trade policy will increase the amount of work. In view of the fact that the Law of Comparative Advantage is made inoperative by such policy, the level of productivity is reduced, and, so, more labor and sweat will be required to produce the same volume of goods previously enjoyed. Consequently, though a reduction in the volume of imports will increase the amount of work, it will not augment the level of national income. (Vide J. B. Condliffe, "The Value of International Trade," Economica, V (N.S.) 18, May, 1938, p. 130. Also Cf. J. M. Keynes, "Free Trade and Unemployment," op. cit., pp. 335-336.)

For if there is one thing that Protection cannot do, it is to cure Unemployment....

There are some arguments for Protection, based upon its securing possible but improbable advantages, to which there is no simple answer. But the claim to cure Unemployment involves the Protectionist fallacy in its grossest and crudest form.

Protection must mean - to this there is no exception - an attempt to limit the volume of trade; it must mean charging the foreigners more at the expense of doing less trade with him. And insofar as the keeping out of an import does not involve a corresponding restriction of export, it must drive some capital out of the country.[1]

Imports are receipts and exports are payments. How, as a nation, can we expect to better ourselves by diminishing our receipts? Is there anything that a tariff could do, which an earthquake could not do better?[2]

Although Keynes was becoming an increasingly outspoken critic of laissez-faire economics[3] in the period of the middle 'twenties,

---

1. J. M. Keynes, "Free Trade for England," op. cit., p. 87.
2. J. M. Keynes, "Free Trade and Unemployment," op. cit., p. 336.
3. The reason why Keynes adopted this attitude is that the environment for which laissez-faire was appropriate no longer existed in the period after World War I. Accordingly, he said, "In my opinion there is now no place except in the left wing of the Conservative Party, for those whose hearts are set on old-fashioned individualism and laissez-faire in all their rigour - greatly though these contributed to the success of the 19th century. I say this not because I think that these doctrines were wrong in the conditions which gave birth to them, but because they have ceased to be applicable to modern conditions." (Vide J. M. Keynes, "Am I a Liberal?" (An Address to the Liberal Summer School at Cambridge in August, 1925), The Nation and Athenaeum, XXXVII, 19, August 8, 1925, p. 564.)

he remained a staunch supporter of free trade.¹ Keynes continued to adhere to the free trade argument, not because of the laissez-faire philosophy in which it was steeped, but because of his own conviction that a nation enjoys the greatest advantage when it employs its resources in those areas where it has a comparative advantage. Keynes indicates his confidence in the efficacy of the free trade argument per se in the following assertion.

> I no longer believe in the political philosophy which the Doctrine of Free Trade adorned. I believe in Free Trade because, in the long run and in general, it is the only policy which is technically sound and intellectually tight.²

These, though, are among Keynes' last published words in defense of free trade, as we shall see in the subsequent chapters of this section.

---

1. J. M. Keynes, "The End of Laissez-Faire II," The New Republic, XLVIII, 613, Sept. 1, 1926, pp. 37-41. (Also vide J. M. Keynes, "Laissez-Faire Versus Nation Building," The New Republic, XXXVII, 472, Dec. 19, 1923, editorial page. And Cf. J. M. Keynes, "The End of Laissez-Faire I," The New Republic, XLVIII, 612, Aug. 25, 1926, pp. 13-15.)
2. J. M. Keynes, "Am I A Liberal?" op. cit., p. 564.

CHAPTER VIII

THE TREATISE ON MONEY

During the next few years of his career, Keynes lost faith in the free trade argument which he had so ably upheld in the past, and gave his support, instead, to the protectionist cause.[1] This shift of allegiance was motivated largely by domestic considerations. For during the period of the late 'twenties, Great Britain was plagued by a chronically high level of unemployment and a depressed state of trade,[2] a condition which Keynes attributed in no small measure to the restoration of the gold standard at the pre-war parity of exchange.[3] In addition, she was finding it increasingly difficult to attain equilibrium in her foreign balance of payments. In fact, it was the contention of many English economists, who were in close contact with the prevailing economic situation, v.g. W. H. Beveridge, J. R. Hicks, L. C. Robbins, and F. C. Benham, that Keynes' advocacy of protection was primarily motivated by a desire to correct this condition of external disequilibrium.[4] Later on, of course, Keynes was to

---

1. R. Hinshaw, op. cit., p. 316.
2. J. M. Keynes and H. D. Henderson, Can Lloyd George Do It? London, The Nation and Athenaeum, 1929, passim.
3. For a consideration of this matter refer to Chapter 5 of this thesis. Also see especially J. M. Keynes, The Economic Consequences of Mr. Churchill, op. cit., passim.
4. W. H. Beveridge and others, Tariffs: The Case Examined, London, Longmans, Green and Co., 1932, pp. 76-77.

favor a protectionist policy for other reasons as well, v.g. as an alternative to devaluation,[1] as a means of augmenting the national revenue and as a stimulant to domestic employment.[2] Be that as it may, the fact remains that during the latter part of the 'twenties Keynes' foreign trade views started to undergo reformulation, and from this time forward he could no longer be classified as a free trader in the classical tradition.

The first statement of Keynes' new foreign trade position is to be found in the Treatise on Money.[3] Herein he makes a "rather tentative and hesitant case for the tariff."[4] To elicit this conclusion is by no means an easy task, for as Sir William Beveridge points out, it is entirely possible for a protectionist to read the Treatise without finding any support herein for protection. "To anyone, indeed," avers Sir William, "who believed almost any of the common arguments for Protection, the whole of Mr. Keynes' treatise with its subtle analysis of economic reactions, would be incomprehensible."[5] However, if one can get close enough to peer through the finely spun veil of Keynesian subtlety, one may readily discern a partiality on his part for such a commercial policy.

As noted above, Keynes was first attracted to the tariff

---

1. Ibid., p. 77.
2. J. M. Keynes, "Proposals for a Revenue Tariff," New Statesman and Nation, I (N.S.), 2, March 7, 1931, pp. 53-54.
3. R. Hinshaw, op. cit., p. 316.
4. Ibid.
5. W. H. Beveridge et al., op. cit., p. 81.

device because he thought that it could be utilized as an instrument for attaining international equilibrium. It could be employed, in his view, either as an alternative or supplement to those measures of monetary control designed to attain this external balance.[1] In view of the important role played by considerations of external equilibrium in Keynes' conversion to protectionism, a knowledge of this concept is essential for understanding his change of attitude.

There are two important elements which enter into Keynes' notion of external equilibrium. These are the volume of foreign lending and the size of the foreign balance. By foreign lending Keynes means the excess of the amount of money put at the disposal of foreigners by nationals of a particular country through the net purchase of investments located abroad over the corresponding amount expended by foreigners for investments situated in that country.[2] The foreign balance, as defined by Keynes, refers to the difference between the amount due to a nation from abroad in payment for its exports and loan interest and the amount which it in turn owes to foreigners for imports and loan interest.[3] This really amounts to the balance of trade on income account which arises when a part of current national output is transferred to foreigners instead of being consumed at home.[4]

In view of the fact that the international balance sheet must

---

1. Ibid., pp. 76-77.
2. J. M. Keynes, A Treatise on Money, op. cit., vol. I, pp. 131-132.
3. Ibid., p. 132.
4. Ibid.

always be in equilibrium, gold is required as a balancing item to account for any discrepancy between the amount of foreign lending and the value of the foreign balance. With gold movements thus introduced, we find that when the amount of foreign lending exceeds the value of the foreign balance, equilibrium in the balance sheet is achieved by an exportation of gold equal to this difference. (In this case, Foreign Lending = Foreign Balance $\neq$ Gold Export.) When the foreign balance exceeds the amount of foreign lending, equilibrium in the balance sheet is achieved by an importation of gold equal to this difference. (In this case, Foreign Balance = Foreign Lending $\neq$ Gold Import.)[1]

Although both of the above cases illustrate a balance in the international account, they do not demonstrate a true condition of external equilibrium. For such an equilibrium cannot exist so long as there occurs any movement of gold, be it into or out of the country.[2] Therefore, external equilibrium can obtain only when the value of the foreign balance is exactly equal to the amount of foreign lending, since in this case gold flows are non-existent. When this identity between the foreign balance and the value of foreign lending is realized, it may be said that foreign investment is equal to foreign borrowing.[3] This latter equality is another way of expressing a condition of international balance.

---

1. Ibid., p. 132.
2. Ibid., p. 163.
3. Foreign lending or foreign borrowing constitutes that part of total savings made available to foreigners. Cf. J. Robinson, Essays in the Theory of Employment, op. cit., p. 187.

Given external equilibrium, internal equilibrium would obtain when home savings were exactly equal to home investment.[1] This, of course, is the same thing as saying that both internal and external equilibrium will be realized when total savings are exactly equal to total investment.[2]

Insofar as the foreign balance and foreign lending are concerned, there is no direct or automatic relationship between them.[3]

---

1. There are a number of additional ways of expressing this simultaneous existence of equilibrium in both sectors. For example, it may be said that both internal and external equilibrium obtain when home investment equals home savings and foreign investment (foreign balance) is equal to the excess of total savings over home savings (foreign lending).

    In view of the fact that the foreign balance is equal to foreign investment and foreign lending is equal to part of total savings, it may be readily seen that Keynes' concept of external equilibrium, like that of internal equilibrium, is really based on his notion of equality between savings and investment. When the foreign balance is equal to foreign lending, this equality may be likened to the identity between savings and investment.
2. J. M. Keynes, A Treatise on Money, op. cit., vol. I, pp. 151-163.
3. Counter to the popular British view, Keynes held that the size of the foreign balance is not directly a function of the amount of foreign lending, but is determined, instead, by relative price levels at home and abroad. The fact that the volume of foreign lending varies, argued Keynes, does not mean that the foreign balance will adjust itself to it immediately and without any appreciable disturbance of internal prices and income. On the contrary, he contended that equilibrium between these quanta was insured, not by an automatic adjustment of the foreign balance in response to an increase or decrease in the amount of foreign lending, but by gold movements and the consequent alteration of interest rates. (Vide J. M. Keynes, A Treatise on Money, op. cit., vol. I, pp. 329-330.)

    According to certain neo-classicists, v.g. Ohlin and Beveridge, Keynes underestimated the degree to which it was possible for the foreign balance of a country to adapt itself to foreign transfers without any special

(F.N. No. 3 continued from p. 136). devices, v.g. gold flows. (Vide W. H. Beveridge et al., Tariffs: The Case Examined, op. cit., pp. 83-84). In their view, variations in the volume of foreign lending stimulate corresponding changes in the size of the foreign balance directly, automatically and with minor assistance from gold movements.

To put the question to the inductive test, Prof. Taussig made a number of studies of nineteenth and early twentieth century examples of countries which experienced wide variations in their volume of foreign lending. As expected, he found that foreign lending and the foreign balance almost inevitably moved together; however, in examining the question of how far monetary adjustments had to be pushed to effect this equality, no conclusion was forthcoming. For at times the evidence appeared to support Professor Ohlin's thesis and at times that subscribed to by Keynes. (Vide J. M. Keynes, A Treatise on Money, op. cit., vol. I, p. 330; F. Taussig, International Trade, New York, Macmillan Co., 1927, passim.)

It was only after the appearance of the General Theory that economists, particularly Mrs. Joan Robinson and Professor R. F. Harrod, began to realize more fully that the rapid adjustment of a country's balance of payments, which Professor Taussig had observed to take place independently of price and monetary changes, was the result of induced movements of income and employment.* The Keynesian income and expenditure analysis was found to provide a far more realistic account of the adjustment mechanism of the balance of payments than did the traditional price-specie-flow doctrine.

* The income approach to international trade was not an original Keynesian contribution. Writers on international economics had been aware of the effects occasioned by changes in purchasing power or changes in relative demand for over one hundred years. However, Keynes' approach seemed to give a far more comprehensive and consistent account of international monetary relations than did any previous explanation.

For a more extensive treatment of the income approach to the restoration of equilibrium in the balance of payments consult the following sources: L. A. Metzler, "The Theory of International Trade," A Survey of Contemporary Economics, (ed. H. S. Ellis), Philadelphia, Blakiston Co., 1948, pp. 211-222; J. Robinson, Essays in the Theory of Employment, London, Macmillan and Co., Ltd., 1937, Part III, Ch. 1; R. F. Harrod, International Economics, (second edition), London, Cambridge University Press, 1939, Ch. 5; F. Machlup, International Trade and the Foreign Trade Multiplier, Philadelphia, Blakiston Co., 1943, passim; J. Viner, Studies in the Theory of International Trade, New York, Harper & Bros., 1937, Ch. 6; R. Nurkse, "Domestic and International Equilibrium," The New Economics (ed. S. Harris), op. cit., pp. 264-292.

138

Although there are certain cross-connections between them, the volume of foreign lending and the size of the foreign balance vary in response to independent sets of forces.[1] The size of the foreign balance depends on the relative price levels at home and abroad of those goods which enter into foreign trade.[2] And the balance of lending depends upon relative rates of interest at home and abroad and the prevailing state of confidence.[3] Therefore, if there occurs an imbalance between the foreign balance and foreign lending, with the consequence that the economy experiences external disequilibrium, this condition will be due either to a disturbance of relative price levels or to a falling out of line of relative interest rates.[4]

Given a gold standard system, the Central Bank has no direct means of coping with the former type of disturbance. It can influence relative price and income levels only indirectly through its power of altering interest rates and the terms of lending generally.[5] For purposes of illustration, let us assume that there occurs a price decline in foreign countries. This will cause an increased demand for imports and a reduced demand for exports of the country in question.[6] This obviously leads to a

---

1. J. Robinson, Essays in the Theory of Employment, op. cit., p. 187.
2. J. M. Keynes, A Treatise on Money, op. cit., vol. I, p. 163.
3. J. Robinson, op. cit., pp. 187-188.
4. J. M. Keynes, A Treatise on Money, op. cit., vol. I, p. 326.
5. Ibid., p. 163.
6. We are prescinding from the effects which the higher income in the foreign countries would exercise on the demand for the home country's exports, since Keynes was not fully aware of this reaction at this time.

139

reduction in the foreign trade balance, and assuming that there occurs no corresponding change in the value of foreign lending, the former will exceed the latter, with the consequence that gold flows out of the country. However, since the primary duty of the Central Bank is to inhibit such gold movements, it is forced to alter the terms of lending at home.[1] As a consequence of this action, prices and money incomes will be reduced to a level more approximate to that prevailing abroad; however, this will not be accomplished without disturbing internal equilibrium.[2] For if home savings be equal to home investment at the old rate of interest, they will be unequal at the new rate; hence, the first effect of the effort to restore external equilibrium is to upset internal equilibrium.[3] In time, however, a new equilibrium[4]

---

1. J.M. Keynes, A Treatise on Money, op. cit., vol. I, p. 214.
2. Complete equilibrium, as construed by Keynes in the Treatise, requires an equality between home savings and home investment; home investment and the adjusted cost of home investment, which is the same as the actual cost of investment minus the profit on the foreign balance; and the volume of foreign lending and the size of the foreign balance. (Vide J.M. Keynes, A Treatise on Money, op. cit., vol. I, pp. 162-163; vol. II, p. 185.)
3. It was because of this tendency towards disharmony between internal and external equilibrium that Keynes was so vehemently opposed to an international currency system such as the gold standard. (Vide Part I of this thesis.)
4. The degree of disharmony between internal and external equilibrium is largely dependent on the size of foreign lending relative to the amount of total saving* together with its sensitivity to small changes in relative interest rates at home and abroad, and the susceptibility of the foreign balance to small changes in relative prices.**

    The duration of the disharmony between internal and external equilibrium depends on the facility with which changes can be effected in the internal money-costs of production. If the volumes of foreign lending, the foreign balance and the internal money costs of production are sensitive to small variations in the interest rate, prices, and the level of employment, respectively, then the task of maintaining simultaneously both internal and external equilibria will not be an overwhelming one.

140

will be achieved by a decline in the general price level, the volume of home saving, the amount of foreign lending, the size of home investment and the value of the foreign balance to a level below what they were in money terms before prices fell abroad. Nothing will be changed in real terms and apart from the new money values which prevail, the new equilibrium will not differ significantly from the old.[1] Thus, despite the fact that the economy is forced to undergo transitional difficulties, there is always a level of interest rate[2] which will in the long run assure it of equilibrium between the foreign balance and foreign lending, and equality between savings and investment.[3]

In the second type of disorder, viz. a falling out of gear of relative interest rates at home and abroad, The Central Bank must again resort to the bank rate instrument. However, the correction will not be restricted to the interest rate structure alone. It will also entail a modification of price and income levels as well, for when there occurs an alteration in the interest rate, this will induce a change in

---

4. *Keynes considers foreign lending as part of total savings and the foreign balance as part of total investment. (Vide J.M. Keynes, A Treatise on Money, op. cit., vol. I, p. 132.)

  **For a consideration of the influence exerted by demand and supply elasticities on the foreign balance consult Mrs. Robinson's fine article, "The Foreign Exchanges;" vide J. Robinson, Essays in the Theory of Employment, London, Macmillan and Co., Ltd., 1937, pp. 186-213.

1. J.M. Keynes, A Treatise on Money, op. cit., vol. I, p. 326.
2. At the point where both internal and external equilibrium are achieved, the market rate of interest is equal to the international and natural rates of interest. The international rate is that value which obviates gold movements and the natural rate is that value which insures an equality between total savings and investment. (Vide J.M. Keynes, A Treatise on Money, op. cit., vol. I, pp. 331-332.)
3. J.M. Keynes, A Treatise on Money, op. cit., vol. I, p. 214.

the demand for investment abroad relative to the demand at home.[1]

To illustrate this type of disturbance and the manner in which it is corrected, let us suppose that the imbalance is due to a rise in the interest rate abroad. This interest rate differential will obviously increase the volume of external loans, with the result that the amount of foreign lending will exceed the size of the foreign balance. This naturally leads to an outflow of gold and again the bank rate must be increased. Raising the bank rate will succeed in diminishing the amount of foreign lending; however, it will similarly reduce the volume of home investment.[2] As a consequence, the level of savings exceeds the level of investment - a condition which leads to a decline in prices and in the earnings of the productive factors. Because of these lower money production costs relative to those prevailing in other countries, home prices appear more inviting to foreign customers, and so the foreign balance will tend to increase. Thus, the bank rate offers a two-pronged attack against external disequilibrium. On one front it reduces the level of foreign lending and on the other it augments the size of the foreign balance, thereby driving the two closer together until they are again in balance with one another.[3] As in the previous case, equilibrium will again be restored by locating that level of interest rate which will insure equality between the foreign balance and foreign lending and the volume of savings and the volume of investment.

With his theoretical framework thus established, Keynes then

---

1. Ibid., pp. 327-328.
2. Ibid.
3. Ibid., p. 215.

142

turns to an analysis of Great Britain's external equilibrium difficulties of 1929-1930 and the means available for their correction.

In diagnosing the British disorder, Keynes found two factors at work. The first was the existence of higher gold-costs of production in Great Britain relative to those prevailing elsewhere - a condition which he attributed to Great Britain's return to the gold standard at the pre-war parity of exchange. The second was the increased attractiveness of foreign over home investment. The net resultant of the operation of these two forces obviously spelled a condition of disequilibrium. For whereas the size of the foreign balance was forced downward, owing to the higher costs of production obtaining at home, the volume of foreign lending was pushed upward, due to the higher interest rates prevailing abroad.[1]

In view of the fact that the Central Bank had no direct means of increasing the size of the foreign balance, it had no alternative but to try to reduce the volume of foreign lending by increasing the interest rate. In so raising the market rate of interest to the international level, however, the monetary authority inevitably forced it to a point above its natural rate. As a result, the equality between savings and investment would be upset and the amounts of home and total investment would be driven below their equilibrium level. Thus, although a higher interest rate would be efficacious in restoring external balance, it might do so only by engendering internal disequilibrium with its attending profit deflation[2] and unemployment.[3]

---

1. *Ibid.*, p. 185.
2. *Ibid.*
3. Keynes of the *Treatise* era viewed an excess of savings over investment as synonymous with a condition of deflation. In fact, he explained the existence of business fluctuations largely in terms

In the pre-war period, this disharmony was not of long duration insofar as Great Britain was concerned,[1] for the volume of foreign lending, the size of the foreign balance and the internal money costs of production quickly adjusted themselves to small changes in interest rates, prices and the level of employment, respectively.[2] However, these conditions no longer obtained in the post-war era, for the foreign balance and money costs of production became especially insensitive to changes in the external sector.[3] The situation confronting Great Britain in the post-war world is described by Keynes in the following not too optimistic terms.

> In an old country, especially in one in which the population has ceased to expand rapidly, the rate of interest at which borrowers for home investment are able to absorb home savings must necessarily decline. Meanwhile, in the new countries the rate will be maintained, and as these countries get over their early pioneer difficulties, the estimated risks of lending to them - provided they are careful about their reputations as borrowers - will decline. Consequently the old country will tend to lend abroad an ever growing proportion of its total savings. This will be partly cared for by the interest on its previous foreign lending. But for the rest its costs of production must fall so as to stimulate its exports and increase its favourable balance on trading account. If there is a resistance to this fall, gold will flow, bank rate will rise, and unemployment will become chronic. This is particularly likely to happen if the prevalence of tariffs against manufactured goods (and a readiness to raise them where imports of such goods are increasing) renders the foreign demand for the old country's exports inelastic, while at the same time Trade Unions in the old country present great obstacles to a reduction of money wages.[4]

---

3. of the discrepancy between savings and investment. (Vide J.M. Keynes, "Unemployment as a World Problem," *Lectures on the Harris Foundation* (ed. P.Q. Wright), Chicago, University of Chicago Press, 1931, passim. Also Cf. J.M. Keynes, *A Treatise on Money*, vol. I, pp. 279-292.)
1. W.H. Beveridge et al., op. cit., p. 78.
2. J.M. Keynes, *A Treatise on Money*, op. cit., vol. I, p. 165.
3. Ibid., pp. 165-166.
4. Ibid., pp. 347-348.

Although Keynes does not immediately prescribe any explicit solution for this situation, there almost seems to be by the tenor of the following remark a presumption in favor of protection.[1]

> I leave it to the reader to work out in detail what a pickle a country might get into if a higher rate of interest abroad than can be earned at home leads to most of its savings being lent abroad, whilst at the same time there are tariffs abroad against most of its exports and a tendency to raise these tariffs from time to time to balance the gradually rising level of costs in the protected countries due to the outflow of gold from the lending country.[2]

Keynes' position in the above passage is that countries which have a favorable balance of trade on income account, but an unfavorable balance of transactions on capital account, should, by reducing their tariff barriers, permit a lending country, v.g. Great Britain, to increase her level of exports. Unless the lending country is accorded such an opportunity to expand her exports, she will experience a disparity between her foreign balance and her volume of foreign lending. Under these circumstances, she may have no recourse but to augment her foreign balance by reducing imports through the expediency of tariffs.[3]

In the second volume of the Treatise - The Applied Theory of

---

1. In the second volume of his Treatise, Keynes is much less occult in endorsing the imposition of a tariff as a means of helping Great Britain overcome her external imbalance, as we shall have later occasion to see.
2. J. M. Keynes, A Treatise on Money, op. cit., vol. I, p. 348.
3. This interpretation is supported by Sir W. H. Beveridge; (Vide W. H. Beveridge, et al., op. cit., p. 81.)

Money - Keynes is far less cryptic in favoring the imposition of tariffs as a means of assisting Great Britain to restore her external equilibrium.

On the assumption that wages and other production costs cannot be reduced, and that the attractiveness of foreign over domestic investment continues unabated, Keynes points out that the excess of Great Britain's foreign lending over her foreign balance will lead to a condition of chronic depression and unemployment. From this eventuality there are but four ways to escape:

> I. To increase the value of the foreign balance by reducing money costs of production through increased efficiency.[1]
>
> II. To increase the value of the foreign balance by diminishing the volume of imports through tariffs or similar measures.
>
> III. To increase home investment by establishing through means of a subsidy, or other similar arrangement, a differential rate of interest for home investment as compared with foreign investment.
>
> IV. To stimulate investment throughout the world, both home and abroad, by an international cheap money policy.[2]

Although a good case could be made in behalf of each of these methods, Keynes is more favorably disposed towards the second and third alternatives. With respect to the second remedy, he

---

1. This was referred to as "Rationalization" in Great Britain during the decade of the 'twenties.
2. J. M. Keynes, *A Treatise on Money*, op. cit., vol. II, pp. 186-187.

maintains that the application of this device would probably not result either in a reduction of exports commensurate with the decrease in the size of imports or in a decline of home investment. In fact, he believes that there would result some increase in the level of foreign investment[1] which would represent "a net gain to the wealth[2] of the community."[3] Insofar as the third alternative is concerned, this, too, would add to the wealth of the community. For by offering a lower rate of interest to prospective home investors, by means of a subsidy or other equivalent arrangement, the excess savings which obtained at the higher rate of interest (which was required in order to restrict foreign lending) would be siphoned off by worthwhile investment schemes instead of being

---

1. Foreign investment, as defined by Keynes, really refers to the positive balance of trade. (Vide J. M. Keynes, A Treatise on Money, op. cit., vol. I, p. 132.) From the point of view of the home economy, a favorable balance of trade is equivalent to investment, for it has the same influence as investment upon the level of effective demand. It represents an increased demand for current home output while at the same time it adds nothing to the supply of goods entering the home market. (Vide J. Robinson, Essays in the Theory of Employment, op. cit., p. 186.)
2. Keynes' contention that an increase in the favorable balance of trade adds to the wealth of the community may be justified by the following reasoning. An increase in the positive balance of trade is synonymous with an increase in investment, but an increase in investment normally leads to an improvement in employment and income; therefore, an increase in exports or a reduction of imports will for any one country raise its level of income and employment. An expansion of activity in the export or import-competing industries will cause a primary increase in employment, while the expenditure of the added incomes earned in these industries will lead, insofar as they are spent for home-produced goods, to a secondary increase in employment and income. (Vide J. Robinson, Essays in the Theory of Employment, op. cit., p. 210.)
3. J. M. Keynes, A Treatise on Money, op. cit., vol. II, p. 186.

wasted in the form of business losses.[1]

In both cases, it will be noticed, Keynes prefers concentrating on an expansion of home activity rather than on an increase of foreign trade, as would have been the case had he selected the first and fourth alternatives. In explaining the reasons for his choice, Keynes gives us one of the earliest indications of his thinking on the mature economy thesis.

Keynes points out that Great Britain is an old country whose population will soon cease to grow. But despite this maturity, her people continue to save about 10 per cent of national income - a ratio far in excess of internal needs. Were England a closed system, the natural rate of interest, i.e. the rate which equates total savings and total investment, would fall much faster here than in other countries. Consequently, with a higher interest return obtainable abroad, equilibrium under conditions of laissez-faire would require that a large and ever-increasing proportion of British savings find its way overseas. In time, this increase in foreign lending could be offset by enlarged interest receipts from previous investments; hence, there would be no need to strive for greater exports. The foreign balance, through the medium of these expanded investment earnings, could keep pace with the enhanced amount of foreign lending, and so equilibrium would be achieved without difficulty. However, there is an interim period to contend with wherein this increased foreign lending cannot be readily

---

1. Ibid., p. 187.

matched by augmented earnings on external investments.[1] In this circumstance, there is no alternative but to increase exports relatively to imports. But can this greater export volume be attained?

It is unlikely, says Keynes, that this objective can be realized if one takes into consideration, apart from the existing international slump, the prevalence of high tariff walls, the disappearance in an industrialized world of the special advantages once peculiar to British manufacture, and the existence of higher real wages in Great Britain relative to elsewhere. In such an environment, he avers, "one cannot but feel a doubt whether the attainment of equilibrium on the lines of an expanding trade surplus will in fact be practicable";[2] hence, the reason for his favoring a restrictionist rather than an expansionist trade program for Great Britain.

To be sure, Keynes agreed that the attainment of equilibrium through the instrumentality of the traditional principles would be the ideal solution; however, if social and political forces precluded such a possibility, he would not be averse to achieving it via the unorthodox media of offering differential terms of interest for home as opposed to foreign investment and the imposition of tariffs. Thus, with no other alternatives in sight, Keynes is entirely disposed to embracing protection as the following important passage will testify.

---

1. *Ibid.*, pp. 188-189.
2. *Ibid.*, p. 189.

> It may be that the attainment of equilibrium in accordance with our traditional principles would be the best solution, - if we could get it. But if social and political forces stand in the way of our getting it, then it will be better to reach equilibrium by such a device as differential terms for home investment relatively to foreign investment, and even, perhaps, such a falling from grace as differential terms for home-produced goods relatively to foreign-produced goods, than to suffer indefinitely the business losses and unemployment which disequilibrium means. Of the two types of devices indicated above, I much prefer that of differential rates for home and foreign lending to that of differential prices for home and foreign goods, for I believe that there is a much greater scope for this device without risking injurious reactions in other directions, and, in some cases indeed, with positive social advantage. But I am coming around to the view that there is also room for applying usefully some method of establishing differential prices for home and foreign goods.[1]

Although Keynes does not explicitly state that he favors the imposition of protective duties on imports or subsidies on exports, this inference is clear, for how else would he hope to establish "differential prices for home and foreign goods?" Insofar as tariffs would lead to a reduction of imports without similarly affecting exports, and insofar as subsidies would encourage an increase in exports without similarly affecting imports, they would both bring about an increase in the foreign balance and thus help the economy to achieve its external equilibrium, i.e. equality between its foreign balance and foreign lending.[2]

---

1. Ibid., p. 189.
2. W. H. Beveridge, et al., op. cit., pp. 81-82.

Summary

On the basis of the foregoing evidence, we may conclude that as early as 1930 Keynes' concern for the national welfare drove him to a consideration of protectionism as a means of helping Great Britain to overcome her economic difficulties.

Keynes' inclination towards protection illustrates well his desire to service first the needs of the internal economy. Bogged down throughout the entire decade of the 'twenties and presently confronted with economic maturity and a loss of foreign markets, due to increased competition and industrialization abroad, Great Britain could no longer survive under a regime of laissez-faire. However efficacious free trade may have been in the past, it no longer served the best British interests of the present. And being primarily concerned with what was best for Great Britain, Keynes was entirely disposed to supplant it with a more consciously controlled trading system.

During the time that Keynes believed free trade to be promotive of the national (British) welfare, he defended it with all his brilliance. But fully aware now of the reality that such a system could lead only to a prolonged suffering of business loss and unemployment for his country, he was entirely willing to overthrow it. Had Great Britain continued to wax prosperous in the late 'twenties, as she had in the nineteenth and early twentieth centuries under a system of free trade, would he have similarly advocated such a restriction of trade? It is hardly likely that he would have done so; hence, the justification for our contention that Keynes made foreign trade policy a function of the domestic well-being - a fact which becomes increasingly obvious during the next few years of his life.

CHAPTER IX

ADDENDUM I TO THE MACMILLAN REPORT

Although Keynes' support for a tariff in the *Treatise* is enshrouded in "elaborate theoretical language,"[1] his defense of this measure is much less disguised in his later writings. This is particularly true of his contributions to the *Report of the Committee on Finance and Industry*.

In November, 1929, Keynes was appointed to the Committee on Finance and Industry[2] by Mr. Snowden, the Labor Chancellor of the Exchequer.[3] This Committee,[4] under the chairmanship of Lord H. P. Macmillan, was set up to inquire into the abnormal industrial depression and widespread unemployment[5] prevailing in Great Britain at the time. It was hoped that, as a result of its investigation of the financial aspects of the problems involved, the Committee would be able to devise, if not remedies, at least

---

1. R. Hinshaw, op. cit., p. 316.
2. Keynes enjoyed a great initial advantage in working on this Committee, for he had just completed four years of intensive research and study on the central problems of money and finance in preparing the *Treatise on Money*, which was shortly to make its appearance. (Vide R. F. Harrod, *The Life of John Maynard Keynes*, op. cit., p. 413.) As a matter of fact, the theoretical framework supporting Keynes' thinking in the *Report*, especially in *Addendum I*, was taken directly from the *Treatise*.
3. A. E. Robinson, op. cit., p. 38.
4. The members of this Committee were Lord Macmillan, J. M. Keynes, Lord R. H. Brand, R. McKenna, J. F. Taylor, A. A. G. Tullock, Sir T. Allen, E. Bevin, W. Raine, J. T. W. Newbold, L. B. Lee, C. Lubbock, and Lord Bradbury.
5. There were over one million unemployed British workers at this time.

some means of alleviating the situation.[1] The Committee did not confine its deliberations to purely domestic problems, for shortly after the date of its appointment, these difficulties were made worse by the world-wide economic collapse. Consequently, in order to take cognizance of the effects of these external disturbances, the Committee had to include the international situation within the scope of its inquiry.[2]

Although the Committee offered in its Report[3] a number of

---

1. More specifically, the Treasury Minute of November 5, 1929, states that this Committee was formed "to inquire into banking, finance and credit, paying regard to the factors both internal and international which govern their operation, and to make recommendations calculated to enable these agencies to promote the development of trade and commerce and the employment of labour." (Vide Committee on Finance and Industry: Report, Cmd. 3897, London, H. M. Stationery Office, June, 1931, p. 1.) (Hereafter this work will be referred to as the Macmillan Report.)
2. Macmillan Report, op. cit., p. 6.
3. Keynes played an extremely important role in the drafting of the Report. In fact, he personally wrote many of its sections. The final Report, though bearing some marks of compromise, may be said to be broadly on Keynesian lines,* since it incorporates a majority of the proposals made by Keynes in his numerous publications of the 'twenties and in the Treatise on Money. (Vide R. F. Harrod, The Life of John Maynard Keynes, op. cit., p. 423.) Among Keynes' recommendations accepted by the Committee were: a managed currency system which would seek to stabilize output and employment at a high level by influencing the flow of savings into home and foreign investments (Macmillan Report, op. cit., pp. 118-119); control over the long-term investment market (Ibid., pp. 119-120); rejection of the gold coin standard (Ibid., pp. 121-122); divorce of gold reserves from the note issue (Ibid., pp. 137-143); utilization of gold reserves exclusively for meeting deficits in the international balance of payments** (Ibid., p. 122); national monetary autonomy (Ibid., p. 132); and the granting of permission to the Central Bank to allow a wider fluctuation in the size of its gold reserves so that it might more readily reconcile foreign exchange stability with domestic credit stability (Ibid., p. 141.). Keynes was not equally successful, though, in convincing the Committee of the need for a larger spread between the gold points and for fixing the forward exchange rates on selected financial

recommendations, many of which were of a Keynesian nature, for relieving British as well as world difficulties, Keynes was of the opinion that these suggestions were not sufficiently exhaustive. Therefore, in concert with a number of other dissident members of the Committee,[1] he prepared an appendix to the Report in which he gave wider scope to his views than was possible in the Report proper. In this effort, known as Addendum I to the Report of the Committee on Finance and Industry, Keynes gave more tangible expression to the protectionist position first entertained by him in the pages of the Treatise on Money. Therefore, to pursue the evolution of his foreign trade thinking, an examination of the evidence contained in this appendage to the Macmillan Report is imperative.

The best hope of a remedy for the world as a whole, according

---

3. centers. (Vide H. R. Burrows, op. cit., p. 162.) Neither was he able to win the full Committee's endorsement of his public works plan nor his suggestion of a tariff and bounty scheme; hence, the reason for stating his views on these questions in a special appendage to the Report.

Strange as it may seem, the Committee gave no consideration to the abandonment of the existing gold standard. But this was only because Keynes and other members of the Committee, v.g. Ernest Bevin, felt that there wasn't the remotest change of the public's accepting such a solution at this time. Ironically, only three months after the publication of the Committee's Report (June, 1931), the gold standard was in fact abandoned. (Vide R. F. Harrod, The Life of John Maynard Keynes, op. cit., p. 414.)

*Despite the fact that this Report was in line with his thinking, Keynes felt that it was incomplete without certain additional observations which he makes in Addendum I.

**This was considered to be the boldest piece of advice in the Report. (Vide J. Stamp, "The Report of the Macmillan Committee," The Economic Journal, XLI, 163, Sept. 1931, p. 425.)

1. These gentlemen were R. McKenna, J.F. Taylor and A.A. Tullock, who signed the appendage without exception, and Messrs. E. Bevin and I. Allen who signed with some reservation.

to the findings of the full Committee, rested in a money policy designed to augment the volume of purchasing power, to ease credit conditions by reducing the short as well as the long-term rate of interest and to encourage in every way possible the spirit of enterprise and the undertaking of new investment.[1]

Keynes and his dissenting colleagues felt that, although this would be good advice for a closed system, it could not satisfy the requirements of Great Britain in particular, since her economic affairs were largely intertwined with those of an international system. In consequence of her membership in such an open system, the power of the Bank of England to initiate an independent monetary policy, irrespective of foreign considerations, was entirely limited.[2]

Should the monetary authority reduce the level of interest on long-term undertakings or the State provide the economy with some kind of direct stimulus, v.g. a public works program, either of these actions would put a strain on the international position of the Bank of England, unless, of course, these policies were similarly pursued in other countries.[3] A cheap money policy at home would make foreign investments more attractive and thus lead to a volume of foreign lending in excess of the foreign balance. A public works program would increase the level of national income,

---

[1] J. M. Keynes et al., *Addendum I to the Report of the Committee on Finance and Industry*, Cmd. 3897, London, H. M. Stationery Office, June, 1931, pp. 190, 196.
[2] *Ibid.*, p. 190.
[3] *Ibid.*, p. 191.

but in doing so, would stimulate the demand for imports and thereby reduce the foreign balance.¹ Thus, by initiating either or both of these policies unilaterally, a nation might disturb the equality between its foreign balance and foreign lending, with the result that gold flows would be set in motion and external equilibrium would be upset. Under such a condition of external disequilibrium, the Central Bank could not pursue for very long an easy money policy. But if it were thus forced to terminate its cheap money program, it would surely bring recovery to a halt.

The implications of external equilibrium for a domestic recovery program are quite clear. When such equilibrium obtains in the foreign sector, i.e. when the excess of total savings over home investment is equal to the surplus on the balance of trade, there cannot occur any gold movements, and so there need be no incumberance in the way of the Central Bank's promotion of an expansive monetary program which will insure a condition of full employment of manpower and resources.²

To guarantee such external equilibrium, a strengthening of the expanding country's balance of trade surplus or a reduction in its volume of foreign lending is clearly indicated; however, Keynes and his associates doubted that this could be accomplished with the

---

1. This spilling over of domestic expansion into the foreign sector by way of increased imports creates higher incomes for foreigners. And unless some portion of this added income is spent for the exports of the expanding country, income in the latter will be reduced by the same amount as the improvement in the foreign sector.
2. J. M. Keynes, et al., Addendum I, op. cit., p. 192.

existing monetary instruments.[1] In short, their contention was that, if the Central Bank and the State were to pursue policies designed to abate the depression and restore employment to a more satisfactory level, other practicable measures, whether of a monetary nature or not, would have to be devised to augment the foreign balance or reduce the volume of foreign lending, so that external equilibrium[2] might be safeguarded.[3]

Turning their attention to a consideration of these measures, Keynes and his associates concluded that there were really three alternatives available, two for increasing the foreign balance and one for reducing the volume of foreign lending or augmenting the amount of home investment.[4] These were as follows:

    (i) A reduction of salaries and wages.

    (ii) Control of imports and aids to the export industries.

    (iii) Domestic enterprise assisted by

---

1. *Ibid.*, p. 190.
2. N. B. How closely related Keynes' thinking in the Addendum was to his equilibrium analysis of the *Treatise on Money*. In effect, Keynes' work on the Committee, particularly in drawing up this appendix, gave him an excellent opportunity to apply the tools which he had fashioned in the *Treatise* to the concrete British problems of the day.
3. J. M. Keynes et al., *Addendum I, op. cit.*, pp. 191-192.
4. The volume of foreign lending may be reduced only by diverting savings from the foreign sector to new domestic outlets. This, Keynes thought, could be achieved either by increasing the enterprise of borrowers or by offering them some kind of subsidy to help defray the cost of borrowing - a suggestion he first advanced in the *Treatise*. (Vide J. M. Keynes, *A Treatise on Money, op. cit.*, vol. II, pp. 186-187.)

State action, or subsidies to private investment at home.[1]

In assaying the value of these alternatives to the British economy in 1930, Keynes and his confederates did not place too much confidence in the first course of action. This is not at all surprising, for, it will be recalled, Keynes had been vehemently opposed to the restoration of the gold standard precisely because it would entail a similar deflation of labor's income.[2] As in his writings of the 'twenties, Keynes argued against a reduction of wages and salaries, because he could see no way of resolving the problem of social justice created by a proposal that would reduce these payments, while leaving unaffected those money-incomes fixed by contract.[3] Furthermore, if all countries were to seek their international equilibrium by competitive wage cuts, this action would benefit no one. In fact, such universal wage cutting would merely reduce prices further and "rivet on the shoulders of the debtors a heavier burden of monetary obligation."[4]

---

1. J.M. Keynes et al., *Addendum I, op. cit.*, p. 192.
2. This reduction of wages and salaries would be accomplished through the instrumentality of bank rate. An increase in the rate of interest would contract credit, thereby affecting adversely current business activity and investment. This reduction of activity would lead in turn to a diminution of employment and a decline in the wage level. Note, however, that this method of adjustment would not affect all classes of income. In fact, rentiers, bondholders and other fixed income recipients would stand to realize an increase in their level of real income as a result of the deflation.
3. J.M. Keynes et al., *Addendum I, op. cit.*, pp. 193-194, 208.
4. Ibid., pp. 197, 208.

Then, too, it must be remembered that Keynes was more favorably disposed towards inflation than deflation. Accordingly, he sought a solution to the problem via an increase rather than a decrease in world prices, as the following excerpts will testify.

> It is not easy to see how we can expect a revival in our foreign trade, on a sufficient scale to be of much value to us, by any other means than through a revival of world demand. To meet the immediate problems, arising out of the world slump, a policy intended to direct increased purchasing power into the right channels, both home and abroad, with a view to restoring equilibrium at the present level of costs, would, therefore, be much wiser, in our judgment, than a policy of trying to cut our costs faster than the rest of the world can cut theirs....[1]
>
> We prefer, therefore, to pin all our hopes on a recovery of world prices, and to strain all our efforts to secure it.[2]

Thus, Keynes and his friends definitely rule out a general wage reduction as a means of restoring external equilibrium.[3] Moreover, they also question whether such a policy would be an effective means of stimulating the level of home employment, as note their following observation.

---

1. Ibid., p. 196.
2. Ibid., p. 209.
3. Keynes had expressed the conviction that wage reductions should not be used as a means of achieving equilibrium throughout the 'twenties. He reaffirmed this view in two articles which appeared early in 1930. (Vide J. M. Keynes, "The Question of High Wages," Political Quarterly, I, 1, Jan. 1930, pp. 118-119; J. M. Keynes, "British Industry, Unemployment and High Wages," Barrons - The Financial Weekly, X, 12, March 24, 1930, p. 22.)

160

> It is impossible to calculate in advance what increase of employment could be expected from a given average reduction of wages. But the relation of the one to the other might disappoint the expectations of many people, inasmuch as a false analogy is often drawn from the obvious great advantages to an individual employer of a reduction of the wages which he has to pay. For each employer perceives quite clearly the advantages he would gain if the wages which he himself pays were to be reduced, but not so clearly the disadvantages he will suffer if the money-incomes of the customers are reduced. Just as it is to the advantage of each producer that every product should be cheap except his own, similarly it is to his advantage that all costs and wages should be high except those which he himself incurs - since the demand for his product comes from the incomes which are paid out as costs by other producers.[1]

Although Keynes and his associates oppose a reduction of money wages, they recognize that, if external equilibrium was to be insured, some adjustment of money incomes was unavoidable, as witness their following statement.

---

1. Thus, although it is popularly thought that Keynes first advanced the argument that wage reductions do not lead directly* to an increase in employment in the General Theory, the germs of this thesis are clearly to be found in the Addendum to the Macmillan Report.

    * Indirectly, however, wage reductions may lead to an increase in employment. The reasoning is as follows. As wages are reduced, the transactions motive for holding money is similarly reduced. But such a weakening of the liquidity preference for money at a given supply of it will cause the rate of interest to fall. This reduction in the cost of borrowing will better equate the interest rate with the marginal efficiency of capital and thus stimulate investment, which will in turn induce an increase in output, employment, and income. (Vide J. M. Keynes, The General Theory of Employment, Interest and Money, op. cit., Chapter 2.)
2. J. M. Keynes et al., Addendum I, op. cit., p. 194.

> Whatever efforts we may make and however high the hopes we entertain, it remains true, unfortunately, that our efforts and hopes may be defeated. It would be absurd to maintain that we can continue to adhere to the existing level of money-incomes irrespective of the value of money.[1]

But if wage reductions be excluded as a means of effecting the correction, what other alternatives are there available for contracting the gold value of money incomes in general?

Keynes and his friends suggested three alternative measures to a reduction in wages and salaries - devaluation, a national treaty and a scheme of tariffs plus bounties.[2] Through these means it was hoped that money-incomes and costs might be sufficiently reduced to stimulate the size of the foreign balance and thereby enable the Bank of England to pursue without embarrassment a program of monetary expansion.[3]

The first of these alternatives was considered to be the most advantageous method, because it would change the monetary standard, e.g. by diminishing by 10 per cent the gold parity of sterling, while leaving all types of money-income at their current levels. It would affect all classes of income uniformly without recourse to any special measures. And lastly, it would have the advantage of according immediate, direct benefit to the export and import-competing industries which were in dire need of assistance at this time. But despite these advantages, this technique was not

---

1. J. M. Keynes et al., *Addendum I, op. cit.*, p. 198.
2. *Ibid.*, pp. 199-200.
3. *Ibid.*, p. 193.

completely satisfactory for an international banking country such as Great Britain. Being a creditor nation, she was owed large sums from abroad fixed in terms of sterling, and to effect such a devaluation would mean that external debts would be written down by an amount equal to the depreciation of the pound.[1] Moreover, it was reasoned that such action would further impair international confidence and so was rejected by all the members of the Committee.[2]

In reference to the second alternative, a national treaty, it was believed that the level of money incomes could be reduced by the imposition of a tax on those incomes which would be exempt from the general wage reduction. But though this solution was theoretically plausible, Keynes and his confreres felt that there would be many practical difficulties in its way, and so they similarly rejected this course of action.[3]

This meant, therefore, that reliance would have to be placed entirely on the third alternative which called for a scheme of import tariffs and export bounties. Keynes and his associates were of the conviction that the same benefits as those that would be forthcoming from a devaluation of sterling by a given amount could be achieved by a tariff of the same percentage on all imports together with a like subsidy on all exports. Besides, this scheme would have the added advantages of leaving sterling

---

1. Ibid., p. 199.
2. Macmillan Report, op. cit., pp. 110-111.
3. J. M. Keynes et al., Addendum I, op. cit., pp. 199-200.

international obligations unchanged in terms of gold and of avoiding injury to the national credit.[1]

The proposed plan would, by reducing the value of a given level of money income through the agency of higher import duties, serve to reduce the demand for imports. However, this contraction of real income would not be of any direct advantage to the export industries, since their money costs of production would remain unaltered. How, then, could the volume of exports be increased? The answer rests in the second measure of the proposal, viz. the provision for export bounties. By according the export or import-competing industries a subsidy or some form of indirect assistance,[2] home producers would be in a better position to compete with foreigners than would be warranted by the existing money costs of production. In effect, the proceeds realized from the imposition of duties on imports would be made available to the export industries in the form of governmental assistance. Thus, a system of import tariffs plus export bounties would discourage imports, encourage exports and increase the foreign balance without seriously disturbing either internal or external economic relationships.

---

1. J. Stamp, op. cit., p. 432.
2. In view of the fact that foreign countries might impose special duties on these British goods, in order to offset their bounties, it was suggested that direct export bounties should be replaced by sundry forms of indirect assistance. (Vide P. B. Whale, International Trade, London, Thornton Butterworth, Ltd., 1932, pp. 183-184.)

The increased trade surplus thus realized would then stand in better relation to the volume of foreign lending, and would, therefore, facilitate the attainment of external equilibrium. Protected in this manner from a loss of the precious metal, the Central Bank could then continue to promote the cheap money policy designed by it to secure full employment of manpower and resources. But apart from safeguarding external equilibrium and thus permitting the continuance of an easy money policy, a protectionist trade policy, by causing home produced goods to be substituted for foreign commodities, helps to bring about a direct increase in the level of home employment and income.

Thus, given an economic environment such as that prevailing in Great Britain in early 1930 - a condition in which she had a surplus of labor and plant which she was unable to utilize, because of the standing of relative interest rates and money costs at home and abroad[1] - Keynes and the other signatories to the Addendum argued that the free trade argument could not apply unconditionally. For under these circumstances, production, employment and productivity can be more readily augmented by a restricted than by a free system of trade. This may be evidenced in their following observations.

---

1. J. M. Keynes et al., Addendum I, op. cit., pp. 200-201.

> The fundamental argument for unrestricted Free
> Trade does not apply without qualification to
> an economic system which is neither in equili-
> brium nor in sight of equilibrium. For if a
> country's productive resources are normally
> fully employed, a tariff cannot increase output,
> but can only divert production from one direc-
> tion to another.... But if this condition of
> full employment is neither fulfilled nor likely
> to be fulfilled for some time, then the position
> is totally different, since a tariff may bring
> about a net increase of production and not merely
> a diversion.
>
> It appears to us, therefore, that, if imports
> were to be controlled, whether by a tariff with
> compensation for exports, by Import Boards, or
> in some other way and home produced goods sub-
> stituted for them, there is a presumption, so
> long as present circumstances last, that this
> would mean a net increase of employment and of
> national productivity.[1]

The above statement gives positive proof that Keynes abandoned the view which he expressed in 1923, viz. protectionist measures cannot increase the level of home employment. Professor R. F. Harrod[2] is of the opinion that Keynes' new attitude towards protectionism was largely the result of his savings and investment analysis of unemployment which he had recently developed.[3] According to this analysis, the foreign trade balance is synonymous with foreign investment.[4] But an improvement in the latter exercises

---

1. Ibid., p. 201.
2. R. F. Harrod, The Life of John Maynard Keynes, op. cit., p. 425.
3. For a consideration of the effects exerted by a disparity between savings and investment on business activity and employment, see J. M. Keynes, A Treatise on Money, op. cit., vol. I, pp. 171-184, pp. 279-292; vol. II, pp. 206-208; J. M. Keynes, An Economic Analysis of Unemployment, op. cit., pp. 20-29; and R. F. Harrod, The Life of John Maynard Keynes, op. cit., pp. 404-413.
4. J. M. Keynes, A Treatise on Money, op. cit., vol. I, p. 132.

the same beneficial effect on the level of home employment as an increase in the volume of home investment, which is, of course, the principal means of stimulating recovery in the Keynesian system. Therefore, to the extent that restrictive trade measures increase the foreign balance of trade, they enhance the level of domestic employment. Moreover, protection helps to revive business confidence and in this way further encourages domestic investment activity. Add to this the fact that a restrictive trade policy accomplishes all these things without reference to a reduction of money wages and without turning the terms of trade against the home country,[1] and it becomes even more apparent why Keynes should now turn away from free trade.

Keynes further revealed his partiality towards protectionism at this time by his support of a domestic capital expansion program which he and his group had suggested as a third alternative means of achieving external equilibrium. It was reasoned by them that, if savings could be diverted from the foreign to the domestic sector, this would reduce the volume of foreign lending and thus bring it into better balance with the foreign trade surplus.

But though an increase in the level of domestic investment might help to reduce the volume of foreign lending and stimulate home employment as well, it might not succeed in restoring external equilibrium, because of its adverse effects on the trade balance. In the first place, a capital development scheme puts a burden on

---

1. R. F. Harrod, *The Life of John Maynard Keynes*, op. cit., p. 426.

the balance of trade by increasing expenditures on imports. These will have to be increased both to furnish needed raw materials and additional consumer goods, especially foodstuffs, to satisfy the demands of the newly employed.[1] Secondly, an expanded investment program subjects the foreign trade balance to greater stress, because it has a propensity to reduce the level of exports. This it may do either by causing resources to be diverted to it from the export industries or by causing an increase in their prices.[2] Therefore, because of its propensity to increase imports and reduce exports, a domestic capital expansion program tends to diminish the foreign trade surplus - an eventuality which will not only impair the maintenance of international equilibrium, but which will reduce the level of home employment as well.

Were it not for this burden which it places on the foreign trade balance, home employment would receive a decided stimulus from such a domestic investment program.[3] Therefore, to ease this pressure on the trade surplus and thereby permit the economy to take advantage of the benefits forthcoming from increased capital formation, Keynes and his friends suggested that imports

---

1. J. M. Keynes et al., Addendum I, op. cit., p. 205.
2. Ibid., p. 204.
3. Keynes and his fellow signatories to the Addendum give us some intimation of the workings of the multiplier, which had not yet been fully formulated, in their following observation. "For in addition to the men directly employed and to the men occupied in making and transporting the materials required, there will be a further set of men put into work to supply the needs created by the additional purchasing and consuming power of the first set of men and so on." (Vide J. M. Keynes et al., Addendum I, op. cit., p. 203.)

be made subject to conscious control.¹ In this way, not only would external equilibrium be preserved, but the home economy could then enjoy the employment benefits derivable from both the increased level of investment and the favorable balance of trade, as note their following contention.

> If, therefore, we were to expand investment at home and control imports,² we should get the favourable effects of both schemes on domestic employment and avoid the disturbing effects of both on our international balance.³

Summary

In assaying the above findings we perceive that Keynes was led to protectionism, as an alternative to wage reductions, on grounds that such a policy would safeguard Great Britain's external equilibrium, provide for increased employment and make possible the undertaking of a capital expansion program which would further add to the level of home employment.

Ever mindful of the domestic welfare, Keynes rejected a reduction of wages and salaries as a means of increasing domestic employment and restoring the external balance, because such a deflation would be too disruptive of internal economic relationships.

---

1. J. M. Keynes et al., <u>Addendum I</u>, <u>op</u>. <u>cit</u>., p. 203.
2. In addition, Keynes and his accomplices urged that the Bank of England regulate the net rate of foreign lending so that it would not exceed the surplus on the trade balance. In this way, external balance could be preserved. (Vide J. M. Keynes et al., <u>Addendum I</u>, <u>op</u>. <u>cit</u>., p. 205.) Incidentally, this, too, was a suggestion preferred by Keynes in the <u>Treatise</u>. (Vide J. M. Keynes, <u>A Treatise on Money</u>, <u>op</u>. <u>cit</u>., vol. II, pp. 313 et seq.)
3. J. M. Keynes et al., <u>Addendum I</u>, <u>op</u>. <u>cit</u>., p. 203.

Instead, he preferred that the correction be made in the external sector through a decrease in imports and an increase in exports. Such an improvement in the foreign trade balance would augment domestic employment and restore external equilibrium without dependence upon deflation and the upsetting of domestic equilibrium.

That Keynes attempted to resolve Great Britain's internal and external economic problems with a minimum of shock and disturbance to the domestic economy illustrates once again his abiding concern for the national welfare. And the fact that he favored a protectionist trade policy as the most facile and most convenient course for Great Britain to follow in overcoming these difficulties substantiates further our contention that his foreign trade thinking was largely determined by national considerations. But whether this view be accepted or not, the fact remains that as of 1930-1931 Keynes was an established protectionist. This much is incontrovertible.

CHAPTER X

THE REVENUE TARIFF EPISODE

During the early part of 1931, the economic situation in Great Britain continued to grow worse. One-fourth of her industrial plant was shut down and a similar proportion of her industrial labor force remained unemployed.[1] In addition, her international position became more unstable,[2] the status of her Budget became more precarious and national confidence sagged even further. To cope with this state of affairs, Keynes urged the enactment of a so-called revenue tariff.[3]

In the past, Keynes had consistently recommended a domestic expansion program as a means of remedying such a situation;[4]

---

1. J. M. Keynes, "Proposals for a Revenue Tariff," The New Statesman and Nation, N.S. I, 2, March 7, 1931, p. 53.
2. Great Britain was being rapidly forced into the position of a debtor country. In 1930, its surplus balance on international account fell from ₤ 138,000,000 to ₤ 39,000,000 and in early 1931 was just about extinct. (Vide J. M. Keynes, "A Gold Conference," op. cit., p. 300.)
3. Although Keynes openly came out in favor of a revenue tariff on March 7, 1931, the London Economist claimed that he had supported such a measure as early as August, 1930. Said the Economist, "It has been known in political circles that it was Mr. Keynes who inspired Mr. E. D. Simon's proposal of last August of a 10 per cent revenue tariff;* but Mr. Keynes has now let the cat out of the bag in public and propounds a scheme of his own." (Vide "The Inconsequences of Mr. Keynes," The London Economist, CXII, 4568, March 14, 1931, p. 549.)
  * The proposal offered by Mr. Simon called for a flat 10 per cent duty on all imports. For a statement of the defense of such a measure vide "A Revenue Tariff," The London Economist, CXI, 4537, August 9, 1930, pp. 267-268.
4. Vide, for example, J. M. Keynes, "Can Lloyd George Do It?" op. cit., passim.

however, such a policy of itself could not be effective in present circumstances, he reasoned, for the difficulties confronting the economy were no longer peculiar to Great Britain alone, but to the world in general.

If the economic ills plaguing Great Britain and the rest of the world were to be solved, averred Keynes, an international prescription would have to be formulated. In diagnosing the world's affliction, preparatory to prescribing a cure for it, he found that the root-cause of the international slump rested in the heavy financial burden placed on London by the reluctance of other creditor nations[1] to lend to other members of the international community.[2] Therefore, reasoned Keynes, a return of London to its former position of financial ascendancy is absolutely required for world recovery. This he makes clear in the following passage.

---

1. Keynes placed much of the blame for the prevailing international depression on the reluctance of the United States and France to lend their surplus balance on international account to other countries, as Great Britain was accustomed to doing in the past. As a result of this refusal to lend abroad, the United States was able to amass one-half the world's gold stocks and France was able to acquire about one-fourth of the total supply.* Keynes believed that this concentration of gold in the hands of the United States and France was the primary factor responsible for the disastrous fall in the level of international prices and the attending economic collapse.

    * In December, 1930, the United States possessed ₤ 944,000,000 and France owned ₤ 431,000,000 worth of gold. (Vide J. M. Keynes, "A Gold Conference," The New Statesman and Nation, N.S. II, 29, Sept. 12, 1931, p. 300.)

2. J. M. Keynes, "Proposals for a Revenue Tariff," op. cit., p. 53.

> No domestic cure today can be adequate by itself. An international cure is essential; and I see the best hope of remedying the international slump in the leadership of Great Britain. But if Great Britain is to resume leadership, she must be strong and believed to be strong. It is of paramount importance, therefore, to restore full confidence in London.... For these reasons I...believe that our exchange position should be relentlessly defended today, in order, above all, that we may resume the vacant financial leadership of the world, which no one else has the experience or the public spirit to occupy, speaking out of acknowledged strength and not out of weakness.[1]

Keynes' contention in the above passage seems to be that, if London's financial power and prestige is to be restored, two conditions must be satisfied. First, Great Britain's economic position must be made strong, and, secondly, the fixed value of sterling must remain inviolate.[2] To accomplish the first objective, the assistance of an expansionist program at home is clearly indicated. But if such an expansive policy be undertaken in a seriously depressed world, this will threaten the sterling exchange rate and thereby jeopardize the realization of a strong financial London.[3] Moreover, such a policy is neither safe nor practicable, if undertaken alone in present circumstances, because of its

---

1. Ibid., p. 54.
2. Heretofore, Keynes had been in favor of a flexible exchange rate; however, he recognized that, if confidence was to be restored in London as an international financial center, the fulfillment of this prerequisite was absolutely required; hence, he accordingly altered his position.
3. J. R. Bellerby, "Correspondence - A Revenue Tariff," The New Statesman and Nation, N.S. I, 6, April 4, 1931, p. 215.

ramifications on the trade balance, the Budget and the state of confidence.

The promotion of an expansive program at this time would raise prices at home and consequently further hamper the export industries in competing in foreign markets. On the other hand, increased domestic activity coupled with a higher level of internal prices would increase the level of imports.[1] The reduced volume of exports and the increased volume of imports would naturally diminish the size of the foreign balance. But this is not the only effect which a domestic expansion program has on a country's external sector. For, by promoting a low level of interest rates, an expansionist policy encourages a flight of capital to abroad. Thus, the consequences of increased domestic activity on a nation's external sector are a diminished foreign balance and an increased volume of foreign lending. If these pressures be strong enough, a disparity will occur between them, and so, there results a condition of international disequilibrium. This imbalance will lead to an outflow of gold and will thereby impair the value of the exchange rate. If sufficiently strong, this loss of gold may even drive the country off the gold standard.[2]

---

1. Note once again Keynes' thinking on the multiplier and the income effect on imports associated with an increase in economic activity. As yet, he had not fully refined his thinking on the multiplier and the multiple expansion of income which he had first intimated in 1929 in the pamphlet, Can Lloyd George Do It?
2. N. B. Great Britain was still on an international gold standard at this time. And it was imperative that she continue to adhere to it if full confidence was to be restored in London.

Insofar as an expansionist program requires some increase in government borrowing for the purpose of financing public works and other employment-creating schemes, such a policy would place a further burden on the Budget. Moreover, the prospect of increased taxation attending such deficit spending would have a bad psychological effect on investors and would, therefore, cause a further loss of business confidence. Thus, an expansionist policy in the prevailing world climate would aggravate international stability, the want of confidence and the burden of taxation, which many considered to be the underlying causes of Great Britain's difficulties.[1]

These objections to a domestic expansion program could not be taken lightly. Consequently, a policy of internal expansion, which was the "sine qua non" for recovery in Keynes' estimate,[2] could not be pursued unless it was "accompanied by other measures which would neutralize its dangers."[3] For Keynes it was particularly important that the trade balance be protected and the pressure on the exchange rate be relieved;[4] otherwise, the restoration of London to her former position of financial supremacy would be impossible.

Keynes believed that the dangers to the Budget, the state of confidence and the maintenance of external equilibrium could be largely obviated by the imposition of a substantial revenue

---

1. J. M. Keynes, "Proposals for a Revenue Tariff," op. cit., p. 53.
2. J. R. Bellerby, op. cit., p. 215.
3. J. M. Keynes, "Proposals for a Revenue Tariff," op. cit., p. 54.
4. L. C. Robbins, "Correspondence - A Revenue Tariff," The New Statesman and Nation, N.S. I, 8, April 18, 1931, p. 280.

tariff.[1] In his estimate, there was no other measure available at this time which would permit the execution of a domestic expansion program and at the same time offset all the dangers inherent in it. But this was not its only advantage, for, according to Keynes, it was also designed to augment the level of home employment.[2] Keynes sets forth all of the benefits to be derived from such a measure in the following passage.

> Compared with any alternative which is open to us, this measure is unique in that it would at the same time relieve the pressing problems of the Budget and restore business confidence. I do not believe that a wise and prudent Budget can be framed today without recourse to a revenue tariff. But this is not its only advantage. Insofar as it leads to the substitution of home-produced goods for goods previously imported, it will increase employment in this country. At the same time, by relieving the pressure on the balance of trade it will provide a much needed margin to pay for the additional imports which a policy of expansion will require and to finance loans by London to necessitous debtor countries. In these ways, the buying power which we take away from the rest of the world by restricting certain imports we shall restore it with the other hand. Some fanatical Free Traders might allege that the adverse effect of import duties on our exports would neutralize all this; but it would not be true.[3]

The revenue tariff suggested by Keynes would ease the pressure

---

1. J. M. Keynes, "Proposals for a Revenue Tariff," op. cit., p. 54.
2. Keynes appears to have been the first economist of note to make a serious case for the tariff as a means of increasing domestic employment and income. (Vide R. Hinshaw, op. cit., pp. 315-316. Also Cf. Prof. Haberler's treatment of this subject in his Theory of International Trade, London, William Hodge and Co., Ltd., 1936, pp. 259-273.)
3. Ibid., p. 54.

on the Budget by providing the funds required for the promotion of an expansionist program[1] from outside sources.[2] Keynes estimated that the revenue forthcoming from this measure would amount to between 50 and 75 million pounds. These funds would be realized by the imposition of two flat rates of duty on the whole range of imports of food, raw materials and manufactures. Foodstuffs and raw materials could be taxed at 5 per cent and semi-manufactured and manufactured goods would be subject to a 15 per cent ad valorem levy.[3]

To the extent that Keynes' proposal would procure revenue for the Government from outside sources, it would lessen the need for higher taxes on personal and business income and so would serve to bolster up business confidence. It would further engender confidence in the business community by lessening competition from abroad. The import-competing industries would especially benefit from such a diminution of foreign competition.

Although Keynes tried to present his tariff proposal as a revenue measure, it was nothing more than a disguised form of protection,[4] for the real objectives behind his tariff scheme

---

1. "The Week," The New Republic, LXVI, 853, April 8, 1931, p. 190.
2. It should be borne in mind that the reason why Keynes proposed securing these funds through this medium rather than through deficit financing, as is customary nowadays, is that the latter alternative would add to the Budget difficulties and, therefore, further jeopardize business confidence.
3. J. M. Keynes, "Proposals for a Revenue Tariff," op. cit., p. 54.
4. L. C. Robbins, "Correspondence - A Revenue Tariff," The New Statesman and Nation, N.S. I, 4, March 28, 1931, p. 178.

were an increase in the level of home employment[1] and an improvement in the foreign balance.[2]

Contrary to his conviction of 1923, Keynes argued that the imposition of a tariff on incoming goods would promote an increase in the level of home employment[3] to the extent that such a device would lead to the substitution of home-produced goods for commodities

---

1. "Tariffs, Wages and Exports," The London Economist, CXII, 4572, April 11, 1931, p. 771.
2. W. H. Beveridge et al., Tariffs: The Case Examined, op. cit., pp. 81-82.
3. Keynes' adversaries pointed out that his claim, to the effect that a tariff device would increase employment by causing home-produced goods to be substituted for foreign-made commodities, did not appear to be consistent with his previous allegation that this proposal would increase the Treasury's receipts by 50 to 75 million pounds. For it is impossible to increase revenue by taxing imports and at the same time increase domestic employment by keeping these same goods from entering the country.* If a nation wants to augment its revenue from tariffs, it must permit foreign-made goods to enter its boundaries, whereas, if it wants to increase its level of employment, by substituting home-produced for foreign-manufactured goods, it must obviously keep them out. But it cannot do both, as Keynes seemed to contend. (Vide C. L. Schwartz, "Correspondence - A Revenue Tariff," The New Statesman and Nation, N.S. I, 3, March 14, 1931, p. 104; and B. A. Levinson, "Correspondence - A Revenue Tariff," The New Statesman and Nation, N.S. I, 4, March 21, 1931, p. 145.)

Although Keynes did not formally admit the contradiction, subsequent evidence shows that he really favored a tariff for its protective rather than for its revenue advantages.

* The London Economist pointed out that, in order to realize even the minimum 50 million pounds of revenue aimed at by Keynes, it would be necessary to keep the level of imports intact. But if such were the case, home-produced goods could not be substituted for foreign-produced commodities, and, so, it would not be possible to augment local employment via this medium, as Keynes maintained. (Vide "The Inconsequences of Mr. Keynes," op. cit., p. 550.)

previously purchased from abroad.[1] But in order for this to be true, Keynes would have to assume that exports would remain constant or, at least, not decline as much as imports. This he affirmed[2] and in doing so opened his attack on the doctrine that "imports must buy exports"[3] - the keystone in the arch of Free Trade thinking.[4]

Briefly, the general free trade argument is that, since international trade constitutes exchange, imports of goods and services are used to pay for each other. A reduction of imports into a particular country spells a reduction in the amount of purchasing power which foreigners have available for expenditure in that country; hence, exports from that country must necessarily decline.[5] Any extension of employment in the import-competing industries would be quickly counterbalanced by a contraction in

---

1. J. M. Keynes, "Proposals for a Revenue Tariff," op. cit., p. 54.
2. Keynes first gave affirmation to this point of view in his Treatise on Money wherein he stated that a reduction of imports "in present circumstances would probably not result either in a diminution of our exports to an extent equal to the diminution of imports, or in a diminution of home investment, but in some increase of foreign investment, which increase would be mainly a net gain to the wealth of the community." (Vide J. M. Keynes, A Treatise on Money, op. cit., vol. II, p. 186.)
3. To give some indication of how much Keynes' views changed on the question of free trade between 1923 and 1931, his earlier position on the "imports equal exports" thesis is cited. "Imports are receipts: and exports are payments. How as a nation can we expect to better ourselves by diminishing our receipts? Is there anything a tariff could do which an earthquake could not do better?" (Vide J. M. Keynes, "Free Trade and Unemployment," op. cit., p. 336.)
4. E. M. F. Durbin, "Correspondence - A Revenue Tariff," The New Statesman and Nation, N.S. I, 5, March 28, 1931, p. 144.
5. W. H. Beveridge, "The Case for Free Trade," The London Times, March 26, 1931, p. 10.

the export trades.[1] Consequently, the exclusion of imports by tariffs or other restrictionist devices cannot mean an increase of output and employment, but only a diversion of manpower and resources from the export to the home industries. Moreover, such a diversion is disadvantageous for the economy as a whole, because it sacrifices the principle of comparative advantage.[2]

In presenting his case, Keynes argued that such a nice balancing of imports and exports can obtain only in a hypothetical economic system which possesses an inherent capacity for stable equilibrium and such a degree of elasticity that any disturbance would be attended to so quickly that the system could not depart appreciably from equilibrium.[3] However, in the real economic world, asserted Keynes, there is "no simple or direct relationship between the volume of imports and the volume of exports."[4]

It is a rather complicated matter to explain the various reactions, internal and external, which may be set in motion by a change in the level of imports and its possible effects on the level of exports. Perhaps, it will suffice to indicate some of the more important considerations which, in Keynes' estimate, enter into the determination of the final outcome. When a nation curtails the volume of its imports, through the imposition of a

---

1. L. C. Robbins, "Correspondence - A Revenue Tariff," The New Statesman and Nation, N.S. I, 5, March 28, 1931, p. 179.
2. W. H. Beveridge, "The Case for Free Trade," op. cit., p. 10.
3. J. M. Keynes, "Economic Notes on Free Trade - The Reaction of Imports on Exports," The New Statesman and Nation, N.S. I, 7, April 11, 1931, p. 242.
4. J. M. Keynes, "Revenue Tariffs - Effects on Home Production," The London Times, April 2, 1931, p. 6.

tariff, the effect of this action on the level of its exports is largely determined by whether the economy was in a position of equilibrium or not when the decline in its imports took place.[1] The type monetary policy pursued by it consequent upon this cutback in the volume of its imports is also of importance. For example, if the home country promotes a tight money policy, while all other countries continue to adhere to a cheap money policy, it is not likely that it will experience a reduction in exports commensurate to the decline in its imports. If, however, the Central Bank in the home country lowers its bank rate, following the imposition of import restrictions, this action may be expected to cause an improvement in domestic activity which will, in turn, bring about an increase in the volume of imports.[2] Insofar as the effect of this cheap money policy on the home country's level of exports is concerned, it is necessary to take into consideration the reaction of this policy on the level of internal prices.[3] But to do this it is necessary to ascertain whether there exists any surplus productive capacity, and, if so, how much of it can be brought into use at approximately the same money rate of remuneration per unit of efficiency as the productive plant and labor previously employed.[4]

Clearly, it is not easy to determine precisely what the net

---

1. J. M. Keynes, "Economic Notes on Free Trade - The Reaction of Imports on Exports," op. cit., p. 242.
2. N. B. the income effect on imports.
3. J. M. Keynes, "Economic Notes on Free Trade - The Reaction of Imports on Exports," op. cit., p. 242.
4. Ibid.

effect of all these factors will be on the level of a nation's exports, following a curtailment of her imports. In Keynes' view, the question cannot be answered "merely on a priori considerations, but must be determined by applying a sound theoretical apparatus to a knowledge of many current facts, and an estimation by the practical judgment of the probabilities suggested by this application."[1] Keynes reasons that there are cases where a reduction in imports would lead to an increase in exports as well as cases where they would be decreased. But in any event, it would be highly improbable that a change in the value of imports would induce an equal change in the value of exports.

In addition to this argument, Keynes posed a number of others against the "imports must equal exports" thesis of the Free Traders.[2] He pointed out that if this contention be true, then there would be no need to be concerned about the trade balance, as he was, during a period of domestic expansion. An increase in domestic activity, as noted repeatedly in this thesis, will lead to an increase in the level of imports. Such an eventuality will weaken the trade balance and might lead to an outflow of gold. But, counters Keynes, if it be true that

---

1. *Ibid.*
2. For additional arguments in support of Keynes' position consult those presented by Mr. Keynes' brilliant pupil, R. F. Kahn, in the pages of *The New Statesman*. (Cf. R. F. Kahn, "Correspondence - A Revenue Tariff," *The New Statesman and Nation*, N.S. I, 6, 8, April 4, 1931, April 18, 1931, p. 214, p. 280.)

there is an identity between imports and exports, then to the extent that imports are increased, exports must be raised correspondingly; hence, a domestic expansion program would have a double advantage, for besides promoting recovery in the home industries it would augment employment in the export sector as well. This, of course, is counter to experience.[1]

Keynes further observed that, if there were a necessary equality between imports and exports, there would be little sense in trying to raise home employment by reducing production costs in the import-competing industries. For, to the extent that imports were diminished and the ability of foreigners to buy in Britain reduced correspondingly, this would increase the number of unemployed in the export sector by an amount equal to the improvement in the import-competing trades.[2] But would common sense agree with the Free Traders?[3]

---

1. J. M. Keynes, "Mr. J. M. Keynes' Rejoinder," (Letter to the Editor), The London Times, March 27, 1931, p. 10.
2. Ibid.
3. It is the humble opinion of the writer that the "import equals export" difficulty is best resolved by an explanation tendered by Mr. L. J. Cadbury. The statement is as follows: "To give a meaning to the statement that imports are paid for by exports, it is necessary to define the period of time over which the transaction takes place. Over a short period of time it is quite obviously inaccurate. Imports can be paid for by raising a foreign loan, by cancelling a foreign credit, and by many other means, without a number of years having to export goods or services of a corresponding value.

    If, however, we qualify the proposition and say that over a long period of time, or sooner or later, imports are paid for exports the truth of our statement is obvious." (Vide L. J. Cadbury, "Correspondence - A Revenue Tariff," The New Statesman and Nation, N.S. I, 6, April 4, 1931, p. 213.)

Lastly, Keynes maintained that, so long as there does not occur any change in the prices of exports, there is another factor at work which will keep their volume from falling off commensurately with the decline in the level of imports. This is the utilization of the export surplus for financing loans to foreigners. If the favorable balance of trade be used in this way, then the buying power taken away from other countries by a restriction of certain imports will be returned to them via an increase in the volume of loans.[1] Therefore, so long as the improvement in the foreign balance is not used to draw gold from abroad, but is used instead to augment the amount of foreign lending,[2] there need be no adverse effect on the level of exports.[3]

To summarize Keynes' position, it may be said that, because a restriction of imports does not necessarily lead to a similar curtailment of exports, a tariff on incoming goods can, by causing

---

1. J. M. Keynes, "Proposals for a Revenue Tariff," op. cit., p. 54.
2. Note the change that took place in Keynes' attitude towards foreign investment. Whereas he now strongly favored an increase in foreign lending, back in 1923 he considered such foreign investment detrimental to the home economy, because it drove capital out of the country. Keynes' adversaries were quick to point out this inconsistency to him, as note the following comment made by Prof. Robbins. "It is not many years ago since Keynes, with his customary Cassandra-like vehemence, was warning us to regard foreign investment as almost wholly undesirable. What queer irony of circumstance is this which, in his present mood, brings him to urge, with equivalent vehemence, just that form of foreign investment which most sane men would agree to be without any redeeming feature!" (Vide L. C. Robbins, "A Reply to Mr. Keynes," The New Statesman and Nation, N.S. I, 3, March 14, 1931, p. 99.)
3. J. M. Keynes et al., Addendum I, op. cit., p. 201.

home-produced goods to be substituted for commodities previously purchased from foreign countries, enhance the level of home employment. In addition to providing this direct stimulus to the domestic employment situation, Keynes believed that a tariff could, through its influence on the interest rate, make possible a further improvement in the level of employment. The increased trade surplus forthcoming from such a tariff would, by providing a larger offset to the volume of foreign lending, insure the maintenance of external equilibrium. Thus assured of its external balance, the Bank of England could then reduce the structure of interest rates without bringing pressure to bear against the exchange rate.[1] Given the existence of these lower interest rates, much of the nation's idle manpower and capital resources could be restored to productive activity.[2]

The Free Traders, however, were unwilling to concede to Keynes' reasoning. Accordingly, they countered with the argument that even if it be admitted in some circumstances that imports may be curtailed without a corresponding decline in the level of exports and that the volume of foreign lending may be increased to fill the

---

1. The maintenance of the sterling exchange value was of pivotal importance in Keynes' current recovery scheme, because one of its primary objectives was the restoration of full confidence in London as an international financial center.
2. In view of the surplus labor and industrial capacity available in Great Britain at this time, it was unlikely that this expansion of domestic activity would cause an upsurge in prices and a consequent discouragement of exports, which might otherwise neutralize the improvement of employment in the home industries. (Vide J. M. Keynes, "Economic Notes on Free Trade - The Reaction of Imports on Exports," op. cit., p. 242.)

void between the two, the raising of tariff barriers will still fail to increase the level of home employment.¹ According to Sir William Beveridge, one of the chief spokesmen for the Free Traders in the early 'thirties, even if the foreign balance becomes more favorable, it remains "unproved that an increase of lending abroad could take place without harmful contraction of lending at home."² Thus, whatever advantage home employment gains through foreign investment it loses through a reduction in domestic investment.

It seems that Sir William was of the view that the total amount of savings available for investment is fixed. The more is loaned to abroad, the less can be loaned to investment undertakings at home. This belief is indicated in the following passage.

> Insofar as these circumstances did continue and exports were maintained by increased lending, it would mean the diversion of British capital abroad and the probable further cramping of home investment.³

In the light of subsequent Keynesian thinking, this position can be shown to be quite erroneous. According to Mrs. Joan Robinson, when a tariff causes an improvement in the foreign balance, the consequent increase in the volume of foreign lending (which Keynes assumed in his analysis) can be brought about only on condition that the rate of interest at home be lower than that prevailing abroad. But if the cost of borrowing money be low,

---

1. E. M. F. Durkin, op. cit., p. 144.
2. J. M. Keynes, "Mr. Keynes' Rejoinder," op. cit., p. 10.
3. W. H. Beveridge et al., Tariffs: The Case Examined, op. cit., p. 57.

then this will serve to increase, not decrease, the amount of home investment. And insofar as this enhanced domestic investment activity generates a higher national income, the level of savings will be increased.[1] For in the Keynesian system savings are a function of income. Consequently, the increased foreign lending is not made at the expense of home investment, but is realized through the increased savings made possible by a higher national income.[2]

In arguing that a restrictive trade policy was capable of increasing the level of home employment during periods of depressed activity, Keynes gave advance notice to one of the most important contributions of the General Theory to economic theory, namely, that the conclusions of classical and neo-classical economics can hold true only on condition that full employment obtains.

Keynes asserts that, given a condition of full employment of manpower and resources, there can be no questioning the orthodox argument that a policy of free trade will best promote the

---

1. J. Robinson, "Beggar-My-Neighbour Remedies for Unemployment," Essays in the Theory of Employment, op. cit., p. 212.
2. In supporting Keynes' position that a decrease in imports can lead to an increase in domestic employment, Mrs. Robinson contends that it was never the true orthodox view that a tariff could not bring about an increase in employment in the short run. Her contention is that "Classical trade simply tells us of the advantages of specialization .... It cannot tell us that when one country increases its share in world employment, at the expense of reducing output per unit of employment, its total output will be reduced. Still less can it tell us that employment in any one country cannot be increased by increasing its balance of trade." (Vide J. Robinson, Essays in the Theory of Employment, op. cit., p. 212.)

economic welfare of the country. In circumstances where a nation's productive resources are likely to be fully employed, a protectionist policy will cause only a diversion and not a net increase of output. In fact, the volume of goods and services produced is likely to be reduced because of the lessened efficiency. But for a country plagued with widespread industrial inactivity and labor displacement, it is another question entirely whether the advantages accruing to increased employment, the state of business confidence, the trade balance and the Budget can be offset by the greater output per unit of employment[1] which results from a policy of free trade. The following statement made by Keynes in the pages of the London Times corroborates this contention that he made the validity of the free trade argument contingent upon the existence of a condition of full employment.

> In ordinary circumstances, when abnormal unemployment is expected to be quite temporary, it is impossible to justify a tariff by reference to its effect on employment. For when the productive resources of the country are likely to be almost fully employed in most directions, a tariff means a diversion of output, not a net increase. I have often argued the free trade case on these lines, and would do so again in the appropriate circumstances. But at present the necessary conditions are not fulfilled. The unemployment of men and plant is so large and so widespread, has lasted so long, and looks like lasting so much longer, that I should expect a tariff to increase employment now, and for some time to come; while the advantages to business confidence, the balance of trade, and the Budget are too obvious to need emphasis. Uncompromising free-traders are entitled to claim that they are taking a long view, but they are on weak ground when they deny the immediate advantages[2] of a tariff.[3]

---

1. Ibid.
2. N. B. Keynes' concern with the short run period.
3. J. M. Keynes, "The Issues for Free Traders," op. cit., p. 8.

Thus, Keynes leaves one with the conclusion that "the existence of an unemployed surplus of plant and labor destroys the free trade case,"[1] and that a policy of unrestricted trade can be promotive of a nation's best economic interests only in a condition of full employment. In this contention, then, is to be found the first intimation of Keynes' all important contribution to economic theory, namely, that the conclusions of classical and neo-classical economics hold true only under conditions of full employment and that, therefore, theirs is the economics of a special case.

From this it may be inferred that Keynes' position on the question of free versus restricted trade was largely dependent upon the status of employment in the home economy.[2] If there obtains a condition of widespread unemployment and inactivity, a strong case can be presented in behalf of a protectionist policy, whereas if there prevails a condition of full employment of manpower and resources, the free trade argument comes back into its own once again. Thus, at this juncture at least, it seems that Keynes' views respecting foreign trade policy were contingent upon the economic climate prevailing in the home economy.

The last claim made by Keynes for his tariff proposal was that it would secure an improvement in the favorable balance of trade.[3] If Great Britain was to carry out her program of internal expansion, it was necessary that she augment the size of her foreign balance.

---

1. W. H. Beveridge, "The Case for Free Trade," op. cit., p. 10.
2. More will be said in this connection in the next section of this thesis.
3. J. M. Keynes, "Further Reflections on a Revenue Tariff," The New Statesman and Nation, N.S. I, 4, March 21, 1931, p. 143.

For in promoting such an expansive program, she would experience an efflux of capital to the higher interest paying centers abroad. And unless this increase in the volume of foreign lending were offset by an improvement in the foreign balance, Britain might well experience a condition of disequilibrium and an impairment of her exchange position - the very things to be avoided if London was to be made strong.

Granted the need of a favorable balance for the maintenance of external equilibrium and the stability of the exchange,[1] why does Keynes propose that it be obtained via the imposition of a tariff? Why not try to realize it through an increase in the level of exports?

Keynes ruled out an increase in the level of exports, as a means of increasing the foreign balance, because British prices and costs were too high relative to elsewhere. Although it was argued that the problem could be solved by a readjustment of wages and an increase in efficiency,[2] he rejected such a solution on grounds that it would

---

1. Although there were some like the London Economist who believed that the primary purpose of Keynes' tariff proposal was to put unemployed British workers back into remunerative employment, Sir W.H. Beveridge and his orthodox colleagues, v.g. J.R. Hicks, G.L. Schwartz and F.C. Benham, argued that Keynes knew too much about the actual facts of British unemployment to make such "extravagant claims." They asserted that an increase of employment through the tariff device was "for him only a subsidiary gain." His primary object, they averred, was to use the tariff as a means of securing international equilibrium. Prof. Robbins was also of this conviction, his claim being that Keynes' main reason for favoring a tariff was "that it would increase our favourable balance of trade and relieve the pressure on the exchanges." (Vide "Tariffs, Wages and Exports," The London Economist, CXII, 4572, April 11, 1931, p. 771; W.H. Beveridge et al., Tariffs: The Case Examined, op. cit., p. 57; and Robbins "Correspondence - A Revenue Tariff," The New Statesman and Nation, N.S. I, 8, April 18, 1931, p. 280.)
2. L. C. Robbins, "A Reply to Mr. Keynes," op. cit., p. 100.

present a problem of justice, so long as many types of money income remained protected by contract and could not, therefore, be adjusted.[1] Moreover, he maintained that, even if internal wages and other costs could be reduced, there was no guarantee that other nations would not retaliate with similar or greater reductions;[2] hence, he saw little positive hope for exports along these lines.[3]

In view of the impossibility of revitalizing the British export industries,[4] Keynes was forced to turn to a restriction of imports as a means of achieving the required improvement in the foreign balance. This he makes clear in the following statement.

> If I knew of a concrete, practicable proposal for stimulating our export trades, I should welcome it. Knowing none, I fall back on a restriction of imports to support our balance of trade and to provide employment.[5]

---

1. J.M. Keynes, "Further Reflections on a Revenue Tariff," op. cit., p. 143.
2. Ibid.
3. J.M. Keynes, "Economic Notes on Free Trade - The Export Industries," The New Statesman and Nation, N.S. I, 4, March 28, 1931 p. 175.
4. The London Economist contends that Keynes' loss of hope in restoring the British export industries to a competitive position was the underlying reason for his turning to a protectionist policy. With the export industries doomed, Keynes was forced to seek new opportunities for these trades in the home market. But, if the manpower and capital formerly engaged in the export sector were to produce for the domestic economy, it is obvious that there would have to occur some restriction of Great Britain's foreign trade. Keynes' recommendation of a protectionist policy under the euphemistic title of a revenue tariff, asserts the Economist, was, the inevitable outcome of such a pessimistic attitude. (For a fuller development of the Economist's position on Keynes' revenue tariff vide "The Inconsequences of Mr. Keynes," The London Economist, CXII, 4568, March 14, 1931, pp. 549-550; "Mr. Keynes and Tariffs," The London Economist, CXII, 4571, April 4, 1931, p. 722; and "Tariffs, Wages and Exports," The London Economist, CXII, 4572, April 11, 1931, pp. 771-772.)
5. J. M. Keynes, "Economic Notes on Free Trade - The Export Industries," op. cit., p. 176.

Thus, with all hopes of an immediate increase in the level of exports precluded, Keynes reasoned that the required increase in the favorable balance, which he estimated at 50 million pounds,[1] could be more easily obtained by checking imports than by stimulating exports. To achieve this objective, he recommended, of course, the implementation of his tariff proposal.[2]

The realization of this improvement in the British foreign balance would clearly enhance the financial position and prestige of London, for it would guarantee the maintenance of external balance, by providing a larger offset to the increased foreign lending which would follow the initiation of a cheap money policy. The insurance of such external equilibrium would, in turn, promote the stability of the foreign exchange which Keynes deemed so important for the restoration of London to her former position of financial supremacy.

Through the advantages thus accorded by the tariff to the Budget, the state of confidence, the level of home employment and the trade balance, Keynes hoped to make Great Britain economically strong and London financially powerful. He did not believe, of course, that exclusive reliance on the tariff would solve all of Great Britain's difficulties; however, he supported it because he thought that it would accord her some margin of strength and a

---

1. J. M. Keynes, "The Issues for Free Traders," The London Times, March 21, 1931, p. 8.
2. J. M. Keynes, "Economic Notes on Free Trade - The Export Industries," op. cit., p. 175.

breathing space in which to formulate a program with which to combat both domestic and international problems.[1] Keynes expresses this sentiment in the following passage.

> I have reached my own conclusion as a result of continuous reflection over many months, without enthusiasm, as the result of the gradual elimination of the practicable alternatives as being more undesirable. Nor do I suppose for one moment that a revenue tariff by itself will see us out of our troubles. Indeed, I mainly support it because it will give us a margin of resources and a breathing space, under cover of which we can do other things.[2]

Keynes' conversion to protectionism, however expedient, evoked a great deal of criticism from his Free Trade friends. He was taunted for having abandoned "the service of high and worthy ideals in international relations"[3] and charged with inconsistency.

To the former charge Keynes retorted that it is easy to go on repeating, as they did, the same standard prescriptions "unaccompanied with any new process of cerebration."[4] He pointed out that the problem facing Great Britain was how to get out of a very tight situation and not, as the Free Traders thought, what the best long run policy would be for her to pursue under conditions of equilibrium.[5] Unfortunately, the Free Traders could not appreciate the

---

1. J. M. Keynes, "Proposals for a Revenue Tariff," op. cit., p. 54.
2. J. M. Keynes, "Economic Notes on Free Trade - The Export Industries," op. cit., p. 175.
3. L. C. Robbins, "A Reply to Mr. Keynes," op. cit., p. 100.
4. J. M. Keynes, "Economic Notes on Free Trade - A Revenue Tariff and the Cost of Living," The New Statesman and Nation, N.S. I, 6, April 4, 1931, p. 211.
5. Ibid.

fact that the conditions of the British problem were different from what they were in the past and that therefore its solution might no longer rest in free trade. Keynes indicates all this in the following highly expressive language.

> My critics have not taken any notice of, or shown the slightest interest in, the analysis of our present state.... Is it the fault of the odium theologicum attaching to Free Trade? Is it that Economics is a queer subject in a queer state? Whatever may be the reason, new paths of thought have no appeal to the fundamentalists of Free Trade. They have been forcing me to chew over again a lot of stale mutton, dragging me along a route I have known all about as long as I have known anything, which cannot, as I have discovered by many attempts, lead one to a solution of our present difficulties - a peregrination of the catacombs - with a guttering candle.[1]

Although Keynes was by no means unmindful of the advantages of free trade in conditions of equilibrium, he felt that in the prevailing circumstances such a policy could not promote the best economic interests of Great Britain. Keynes was eminently practical and when convinced that the solution of his country's difficulties was not to be found in a free trade policy, he had sufficient strength of conviction to alter his views, even if it meant leaving himself open to the charge of inconsistency. Consistency for consistency's sake had no place in Keynes' thought; nor could he justify it in the thinking of others. Thus, to those who charged him with inconsistency he directed the following terse retort.

---

1. J. M. Keynes, "Economic Notes on Free Trade - The Reaction of Imports on Exports," op. cit., p. 242.

> May I also register a mild complaint against the undercurrent of moral reprobation which I detect in some quarters? I seem to see the elder parrots sitting round and saying: "You can rely on us. Every day for 30 years, regardless of the weather, we have said 'what a lovely morning!' But this is a bad bird. He says one thing one day, and something else the next."[1]

Summary

In appraising Keynes' thinking during the revenue tariff episode of his career, we find that his break with classical free trade was motivated not so much by his desire to have Great Britain assist the world back to recovery as by his desire to have her resolve her own particular internal and external economic problems. His contention that a revenue tariff would, by creating a trade surplus for Great Britain, enable her to make external loans on a large scale once again and thus help her to foster recovery on an international level was entirely specious. For his primary consideration in urging this measure was simply to gain some advantage for Great Britain, however temporary, for putting her own economic affairs in order.

Keynes recognized that, if Britain was to overcome her economic difficulties, it was imperative that she undertake some consciously directed recovery program. However, the initiation of an expansive program in a depressed world environment would have serious implications for the internal and external sectors of the economy. To

---

1. J. M. Keynes, "Economic Notes on Free Trade - A Revenue Tariff and the Cost of Living," op. cit., p. 211.

the extent that such a program would require some increase in borrowing for the financing of public works projects, it would place an additional burden on the Budget and would further undermine business confidence.

An expansive policy would also have adverse effects on the foreign trade balance, because it has a tendency to encourage imports and discourage exports. This deterioration of the trade surplus would not only cause a reduction in the level of home employment, but would also lead to an imbalance between it and the volume of foreign lending. Such a condition of external disequilibrium, if sufficiently prolonged, would impair the stability of the exchange, and would thus threaten the expansion program.

Therefore, if Great Britain was to profit from the promotion of an expansive policy, it is evident that something would have to be done to correct the adverse effects which such a policy would exercise on the Budget, the state of confidence and the level of home employment. Attention would also have to be given to the maintenance of external equilibrium and to the fixity of the exchange rate if Great Britain was to remain on the gold standard and full confidence was to be restored in London.

In Keynes' estimate, the answer to all these problems rested in the realization of an increase in the size of the foreign balance of trade - an objective which he thought could be attained through the imposition of a revenue tariff. Such a measure would help to ease the pressure on the Budget by making available from customs receipts at least a portion of the funds required for the undertaking of an expansive public works program. It would generate confidence in the business community by restricting the degree of foreign competition. And it would increase the level of home employment by causing home-produced goods to be substituted for foreign-made commodities.

In the external sector, a revenue tariff would, by making possible an increase in the export surplus, bring it into better balance with the volume of foreign lending. The attainment of such external equilibrium would insure the maintenance of the exchange value of the pound at a stable level and would enable the Bank of England to pursue an expansionist monetary policy without anxiety.

CHAPTER XI

GREAT BRITAIN'S ABANDONMENT OF THE GOLD STANDARD

As the year, 1931, wore on, Great Britain became immersed in even greater economic difficulties, particularly with respect to her foreign trade balance.[1] The surplus on the foreign trade account was so diminished that she was now rapidly approaching the status of a debtor country.[2]

The rapid deterioration of the British foreign trade balance was largely caused by the world-wide economic holocaust which took place after 1929. The specific source of the difficulty was that whereas the foreign demand for British-made goods fell off, due to the reduced volume of activity and income, British demand for foreign raw materials and foodstuffs, being less elastic, did not fall off commensurately. Add to this the fact that interest payments by foreigners on British overseas holdings were largely contracted, and it becomes clear why Great Britain should experience the financial crisis that she did.[3]

To alleviate the trade balance difficulty, the National Government proposed the undertaking of an economy program.[4] It

---

1. In 1930, the British surplus balance on international account amounted to only ₤ 39,000,000 and by Sept. 1931 it was practically extinct.
2. J. M. Keynes, "A Gold Conference," op. cit., p. 300.
3. A. C. Pigou, Economics in Practice, London, Macmillan and Co., Ltd., 1935, p. 67.
4. J. M. Keynes, Essays in Persuasion, New York, Harcourt, Brace and Co., 1932, p. 285. (Many of these essays first appeared in 1931 as periodical and newspaper articles.)

was believed that a curtailment of governmental expenditures, v.g. a reduction in the road-building and home-building programs, the dole and the salaries of public servants,[1] would not only help to delete the Budget deficit, but would also be of indirect benefit to the trade balance. For if the level of British purchasing power could be diminished, as the Report of the Economy Committee (The May Committee) suggested, some part of the reduction in purchasing power would cause a cutback in the purchase of imported goods.[2]

Although Keynes agreed that the purchase of foreign-produced goods could be so reduced, he felt that this was "an extraordinarily indirect and wasteful way of reducing imports."[3] For a curtailment of purchasing power would induce not only a reduction in the consumption of imports, but of home-produced goods as well. In fact, the consumption of domestically produced goods would be far more adversely affected. For, of the total reduced spending, Keynes estimated that about twenty per cent would be at the expense of imports[4] and the remaining eighty per cent at the expense of home-produced commodities.[5] Thus, a large reduction

---

1. R. F. Harrod, The Life of John Maynard Keynes, op. cit., p. 438.
2. J. M. Keynes, "Some Consequences of the Economy Report," The New Statesman and Nation, N.S. II, 25, August 15, 1931, p. 189.
3. J. M. Keynes, Essays in Persuasion, op. cit., p. 281.
4. But even this reduction of imports would not help, quips Keynes, if it be true, as the Free Traders contend, that a reduction of imports leads to a corresponding reduction in the level of exports. (Vide J. M. Keynes, "The Budget," The New Statesman and Nation, N.S. II, 30, Sept. 19, 1931, p. 329.)
5. J. M. Keynes, Essays in Persuasion, op. cit., p. 282.

in the level of home income and employment would be required to bring about a better balancing of imports and exports.[1]

Keynes, being an expansionist, argued that such a contractionist program would be extremely wasteful and would not help to solve the twin problems of unemployment and an adverse balance.[2] Such a policy, by reducing expenditures, would obviously increase, rather than abate, the level of unemployment and insofar as the trade balance is concerned, Keynes pointed out that "cutting the school-teacher's salaries will not help us to recapture the markets of the world," for such a scheme will leave the cost of production in the export industries unchanged.[3] Accordingly, Keynes offered his own plan for improving the current balance of trade on income account and for dealing with the problem of unemployment. His first recommendation called for a devaluation of sterling;[4] however, he recognized that this alternative did not have too much support in the country and so he was constrained to turn once again to the tariff device.[5] Keynes' support of a restrictionist policy was couched largely in the same language as that used by him earlier in the year in support of the revenue tariff. In advancing his case for a tariff, in lieu of a

---

1. F. C. Benham, "The Muddle of the Thirties," *Economica*, N.S. XII, 45, Feb. 1945, p. 6.
2. J. M. Keynes, *Essays in Persuasion*, op. cit., p. 166.
3. Ibid.
4. W. H. Beveridge et al., *Tariffs: The Case Examined*, op. cit., p. 77.
5. J. M. Keynes, *Essays in Persuasion*, op. cit., p. 283.

reduction in wages and salaries, Keynes cites the following highly familiar arguments.

> Now the latter course (a reduction in wages and salaries), if it were to be adequate, would involve so drastic a reduction of wages and such appallingly difficult, probably insoluble, problems, both of social justice and practical method, that it would be crazy not to try first the effects of the alternative, and much milder, measure of restricting imports.
>
> It happens that this course also has other important advantages. It will not only relieve the strain on the foreign exchange. It would also do more than any other single measure to balance the Budget; and is the only form of taxation open to us which will actually increase profits, improve employment, and raise the spirits and the confidence of the business community.[1]

In view of the many advantages associated with a tariff, it was inconceivable to Keynes that the National Government should avoid such a solution and pursue, instead, an economy program whose effect would be "to reduce the standard of life of as many people as are within their reach in the hope that some small portion of the reductions of standards will be at the expense of imports."[2] Thus concluded Keynes, "Deliberately to prefer this to a direct restriction of imports is to be non compos mentis."[3]

As circumstances turned out, it wasn't necessary for Keynes to become further embroiled in controversy with the Administration, for in September, 1931, Great Britain went off the gold

---

1. *Ibid.*, pp. 283-284.
2. *Ibid.*, p. 285.
3. *Ibid.*

standard and as a result of that action the pound was automatically devalued. Let us review briefly some of the events that led to Great Britain's decision to abandon the gold standard.

Although there were many deep-seated factors[1] behind Britain's divorce from gold, the proximate cause of the suspension of gold payments by the Bank of England was the wave of distrust that engulfed the pound following the banking crisis in Central Europe.

The crisis began in mid-summer with the collapse of the highly regarded Austrian Creditanstalt. This development led to a great feeling of uneasiness and a consequent withdrawal of funds from Central Europe. This caused the Darmstadter und Nationalbank to get into difficulties of great magnitude and on July 13 it, too, was forced to suspend payments. To prevent a complete collapse of the German banking system and the reichsmark, the Government imposed a restriction upon external payments. This action had serious bearing on London, for a considerable part of the assets of a number of City banks was thus immobilized.[2]

---

1. Dr. Paul Einzig, noted British banking authority, cites the following basic causes for Great Britain's departure from gold.
    (1) The discrepancy between the cost of production in Great Britain and other foreign countries.
    (2) The downward trend of world prices.
    (3) The existence of excessive taxation in Great Britain as compared with other nations.
    (4) Gold hoarding practices on the part of the United States and France.
    (5) The abnormal international transfer of funds, especially as required by reparations and war debts.
    (Vide P. Einzig, The Tragedy of the Pound, London, Kegan Paul, French, Trubner and Co., Ltd., 1932, pp. 9 et seq.)
2. P. Einzig, The Comedy of the Pound, London, Kegan Paul, French, Trubner and Co., Ltd., 1933, p. 17.

In the meantime, the pound also was being subjected to pressure. To stem the outflow of gold, the Bank of England utilized its supply of foreign exchange reserves; however, this sum was hardly adequate for the task. Consequently, in the last days of July, the British authorities were forced to enlist the assistance of the Bank of France and the Federal Reserve System. According to the terms of the agreement concluded on July 31, 50 million pounds was to be made available by these institutions to the Bank of England.[1]

Rearmed with these reserves, the British Central Bank was able to re-enter the foreign exchange market and lend support to the pound.[2] Unfortunately, the credit set up for the Bank was inadequate, and so within a matter of weeks another advance of 80 million pounds was made available to it by the French and American Central Banks. But still the drain continued. Only the possession by the Bank of hundreds of millions of pounds could have saved sterling from its inevitable fate.[3] Thus, on September 21, 1931,[4] the Bank

---

1. Ibid., p. 19.
2. For a short time after the conclusion of this agreement the Bank of England withdrew its support of sterling. It even permitted its value on August 3rd to depreciate for a short while below the gold export point.
   The Bank authorities were of the opinion that the psychological effects resulting from the negotiation of this agreement would be enough to stem any further run on the Bank's reserves. Such, though, was not the case. The fact that the depreciation was allowed to occur was, indeed, a serious blunder, for it caused a further loss of confidence in the pound.
3. In the course of the crisis, the Bank of England paid out ₤200,000,000 in gold or its equivalent. This sum constituted about one-half of the total claims of foreigners on London. (Vide J.M. Keynes, Essays in Persuasion, op. cit., p. 289.)
4. Prof. Harrod believes that, if the gold standard had broken down early in 1930 instead of September 1931, Keynes would have remained a free trader. (Vide R. F. Harrod, The Life of John Maynard Keynes, op. cit., p. 431.)

of England had no recourse but to suspend the gold standard.[1]

This unexpected turn of events caused an important change in Keynes' economic thinking. In a letter written to the *London Times* a week after Great Britain's departure from the gold standard, he asked that consideration of the general tariff which he had recently supported be postponed.[2] In the prevailing circumstances, proposals for high protection ceased to be urgent, asserted Keynes, for it was no longer necessary to utilize such a device for mitigating the disequilibrium existing between British and foreign prices.[3] At the prevailing gold-value of sterling, British products were again among the cheapest in the world; hence, for the time being, at least, there was no pressing need for the imposition of a general tariff.

The important consideration for the present, he averred, was the currency question. Additional attention would have to be given to the probable future level of sterling in relation to gold and how many other countries were likely to follow Great Britain's lead. Keynes also suggested that consideration be given to the possibility of formulating a sound international

---

1. P. Einzig, *The Comedy of the Pound*, op. cit., pp. 21-24.
2. J. M. Keynes, "Letter to the Editor," *The London Times*, September 28, 1931, p. 15.
3. For a fuller consideration of why protection became an obsolete issue after Great Britain's going off the gold standard. Cf. "The Election and Fiscal Policy," *The London Economist*, CXII, 4597, Oct. 10, 1931, pp. 645-646; "Sanity versus Tariffs," *The London Economist*, CXII, 4598, Oct. 17, 1931, pp. 696-697; "Stark and Unashamed," *The London Economist*, CXIV, 4615, Feb. 6, 1932, pp. 283-284; and W. H. Beveridge et al., *Tariffs: The Case Examined*, op. cit., Epilogue.)

currency policy to take the place of gold - one that would help to "rebuild the financial supremacy of London on a firm basis." Only when these questions are resolved, he concluded, will it be possible to determine whether or not Great Britain should return to a protectionist policy.[1]

It is not at all surprising that Keynes should modify his position on the tariff question. His own personal recommendation for alleviating Great Britain's difficulties, it will be recalled, was precisely devaluation. The only reason why he did not urge this solution more strongly is that he did not believe it to be too popular with the City,[2] the political parties and the general public.[3] But now that it was an accomplished fact why shouldn't he prefer it to a tariff? Certainly, Great Britain stood to gain far more from it than from a general tariff. For whereas the latter could only influence the level of imports, devaluation would encourage exports and discourage imports. And most important, it could accomplish this without reference to a reduction in money incomes. Keynes points out all the advantages of devaluation in the following glowing terms.

> For, if the sterling exchange is depreciated by, say, 25 per cent, this does as much to restrict our imports as a tariff of that amount; but whereas a tariff could not help our exports and might hurt them, the depreciation of sterling affords them a bounty of the same 25 per cent by which it aids the home producer against imports.

---

1. J. M. Keynes, "Letter to the Editor," The London Times, September 28, 1931, op. cit., p. 15.
2. J. M. Keynes, Essays in Persuasion, op. cit., p. 288.
3. Ibid., p. 284.

> In many lines of trade the British manufacturer
> today must be the cheapest producer in the world
> in terms of gold. We gain these advantages with-
> out a cut of wages and without industrial strife.[1]
> We gain them in a way which is strictly fair to
> every section of the community, without any
> serious effects on the cost of living. For less
> than a quarter of our total consumption is repre-
> sented by imports; so that sterling would have to
> depreciate by much more than 25 per cent before
> I should expect the cost of living to rise by as
> much as 10 per cent. This would cause hardship
> to no one, for it would only put things back
> where they were two years ago. Meanwhile, there
> will be a great stimulus to employment.[2]

This change of attitude on the question of protection illustrates once again how Keynes' thinking on foreign trade was conditioned by national requirements. During the period that Great Britain appeared to have no other recourse for dealing with her internal and external problems, Keynes marshalled all the powers of his mighty intellect to develop a water-tight case for British protection. But given devaluation and the possibility of a more favorable solution to her problems, he was quick to seize it and set aside, if not abandon completely, the protectionist argument.

To the uninitiated in the way of Keynes this action might appear inconsistent, and yet, it was not. Being primarily concerned with advancing the national well-being, it was entirely congruous for him to favor a postponement of any discussion of the tariff issue[3] and lend his support, instead, to the policy of devaluation. For

---

1. This was always one of Keynes' primary considerations.
2. J. M. Keynes, Essays in Persuasion, op. cit., pp. 289-290. (This comment first appeared in the Sunday Express on Sept. 27, 1931.
3. J. M. Keynes, "Letter to the Editor," The London Times, September 28, 1931, op. cit., p. 15.

the benefits forthcoming to Great Britain from a depreciated currency would far exceed those that might accrue from a tariff. During the course of his life, John Maynard Keynes may have been dissonant in both theory and practice, but this was so because only in this way could he remain consistent in the one thing that mattered most - the furtherance of the national welfare.

CHAPTER XII

THE MEANS TO PROSPERITY

For a period of approximately two years following Great Britain's abandonment of the gold standard, it is difficult to determine just what Keynes' views were on the protection versus free trade issue. One of the main reasons for this is that, after his recommendation that consideration of the tariff question be postponed, he said little else on the matter. And when he did make some pronouncement on the question of foreign trade it was difficult to determine whether he was moving closer to protectionism or back to free trade.

Nowhere is this uncertainty more to be found than in the pages of the Means to Prosperity.[1] There are certain passages herein which would lead one to believe that Keynes was moving closer to protection, while others would cause one to believe that he was reverting to freer trade. To give some indication of Keynes' inconsistency, an effort will be made to cite those aspects of his work which lend support to freer trade and those which favor more restricted trade.

The message of the Means to Prosperity is not unlike that of Keynes' 1929 pamphlet, Can Lloyd George Do It? Basically, Keynes' theme is that the nations of the world must undertake extensive

---

1. This work consists largely of four articles which Keynes contributed to the London Times and one which he contributed to the New Statesman and Nation in March and April, 1933. These articles were written in anticipation of the full-scale international economic conference which was to be held in London during the coming summer.

loan expenditure programs as a means of combatting unemployment and reflating prices.[1] It is in conjunction with filling in the details of this proposal that Keynes makes certain observations which at times may be interpreted in favor of a relaxation of trade restrictions and at other times in favor of more regimented trade. In making these observations, Keynes is very much influenced by the working of the multiplier and the consumption and income effects resulting from a loan-expenditure program. Therefore, to appreciate more fully his attitude towards protection and free trade at this time, it is necessary that we make a brief digression to consider the multiplier concept and the multiple generation of income.

The Multiplier

On the basis of the multiplier concept formulated by Mr. R. F. Kahn,[2] who was one of his most brilliant pupils at Cambridge, Keynes was able to show that, if there occurs a net increase in expenditure, the resulting increase in income and employment will not be restricted to the amount of new spending.[3] For the added wages received by the newly employed workers will be spent for additional goods and services which will in turn lead to increased employment and income in those industries which produce them. And,

---

1. E. T. Grether, "The Means to Prosperity - A Review," *American Economic Review*, XXIII, 2, June, 1933, p. 347.
2. For a full treatment of Mr. Kahn's contribution, vide R. F. Kahn, "The Relation of Home Investment to Unemployment," *The Economic Journal*, XLI, 162, June, 1931, pp. 173-198.
3. J. M. Keynes, *The Means to Prosperity*, New York, Harcourt, Brace and Co., 1933, p. 6.

of course, these newly employed workers, who service the increased consumption of those employed on the new capital works projects, will similarly spend more and thus generate a further increase in income[1] and employment.[2]

At first blush, one might think that the process would continue ad infinitum. Unfortunately, such is not the case, for at each stage of the creation and spending of income there occurs a certain amount of leakage. At each round, a certain proportion of the increased income fails to generate a similar increase, for some portion of it may not be spent, or spent in a way as not to create a net improvement in home income and employment.[3] A part of the newly acquired income will be saved; some of it will be spent for imports; some might merely cause prices to rise for certain classes of goods, and some portion of it might be a substitution for expenditures heretofore financed by the dole or personal savings.[4]

As a result of these leakages from the income stream, there is a limitation on the amount of employment and income that may be realized from a primary expenditure. Just how much employment and

---

1. Ibid., p. 7.
2. Keynes is working on the assumption that there exist idle manpower and resources. For if these added expenditures were to take place in an environment of full employment, the consequences would be higher prices and increased imports instead of higher income and employment.
3. If there were no leakages, the total amount of income and employment generated by a net increase of expenditure would, from a theoretical standpoint, be infinite. Practically, of course, real income and employment could increase only up to the point where the economy achieved full employment of manpower and resources.
4. J. M. Keynes, The Means to Prosperity, op. cit., p. 7.

income will be forthcoming from an additional outlay will be determined by the multiplier.[1] And its value will depend upon the magnitude of the leakages which are associated with the primary expenditure and the spending and re-spending of income which it sets in motion. If the size of the leakages be high, the multiplier will be low and the greater will have to be the value of the primary expenditure to insure a desired level of employment and income. On the other hand, if the value of the leakages be low, the multiplier will be high and the lower will have to be the amount of the primary expenditure to guarantee a particular level of employment and income.

To explain how the size of the multiplier is determined, let us assume that there occurs an additional primary expenditure of ₤ 100. This outlay is divided into two parts. The first part consists of that money which does not become additional income in the hands of home citizens and the second part consists of that money which does become additional income for them.[2] The first part is largely comprised of the following.

    (i) The cost of imported materials.

    (ii) The cost of goods, which are not newly produced but merely transferred, such as

---

1. The multiplier simply relates the total employment to the primary employment. If ₤ 200 of primary expenditure will provide one man-year of primary employment and the multiplier is 2, then total expenditures resulting from this outlay will ultimately reach ₤ 400 which means that the primary expenditure and its repercussions will provide for the two man-years of employment.
2. J. M. Keynes, The Means to Prosperity, op. cit., pp. 8-9.

land or goods taken out of stock which are
not replenished.

(iii) The cost of productive resources of
men and plant which are not additionally
employed but are merely drawn away from
other jobs.

(iv) The cost of wages which take the place
of income previously provided out of funds
borrowed for the dole.[1]

With respect to the second part, that which does become income for home citizens, this must again be divided into two parts, depending upon whether it is saved or spent.

In order to obtain the value of the multiplier, it is necessary to estimate the values of these two proportions, i.e. what per cent of the expenditure actually becomes someone's income and what per cent of that income so received is spent. The product of these two proportions will give us the ratio of the second flow of expenditure to the primary flow, which Keynes refers to as "the ratio of the first repercussion to the primary effect."[2] Insofar as the third flow of expenditure is concerned, this will bear the same relationship to the second flow of expenditure as the latter bore to the initial flow, and so on. By then summating this infinite number of repercussions, it will be possible to determine the size of the multiplier.[3]

For purposes of illustration let us assume that the proportion of the primary expenditure, as well as that of all subsequent ones,

---

1. Ibid., p. 9.
2. Ibid.
3. Ibid.

which actually becomes income is equal to 70 per cent and that of this income so received 30 per cent is saved and 70 per cent is spent. This means, therefore, that the first repercussion resulting from the primary expenditure will be 49 per cent (.70 .70 = .49) or a ratio of about one-half. The second repercussion, i.e. the third flow of expenditure, will be equal to one-half the second flow of expenditure or to one-fourth of the primary effect, and so on. We may represent these repercussions by the following infinite geometric progression, (1 + 1/2 + 1/4 + 1/8 + etc.). The sum of this series is equal to 2 and so it may be concluded that the multiplier in this instance has a value of 2.[1] Every pound of primary expenditure will generate a total income of two pounds.

If the leakages were smaller, a larger proportion of the expenditures would remain in the income stream with the result that the multiplier would be greater. For example, if the proportion of the additional expenditures which became income were equal to 80 per cent, and the portion of this income which was spent was similarly equal to 80 per cent, the multiplier would be approximately 3. This is so, for the first repercussion would be approximately equal to two-thirds of the primary effect and the second repercussion would be equal to approximately two-thirds of the first, and so on. This series of repercussions may be represented by the following geometric progression, (1 + 2/3 + 4/9 + 8/27 + etc.), whose sum is equal to 3; hence, the value of the

---

1. *Ibid.*, p. 10.

multiplier in this case is 3.

Equipped with this understanding of the multiplier concept and the fashion in which an additional primary expenditure can lead to a multiple increase of incomes, we may now turn to a consideration of some of the observations which Keynes made respecting foreign trade.

Arguments that might be adduced from the Means to Prosperity in favor of protection.

From the above consideration of the multiplier concept it is obvious that the smaller is the portion of additional income spent for imports, the less will be the amount of leakage and the greater, therefore, will be the effect of the primary outlay in increasing home income and employment. On the basis of this, one can make a strong case for protection, since such a policy, by restricting the volume of imports, would reduce the proportion of expenditure which becomes income for foreigners, enhance the size of the multiplier and thereby increase the amount of domestic income and employment forthcoming from each additional loan-expenditure.

An even stronger argument may be presented for protection in those circumstances wherein only the home country is undertaking a loan-expenditure program. For whereas the expanding country incurs all the expense of such a program, the non-expanding nations enjoy much of the benefit in the form of increased exports to it. The country undertaking the increased expenditures does not, of course, have an equal opportunity to augment its level of exports,[1] since these other countries are not pursuing expansive policies; hence, its foreign balance will be impaired.[2] In these conditions, a restrictive trade policy which is designed to protect the foreign balance would be entirely justified. For such a policy would not constitute an attempt to gain an unfair advantage, i.e. a beggar-my-neighbor practice, but only an effort to insure that the advantages forthcoming from a domestic expansion program rightfully remain at home.

A restriction of foreign trade under such circumstances would, by reducing the import leakage, enhance the value of the multiplier and this, in turn, would serve to increase the benefits which accrue to home employment from a public expenditure program. Although Keynes does not state explicitly that he would favor a curtailment of imports as a means of augmenting the multiplier and in this way confining the employment and income effects of an expansion program to the home economy, he is, nonetheless, quite aware of this advantage to be derived from limited participation in international trade. This may be indicated in the following observation which he makes in the preface to the American edition of the *Means to Prosperity*.

---

1. To the extent that the increased export activity in the non-expanding countries raises their level of income, there will occur some increase in their demand for imports. Undoubtedly, they will obtain some of these imports from the country which is pursuing an expansive policy; however, it is not at all likely that the value of these purchases will equal the value of the exports which they sell to the expanding country.
2. If all nations were to pursue an expansive policy at the same time, the pressure on each country's foreign balance would cancel out; hence, this is the reason why Keynes urged that all nations undertake loan-expenditure programs simultaneously.

> The more nearly an economic system is self-sufficient, and the smaller the relative importance of its international trade, the larger will be the multiplier by which we obtain the total effect of additional expenditure on employment. For the smaller are the deductions to be made in respect of imports.[1]

From this statement one may well deduce that, in order to obtain the maximum advantage from its loan expenditure program, a country should restrict its volume of imports. Although Keynes does not explicitly sanction a protectionist policy in the above passage, the reader cannot help but infer that this is what he really has in mind.

Keynes lends further substance to the view that he was partial to protection at this time by the emphasis which he places on the need for a favorable balance of trade as a means of insuring the success of the loan-expenditure program. From our knowledge of the multiplier concept it may be readily reasoned that, if there occurs a deterioration of the foreign balance, i.e. a substantial increase in the volume of imports unaccompanied by a corresponding increase in the level of exports, the increased employment and income to be enjoyed by the home economy from an expanded loan expenditure program will be transferred, instead, to other countries. Thus, argues Keynes, if a nation is to profit from an expansive domestic program, it is absolutely essential that it maintain, simultaneously, a favorable balance of trade.[2]

---

1. J. M. Keynes, The Means to Prosperity, op. cit., p. v.
2. J. M. Keynes, The Means to Prosperity (British edition), 1933, Macmillan and Co., Ltd., London, p. 16.

In fact, Keynes places the blame for the failure of previous British loan-expenditure efforts to raise the level of employment precisely on the fact that these outlays were completely offset by a deterioration of the foreign trade balance, as note his following contention.

> We are, I think, too much discouraged as to the potentialities of fruitful action along these lines, because the effect of previous efforts has been masked by offsetting influences.
>
> It is most important to understand that the effects of loan-expenditure and of the foreign balance are 'in pari materia'. Thus it was the rapid decline of the foreign balance by £ 75,000,000 in 1930, and by £ 207,000,000 in 1931 as compared with 1929, which defeated the attempt of the Labour Government to increase employment by loan-expenditure; the additional loan-expenditure for which they were responsible being on a much smaller scale than this.[1]

But though there occured an improvement in the British balance of payments after the abandonment of the gold standard, this was not accompanied by an increase in the level of employment, as might be expected, because the National Government greatly curtailed the volume of loan-expenditures.[2] In effect, there occurred in 1932 a reversal of the situation which obtained in 1930, thus leading Keynes to quip,

> Heaven knows to what plight a combination of the policy of the Labour Government in

---

1. J. M. Keynes, The Means to Prosperity (American edition), op. cit., p. 36.
2. Ibid.

>   doing nothing to protect the foreign
>   balance, with the policy of the National
>   Government to curtail loan-expenditure
>   might not have brought us![1]

Apparently, both parties overlooked the fact that, if recovery was to be achieved, two requirements would have to be satisfied simultaneously - an expansion of domestic expenditures and protection of the foreign balance. Thus, the combination still untried by Great Britain, according to Keynes, was "the policy of protecting the foreign balance and at the same time doing all in our power to stimulate loan-expenditures."[2]

But this assertion leads one to ask, "How does Keynes propose to protect the foreign balance?" By his own admission, he cannot expect too much assistance from an increase in the volume of exports, because of depressed world conditions.[3] Therefore, there is a strong possibility that he may still have been amenable at this time to a restriction of imports through a protectionist policy.

Arguments that might be adduced from the Means to Prosperity in favor of free trade.

The free traders, like the protectionists, can find arguments in the Means to Prosperity to prove that Keynes supported their point of view, as witness the following contention voiced by L. R. Klein.

---

1. Ibid.
2. Ibid., pp. 36-37.
3. Ibid., p. 35.

> He (Keynes) also began to see more clearly the working of economic systems as wholes. Only a few years before the *Means to Prosperity*, he had announced a distinct favoritism for a protectionist policy in Great Britain. Now he was willing to give up this idea since he realized that successful attempts by England to improve her foreign balance would only be at the expense of other countries. Furthermore, he realized that competitive protection applied by all countries simultaneously would only be harmful to all. What he now proposed was world-wide inflationary loan expenditures to stimulate the world as a whole.[1]

In considering the question of how to raise world prices and output, Keynes suggests that aggregate spending power be augmented. This may be done, he asserts, either by increasing loan-expenditures or by improving the foreign balance.[2] Although the effects on domestic activity resulting from a loan-expenditure program and a favorable balance of trade are the same, Keynes cautions that only the first method is valid for the world as a whole. For the second method merely means that one country is withholding employment and purchasing power from other countries. If one country improves its foreign balance, it is obvious that the balance of some other country or countries must be reduced. Consequently, the favorable balance of trade device cannot be counted on to increase total output or raise world prices.[3] In this connection, Keynes also takes exception with many of the restrictive trade devices which

---

1. L. R. Klein, op. cit., pp. 41-42.
2. J. M. Keynes, The Means to Prosperity, op. cit., p. 20.
3. Ibid., pp. 20-21.

were fashioned in the early 'thirties for the purpose of achieving a favorable trade balance. This may be indicated in the following passage.

> Currency depreciation and tariffs were weapons which Great Britain had in hand until recently as a means of self-protection. A moment came when we were compelled to use them, and they have served us well. But competitive currency depreciations and competitive tariffs, and more artificial means of improving an individual country's foreign balance such as exchange restrictions, import prohibitions, and quotas, help no one and injure each, if they are applied all round.[1]

One may discern a further partiality on Keynes' part towards freer trade from a consideration of the conditions which he would stipulate for participation by nations in his International Note Issue scheme. A consideration of this proposal need not detain us at this time, for many of its features were later incorporated into the Clearing Union plan, which we shall have occasion to examine in a subsequent chapter. For now, suffice it to say that the primary purpose of this plan was to increase the reserves of Central Banks, so as to enable them to promote loan-expenditure programs without undue anxiety.[2]

To participate in this scheme, Keynes suggests that prospective member nations be made to promise that they will utilize the assistance accorded them by the plan "to abate certain unsound international practices which have become common under stress of hard

---

1. Ibid.
2. Ibid., p. 31.

circumstances."[1] Participating nations should abolish exchange restrictions and replace standstill agreements by concrete schemes for gradual liquidation. Member countries, especially the financially strong, should make every effort to re-open their money markets to foreign loans. And most important of all, "tariffs and quotas imposed to protect the foreign balance, and not in pursuance of permanent national policies, should be removed."[2]

The above pre-requisites, urged by Keynes for membership in his International Note Issue scheme, would hardly qualify him as a protectionist. In fact, the last cited condition, in particular, could well be interpreted as a repudiation by him of his recommendation of 1931, viz. that tariffs be imposed to increase the surplus on the trade balance as a means of achieving external equilibrium, a balanced Budget, a higher level of business confidence, and a diminution in the number of unemployed.

Summary

One is truly left in a dilemma in trying to determine Keynes' foreign trade position from the views expressed by him in the *Means to Prosperity*. For though arguments may be marshalled to show that he was still inclined towards protection, others may be cited to prove that he was now more favorably disposed towards freer trade.

One thing, however, is certain and that is that Keynes'

---

1. Ibid.
2. Ibid.

enthusiasm for a tariff in the **Means to Prosperity** was definitely not so strong as that expressed by him in 1930 and 1931. But how is this moderate, though by no means complete, reversal of form to be explained? Insofar as the writer can determine - and this view is neither substantiated nor disproved by any of the sources of information consulted by him - there is but one plausible explanation for Keynes' slight defection. This is to be found in the fact that his economic thinking was always oriented to national needs.

As already noted in the previous chapter, once Great Britain went off the gold standard there was little need for Keynes to continue agitating for a protectionist trade policy. For all the advantages to be enjoyed from the imposition of a tariff, and more, could be had from the devaluation of sterling which followed the abandonment of the gold standard. As a result of this depreciation of sterling, the British foreign trade balance improved by ₤74,000,000 in 1932 over 1931.[1] Thus, given an even more satisfactory solution to Great Britain's problems than a tariff, it was only natural that Keynes should lose some interest in a protectionist trade policy.

Were it not for the fact that there was much uncertainty as to how long countries still on the gold standard, v.g. France and the United States, would permit Great Britain to profit from a devalued currency, it would have been entirely consistent for

---

1. Ibid., p. 36.

Keynes to argue now for multilateral free trade. For such a policy would have permitted British exporters to take greater advantage of their lower prices than would have a restrictive trade policy. If this be considered, then one should not be so much surprised by Keynes' slight defection from protection as by the fact that he did not revert completely to free trade. For such a policy, by improving further the trade balance, would have resolved even more effectively many of Great Britain's external as well as internal difficulties.

Thus, while we are unable, on the basis of his observations in the *Means to Prosperity*, to classify Keynes categorically as a free trader or a protectionist, we can conclude that his views respecting commercial policy were becoming more and more conditioned by what would best suit the economic needs of Great Britain. In the period 1930-1931, when the domestic economy was seriously bogged down and the surplus on the trade balance was practically non-existent, Keynes fought in earnest for a restrictive trade policy. This, he argued, was the only means of survival available to the nation. But as the British economy started to make recovery and as the balance of trade became positive once again, his enthusiasm for a tariff waned somewhat, since the need for a protectionist policy was no longer quite so urgent. In short, Keynes' foreign trade views were being reduced to a function of the domestic prosperity - a fact which becomes even more apparent in his subsequent pronouncements.

CHAPTER XIII

NATIONAL SELF-SUFFICIENCY

As a result of the collapse of the World Economic Conference[1] which took place in London in June, 1933, Keynes gave up all hope that the world was prepared to accept any of his recommendations for achieving full recovery, v.g. the world-wide loan-expenditure program which he had recommended in the Means to Prosperity.

---

1. The failure of the World Economic Conference was largely attributed to President Roosevelt who doomed any hope for international cooperation by advising the conferees that he was opposed to restoration of a rigid international standard and that he favored, instead, a management of the currency which would give preference to domestic considerations, v.g. attainment of a dollar with stable purchasing power. (A. W. Crawford, International Monetary Developments between the First and Second World Wars, Finance Department, Chamber of Commerce of the United States, June, 1944, p. 7.)

    Although Keynes was anxious that the World Economic Conference find some way of alleviating the international slump, he could not take exception with Mr. Roosevelt's position, for the President acted much in the same fashion that he himself would have acted. (A. Smithies, op. cit., p. 587.) It will be remembered that Keynes had long supported a currency system that would be managed with a view towards achieving a stable internal price level rather than a fixed rate of exchange. Accordingly, he wrote in the Daily Mail, "It is a long time since a statesman cut through the cobwebs as boldly as the President of the United States.... He has told us where he stands, and he invited the Conference to proceed to substantial business. But he is prepared to act alone if necessary; and he is strong enough to do so.... The President's message has an importance which transcends its origins. It is, in substance, a challenge to us to decide whether we propose to tread the old, unfortunate ways, or to explore new paths; paths new to statesmen and to bankers, but not new to thought. For they lead to the managed currency of the future, the examination of which has been the prime topic of post-war economics." (R. F. Harrod, The Life of John Maynard Keynes, op. cit., p. 445.)

Unable to conduct his experiment for attaining full employment on a world-wide level, he suggested that Great Britain put his suggestions to the test on a purely national basis.[1] But to insure the success of these experiments all relationships with the outside world would have to be severed;[2] hence, Keynes was forced once again to move closer towards a protectionist position. This he did unequivocally in two articles which he wrote shortly after the breakdown of the Conference.

In restating his position on the question of commercial policy, Keynes asserts that he would not dispute the fundamental truths of free trade any more than he did in 1923.[3] However, he points out that his "background of economic theory" is now somewhat different from what it was at that time, and, so, he would not charge Mr. Baldwin, as he did then, with being "a victim of the protectionist fallacy in its crudest form"[4] for believing that a tariff could relieve the British unemployment situation. But more important, Keynes attributes his change of attitude to the fact that the conditions of the present are unlike those of the pre-war era.[5]

---

1. R. F. Harrod, The Life of John Maynard Keynes, op. cit., p. 446.
2. This view is subscribed to by Prof. Harrod and the London Economist. The latter contends that "the real secret of the new isolationism is evidently a desire to conduct experiments with the national economy, which it is feared may be rendered impossible if full economic relations with the outside world are maintained. The isolationist wishes, in short, to 'plan' whether in the monetary or economic sphere, or both, and would like a vacuum in which to do it." ("The Gospel of Self-Sufficiency," The London Economist, CXVII, 4691, July 22, 1923, p. 171.)
3. J.M. Keynes, "National Self-Sufficiency," The Yale Review, XXII, 4, June, 1933, p. 755.
4. J.M. Keynes, "Free Trade for England," op. cit., p. 87.
5. J.M. Keynes, "National Self-Sufficiency," op. cit., pp. 755-756.

Keynes believed that many of the arguments presented in behalf of free trade by its supporters during the nineteenth century were no longer applicable in the 'thirties. Among the arguments so advanced by them were the following: a policy of free trade would employ the world's manpower and resources to their greatest advantage, thereby increasing the total wealth of all nations; it would advance the cause of freedom; promote personal initiative; serve as a bulwark against the forces of privilege, monopoly and obsolescence; and assure peace, concord and economic justice between nations.[1]

Keynes doubted that these claims were valid in the prevailing economic environment. He was especially skeptical of the assertion that a policy of free trade was promotive of international tranquility. For it was difficult to understand how the struggle for foreign markets, the penetration of economic boundaries by the resources and the influence of foreign capitalists and the dependence of domestic well-being upon the fluctuating economic policies of foreign countries could possibly serve as instruments of international peace.[2]

It was Keynes' contention that economic internationalism leads to international strife rather than to world-wide peace. To maximize the degree of international specialization and the geographical diffusion of capital, it is necessary to protect a country's existing foreign interests, capture new markets, and in

---

1. J. M. Keynes, "National Self-Sufficiency - I," The New Statesman and Nation, N.S. VI, 124, July 8, 1933, p. 36.
2. Ibid., p. 37.

general, pursue an imperalistic economic policy; however, these policies are hardly promotive of peace. Another factor, in Keynes' estimate, which is responsible for a great degree of international enmity is the separation between ownership and management of foreign capital. This principle of seperation between ownership and management of capital is injurious enough within a country, but it is far more damaging when applied internationally. The foreign investor, as a rule, lacks knowledge and responsibility towards what he owns. His primary preoccupation is that his savings be invested in that area where he can realize the highest rate of return. He is not too much concerned with the effects which his capital transfers are likely to have on the well-being of the countries from which he withdraws his funds. But such an attitude, contends Keynes, can hardly be deemed promotive of cordial international relations.[1]

As a result of these obstacles placed in the way of world peace by economic internationalism, Keynes favored, instead, a policy of economic isolation. This is indicated in the following passage.

> I sympathize, therefore, with those who would minimize, rather than those who would maximize, economic entanglements between nations. Ideas, knowledge, art, hospitality, travel - these are the things which should of their nature be

---

1. *Ibid.*, p. 37.

international. But let goods be homespun whenever it is reasonably and conveniently possible; and, above all, let finance be primarily national.[1]

If nations can thus become more self-sustaining, avers Keynes, the possibility of achieving world peace will be greatly enhanced.

In Keynes' opinion, another free trade argument which was entirely valid in the nineteenth century, but of questionable merit in the economic environment of the 'thirties was the principle of comparative cost. In the nineteenth century, there were substantial differences in the degree of industrialization in different areas of the world; hence, there were considerable advantages associated with national specialization. However, Keynes did not believe that the advantages forthcoming from the international division of labor in the prevailing circumstances were at all comparable with what they were in the nineteenth century, for, industrially, there now remained little difference between national efficiencies. Unlike the pre-war period, mass production processes could now be performed in most countries and climates with equal efficiency.[2] In view of the important character of Keynes' new position on the principle of comparative advantage, it would be well to quote his pronouncement on this issue in full. His statement is as follows.

---

1. *Ibid.*
2. *Ibid.*

> At a time when there were enormous differences in degree in the industrialization and opportunities for technical training in different countries, the advantages of a high degree of national specialization were very considerable.
>
> But I am not persuaded that the economic advantages of the international division of labour today are at all comparable with what they were. I must not be understood to carry my argument beyond a certain point. A considerable degree of international specialization is necessary in a rational world in all cases where it is dictated by wide differences of climate, natural resources, native aptitudes, level of culture and density of population. But over an increasingly wide range of industrial products, and perhaps of agricultural products, also, I become doubtful whether the economic cost of national self-sufficiency is great enough to outweigh the other advantages of gradually bringing the producer and the consumer within the ambit of the same national, economic and financial organization. Experience accumulates to prove that most modern mass-production processes can be performed in most countries and climates with almost equal efficiency.[1]

An additional reason advanced by Keynes for the limited applicability of the comparative cost principle in the twentieth century is that, as the wealth of a nation increases, both primary and manufactured goods play a smaller and smaller part in the standard of living as compared to houses, personal services and other items which do not enter into foreign commerce. Consequently, even if there were to occur some small increase in the cost of producing at home those goods previously imported, the national standard of living would not be appreciably affected. Moreover, even if there were to occur some deterioration of the standard, this would be

---

1. *Ibid.*

more than offset by the advantages forthcoming from self-sufficiency. Thus, concludes Keynes, "National Self-Sufficiency, in short, though it costs something, may be becoming a luxury which we can afford if we happen to want it."[1]

In developing further his case for national self-sufficiency and more restricted trade, Keynes argues that such a policy is made necessary by the failure of international capitalism. He indicates this failure of capitalism in the following terms.

> The decadent international but individualistic capitalism, in the hands of which we found ourselves after the war, is not a success. It is not intelligent, it is not beautiful, it is not just, it is not virtuous - and it doesn't deliver the goods.[2]

As a result of the shortcomings associated with this politico-economic system, many nations were being forced to experiment with different forms of political economy. This was particularly true of Germany, Italy, Russia and Ireland. The United States and Great Britain, too, though largely conforming to the old model, were seeking, under the surface, a new form of economic organization.[3]

The point that Keynes wanted to make was this. In order for Great Britain to achieve that type of economic system which would best suit it, a certain amount of testing would have to be done. But if these experiments were to be successful, it was absolutely essential that the home economy be free of those world forces

---

1. Ibid.
2. J. M. Keynes, "National Self-Sufficiency - II," The New Statesman and Nation, N.S. VI, 125, July 15, 1933, p. 65.
3. Ibid.

which sought to achieve some pattern of uniform equilibrium in accordance with the so-called principles of laisser faire capitalism. Keynes argued that, during this transitional period, it was extremely important "to be our own masters, and to be as free as we can make ourselves from the interferences of the outside world."[1] The attainment of such national self-sufficiency and economic isolation, as advocated by Keynes, would not only enable Great Britain to conduct her own experiments, but it would also make her task easier insofar as they could be accomplished without excessive economic cost.

Granted the need for replacing laisser faire capitalism with some other form of political economy, what did Keynes have to offer in its place?

The type system suggested by Keynes would retain "as much private judgment and initiative and enterprise as possible."[2] However, this retention of private enterprise would be contingent upon a sizable reduction in the rate of interest.[3] To insure this reduction, Keynes suggests a separation of the British capital market from that of the rest of the world.[4] Should Great Britain reject this course of action and re-subscribe, instead, to a policy of economic internationalism, this would have dire consequences for it, as witness the following contention voiced

---

1. Ibid.
2. Ibid.
3. Keynes stipulated that the rate of interest should reach the vanishing point within a period of the next thirty years.
4. "The Gospel of Self-Sufficiency," The London Economist, op. cit., p. 171.

by Keynes.

> Economic internationalism embracing the free movement of capital and of loanable funds as well as of traded goods may condemn this country for a generation to come to a much lower degree of material prosperity than could be attained under a different system.[1]

Another feature of the system proposed by Keynes to take the place of laisser faire capitalism is increased participation by the State in the economy. Economic activity, he asserted, should not be determined exclusively by the test of the accountant's profit, for such a criterion does not permit a nation to exploit its economic potentialities to their fullest extent. Judged from this pecuniary standard, the important consideration is not whether there are resources, manpower and technique available for undertaking a particular project, v.g. slum clearance, but whether such a program will be worthwhile from a financial standpoint. Thus, quips Keynes, "We have to remain poor because it does not 'pay' to be rich."[2] To eliminate this tremendous loss of wealth to the nation, Keynes advocates a modification of the State's view towards the undertaking of many socially advantageous, though not necessarily financially profitable, economic projects. This, though, does not mean that Keynes would do away with the profit test completely, for he readily admits that there are many sectors of private enterprise in which it is still most eminently suited.[3]

---

1. J. M. Keynes, "National Self-Sufficiency - II," op. cit., p. 65.
2. Ibid., p. 66.
3. Ibid.

Insofar as the increased role of government participation in the economy is concerned, this has definite implications for foreign trade policy, as Keynes' comment will bear out.

> Now if the functions and purposes of the State are to be thus enlarged, the decision as to what, broadly speaking, shall be produced within the nation and what shall be exchanged with abroad, must stand high amongst the objects of policy.[1]

There can be no misinterpreting this particular statement. For it can only mean that, if the State is to take a more effective role in economic matters, it must exercise greater discretion not only in purely domestic affairs, but also in determining the character of the country's foreign trade. But once this State control is introduced in the foreign sector, free trade, as understood by the orthodox economists, can no longer be said to exist.

Summary

To sum up Keynes' position on the question of foreign trade policy at this time, it may be said that, as of July, 1933, he had definitely cast his lot with the protectionists. His position in the period following the collapse of the World Economic Conference, unlike that of The Means to Prosperity, was clear and emphatic. There could be no mistaking the fact that Keynes had resolved the issue between free trade and protection in favor of the latter.

To substantiate this contention, reference is made to Keynes'

---

1. Ibid.

assertion that the economic environment of the twentieth century is unlike that of the nineteenth; hence, many of the arguments in support of free trade, which may have been valid in the earlier period, did not necessarily hold true in the later period. More specifically, Keynes expressed opposition to free trade, because, contrary to the claims of the nineteenth century free-traders, he believed that in the prevailing environment it served only to engender international enmity. Secondly, Keynes abandoned free trade, because he no longer believed that the advantages associated with the international division of labor in the prevailing environment were at all comparable with what they were in the nineteenth century. This Keynes attributed to the introduction of mass production techniques practically throughout the entire world. Thirdly, Keynes argued that, although the economic internationalism of the nineteenth century free trader assumed the existence of an efficient world-wide capitalism, such a condition no longer obtained in the twentieth century. A new politico-economic system would have to be devised to take its place. And to insure the success of this operation, international trade and finance would have to be severely restricted. Lastly, Keynes was opposed to the free international movement of capital and goods, because the type system envisaged by him to take the place of laissez-faire capitalism required an autonomous monetary policy for the maintenance of low interest rates and a greater participation by the State in domestic as well as foreign commerce.

Summary - Part II

To summarize our findings on the evolution of Keynes' thinking on international economics between the pre-World War I era and the 'thirties, it may be said that he moved from a position of classical free trade to one of absolute protection.

In the immediate pre-World War I period, which marks the beginning of his career as a professional economist, Keynes was entirely orthodox in his thinking on the question of commercial policy. Although this statement cannot be explicitly corroborated by any of Keynes' pre-war contributions, its validity may be substantially established by the fact that he is classified as a classical economist during this time. He was a protege of Alfred Marshall, and as such, it is hardly likely that he would have subscribed to the tenets of protectionism at this stage of his career.

Another fact which tends to give credence to this assertion is that when Keynes did take an explicit position on the question of commercial policy in the post-World War I period, he definitely gave his support to the free trade doctrine. This is very much evident in his first major post-war work, The Economic Consequences of the Peace.

In the 'twenties, Keynes became extremely critical of the international gold standard and the British decision to return to it at the pre-war parity of exchange; nonetheless, he remained a staunch supporter of free trade, as witness his two articles of 1923 repudiating the protectionist arguments of Prime Minister

Baldwin. But, as Great Britain found it increasingly difficult in the late 'twenties to achieve internal and external equilibrium, a condition largely attributable to her imprudent decision to return to an over-valued pound, Keynes became more and more skeptical that the nation could resolve her economic problems by adhering to free trade.

Keynes first gave indication of this change of attitude in the pages of his *Treatise on Money* - a work which he largely thought out in the depressed British environment of the late 'twenties. In this tract, he pointed out that, in view of the impending maturity of the British economy, more and more savings will seek foreign outlets. But while the volume of foreign lending is thus increasing, the surplus on the trade balance will not keep pace with it, because of the higher British production costs and the existence of tariff barriers abroad. This disparity between the amount of foreign lending and the size of the foreign balance constitutes a condition of external disequilibrium.

To achieve balance between these two quanta and thus restore external equilibrium, it would be necessary either to reduce the volume of foreign lending, through an increase in the level of interest, or to increase the surplus on the foreign trade balance, through an increase in exports or a reduction in imports. Keynes was very much opposed to the first alternative, because a rise in the interest rate would further discourage home investment; hence, he urged that the correction be made in the size of the foreign balance. But because of the relatively high British production costs which prevailed in the late 'twenties, there was little hope of improving the trade surplus through an increase in exports; therefore, a reduction in the volume of imports was clearly indicated. And to realize this, he suggested that consideration be given to the tariff device.

By bringing the foreign trade surplus into better balance with the volume of foreign lending, the tariff would effectively serve as a means of restoring equilibrium in the external sector. It would also assist in the attainment of internal equilibrium, i.e. an equality between home savings and investment, by making possible the maintenance of a rate of interest sufficiently low to insure that the volume of investment would offset the level of savings. These, as a matter of fact, are the primary reasons why Keynes turned to a consideration of protectionism at this time.

By keeping the foreign balance equal to the volume of foreign lending, a protectionist policy would eliminate gold movements either into or out of the country in question. And so long as a Central Bank's gold reserves remained intact, it could pursue an autonomous monetary policy.

Keynes gave further support to the tariff as a device for maintaining or restoring equilibrium in his work with the Macmillan Committee during the closing months of 1929 and the early part of 1930. Confronted with a depression which was no longer peculiar to Great Britain alone, but to the world in general, Keynes suggested that Britain's best hope for recovery rested in a widespread expansion program. But the prevalence of low interest rates required by such a program would increase the amount of foreign lending and, insofar as it would lead to a rise in prices, would discourage exports and encourage imports, thereby reducing the size of the trade surplus. Such an increase in the volume of foreign lending and decrease in the size of the foreign balance would eventually lead to a condition of disequilibrium. To preclude such a prospect, Keynes recommended in the special appendix to the Macmillan Report that the foreign balance be protected through the imposition of tariffs on imports and the granting of bounties on exports. In this way, the foreign balance could be made to equate more readily with the volume of foreign lending, and thus insure the maintenance of external equilibrium, while the economy pursued an expansive policy internally.

In the following year, 1931, Keynes came out in favor of a revenue tariff. This time, however, he pleaded his case not on grounds that it would help to restore equilibrium, but that it would bolster business confidence, relieve the pressure on the Budget, increase the surplus on the foreign trade balance, and reduce the level of unemployment. By so restoring Great Britain to economic health, Keynes felt that she would be able to resume her position of chief creditor nation and, through the extension of loans to other countries, would help to promote world-wide recovery.

With the departure of Great Britain from the international

gold standard in September, 1931, Keynes asked that consideration of the tariff issue be postponed. For the devaluation of the pound which followed Great Britain's abandonment of the gold standard made possible the realization of all those advantages which he had hoped Great Britain could achieve through the imposition of a tariff. In fact, devaluation was superior to the tariff, because it not only discouraged imports, but encouraged exports, thereby making for an even greater trade balance.

In the period immediately following Great Britain's divorce from the gold standard, Keynes said little else on the question of protection. Although he did not dissociate himself from the protectionist cause, neither did he support it with the same conviction that he did in 1931. Keynes' position on the question of commercial policy becomes extremely nebulous in The Means to Prosperity. For herein are to be found arguments both in support of free trade and protection. No doubt, Keynes' more favorable attitude towards free trade was largely conditioned by the fact that in the period after 1931 the British balance of trade showed sizable improvement. Moreover, with the restoration of her export industries to a more competitive position, Great Britain stood to gain more from freer trade than from protection. This change of attitude was, of course, simply a reflection of Keynes' desire to promote above all else the well-being of the national economy.

It is only after the collapse of the World Economic Conference in the early summer of 1933 that it is possible to state categorically, that despite his irresolution in The Means to Prosperity,

Keynes was still to be identified with the protectionists. Convinced that the world was not yet prepared to undertake any of his policies for achieving full employment, he sought to have them implemented on a national level. Accordingly, he prepared two articles, shortly after the demise of the London Conference, exhorting Great Britain to experiment with new politico-economic systems. To insure the success of these experiments Keynes urged a restriction of international intercourse. He also recommended a greater degree of national self-sufficiency on grounds that such a policy would be more promotive of world-peace and that the advantages associated with free trade no longer obtained, for the economic conditions of the twentieth century were unlike those of the nineteenth.

As of mid-1933, then, it may be concluded that Keynes was a confirmed protectionist. What his position was immediately after this date is difficult to determine, for he had little else to say on the matter. Whether this silence was due to the fact that he still adhered to this belief and that, therefore, no further explanation was necessary or that he was too preoccupied with the preparation of the General Theory is entirely problematic.

To ascertain more definitely Keynes' views on the question of free trade versus protection after 1933 it is necessary to direct our attention to a consideration of his General Theory of Employment, Interest and Money. Specifically, our task in the next section will be to assay his thinking in this work as it relates to the question of foreign trade theory and policy.

PART III

KEYNES' FOREIGN TRADE VIEWS DURING
THE ERA OF THE GENERAL THEORY

Scope of Part III

Although the General Theory is fundamentally concerned with domestic economics, it has many significant applications to international economic theory and policy.[1] Of particular significance to international economics are Keynes' theory of employment, the question of chronic unemployment, the problem of investment, especially in an advanced state, the multiplier and income effect,[2] and his treatment of mercantilism. Our task in this part of the thesis is to examine these contributions and their implications for foreign trade theory and policy. When this analysis of the relationship between the General Theory and international economics has been completed, we shall turn to a consideration of Keynes' views respecting international economic policy in the period from the publication of the General Theory to the outbreak of World War II.

---

1. D. Dillard, op. cit., p. 279.
2. Keynes also dealt with the multiplier and income effect in a number of other works and since these concepts are developed at some length in other sections of this thesis, there is no need to repeat the analysis here.

CHAPTER XIV

THE THEORY OF EMPLOYMENT AND ITS

IMPLICATIONS FOR INTERNATIONAL ECONOMICS

a. *Keynes refutation of the classical postulate of full employment.*

Keynes' criticism of the accepted classical theory of economics consisted not so much in finding logical flaws in its analysis as in pointing out that its tacit assumption of full employment is seldom or never satisfied, with the result that it is ill-equipped to solve the economic problems of the real world.[1] Because a condition of full employment does not ordinarily exist, the attempt to apply economic theories predicated on the existence of such a condition will not be effective in solving the problems of actual experience. Keynes expresses dissatisfaction with the classical assumption of full employment in the opening passage of his work, which runs as follows.

> I shall argue that the postulates of the classical theory are applicable to a special case only and not to the general case, the situation which it assumes being a limiting point of the possible position of equilibrium. Moreover, the characteristics of the special case assumed by the classical theory happen not to be those of the economic society in which we actually live, with the result that its teaching is misleading and disastrous if we attempt to apply it to the facts of experience.[2]

---

1. J. M. Keynes, *The General Theory of Employment, Interest and Money*, New York, Harcourt, Brace and Co., 1936, p. 378.
2. Ibid., p. 3.

What Keynes is saying in the above is that classical theory is based upon the existence of full employment - a condition which obtains only in special circumstances. The doctrines of classical economics can apply only in a full employment economy; therefore, any attempt to apply them in all conditions, v.g. at positions of equilibrium below full employment, is invalid.[1] But one of the teachings of classical economics which depends upon the assumption of full employment is free trade; hence, according to Keynes' reasoning, this doctrine is erroneous if it be applied to the general case. In effect, classical free trade is efficacious only under conditions of full employment. Given less than full employment, its validity becomes questionable.

To disprove the classical postulate of general full employment, Keynes was forced to attack Say's law, since this assumption was largely dependent upon it. But before taking issue with the law itself, Keynes directed his attention to the classical analysis of the manner in which wage rates are adjusted, for this was an essential mechanism by which the Law of Markets was supposed to operate.[2]

According to the classical doctrine, widespread unemployment

---

1. Apart from the doctrine of employment, Keynes considered most of the classical theories entirely satisfactory. For example, he completely subscribed to the marginal utility theory of value and to the marginal productivity theory of distribution. (Vide R. L. Meek, "The Place of Keynes in the History of Economic Thought," The Modern Quarterly, N.S. VI, 1. Winter, 1950-1951, p. 44.)
2. A. H. Hansen, A Guide to Keynes, op. cit., p. 20.

could not exist, provided that workers were prepared to accept a reduction in money wages. Such an adjustment would insure an equality between wages and the lower marginal productivity of labor, which attends an increase in employment, and would thereby enable the entrepeneur to engage additional workers. Output and employment could be increased "up to the point where the reduction which labor has agreed to accept in money-wages is just offset by the diminishing marginal efficiency of labor as output is increased."[1]

Although Keynes does not dispute the classical postulate that "the wage is equal to the marginal product of labor,"[2] he questions whether a general reduction in money-wages could directly lead to an increase in the level of employment.[3] For

---

1. J. M. Keynes, The General Theory of Employment, Interest and Money, op. cit., p. 257.
2. Ibid., p. 5.
3. Ibid., pp. 259-260. Although Keynes denies that a reduction in money-wages has a tendency to increase employment directly, he points out that such an adjustment may do so indirectly. According to his analysis, a reduction in the level of wages, accompanied by some reduction in prices and in money-incomes generally, will lessen the cash needs for transactions purposes. This will serve to reduce the community's schedule of liquidity-preference which will cause, in turn, a reduction in the rate of interest.* This lower cost of borrowing will stand in better relation to the marginal efficiency of capital and will thus prove favorable to investment. And the increase in investment will, of course, enhance the level of employment.

* A far less painful way of attaining a lower rate of interest is to increase the amount of money in circulation. When this happens, the ratio of the amount of money which individuals and business entities will want to retain in

if money-wage rates are reduced, the level of aggregate effective demand will be less than it was prior to the money-wage adjustment. But if the money-demand function for goods is reduced, the demand function for labor will have to be similarly reduced.[1] Thus, concludes Keynes, unless a reduction in money-wages is accompanied by the same aggregate effective demand as before,[2] classical theory is wholly unable to determine what effect a reduction in money wages will have on employment,[3] and, so, its assumption of general full employment is seriously open to question.

Having rejected the classical notion that an adjustment of money-wage rates can serve as a remedy for unemployment,[4] Keynes next turns to a consideration of Say's Law.[5] Specifically, he

---

3. liquid form will decline and thereby bring about a reduction in the rate of interest. (For an exhaustive treatment of all the repercussions which a decline in money-wages is likely to have on the propensity to consume, the marginal efficiency of capital and the rate of interest vide J. M. Keynes, The General Theory, op. cit., pp. 262-269.)
1. A. H. Hansen, A Guide to Keynes, op. cit., p. 23.
2. Although the level of aggregate effective demand might remain constant for a particular firm or industry which decides to cut money-wage rates, it will not remain the same if all industries try to reduce money-wages at the same time.
3. J. M. Keynes, The General Theory of Employment, Interest and Money, op. cit., p. 260.
4. Although Keynes rejects this notion in Chapter 2, he does not completely refute it until he reaches Chapter 19 of the General Theory.
5. Keynes believes that Say's doctrine is very well set forth by J. S. Mill in his Principles of Political Economy (Book III, Ch. XIV.) The law is explained in the following terms. "What constitutes the means of payment for commodities is simply commodities. Each person's means of paying for the productions of other people consist of those which he himself

takes exception[1] to the law on the ground of its assumption that the aggregate demand price is equal to the aggregate supply price of production for all levels of employment and output. According to Keynes, there is no necessary identity between these two quanta. The reason for supposing that there is arises from the confusion of an indubitable proposition, namely, that the income obtained in the aggregate by all the elements engaged in productive activity must necessarily be equal to the value of the output, with the invalid proposition that, therefore, all costs of producing the output will be covered by the expenditure of this income.[2] The latter proposition is erroneously inferred from the former, for, although it be true that income is derived from production, there is no absolute necessity that this income be entirely spent to cover all costs of production.

---

5. possesses. All sellers are inevitably, and by the meaning of the word, buyers. Could we suddenly double the productive powers of the country, we should double the supply of commodities in every market; but we should, by the same stroke, double the purchasing power. Everybody would bring a double demand as well as supply; everybody would be able to buy twice as much, because everyone would have twice as much to offer in exchange."
1. Keynes was not the first to attack Say's Law. The Rev. Thomas Malthus had seriously questioned it in the early part of the 19th century. John A. Hobson, a proponent of the underconsumption theory of economic fluctuations, also took exception with it, as did Albert Aftalion in the early part of the 20th century. Unfortunately, their theoretical tools were inadequate to upset completely the validity of the law, and, so, the task was essentially left up to Keynes. (Vide A. H. Hansen, *A Guide to Keynes*, op. cit., p. 6; and *Business Cycles and National Income*, New York, W. W. Norton and Co., 1951, Chapters 14 and 18.)
2. A. H. Hansen, *A Guide to Keynes*, op. cit., p. 28.

Keynes is able to establish the truth of this proposition with the assistance of some of the tools which he fashioned in the *General Theory*. On the basis of the consumption function, Keynes shows that, although consumer demand is determined by income, it is not equal to income, because it does not increase at the same rate as income. And insofar as the difference between income and consumption, i.e. savings, is concerned, there is no nexus which equates decisions to save with decisions to invest.[1] For the motives which determine decisions to save are not the same as those which determine decisions to invest, as note the following

---

1. The classicists believed that decisions to save and invest were equated through variations in the rate of interest. For example, if the demand for investment increased, the volume of savings was increased correspondingly through an increase in the level of interest. The classicists reasoned that it was painful to save or abstain from consumption; hence, the only way to encourage income recipients to forego consumption was to offer them a higher premium for their abstinence. The rate of interest so offered them would exactly balance the volume of savings with the amount of investment. Under these circumstances, a smaller portion of income would be used for consumption and a larger share would be utilized for financing investment undertakings; nonetheless, the aggregate demand would be equal to the aggregate supply.

    If, on the other hand, the demand for investment funds slackened, the rate of interest would fall. However, income recipients would not save as much at this lower level of interest as at the previous one, for it would not be sufficiently high to compensate them for abstaining from consumption. The lower rate of interest so offered would equate the reduced volume of investment with a smaller amount of savings. Under these circumstances, a larger portion of the income received would be destined for consumption and a smaller share would be utilized for financing investment, but again, the aggregate demand, though of a different composition, would be equal to the aggregate supply. (For a fuller treatment of this point vide A. H. Hansen, *Recovery or Stagnation?* New York, W.W. Norton and Co., 1938, pp. 18-19.)

assertion made by Keynes.

> Those who think in this way are deceived, nonetheless, by an optical illusion, which makes two essentially different activities appear to be the same. They are fallaciously supposing that there is a nexus which unites decisions to abstain from present consumption with decisions to provide for future consumption; whereas the motives which determine the latter are not linked in any simple way with the motives which determine the former.[1]

In effect, a person or enterprise does not necessarily refrain from consumption with the understanding that he or it will necessarily invest the amount of realized savings.[2] These decisions to save and to invest are largely made by different sets of people and are determined by different considerations.[3] The volume of savings, though primarily a function of income, is also determined by considerations of liquidity, which in turn depend upon transactions, precautionary and speculative motives.[4] The volume of investment, on the other hand, is not determined by the level of income[5] and the other factors which condition decisions to save; rather, it is primarily dependent upon the relationship between the rate of interest and the schedule of the marginal efficiency of capital,[6]

---

1. J. M. Keynes, The General Theory, op. cit., p. 21.
2. G. A. Elliott, "The Significance of the General Theory of Employment, Interest and Money," The Canadian Journal of Economics and Political Science, XIII, 3, August, 1947, p. 373.
3. Ibid.
4. J. M. Keynes, The General Theory, op. cit., p. 170.
5. A. H. Hansen, A Guide to Keynes, op. cit., p. 28.
6. J. M. Keynes, The General Theory, op. cit., pp. 27-28.

i.e. the prospects of future yields as currently estimated.[1] As a result of these different factors which enter into the determination of decisions to save and to invest, Keynes reasons that they have no inherent tendency to be equal and that there is no automatic, painless way whereby they may be brought into balance with one another.[2] But if this be true, then the gap between consumption expenditures and income, i.e. savings, may or may not be offset by investment outlays.[3] If they are, the aggregate demand price will be equal to the aggregate supply price and Say's Law obtains; however, if the level of investment forthcoming is less than the volume of savings which the community would like to set aside, the law becomes invalid and the level of output, employment and income will be forced downward.[4] On the assumption that "ex ante" savings exceed "ex ante" investment, the level of economic activity will fall to that point where the volume of savings is being exactly offset by the volume of investment.[5] But

---

1. G. A. Elliott, op. cit., p. 373.
2. W. H. Beveridge, Full Employment in a Free Society, London, George Allen and Unwin, Ltd., 1944, p. 94.
3. This should not be interpreted to mean that savings and investment will remain unequal. For though they may be dissimilar "ex ante", they must of necessity be equal "ex post". This identity between savings and investment will be achieved at a new point of equilibrium through variations in the level of income. (For a very lucid discussion of the manner in which savings and investment are brought into balance vide "Mr. Keynes on Money," The London Economist, CXXII, 4827, Feb. 29, 1936, p. 471.)
4. J. M. Keynes, The General Theory, op. cit., p. 26.
5. Keynes, of course, did not use this "ex ante" and "ex post" approach to the question of equating savings and investment.

at this new point of equilibrium, the economy experiences a condition of less than full employment. By thus destroying Say's assumption of equality between the demand price of total output and its supply price for all levels of output, Keynes was able to prove that the classical postulate of full employment was erroneous.

As a result of the above shortcomings associated with Say's Law, Keynes contended that many of the arguments predicated on it would have to be re-assayed. Among the traditional arguments to be questioned, in his estimate, were the following: the social advantages of individual and national thrift, the rate of interest, the theory of unemployment, the quantity theory of money, and the "unqualified advantages of laissez-faire in respect of foreign trade."[1]

In effect, the doctrine of free trade, as well as all the other classical teachings, have to be questioned, because they are based on the assumption that a condition of full employment generally prevails in the economic system, and that the economy is self-adjusting at that level. In practice, however, such is not the case and the system ordinarily adjusts itself to a level below that of full employment.[2]

Our immediate task, then, is to examine the orthodox doctrine of free trade under conditions of both full and less than full employment. As already intimated, this research should reveal

---

1. J. M. Keynes, The General Theory, op. cit., p. 21.
2. A. L. Rowse, Mr. Keynes and the Labour Movement, London, Macmillan and Co., Ltd., 1936, p. 12.

that, although the classical argument in behalf of free trade is substantially valid under conditions of full employment, it is not entirely applicable to an environment of less than full utilization of manpower and resources.

b. <u>The classical theory of international trade considered under conditions of full employment</u>.

On the assumption that manpower and resources are always fully employed, the important consideration is obviously to utilize them in the most efficient manner possible.[1] The main pre-occupation of the classicists, therefore, was not with considering the factors which determine the size of output and income, but with explaining how the distribution of a given volume of employed resources between competing uses should be made, and with the manner in which their relative rewards and the relative values of their products is determined.[2]

The classical economists' concern with the fashion in which resources are employed in different uses is especially evident in their international trade theory. For according to the law of comparative advantage, which is the basis for their free trade argument, each nation should employ its resources in the production of those goods in which it is relatively best suited. Such an international division of labor would increase productivity[3]

---

1. W. A. Salant, "Foreign Trade Policy in the Business Cycle," <u>Readings in the Theory of International Trade</u>, Phila., The Blakiston Co., 1949, p. 201.
2. J. M. Keynes, <u>The General Theory</u>, <u>op. cit.</u>, p. 4.
3. D. Dillard, <u>op. cit.</u>, pp. 283-284.

and, when complemented by a free trade policy, would maximize real incomes for all trading nations.[1]

The above orthodox reasoning is largely predicated on the opportunity cost analysis. For example, the argument for not producing commodity A is that the same resources applied to the production of commodity B will in the long run yield a higher total real income.[2] This method of analysis presupposes that a factor of production has two or more alternative uses available to it. Given these two or more alternative opportunities, each factor should be employed in that capacity in which its advantage is greatest. In an environment of world-wide full employment, the factors of production do have alternative opportunities open to them; hence, if nations are to maximize their real incomes, then each should utilize its resources and manpower in the production of those goods in which it has the greatest comparative advantage and exchange them freely with other countries for commodities in which they in turn enjoy the greatest comparative advantage.[3]

Under these conditions, viz. that the self-restorative powers of the modern economy are sufficiently strong to guarantee a reasonably high level of employment and income in the trading countries, the opportunity cost analysis is completely valid. For

---

1. J. C. Gilbert, "The Present Position of the Theory of International Trade," Review of Economic Studies, III, 1, Oct., 1935, p. 18.
2. N. S. Buchanan, op. cit., p. 57.
3. Ibid., p. 150.

in such an environment it would be extremely uneconomical to waste manpower and resources in the production of goods that could be more efficiently produced abroad.[1] Thus, given a high level of employment and income, the orthodox arguments in behalf of international specialization and free trade are difficult to refute.[2] Insofar as the allocation of productive factors in a full employment economy is concerned, Keynes readily admits that the classical analysis is entirely correct. This he indicates in the following passage.

> If our central controls succeed in establishing an aggregate volume of output corresponding to full employment as nearly as is practicable, the classical theory comes into its own from this point onwards. If we suppose the volume of output to be given, i.e. to be determined by forces outside the classical scheme of thought, then there is no objection to be raised against the classical analysis of the manner in which private self-interest will determine what in particular is produced, in what proportions the factors of production will be combined to produce it, and how the value of the final product will be distributed among them.... I see no reason to believe that the existing system seriously misemploys the factors of production which are in use.... The result of filling in the gaps in the classical theory is not to dispose of the 'Manchester System' but to indicate the nature of the environment which the free play of economic forces requires if it is to realize the full potentialities of production.[3]

In view of the fact that Keynes is satisfied with the orthodox explanation of the manner in which the factors of production are

---

1. A. H. Hansen, *America's Role in the World Economy*, New York, W. W. Norton and Co., 1945, p. 164.
2. N. S. Buchanan, op. cit., p. 150.
3. J. M. Keynes, *The General Theory*, op. cit., pp. 378-379.

combined under conditions of full employment, it follows that under these circumstances he must necessarily subscribe to the law of comparative advantage and to the doctrine of free trade which is predicated upon it.[1] For the law of comparative advantage, though it applies internationally, is essentially concerned with the optimum allocation and efficient use of the productive factors.

In taking exception to the classical doctrine of free trade, Keynes does not do so because he considers the law of comparative advantage to be erroneous. Rather, his argument is that, while the law is basically correct, the orthodox argument in behalf of free trade is invalidated by the tacit assumption that a condition of full employment always obtains in the trading countries.[2] Keynes' contention is that, if there prevails a condition of worldwide unemployment, the classical doctrine of free trade is subject to question; however, if a condition of general full employment can be shown to exist, then there can be no disputing the orthodox free trade argument.[3] In effect, Keynes makes full employment the prerequisite for a policy of free trade, as witness his following assertion.

---

1. If the validity of the law of comparative advantage in a full employment society be accepted, then Keynes would also have to admit the plausibility of free trade. For given such specialization, exchange is made mandatory and the freer is this exchange of goods, the higher will be the level of real income.
2. J. Eaton, *Marx against Keynes*, London, Lawrence and Wishart, Ltd., 1951, p. 48.
3. *Ibid.*, pp. 48-49.

> If nations can learn to provide themselves
> with full employment by their domestic policy,
> there need be no important economic forces
> calculated to set the interest of one country
> against that of its neighbours. There would
> still be room for the international division
> of labour and for international lending in
> appropriate conditions. But there would no
> longer be a pressing motive why one country
> need force its wares on another or rebuke
> the offerings of its neighbour, not because
> this was necessary to enable it to pay for
> what it wished to purchase, but with the
> express object of upsetting the equilibrium
> of payments so as to develop a balance of
> trade in its own favour. International trade
> would cease to be what it is, namely, a des-
> perate expedient to maintain employment at
> home by forcing sales on foreign markets and
> restricting purchases, which, if successful,
> will merely shift the problem of unemployment
> to the neighbour which is worsted in the
> struggle, but a willing and unimpeded exchange
> of goods and services in conditions of mutual
> advantage.[1]

Briefly, Keynes' argument is simply this. If nations can succeed in attaining internal stability, they are then in a position to enjoy the benefits arising out of the international division of labor.[2] For once full employment is realized, the problem is no longer one of finding some employment for idle workers and resources, but how to select the best possible employment for each resource and worker.[3] At this point, the opportunity cost analysis becomes appropriate and the classical analysis comes into its own once again.

---

1. J. M. Keynes, *The General Theory*, op. cit., pp. 382-383.
2. A. Smithies, op. cit., p. 587.
3. R. Stevens, "The New Economics and World Peace," *Pacifism and Economics*, VI, 1, Phila., The Pacifist Research Bureau, 1944, p. 3.

c. *The classical theory of international trade considered under conditions of less than full employment.*

Given the existence of a condition of less than full employment, the problem confronting the economy is unlike the one that it must face under conditions of full utilization of manpower and resources. The problem which it must consider in the former circumstances is to employ the productive factors in their best alternative uses;[1] whereas, the problem it must solve in the latter circumstances is not how to utilize these factors in the most efficient way possible, but how to engage them at all.[2] In effect, the opportunity cost analysis, though valid under conditions of full employment, is not equally valid under conditions of large-scale unemployment. As a result of the inappropriateness of the opportunity cost analysis in an environment of unemployed manpower and resources, the free trade argument which is based upon it loses a great deal of its force in such a state of depressed activity. In short, much of the orthodox reasoning about foreign trade policy, which is predicated on the existence of full employment, becomes erroneous when applied to an economy experiencing widespread displacement of manpower and resources.[3]

There is an essential difference in the nature of the problems facing a fully employed economy and one that is less than fully

---

1. M. A. Heilperin, *The Trade of Nations*, New York, Alfred A. Knopf, 1952, p. 99.
2. N. S. Buchanan and F. A. Lutz, *Rebuilding the World Economy*, New York, The Twentieth Century Fund, 1947, p. 57.
3. W. A. Salant, *op. cit.*, p. 201.

256

employed; therefore, policies which are suitable for the one may not be suitable for the other.[1] When an economy enjoys full utilization of manpower and resources, maximum productivity or minimum unit costs of production is the proper criterion for determining desirable policy; whereas, when an economy is operating at a level of less than full employment, maximum national income becomes the correct norm for judging right policy.[2]

As already established in the preceding section, maximum productivity can be realized through the international division of labor and free trade. However, insofar as the second objective is concerned, i.e. maximization of income under conditions of less than full employment, this may at times be more readily achieved through a protectionist policy, for if a nation can succeed in increasing its foreign trade surplus, this will represent an increase in foreign investment and an increase in investment, whether it be domestic or foreign, will lead to an increase in employment and income.[3]

According to Keynes, the amount of employment is limited by the extent of the aggregate demand.[4] Consequently, if the level of effective demand is inadequate to provide full employment, it is entirely possible for a nation to increase its level of home employment by diverting demand from foreign to home produced

---

1. A. H. Hansen, *Recovery or Stagnation*? *op. cit.*, pp. 16-18.
2. D. Dillard, *op. cit.*, p. 315.
3. J. Robinson, *Essays in the Theory of Employment*, *op. cit.*, p. 186.
4. J. M. Keynes, *The General Theory*, *op. cit.*, p. 104.

goods.¹ This could be effectively accomplished through the imposition of tariffs and other restrictive measures on the flow of international trade.

Although it be true that a protectionist policy frustrates the optimum international division of labor and thus causes a decrease in productivity, it is also true that such a policy may cause the

---

1. In this regard, too,* Hobson's thinking pre-dates that of Keynes. This may be substantiated by reference to the following passages contained in Hobson's *International Trade.*
"If we once admit the possibility that there exists a larger margin or excess of productive capacity which is proved to exist in most trades during periods of slackness or depression, we begin to comprehend the true underlying source of the plausibility of protection (p. 155).... The real case for protection, as I understand it rests upon this assumption that in normal times there does exist, not the smallest margin of capital and labour needed for current trade adjustments, but an amount considerably larger than this, and that, if a tariff can be framed to substitute the employment of this productive energy for that of foreign capital and labour, the volume of our production will be greater (p. 156).... It is the theoretic possibility of filling this hole of unemployment by an artificial diversion of trade through protection that gives what plausibility attaches to a tariff. It might be a profitable economic policy for a nation to pay a slightly higher price for certain consumable goods, and by reducing to a corresponding extent its demand for other commodities to displace capital and labour in these industries, if the result were to secure full regular employment for considerable quantities of capital and labour which otherwise would be wasted.... It must be borne in mind that the theoretic validity of this remedy for unemployment rests wholly on the hypothesis that there exists a considerable margin of spare available power of capital and labour, an unemployed margin beyond the legitimate needs of ordinary business adjustments, and that, therefore, orders diverted from the foreigner could be executed without causing capital and labour to leave employments where they were more productively engaged." (pp. 157-158.) (Vide J. A. Hobson, *International Trade*, London, Methuen and Co., 1904, pp. 146-169.)

* Vide p. 245 of this thesis.

real income of a country experiencing widespread unemployment to be higher than it would be under a free trade policy.[1] This may be explained by the fact that the gain in national income which is realized from the increased employment may more than offset the loss of income which is caused by the reduction in productivity.[2]

When a nation is plagued with widespread unemployment, the alternative to employing factors less efficiently is not to employ them at all.[3] The opportunity cost analysis is not applicable under these circumstances, for the opportunity cost of employing labor in the production of goods that might be imported more cheaply is virtually zero.[4] In fact, if these workers are drawing public assistance in the form of a dole, the opportunity cost will actually be negative.[5] Therefore, a nation may find it more advantageous to engage its manpower and resources, however inefficiently, than to have them remain completely idle. For, by restoring them to productive activity, it will generate at least some income; whereas, the alternative to not returning them to productive activity is not to create any income at all. Given large-scale labor displacement,

---

1. D. Dillard, op. cit., p. 284.
2. In this regard, Mrs. Joan Robinson says, "Classical trade simply tells us of the advantages of specialization.... It cannot tell us that when one country increases its share in world employment, at the expense of reducing output per unit of employment, its total output will be reduced." (J. Robinson, "Beggar-My-Neighbour Remedies for Unemployment," Essays in the Theory of Employment, op. cit., p. 212.)
3. D. Dillard, op. cit., p. 284.
4. W. H. Beveridge, Full Employment in a Free Society, op. cit., p. 211.
5. N. S. Buchanan, International Investment and Domestic Welfare, op. cit., p. 150.

it would be senseless for a country to economize in the use of manpower by adhering to a free trade policy only to have it go to waste in unemployment.[1] Thus, it may be argued that, when nations are experiencing widespread unemployment, it is not necessarily true, as would be the case under conditions of full employment, that they will be better off in expanding foreign[2] trade.[3]

---

1. This fact was readily recognized during the decade of the 'thirties. As a result, "nations were willing to employ two men to make at home a product that might have been obtained from abroad in exchange for another product that could be made at home by one man, because they did not know how else to employ the other man." (H. Feis, The Changing Pattern of International Economic Affairs, New York, Harper Brothers, 1940, p. 39.)
2. N. S. Buchanan, op. cit., p. 151.
3. By indicating that the free trade doctrine of the classicists is valid only in an environment where there exists full utilization of manpower and resources, Keynes had sizable influence on the formulation of international trade policy in the post-war world. In most official quarters it is now recognized that the prerequisite for the development of a free, multilateral trading system is the existence of world-wide full employment. It is particularly important that such a condition obtain in the major trading countries such as the United States.

   The importance of full employment to the extension of free trade throughout the world is brought out quite emphatically in the following pronouncement of the United States State Department. "The attainment of approximately full employment by the major industrial and trading nations, and its maintenance on a reasonably assured basis, are essential to the expansion of international trade on which the full prosperity of these and other nations depends; to the full realization of the objectives of all liberal international agreements in such fields as commercial policy, commodity problems, restrictive business practices, monetary stabilization, and investment; and therefore to the preservation of world peace and security." (U. S. State Department, Proposals for Expansion of World Trade and Employment, Washington, D.C., U.S. Government Printing Office, 1945, p. 9.)

To determine whether or not it should pursue a protectionist trade policy in a period of mass unemployment, a nation must weigh the advantages and disadvantages which attend such a policy. It must compare the advantage of increased employment and income with the disadvantage of higher unit costs of production. If the gain in national income exceeds the loss in productivity, a restrictive trade policy may be in order; whereas, if the loss in productive efficiency outweighs the increase in income, such a policy may be economically unsound. In general, if unemployment is severe, a protectionist policy will, undoubtedly, be more advantageous; whereas, if the amount of labor displacement is not too great, a free trade policy will be more beneficial for the economy as a whole.[1]

---

3. For a comprehensive treatment of the influence exerted by Keynes' theory of employment on international trade policy consult the following sources. Research Committee of the C. E. D., *International Trade, Foreign Investment and Domestic Employment*, New York, Committee for Economic Development, 1945, passim; A. H. Hansen, *America's Role in the World Economy*, op. cit., pp. 179-180; M. A. Heilperin, *The Trade of Nations*, op. cit., p. 129; R. Nurkse, "Conditions of International Equilibrium," *Essays in International Finance*, No. 4, International Finance Section, Princeton University, Spring, 1945, passim; N. S. Buchanan, *International Investment and Domestic Welfare*, op. cit., p. 235; W. H. Beveridge, *Full Employment in a Free Society*, op. cit., p. 210; B. Banerjii, op. cit., p. 60; W. A. Salant, op. cit., p. 226; "The Principles of Trade," *The London Economist*, CXLVI, 5238, Jan. 15, 1944, p. 64; "The Multilateral Approach," *The London Economist*, CXLVI, 5239, Jan. 22, 1944, p. 94; "Prices and Markets," *The London Economist*, CXLVI, 5242, Feb. 12, 1944, pp. 204-205; "The New Liberalism," *The London Economist*, CXLVI, 5243, Feb. 19, 1944, p. 233; "Trade and Employment," *The London Economist*, CXLVI, 5257, May 27, 1944, p. 702.

1. D. Dillard, op. cit., p. 284.

d. **Keynes must have been amenable to a protectionist policy in the General Theory, because he believed that the economy was characterized by chronic unemployment.**

In the preceding sections of this chapter it has been established that Keynes' attitude towards commercial policy was variable, depending upon the status of domestic employment, i.e. under conditions of full employment he would favor a free trade policy, whereas, in an environment of less than full employment he would be inclined towards protection. But in the General Theory Keynes appears to rule out the former alternative by his contention that the economy is usually characterized by a condition of chronic unemployment. This he establishes in the following passage.

> In particular, it is an outstanding characteristic of the economic system in which we live, that, whilst it is subject to severe fluctuations in respect of output and employment, it is not violently unstable. Indeed it seems capable of remaining in a chronic condition of sub-normal activity for a considerable period without any marked tendency either towards recovery or towards complete collapse. Moreover, the evidence indicates that full, or even approximately full, employment is of rare and short-lived occurrence. Fluctuations may start briskly but seem to wear themselves out before they have proceeded to great extremes, and an intermediate situation which is neither desperate nor satisfactory is our normal lot.[1]

If, then, it be true that a condition of full employment is the exception rather than the rule and that there exists "a chronic condition of sub-normal activity for a considerable period," it

---

1. J. M. Keynes, The General Theory, op. cit., pp. 249-250.

is entirely valid to reason that, at the time of the publication of the General Theory, Keynes must have been amenable to protectionism. For, having rejected the possibility of enduring full employment, he would, by his own admission, have to look with favor upon protection, since under conditions of widespread labor and capital displacement, a restrictive trade policy might enhance the level of employment[1] and income.[2] And this, of course, was his primary concern at the time.

e. Summary

Our first conclusion respecting Keynes' commercial policy views, as set forth in The General Theory, is that they are by no means categorical. As in all cases where Keynes' thinking challenges classical theory, his ultimate position is contingent upon the status of domestic employment. If a condition of full employment obtains, the special case of classical economics is realized and orthodox theory becomes appropriate once again. Under these circumstances, Keynes would unhesitatingly subscribe to free trade. If, on the other hand, the necessary full employment environment is non-existent, then the tenets and policy recommendations of classical economics are not applicable.[3] In this economic setting,

---

1. J. M. Keynes, Ibid., pp. 334-335 and pp. 348-349.
2. L. Metzler, Income, Employment and Public Policy, New York, W. W. Norton and Co., Inc., 1948, p. 251.
3. Keynes was by no means the first economist to make us aware of the relationship between commercial policy and the level of employment. John A. Hobson, for one, recognized the importance of this relationship some 14 years prior to the appearance of the General Theory, as the following excerpts

Keynes might be more inclined towards a restrictive trade policy.

That Keynes' attitude towards commercial policy should be variable does not mean that he was inconsistent, for he simply offered different solutions for different assumptions or conditions. Given a condition of full employment, a free trade policy would be more advantageous for the home economy; whereas, if there existed a condition of widespread unemployment, a protectionist policy might be more beneficial, since it would be a more effective means of increasing the level of employment and income. To understand Keynes' thinking respecting commercial policy, it should not be forgotten that, even from the earliest phase of his career, it was related to what was best for the domestic economy. Keynes' primary concern was always with the attainment of those objectives which would best promote the national welfare, v.g. stability of prices, insulation from external fluctuations and the maintenance of high

---

3. from his *Economics of Unemployment* will bear out. "This argument (protection) will not, I think, hold water under ordinary trade conditions, in which the available productive power of a country may be considered to be fully employed. Under this condition it is evidently better to buy in the cheaper foreign market, for no total increase of employment will result from preferring the home-made goods. But where there is general unemployment both in this country and abroad, the immediate case for employing otherwise unemployed British capital and labour is far more plausible (p. 153).... Given a general depression and unemployment in the industrial world, a tariff might be used to distribute the aggregate volume of employment for the time being favourably to the political area which set it up." (p. 155) (Vide J. A. Hobson, *The Economics of Unemployment*, London, George Allen and Unwin, Ltd., 1922, pp. 153-157.)

levels of domestic employment and income. In short, his thinking on foreign trade policy was largely conditioned by internal requirements. If the economy could gain more from a free trade policy, he would favor it; however, if, as in periods of depressed activity, it could profit more from a restrictive trade policy, he would, instead, espouse it. From the standpoint that Keynes sought always to maximize the national advantage, it can hardly be said that he was inconsistent.

CHAPTER XV

THE NATURE OF INVESTMENT AND ITS
IMPLICATIONS FOR INTERNATIONAL ECONOMICS

a. <u>A favorable balance of trade is synonymous with investment and insofar as investment is the primary determinant of employment and income, a strong case can be made for a protectionist policy as a means of augmenting the favorable balance of trade and thereby the level of home income and employment.</u>

According to Keynes' theory of employment, when the level of employment increases, aggregate real income is also increased. Given this higher income, the community will increase its outlays for consumption; however, its psychology is such that it will not increase these expenditures by so much as the increment of income received. This behavior is explained by the law of

---

1. If a community has a propensity to consume of less than unity, it is important that the volume of savings be offset by a like amount of current investment; otherwise, the prevailing equilibrium will be upset and the level of income will fall. And it will continue to fall until a new equilibrium is reached, i.e. a point at which savings and investment are again equal to one another. (W. B. Reddaway, "The General Theory of Employment, Interest and Money - a Review," <u>The Economic Record</u>, XII, 22, June, 1936, p. 31.)

   The importance of equating savings and investment at a high level is clearly indicated by Prof. Samuelson in the following passage. "Upon one thing all modern economists, of whatever school of thought, are agreed: the amount which the community wishes to save at full employment income levels must somehow be offset, or income will fall until the community is so poor and wretched as to be willing to save no more than can be offset. In terms of time-period analysis, the community must return to the income stream in each period as much as it

consumption¹ which Keynes describes in the following terms.

> The fundamental psychological law, upon which we are entitled to depend with great confidence both 'a priori' from our knowledge of human nature and from the detailed facts of experience, is that men are disposed, as a rule and on the average, to increase their consumption as their income increases, but not by as much as the increase in their income. That is to say, if C_w is the amount of consumption and Y_w is income (both measured in wage-units) C_w has the same sign as Y but is smaller in amount, i. e. $\frac{d\,C_w}{d\,Y_w}$ is positive and less than unity.²

This means that, unless the difference between the amount of income received and the amount of this income spent for consumption is returned to the entrepeneurs, they will incur losses, with the result that they will have to curtail employment and income in the ensuing period.³ Therefore, to warrant any given level of

---

1. received in previous periods, or else there will ensue a cumulative downward spiral of income and employment. We are confronted with the paradox that while no one attempts to save with any thought of investment outlet, or of offsets, yet the amount which all together succeed in saving is brought into alignment by the movements of income and employment.* But the alignment is performed on a cruel Procrustean bed with employment and income being lopped off if the desire to save is excessive in comparison with available offsets, and with an inflationary straining of demand if investment is excessive." (P. Samuelson, "Full Employment after the War," *Post-War Economic Problems*, (S. Harris, editor), New York, McGraw-Hill, 1943, p. 37.)

    * For a further account of the manner in which savings are brought into balance with investment vide "Mr. Keynes on Money," *The London Economist*, CXXII, 4827, Feb. 29. 1936, pp. 471-472.

1. J. M. Keynes, *The General Theory, op. cit.*, p. 27.
2. *Ibid.*, p. 96.
3. *Ibid.*, p. 27.

employment the amount of current investment forthcoming must be sufficient to offset the excess of total output over what the community desires to consume at that particular level of employment.[1]

On the basis of the foregoing, Keynes was able to show that, given the community's propensity to consume, the level of employment will depend on the volume of current investment. And the amount of current investment will depend upon what Keynes calls the inducement to invest. The latter will be determined by the relationship between the marginal efficiency of capital and the structure of interest rates.[2] This, in essence, is Keynes' general theory of employment.

In assaying Keynes' contribution, one cannot fail to note the pivotal importance of investment in the determination of employment and income. When the level of employment increases, the

---

1. It is the contention of Prof. Alvin H. Hansen that the notion of the consumption function is not exclusive with Keynes. Prof. J. M. Clark, for one, indicated in his *Strategic Factors in Business Cycles*, which was published in 1934, that, "there is the probability – which may be taken as a moral certainty – that as the national income increases in the upswing of the business cycle, consumers' expenditures increase less rapidly than the total income, and savings available for expenditures on producers' goods increase more rapidly." (p. 78). Arthur Aftalion also observed that consumption increases absolutely less than output – a fact which he attributed to the law of diminishing marginal utilities. Although both of these men had a clear understanding of the nature of consumer behavior, it remained for Keynes to establish the true importance of this function. This he succeeded in doing, because he was able to integrate it with other relevant functions to formulate a general theory of employment and income. (Vide A. H. Hansen, *A Guide to Keynes*, op. cit., pp. 27-28.)
2. J. M. Keynes, *The General Theory*, op. cit., p. 27.

disparity between the aggregate supply price of the national output and the receipts which entrepeneurs can expect to realize from consumer purchases will grow wider, owing to the operation of the psychological law.[1] Consequently, if there occurs no change in the propensity of the community to consume, the level of employment cannot be augmented, unless, of course, there occurs an increase in the level of current investment. Such an increase in investment expenditures would help fill the ever-widening gap between the supply price of total output and the receipts made possible by consumer expenditures.[2] Keynes indicates the importance of investment as a means of offsetting savings and, therefore, as a means of increasing employment in the following passage.

> Employment can only increase pari passu with an increase in investment; unless, indeed, there is a change in the propensity to consume. For since consumers will spend less than the increase in aggregate supply price when employment is increased, the increased employment will prove unprofitable unless there is an increase in investment to fill the gap.[3]

The key to the employment problem in terms of the Keynesian analysis is to be found in an ever-increasing volume of investment activity. This is more true for a wealthy than for a poor country. Keynes explains this by saying that the richer the community, the greater will be the margin between its consumption and its potential

---

1. Ibid., pp. 29-30.
2. J. M. Keynes, "A Self-Adjusting System," The New Republic, LXXXII, 1054, Feb. 20, 1935, p. 36.
3. Ibid., p. 98.

production and, therefore, the greater the urgency for finding new investment projects. The situation will not be quite so acute in a less affluent country, for a poor community is likely to consume the greater part of this output, with the result that a small amount of investment will suffice to provide full employment.

The Determinants of Investment and the Mature Economy.

The attainment of a sufficiently large volume of investment to offset the increased amount of savings which people desire to set aside in a wealthy economy is not easy. Capital is not a self-subsistent entity which exists apart from consumption; therefore, any permanent weakening of the propensity to consume must also weaken the demand for consumer goods.[1] New capital formation can take place in excess of current capital depreciation only on condition that future consumption expenditures are expected to increase.[2] But in an advanced state there is little likelihood that consumption will be increased in the future. Therefore, given the prospect of a static demand, there is little incentive to bring into existence additional capital goods which will provide for the consumption of tomorrow.

Another reason why it may be difficult to achieve a level of investment which is large enough to offset the community's desire

---

1. Ibid., pp. 105-106.
2. In this regard, Keynes is reminded of "The Fable of the Bees" wherein Mandeville points out that, "the gay of tomorrow are absolutely indispensable to provide a raison d'etre for the grave of today."

to save is that, the greater is the amount of capital expansion which has taken place in the past,[1] the less attractive will opportunities be for further investment in the future.[2] This may be explained by the fact that, as a nation's stock of capital goods is augmented, the marginal efficiency[3] of this equipment tends to diminish.[4] For as the quantity of a particular productive factor increases, there is a tendency for its marginal efficiency to fall. Also, as pressure is exerted on the economy's facilities for producing a particular type of capital good, its supply price will be forced upward.[5] Thus, if, on the one hand, the yield forthcoming from an additional unit of capital is diminished and, on the other, its supply price is increased, it is obvious that the marginal efficiency of that earning asset will be reduced.[6]

A decline in the marginal efficiency of capital is not the only factor which makes for a reduced volume of investment. The

---

1. According to L. R. Klein, the existence of a large stock of previously accumulated capital is one of the main pillars of the mature economy thesis. Klein bases his statement on the results of statistical investigations which reveal a negative correlation between the volume of new investment forthcoming and the amount already in existence. (Vide L. R. Klein, op. cit., pp. 68-69.)
2. J. M. Keynes, The General Theory, op. cit., p. 31.
3. The marginal efficiency of capital may be defined as "the rate of discount which makes the present value of all future returns of a capital asset equal to the supply price of that asset." (B. Ohlin, The Problem of Employment Stabilization, New York, Columbia University Press, 1949, p. 139.)
4. J. M. Keynes, The General Theory, op.cit., p. 136.
5. Ibid.
6. W. B. Reddaway, op. cit., pp. 31-32.

level of interest must also be taken into consideration. Given the aggregate investment demand schedule, i.e. a schedule which relates the rate of aggregate investment to the marginal efficiency of capital corresponding to that rate of investment, and the prevailing structure of interest rates, it is possible to determine just how much capital formation will be forthcoming.[1] According to Keynes, the rate of investment will be pushed to the point on the investment demand schedule where the marginal efficiency of capital just offsets the going rate of interest.[2] In short, the inducement to investment depends upon the marginal efficiency of capital and the prevailing rate of interest. Keynes expresses this more specifically in the following statement.

> There will be an inducement to push the rate of new investment to the point which forces the supply-price of each type capital-asset to a figure which, taken in conjunction with its prospective yield, brings the marginal efficiency of capital in general to approximate equality with the rate of interest.[3]

From the foregoing it is evident that an increase in investment will be forthcoming only on condition that there occurs either an increase in the marginal efficiency of capital or a reduction in the interest rate. The former is ruled out in an economically

---

1. J. M. Keynes, The General Theory, op. cit., pp. 136-137.
2. The rate of interest in the Keynesian system is simply determined by the demand for and supply of money. More specifically, it is determined at the point where the liquidity preference schedule and the available money supply interract. (Vide J. M. Keynes, The General Theory, op. cit., pp. 165-174.)
3. Ibid., p. 248.

advanced state, because as the supply of capital increases its marginal efficiency will tend to diminish, due to the law of diminishing marginal returns and the increased cost of production. Consequently, this means that investment in such a society can be increased only through the medium of a lower interest rate.[1]

So long as the rate of return for new capital undertakings exceeds the market rate of interest, investment will be continued; however, it cannot be presumed that the rate of interest will continue to decline in proportion to the ever-decreasing marginal efficiency of capital. For, in time, the rate of interest will reach a certain level below which it will not fall. According to Keynes, "after the rate of interest has fallen to a certain level, liquidity preference may become virtually absolute in the sense that almost everyone prefers cash to holding a debt which yields so low a rate of interest."[2] But why is this so?

Keynes attributes this failure of the interest rate to fall below a level well above zero[3] to the operation of institutional and psychological factors. In the first place, it is impossible to reduce the rate of interest below a certain level, because there are certain irreducible costs associated with the lending

---

1. According to Keynes, a lower rate of interest can be realized through an increase in the money supply. (Vide J. M. Keynes, The General Theory, op. cit., pp. 172-173.)
2. Ibid., p. 207.
3. Keynes believes that a lower limit of 2 or 2½ per cent is set on the long-term rate of interest. (Vide J. M. Keynes, The General Theory, op. cit., pp. 218-219.)

of money. Consequently, it cannot be forced below a certain minimum without causing loss to the lenders.[1] Also, it must be considered that the rate of interest at which money is lent is not a "pure" rate. Even if it were to be assumed that the "pure" cost of borrowing money were zero, certain risks attending the lending of funds at low rates of interest would have to be taken into consideration.[2] For in the event that the interest rate increases even slightly prior to the maturity of the investment, the capitalized value of that earning asset will be diminished. In fact, it may be reduced to such an extent as to liquidate all of the realized interest earnings. Thus, it may be concluded that "below a certain minimum interest rate complete liquidity will be preferred to financial investment and, for this reason, the rate of interest will fail to fall to that point at which the savings of the community will find a ready outlet in investment."[3]

But even if the rate of interest could be reduced to zero, this might not insure an adequate volume of capital formation to offset the amount of savings which the economy might wish to set aside. For, as the volume of investment increases, its marginal efficiency will in time reach zero.[4] At this point, net capital

---

1. J. S. G. Wilson, Lord Keynes and the Development of Modern Economic Theory, Sidney, The Economic Society of Australia and New Zealand, 1946, p. 26.
2. A. H. Hansen, Full Recovery or Stagnation? op. cit., p. 23.
3. J. S. G. Wilson, op. cit., p. 28.
4. Keynes estimates that in an advanced community the marginal efficiency of capital could be reduced to zero within the span of a single generation. Thereafter, of course, it would become negative. (Vide J. M. Keynes, The General Theory, op. cit., p. 217 and pp. 220-221.)

formation will be non-existent,[1] with the result that the level of employment and income will settle at a new, but extremely low level of equilibrium, viz. at the point where both savings and investment are equal to zero.[2] It is at this juncture that the stagnant state[3] emerges.[4]

---

1. But, if investment be non-existent, then savings must similarly be reduced to zero, for the two are of necessity always equal to each other.
2. A. H. Hansen, *A Guide to Keynes*, op. cit., pp. 217-218.
3. There is considerable difference of opinion as to whether or not Keynes treated explicitly the mature economy concept" in his *General Theory*. Prof. J. F. Bell claims that, although Keynes did not fully develop the concept of a mature economy, it can, nonetheless, be inferred from his theories. (J. F. Bell, *A History of Economic Thought*, New York, Ronald Press Co., 1953, p. 64.) Prof. D. Hamberg is also of the view that the mature economy thesis is not clearly enunciated in the *General Theory*. His contention is that the thesis of secular stagnation was formulated by his American "Mohammed", Prof. A. H. Hansen, and others. (D. Hamberg, *Business Cycles*, New York, Macmillan Co., 1951, p. 136.)

On the other hand, Prof. J. A. Schumpeter feels that Keynes did, in fact, accord the mature economy thesis full theoretical treatment in the *General Theory*, as witness his following observation. "The social vision first revealed in *The Economic Consequences of the Peace*, the vision of an economic process in which investment opportunity flags and saving habits nonetheless persist, is theoretically implemented in the *General Theory* by means of three schedule concepts: the consumption function, the efficiency of capital function, and the liquidity preference function." (J. A. Schumpeter, *The Great Economists*, op. cit., pp. 280-281.)

Prof. J. H. Williams believes that the mature economy thesis is adequately summarized by Keynes on p. 31 of the *General Theory* wherein he states, "The richer the community, the wider will tend to be the gap between its actual and its potential production; and, therefore, the more obvious and outrageous the defects of the economic system.... Not only is the marginal propensity to consume weaker in a wealthy country, but, owing to its accumulations of capital being already larger, the opportunities for further investment are less attractive."

Whether we are dealing with a mature or with an expanding economy, the problem facing both of them is basically the same. For each country, owing to the fixed psychological propensity of its people to save, must find suitable investment projects to

---

3. Moreover, Prof. Williams is of the opinion that the mature economy or stagnation thesis constitutes the very heart of the General Theory. (J. H. Williams, "An Appraisal of Keynesian Economics," American Economic Review, XXXVIII, 2, May, 1948, pp. 275-276.)

    The writer entirely agrees with the position taken by Prof. Schumpeter and would like to add further that the essence of the mature economy concept was stated by Keynes even in his Treatise on Money. It is in this work that he indicates a tendency for savings to outrun available investment and the difficulty of discovering offsets to the amount of savings which the community wishes to keep by it. (J. M. Keynes, A Treatise on Money, op. cit., vol. II, p. 188.) Also vide "Death of a Genius," The Banker, LXXVIII, 244, May, 1946, p. 76.)

    For a more complete treatment of the mature economy thesis, consult the works of Prof. Alvin H. Hansen who is an acknowledged authority on this question. Vide A. H. Hansen, Full Recovery or Stagnation? New York, W. W. Norton and Co., 1938; _____, After the War- Full Employment, Washington, D. C., National Resources Planning Board, 1942; _____, Fiscal Policy and Business Cycles, New York, W. W. Norton and Co., 1941; _____, America's Role in the World Economy, New York, W. W. Norton and Co., 1945; and _____, Economic Policy and Full Employment, New York, McGraw-Hill Book Co., Inc., 1947.

    * Keynes was by no means the first economist to think in terms of a mature state. The classical economists were entirely aware of such a possibility. For example, Adam Smith blamed the prospect of the static state on the capacity of the progressive state to create capital. Malthus and Ricardo attributed this prospect to the failure of resources to move in consonance with demand; or too, on "the niggardliness of nature." John S. Mill also showed an awareness of the stagnant state in his Principles of Political Economy.

4. A. H. Hansen, Full Recovery or Stagnation? op. cit., pp. 19-30.

offset the volume of desired savings. The only difference in
their problems is one of degree, viz. the mature state will find
it more difficult to offset savings than will the more progressive
economy; nonetheless, they must both succeed in locating new
investment outlets if they are to maintain their levels of
employment and income.

Most of these investment outlets will be found in the production of producer durable goods, construction activity and in the manufacture of goods for inventory. As a rule, a sufficiently large volume of investment may be realized from these sources to balance the community's desired level of savings. But suppose that we are dealing with an economy wherein investment in capital equipment and new construction is largely saturated, and wherein the propensity to consume is weak, so that there is no justification for inventory accumulation. What alternative, apart from government spending, would such an economy have to escape the prospect of chronic under-full employment equilibrium?

Foreign investment as an offset to savings and an aid to employment.

A most effective alternative in the case of those countries which conduct a sizable volume of international trade would be an increase in foreign investment. This form of investment is synonymous with the favorable balance of payments on income account between one country and the rest of the world.[1] It arises when

---

1. J. Robinson, Introduction to the Theory of Employment, London, Macmillan Co., Ltd., 1937, pp. 98-99.

the volume of exports exceeds the volume of imports. A trade surplus may be realized either through an increase in exports relative to imports or through a decrease in imports relative to exports. Ideally, this increase in the foreign trade balance should be achieved through the agency of greater exports and a constant level of imports. If, however, it be extremely difficult or even impossible to achieve this increase in the foreign balance through an expansion of exports, it is possible to realize this same objective through a diminution in the volume of imports.[1] Such a reduction in the level of imports could be effectively accomplished through the implementing of a restrictive trade policy.[2]

(1) <u>An increase in foreign investment through an increase in the level of exports.</u>

Insofar as an improvement in the foreign trade balance through an increase in the volume of exports is concerned, this will exert the same effects on the home economy as an increase in the volume of domestic investment.[3] An increase in the volume of exports,

---

1. This statement assumes that the nature of the particular country's imports is such as to admit substitution by similar home-produced goods.
2. In addition to restricting imports by means of tariffs and quotas, it is possible to accomplish the same objective through exchange depreciation or a general wage reduction. For a full consideration of the effects which these measures have on a country's foreign trade balance and on the level of home employment consult Mrs. Joan Robinson's <u>Essays in the Theory of Employment</u>, <u>op. cit.</u>, pp. 211 ff.
3. Professor R. F. Harrod is of the view that it is not the excess of exports over imports which provides the stimulus

unaccompanied by a like increase in the value of imports,[1] will

---

3. to home activity, but the increase in the volume of exports. He bases his contention on the fact than an increase in the level of exports, whether accompanied or not by a like increase in imports, will lead to an increase in the volume of investment. Professor Harrod summarizes his position in the following way. "In my system, the increase in the volume of exports would be rightfully found to have a stimulating effect on employment through consequential reactions in home investment even though no addition to the balance of trade ensued." (p. 102.) For a more exhaustive consideration of Professor Harrod's position on this question vide R. F. Harrod, *Towards a Dynamic Economics*, London, Macmillan and Co., Ltd., 1948, pp. 101-108.

Mrs. Joan Robinson, among others, is of the opposite point of view. She believes that it is the increase in the trade balance and not the increase in the volume of exports, as such, which provides the stimulus to domestic activity. For, whereas the sale of exports adds to the level of demand for home-produced goods, the purchase of imports "with domestically earned income subtracts from the demand which can be potentially exercised against domestically produced goods." If this be the case, then the net advantage or disadvantage accruing to home incomes must be equal to the difference between exports and imports, i.e. the foreign trade balance on income account. (Vide J. Robinson, *Essays in the Theory of Employment*, pp. 210-211.)

Professor J. H. G. Pierson also supports the thesis advanced by Mrs. Robinson. According to him, the volume of exports, as such, has no bearing on the level of domestic employment, for as soon as imports are equal to exports their effects cancel out. This he explains "by the fact that money which is spent on imports subtracts from the home country's market, production and employment just about as much as the money foreigners spend for its imports adds to its market, production and employment." An increase in production and employment, he concludes, can be realized only on condition that the volume of exports exceeds the volume of imports. (Vide J. H. G. Pierson, *Full Employment and Free Enterprise*, Washington, D. C., Public Affairs Press, 1947, pp. 84-87.)

1. J. H. G. Pierson, *Full Employment and Free Enterprise*, op. cit., pp. 190-191.

enhance the demand for home produced goods[1] and thereby make possible an increase in the level of employment.[2] To the extent that it causes a greater demand to be exercised for domestic goods, without adding correspondingly to their current supply, a favorable balance of trade helps to reduce the gap between total output and that part domestically consumed. In this respect, a trade surplus operates precisely like domestic investment, for it serves as "a national outlet for domestic savings."[3] The greater the effectiveness of foreign investment in filling the void between domestic consumption and total output, the closer will aggregate demand move towards equality with the aggregate supply price. And the greater is the assurance that these two quanta will equate with one another at a high level, the greater are the prospects of sustaining the volume of employment and income at that level.[4] All this is clearly indicated by Professor J. H. G. Pierson in the following passage.

> Given a nation's volume of savings, offsets to that savings must be found. Economists tell us that we need a volume of investment and other non-consumption offsets to saving, equal in magnitude to the volume of savings forthcoming at a full employment level of national income; and that we are not likely to come anywhere near attaining such a volume of

---

1. G. Haberler, "The Choice of Exchange Rates After the War," *American Economic Review*, XXXV, 3, June, 1945, p. 309.
2. J. Robinson, *Essays in the Theory of Employment*, op. cit., p. 210.
3. A. Maffry, "Foreign Trade in the Post-War Economy," *Survey of Current Business*, November, 1944, p. 11.
4. R. G. Hawtrey, *Capital and Employment*, London, Longmans, Green and Co., 1937, p. 226.

investment through the unaided operation of
natural forces; and that foreign investment
is a peculiarly strategic kind of investment
for purposes of closing the gap.[1]

(2) *An increase in foreign investment through a decrease in the level of imports.*

If a more favorable balance of trade is realized through a decrease in the volume of imports, the effect on home production, employment and income will still be the same as an increase in home investment.[2] A reduction in imports would, by transferring demand from foreign to home-produced commodities, increase the consumption of domestically-produced goods.[3] Total consumption would remain unaffected, because there simply occurs a change in the composition of the output consumed, i.e. more domestic but fewer foreign-produced goods are demanded. Although such a diversion of demand may not generate an increase in total consumption, it does cause an increase in that part of consumption which is locally produced. And to the extent that there now exists a greater demand for such domestic goods, additional home labor and capital will have to be utilized for their production.

The benefits resulting from the substitution of home produced goods for commodities previously imported are not restricted to an immediate increase in domestic employment and a greater utilization

---

1. J. H. G. Pierson, op. cit., p. 90.
2. W. A. Salant, op. cit., pp. 211-212.
3. N. S. Buchanan, op. cit., p. 171.

of plant capacity. For to service the new demand for goods, heretofore produced and purchased from abroad, it may be necessary to create additional plant and equipment. This activity is, of course, synonymous with an increase in domestic investment, and apart from providing another offset to the volume of the community's savings,[1] will lead to a primary increase in the level of home employment. This primary increase in the level of employment and income will stimulate a further demand for consumer goods and, so long as it is exercised for domestic goods, will induce a secondary increase in home employment and income. The overall increase in national income and employment will, of course, ultimately depend upon the size of the investment multiplier.[2]

---

1. Ibid.
2. A nation's commercial policy can exert a sizable influence on the volume of secondary employment forthcoming from an increase in investment expenditures. A protectionist trade policy, for example, will, by curtailing the volume of imports, reduce the size of the leakage which is associated with the receipt and allocation of income. In effect, a greater proportion of the income received will be spent for home-produced goods and to this extent will increase the size of the multiplier. Such an increase in the value of the multiplier means that each additional dollar spent on capital formation will generate a greater amount of income in the home economy.

   A free trade policy, on the other hand, will, by increasing the level of imports, increase the leakage factor and thereby reduce the size of the multiplier. This means that the secondary employment associated with an increase in investment outlays, under conditions of free trade, will not be so large as under conditions of restricted trade. The inference to be derived from this, therefore, is quite clear - if a nation, which is experiencing less than full employment, is desirous of maximizing the amount of employment and income forthcoming from an additional investment outlay, it should give serious consideration to the pursuance of a restrictive trade policy.

The advantages forthcoming to the home economy from a restriction of imports may also be looked at from another point of view. As already indicated, a reduction in the volume of imports, unaccompanied by a similar diminution in the level of exports, will increase the trade surplus. But an increase in the foreign balance has the same salubrious effects on the home economy as an increase in the level of home investment. Thus, with consumption remaining constant[1] and an expansion occurring in the level of total home investment, owing to the improvement in the foreign trade balance, it follows that the level of aggregate demand will increase. And as aggregate demand increases, the levels of domestic output, employment and income must rise accordingly.

b. <u>Given a condition of widespread unemployment, Keynes' theory of employment is biased towards protectionism, because such a trade policy will enhance the volume of investment which, in turn, will increase the level of domestic employment and income</u>.

As has been established in the preceding sections, an improvement in the foreign trade surplus, whether it be realized through an increase in the volume of exports or a reduction in the level of imports, will exert the same expansive effect on domestic production, employment and income as does an increase in home

---

1. Total consumption remains constant, for, although there occurs a reduction in the purchase of foreign goods, this is counterbalanced by an increase in the consumption of import-substitute goods.

investment.¹ Like an increase in domestic investment, it offsets a part of the economy's savings and immediately generates a primary increase² in the level of home employment and income. And to the extent that this income is then spent for home-produced consumer goods, it will lead, via the multiplier, to a secondary increase of employment and income in the system.³ Thus, from the standpoint of a single country, an improvement in the trade surplus is just as effective a means of bolstering employment and income as is an increase in domestic capital formation.

---

1. Although an increase in foreign investment has the same advantage for the domestic economy as does an extension of home investment, such does not hold true for the world in general. Whereas an increase in home investment generates an increase in employment for the whole world, an improvement in the trade surplus of a particular country will make possible an increase in its employment only by reducing the amount of employment in other countries. For the world as a whole the overall level of employment remains the same, since a decline in the imports of one country represents a decline in the exports of other countries. Consequently, not all countries can hope to achieve at the same time a favorable balance of trade as a means of expanding domestic employment. (Vide R. Stevens, op. cit., p. 40.)
2. Professor N. S. Buchanan claims that the effects on primary employment which result from an improvement in foreign investment are not likely to be so great as those associated with an increase in home investment. For, whereas an increase in domestic expenditure for capital equipment, v.g. rolling stock, will definitely create additional employment and income, "an increase in the volume of foreign investment may be realized out of inventories and to the extent that these are depleted and not replaced there will be no appreciable effect on primary employment." However, Professor Buchanan admits that after the first act of expenditure, the secondary effects for home and foreign investment are the same. (Vide N.S. Buchanan, *International Investment and Domestic Welfare*, op. cit., pp. 144-149 and p. 172.)
3. W. A. Salant, "The Domestic Effects of Capital Export under the Point IV Program," *American Economic Review*, XL, 2, May, 1950, pp. 495-510.

This identity between foreign and domestic investment has definite implications for a country which is experiencing difficulty in locating sufficient investment outlets at home to offset the community's desired level of savings, i.e. the difference between total output and domestic consumption. Because an increase in the foreign trade balance, whether it be achieved through an increase in exports or a reduction of imports, is synonymous with an increase in investment, an economy in such straits may, by instituting a protectionist policy, achieve a higher level of investment and thereby maintain or even increase its level of output and employment.[1]

In view of the strategic role played by the level of investment in the theory of employment, and because a favorable balance of trade is synonymous with investment, there is a strong presumption that Keynes of The General Theory was favorably disposed towards protectionism. According to Keynes' theory, the level of employment is determined by the level of aggregate effective demand which in turn is based upon the propensity to consume and the volume of investment. Given the consumption function, the level

---

1. To this it might be objected that such a restrictive trade policy would not be effective in all countries. This, of course, is entirely correct; however, it must be noted that Keynes was not dealing here with an open system.* Rather, his preoccupation was with the problems of a closed system and for such an economy the protectionist subscription would be effective.

    * (Vide R. F. Harrod, Towards a Dynamic Economics, op. cit., p. 102.)

of employment is dependent upon the amount of investment forthcoming.[1] But since an increase in the foreign trade surplus constitutes an addition to total investment, such an improvement in the foreign balance, by raising the level of aggregate demand, helps to enhance the volume of employment and income. This is explicitly admitted by Keynes in the following passage.

> When a country is growing in wealth somewhat rapidly, the further progress of this happy state of affairs is liable to be interrupted, in conditions of laissez-faire, by the insufficiency of the inducements to new investment. Given the social and political environment and the national characteristics which determine the propensity to consume, the well-being of a progressive state essentially depends, for the reasons we have already explained, on the sufficiency of such inducements. They may be found either in home investment or in foreign investment which between them, make up aggregate investment.[2]

If, then, an increase in foreign investment is desirable for the well-being of an economy which has a weak inducement to invest, it is entirely reasonable that the government should preoccupy itself with the attainment of a favorable balance of trade,[3] as Keynes points out in the following passage.

> In a society where there is no question of direct investment under the aegis of public authority, the economic objectives, with which it is reasonable for the government to be preoccupied, are the domestic rate of interest and the balance of foreign trade.[4]

---

1. J. M. Keynes, The General Theory, op. cit., pp. 260-261.
2. Ibid., p. 335.
3. B. Banerjii, op. cit., p. 64.
4. J. M. Keynes, The General Theory, op. cit., p. 335.

But, since a restriction of imports is one means of achieving an increase in the foreign trade balance, it may be inferred that, from a Keynesian point of view, such a policy is entirely plausible for a country which is trying to overcome widespread unemployment.[1] Thus, the practical conclusion of the Keynesian theory is that, until nations have learned to provide themselves with high levels of employment, a protectionist policy, because it helps to overcome labor and capital displacement, is entirely justified.[2]

---

1. This thesis is ably supported by Professor L. Metzler. It is his claim that the classical argument against a favorable balance of trade as a permanent policy stands or falls with the classical assumption of full employment. And since Keynes rejected the notion that full employment always exists, he was bound to accept the idea that a reduction of imports through tariffs would have a definite influence on the level of employment. For, given a condition of widespread unemployment, a restriction of imports will, by adding to the volume of total investment and, therefore, to the level of aggregate demand, increase the amount of home employment. (Vide L. Metzler, "The Theory of International Trade," op. cit., pp. 250-251.)
2. J. Eaton, op. cit., p. 49.

CHAPTER XVI

KEYNES IS SYMPATHETIC TOWARDS A PROTECTIONIST POLICY IN HIS TREATMENT OF MERCANTILISM.

As in many of his previous writings, Keynes does not, in his treatment of mercantilism, make his position on commercial policy completely clear. For, although he presents several arguments in behalf of a protectionist policy, he also develops one or two arguments which can be construed in favor of free trade. On balance, however, it seems that Keynes does end up on the side of the protectionists.

At the very outset of his consideration of mercantilism, Keynes points out that, contrary to his previous views,[1] a protectionist policy can effectively raise the level of home employment.[2] And since his primary preoccupation in the General Theory is with overcoming unemployment, one is justifiably led to infer that Keynes must have been amenable to a protectionist policy.

Keynes gives further credence to this view by then asserting that, in an economy where there is a gold standard operative, it

---

1. Keynes refers here to his position of 1923 at which time he stated, "If there is one thing that Protection cannot do, it is to cure Unemployment.... There are some arguments for Protection, based upon its securing possible but improbable advantages, to which there is no simple answer. But the claim to cure Unemployment involves the Protectionist fallacy in its grossest and crudest form." (J. M. Keynes, "Free Trade," The Nation and Athenaeum, op. cit., pp. 302-303.)
2. J. M. Keynes, The General Theory, op. cit., p. 334.

is entirely proper that the Government authorities should be preoccupied with the balance of trade. For, by so exercising control over this mechanism, they can affect, both directly and indirectly, the all important investment component of aggregate demand.[1]

In an environment where large external loans and the direct investment of funds abroad are largely restricted and where the authorities have no direct control over the level of interest or the other inducements to home investment, Keynes asserts that "measures to increase the favourable balance of trade" are the only direct means available to them for increasing the level of investment.[2] Although Keynes does not specify what these "measures" are, it is clear that they constitute some form of interference with the free international flow of goods and services. But, such governmental interference with foreign trade, be it via an encouragement of exports through bounties or a restriction of imports through tariffs and other such measures, is certainly not in keeping with the tenets of free trade. Thus, given a situation wherein the inducement to invest is not sufficiently strong to guarantee a high level of employment and output, a strong argument can be advanced to show that Keynes was biased towards a restrictive trade policy as a means of bolstering foreign and thus the overall level of investment.

In addition to increasing investment activity directly, Keynes feels that preoccupation with the trade balance will also

---

1. Ibid., p. 336.
2. Ibid.

help to augment it indirectly through the instrumentality of a lower interest rate. Keynes' contention is that, if the level of wages, the state of liquidity preference and banking conventions be stable, the interest rate in a gold standard country will be largely determined by the quantity of the precious metals which is available to satisfy the community's preference for liquidity. But if the government authorities have no way of affecting the supply of money, the only way whereby this may be done is indirectly through the realization of an export surplus.[1] Therefore, by so promoting those "measures" which will assure a favorable balance of trade, the authorities will stimulate an influx of the precious metals which will help to reduce the interest rate and thus lead to an increase in the volume of home investment. Keynes summarizes his arguments for conscious control of the trade balance in the following terms.

> Thus, as it happens, a preoccupation on the part of the authorities with a favourable balance of trade served 'both' purposes; and was, furthermore, the only available means of promoting them. At a time when the authorities had no direct control over the domestic rate of interest or the other inducements to home investment, measures to increase the favourable balance of trade were the only 'direct' means at their disposal for increasing foreign investment; and, at the same time, the effect of a favourable balance of trade on the influx of the precious metals was their only 'indirect' means of reducing the domestic rate of interest and so increasing the inducement to home investment.[2]

However, no sooner has Keynes finished stating that the

---

1. Ibid.
2. Ibid.

government authorities "should pay close attention to the state of the balance of trade," because of its importance to the maintenance of domestic prosperity,[1] than he makes a complete about-face. After leading the reader to believe that preoccupation with measures which insure a favorable balance of trade is wholly justified, Keynes jolts him by warning that he is not to reach "a premature conclusion as to the 'practical' policy" to which his argument leads up, for

> There are strong presumptions of a general character against trade restrictions unless they can be justified on special grounds.[2] The advantages of the international division of labour are real and substantial, even though the classical school greatly overstressed them. The fact that the advantage which our own country gains from a favourable balance is liable to involve an equal disadvantage to some other country (a point to which the mercantilists were fully alive) means not only that great moderation is necessary, so that a country secures for itself no larger a share of the stock of the precious metals than is fair and reasonable, but also that an immoderate policy

---

1. Ibid., pp. 337-338.
2. It should be noted that Keynes does not completely exclude a protectionist policy. As a matter of fact, it may even be argued that Keynes has not changed his attitude towards a restrictionist trade policy at all, provided it can be demonstrated that a condition of widespread unemployment constitutes an exception or one of the so-called "special grounds" which admits of a protectionist trade policy. If this be the case, then Keynes' position on commercial policy is still substantially the same, viz. given a condition of widespread unemployment, a strong case can be made for a restrictive trade policy, but if this condition be replaced by one of full employment, then the free trade doctrine comes back into its own once again. (Vide Chapter 14 of this thesis for the full statement of this position.)

> may lead to a senseless international competition for a favourable balance which injures all alike.[1]

At first approximation, the reader of the above passage is led to believe that he must have erred in identifying Keynes as a protectionist sympathizer, for the above statement hardly expresses the sentiments of one who is inclined towards a restrictive trade policy. However, as Keynes develops his position, it becomes apparent that he cannot possibly adhere to such a view without contradicting himself, and, so, there still remains some force in our contention that Keynes of the General Theory was inclined towards protectionism. In further elaborating his position, Keynes asserts that he is not opposed to the laissez-faire doctrine of foreign trade, because of its commercial policy implications, but because of "the inadequacy of the theoretical foundations" upon which it rests.[2] Specifically, he takes exception with the orthodox notion that "the rate of interest and the volume of investment are self-adjusting at the optimum level," so that there is no need to be preoccupied with the balance of trade.[3] But whereas he takes exception with the classicists, Keynes praises the mercantilists for recognizing that the interest rate and the volume of investment are not self-equilibrating at the best possible level[4] and that, therefore, their manipulation

---

1. Ibid., pp. 338-339.
2. Ibid., p. 339.
3. Ibid.
4. Ibid., pp. 341-345.

of the balance of trade,[1] as a means of equating them at a high level, was not a "puerile obsession."[2]

Now, if, by his own admission, the mercantilists were justified in preoccupying themselves with the foreign trade balance for purposes of balancing the interest rate and the volume of investment at a high level, then Keynes must necessarily sanction their restrictive trade measures. For, how else could they control the trade balance in a way to insure equality between these two factors at a high level? In short, he who wills the end must will the means, and since the mercantilists had no other measures available, Keynes would have to admit that a restrictionist trade policy is a justifiable means of attaining balance between the interest rate and the level of investment. But, if a protectionist policy be correct in those circumstances wherein the interest rate and the volume of investment are not self-adjusting at an optimum level, then Keynes cannot, without contradicting himself, give a blanket endorsement to the commercial policy of the free traders. At best, he may subscribe to their practical policy only on condition that

---

1. A basic difference between the approach of the mercantilists and that of the orthodox economists of the gold standard era is that whereas the mercantilists employed the trade balance to influence the interest rate, the orthodox economists used the interest rate to affect the balance of trade. Incidentally, it is Keynes' contention that, because the orthodox economists utilized the bank rate as a means of insuring external equilibrium, "the objective of maintaining a domestic rate of interest consistent with full employment was wholly ruled out." (Vide J. M. Keynes, The General Theory, op. cit., p. 339; also vide Chapter 6 of this thesis.)
2. J. M. Keynes, The General Theory, op. cit., p. 339.

the interest rate and the volume of investment equate at an optimum level, i.e. at full employment, for at this point it is quite true that the classical doctrine becomes effective once again.

After taking the classical foreign trade theory to task for its "theoretical" shortcomings, Keynes then moves closer to a protectionist position by asserting that, insofar as dealing with "the economic system as a whole and with securing the optimum employment[1] of the system's entire resources"[2] is concerned, the methods of the mercantilists were more practical than those of the classicists.[3] But the problem of optimum employment which confronted the mercantilists was, of course, the same one which he was trying to solve during the inter-war years. And because the restrictive techniques of the mercantilists did succeed in raising the level of domestic activity, it is not surprising that they should make a favorable impression upon him.

---

1. Although Keynes attaches a high degree of importance to the mercantilists' attempt to secure an optimum level of employment, this was by no means the primary objective of their system.
2. J. M. Keynes, The General Theory, op. cit., p. 340.
3. Although Keynes believes that the mercantilistic contributions to the study of the economic system as a whole and to the determination of employment and output "may have attained to fragments of practical wisdom," he makes it quite clear that classical theory, too, has its place in the study of economics, as note his following observation. "Regarded as the theory of the individual firm and of the distribution of the product resulting from the employment of a given quantity of resources, the classical theory has made a contribution to economic thinking which cannot be impugned." (Vide J. M. Keynes, The General Theory, op. cit., pp. 339-340.)

Keynes is particularly impressed by the mercantilists' attempt to maintain the level of home employment by getting rid of a surplus of domestic goods through the channels of foreign trade.¹ Keynes asserts that the early economic thinkers of the 16th and 17th centuries were justified in so doing, because of the chronic tendency for the propensity to save to be stronger than the inducement to invest.² But this chronic tendency to over-save was the same problem confronting him in the mid-'thirties; hence, if he considered the exportation of excess goods and the attending restriction of imports by the mercantilists as effective means of increasing home employment, there is a strong presumption that he, too, must have looked with favor upon these measures in his own time and place.

Summary

To sum up Keynes' commercial policy views as found in his consideration of the mercantilists, it may be said that, although he showed some hesitancy at one or two points in fully subscribing to their restrictive trade views, it must be concluded that in the overall he was pretty much in accord with their policies.³ And

---

1. Such an attempt to dispose of excessive home-produced goods in foreign markets clearly implies a need for restrictions on imports, for if the inflow of foreign goods increases to the same extent as the outflow of domestic goods, then obviously this effort will be self-defeating.
2. J. M. Keynes, The General Theory, op. cit., pp. 346-348.
3. There are many economists who believe that Keynes read into the mercantilistic doctrines more than was warranted. Prof. R. F. Harrod, for example, states that Keynes appears "to have seized on isolated passages to find wisdom that was not

well he might be, for they sought to solve the same problems that he did, i.e. chronic over-saving and unemployment. Moreover, the mercantilists tried to solve these problems through the same media that he did, viz. the promotion of low interest rates and a high level of investment.

In view of the fact that the mercantilists were more successful in adjusting the interest rate and the level of investment, through their manipulation of the foreign trade balance, than were the classicists, who were content to look upon these factors as self-adjusting, it is only natural to presume that Keynes was more biased towards the restrictionist methods of the mercantilists than towards the laissez-faire policies of the classicists. Thus, albeit Keynes does not explicitly state anywhere in his section on mercantilism that he is in favor of a protectionist policy, his sentiments certainly seem to be inclined more towards it than towards free trade.

---

3. really there." Keynes' own attitude on this matter can be best inferred from his following reaction to Professor Harrod's observation. In a letter to Mrs. Joan Robinson, dated 3rd September, 1935, he wrote, "Roy strongly objects to Chapter 26* as a tendentious attempt to glorify imbeciles." (* Keynes is referring here to an earlier draft of his General Theory. In the published work, his treatment of mercantilism appears in Chapter 23.) (Vide R. F. Harrod, The Life of John Maynard Keynes, op. cit., p. 460.)

CHAPTER XVII

KEYNES' FOREIGN TRADE VIEWS IN THE
PERIOD PRIOR TO WORLD WAR II

In the years between the publication of his General Theory of Employment, Interest and Money and the outbreak of World War II, Keynes' views respecting international economic policy remained essentially biased towards restricted trade. Although his literary output was greatly reduced during this period, especially after the heart attack which he suffered in the summer of 1937, Keynes did, in his limited pronouncements, make it quite clear that he was still inclined towards protectionism.

As during the earlier phases of his career, Keynes, in the period immediately prior to the outbreak of World War II, continued to adhere to the principle that international economic policies should be made subordinate to considerations of a purely national character, v.g. high employment, and not the other way round.[1] To realize this objective, Keynes came to depend more and more upon planned trade.[2] This may be readily established by reference to a

---

1. S. Harris, John Maynard Keynes, Economist and Policy Maker, New York, Charles Scribner's Sons, 1955, p. 187.
2. It will be recalled from our consideration of Keynes' foreign trade views as contained in the Treatise on Money that he started to move in the direction of planned trade as early as 1930. However, it is the view of Professor Harrod that Keynes really reconciled himself to a policy of planned trade after 1933. It was in this year, it will be remembered, that Keynes came out in favor of national self-sufficiency. (Vide R. F. Harrod, The Life of John Maynard Keynes, op. cit., p. 568.)

number of his articles and letters which appeared in the London Times from 1937 to 1939

The economic recovery in Great Britain in early 1937 provides our first illustration of the manner in which Keynes would dovetail foreign trade considerations with those of a domestic nature. He points out that a retractable policy in foreign trade is just as essential as a reversable policy in the fiscal operations of government. With respect to fiscal policy, he says, "Just as it was advisable for the Government to incur debt during the slump, so for the same reasons it is now advisable that they should incline to the opposite policy."[1] And insofar as trade policy is concerned, he points out that, just as it was proper to check imports and undertake other restrictive measures to assist the balance of trade during the slump, so, too, it is now advisable to shift in the opposite direction.[2] However, this does not constitute a blanket endorsement of free trade, for he makes this easing of restrictions contingent upon the level of employment, as note the following qualification.[3]

> I should like to see a temporary rebate on tariffs wherever this could be done without throwing British resources out of employment.[4]

---

1. J. M. Keynes, "How to Avoid a Slump II – Dear Money," The London Times, Jan. 13, 1937, p. 13.
2. Ibid.
3. N. B. Keynes makes this a temporary and not a permanent arrangement.
4. J. M. Keynes, "How to Avoid a Slump II – Dear Money," op. cit., p. 13.

In explaining the implications of such an easing of trade restrictions during a recovery period, Keynes asserts that such a policy must be expected to unbalance the foreign account, due to the higher prices which will have to be paid for raw materials and the general increase in the level of activity. This deterioration of the trade balance under such circumstances should be viewed with equanimity, avers Keynes. In fact, it is highly desirable for the British economy that the raw material countries should be given the opportunity to replenish their gold and sterling reserves by sending their goods to it.[1] This policy is desirable for two reasons. First, the influx of foreign goods will serve to abate the inflationary pressures at home, and, secondly, the accretion of gold and sterling resources in the hands of these foreign countries will help to sustain demand for the products of British industry when home demand starts to fall off. Keynes summarizes the virtues of this policy as follows.

> This policy is doubly desirable. First, because it will help to relieve a temporarily inflated demand in the home market. But secondly, because a policy of allowing these countries to increase their resources in 1937 provides the best prospect of their using these resources to buy our goods and help our export industries at a time when an increased demand in our home market is just what we shall be wanting.[2]

From the foregoing it is clear that Keynes would utilize commercial policy as a means of controlling the movements of the trade cycle. In the case of a large importing and exporting

---

1. *Ibid.*
2. *Ibid.*, p. 14.

country such as England, it would appear that fiscal policy of itself would be inadequate to cope with this problem. Fiscal operations would necessarily have to be supplemented by some form of planned trade,[1] and it appears that this is precisely what Keynes has in mind, as witness his following contention.

> These, (fiscal and commercial policy) I urge, are the methods which will best serve to protect us from the excesses of the boom and, at the same time, put us in good trim to ward off the cumulative dangers of the slump when the reaction comes, as come it surely will.[2]

Keynes' advocacy of planned trade may be further evidenced from a pronouncement made by him in October, 1938 in favor of a barter system of trade.[3] Surprising as it may seem, Keynes' recommendation of barter agreements in international trade was largely motivated by a consideration of the high level of labor productivity which obtained in Great Britain and the United States at this time.

Keynes points out that between 1930 and 1935 there occurred in Great Britain an annual increase of 4 to 5 per cent in worker productivity.[4] In the United States, the results were approximately the same, with productivity per worker increasing at the annual rate of $4\frac{1}{2}$ per cent between 1929 and 1935.[5] Keynes was

---

1. This point will be given additional consideration below.
2. J. M. Keynes, "How to Avoid a Slump II - Dear Money," op. cit., p. 14.
3. J. M. Keynes, "Foreign Trade - The Barter Aspect," The London Times, Oct. 7, 1938, p. 10.
4. Ibid.
5. Ibid.

particularly impressed by the gain in the United States, "because the comparison is between a boom year and one of sub-normal activity, so that no assistance was gained from an increase in the scale of production."[1]

As a result of this increase in productivity in both Britain and the United States, the employment of workers, measured in man-hours, fell by an even greater percentage than the volume of physical production.[2] In the United States, for example, physical production in 1935 fell to 87.4 per cent of what it had been in 1929; whereas, the number of man-hours worked fell by almost a third to 68.7 per cent of the 1929 figure.[3] The inference to be drawn from this is that the increase in labor productivity further aggravated the employment problem in both Britain and the United States, since it made possible an increase in production with fewer workers.

Given these circumstances of rapid technological progress unaccompanied by a corresponding increase in demand, Keynes felt that it would be possible to service Great Britain's economic needs with "an unchanged value of plant."[4] As a result, entrepeneurs should be able to take care of all their new plant costs out of depreciation reserves without having to avail themselves of current net savings. This, though, would cause a further

---

1. _Ibid._
2. _Ibid._
3. _Ibid._
4. _Ibid._

aggravation of the already serious problem of finding sufficient new investment outlets to offset the community's propensity to save.[1]

In addition to this lack of profitable new investment opportunities, other factors, in Keynes' estimate, which were making it difficult for Great Britain as well as the United States to achieve full employment in 1938 were the rate of interest, the psychology of business, the propensity to save and the current distribution of incomes. Under these circumstances, avers Keynes, " It becomes increasingly improbable that anything approaching full employment can be maintained without abnormal loan expenditure by the Government."[2]

However, Keynes cautions that this problem must be attacked on a number of additional fronts. As indicated above, one of these is the foreign trade sector. To keep Great Britain's trade balance from becoming a source of disinvestment and an additional source of labor displacement, Keynes urges that appropriate machinery be established to equate the value of British exports and imports. This means, in effect, that Keynes was favoring a barter system of trade, as may be seen in the following statement.

> In the circumstances of the moment I suggest that the balance of trade position and the net disinvestment in this country's foreign assets which is probably going on also needs particular attention - not, indeed, by an aggravation of tariffs but by a new, and now necessary, machinery for linking up exports with imports, so as to make sure that those from whom we buy spend a reasonable proportion of the proceeds in corresponding

---

1. Ibid.
2. Ibid.

purchases from us.¹ We can no longer afford to leave the barter aspect of foreign trade to look after itself.²

Keynes' advocacy of a bilateral approach was by no means a passing thing,³ for in the spring of 1939 he was still pretty much preoccupied with this question. He now tried to demonstrate the importance of such a mechanism to the successful carrying out of the Government's loan expenditure program.⁴

An increase in domestic expenditures carries with it a threat to the balance of foreign trade, for, although a nation's demand for imports will surely increase as its income is augmented, there is no

---

1. So long as imports and exports are equated through bilateral trade agreements, there is no possibility of incurring an import balance which is, of course, tantamount to foreign disinvestment and therefore harmful to domestic employment and income. With imports and exports in equilibrium, the effect on the domestic economy would at worst be neutral. In fact, there is a strong possibility than an increased demand for exports, although accompanied by a like increase in the volume of imports, will stimulate the level of home employment and income, should the enhanced export activity lead to an increase in capital formation.*

    * This argument has been advanced by Professor R. F. Harrod.
2. J. M. Keynes, "Foreign Trade - The Barter Aspect," op. cit., p. 10.
3. In fact, Keynes was espoused to this bilateral approach at least as late as the autumn of 1941. This may be established from Professor Harrod's brief account of a conversation which he had with him at this time. "I ran into him about this time in a Treasury corridor; he was leaning against a door-post. 'You must give up the bilateralist approach,' I said, 'and come down on the American side.' 'No,' he said, 'I must pursue both lines of thought...both.' His expression was enigmatic. He seemed to be transfixed with a curious immobility that was unlike him. Some deep inscrutable thoughts were proceeding. Even his great brain was baffled by this problem." (Vide R. F. Harrod, The Life of John Maynard Keynes, op. cit., p. 526.)
4. J. M. Keynes, "Crisis Finance - I - Employment and the Budget," The London Times, April 17, 1939, pp. 13-14.

assurance that exports will increase correspondingly.[1] Therefore, because of this lack of any nexus between a nation's volume of imports and level of exports, Keynes feels that the trade balance can, in these circumstances, be safeguarded only through a conscious linking of imports and exports.[2] Accordingly, he says,

> The handling of foreign trade cannot be left to individual enterprise unaided. For individuals have no machinery for the linking of imports to exports which is now essential for our financial strength. This is an urgent problem of immense difficulty - not less so because the solution is so contrary to our traditions and our preferences.[3]

As an additional means of maintaining control over the balance of payments, Keynes urged a tightening up of the embargo on the transfer of capital funds to overseas by British citizens.[4] Keynes recognized that it would be impossible in peace time to plug every loophole. However, he believed that it would be enough simply to issue a directive to all private and institutional investors and to banks and brokers forbidding new transactions on capital account which involve a remittance of funds to abroad, unless approved by the Government. By so restricting the movement of these funds, he felt that the whole of the country's liquid capital resources could be held in reserve to meet adverse trade balances[5] as well as to

---

1. Ibid., p. 13.
2. Ibid.
3. Ibid.
4. J. M. Keynes, "Crisis Finance - II - The Supply of Savings," The London Times, April 18, 1939, p. 15.
5. An embargo on the movement of funds to abroad would not on" enable the Treasury to cope with any eventual deficit in nation's foreign balance, but would also assist it in t' financing of its loan expenditure program. According

provide for foreign political loans. Moreover, such an embargo on capital transfers would enable the Treasury to administer its loan expenditure program without regard to external considerations. For these reasons, concluded Keynes, "It is a small measure of sacrifice to ask from owners of capital: that they should refrain from running away."[1]

Summary

To indicate Keynes' position on foreign trade between the publication of The General Theory and the outbreak of World War II, we may say that he moved even closer to a policy of restricted international trade and finance. Although it be true that Keynes had not been in favor of an open free trade system for some time, he had, nonetheless, held out at least some hope for international cooperation in the

---

5. Keynes, if it be assumed that the volume of current savings cannot escape abroad, because of this stricture on capital movements, then this amount of savings is necessarily available to the Treasury. Should it be further assumed that there is no trade deficit, then the income of the community will be equal to Government plus private expenditures. And the difference between the community's aggregate income and what individuals spend is equal to savings and therefore available to the Treasury for payment of taxes and the extension of loans. If, however, any part of this savings were to be diverted abroad in the form of a foreign loan, this would mean that the Treasury would be financing part of its domestic program with its gold reserves. Thus, to the extent that a nation can avoid a trade deficit and succeed in preventing the leakage of capital resources to abroad, it may finance its domestic expenditures without any loss of gold. In such circumstances, the only concern of the Treasury would be with the physical capacity of the country to carry out the Government's program. (Vide J. M. Keynes, "Crisis Finance - II - The Supply of Savings," op. cit., p. 15.)
1. J. M. Keynes, "Crisis Finance - I - Employment and the Budget," op. cit., p. 14.

monetary sphere. Certainly this may be evidenced from his writings as late as 1935.[1] However, in the period following the publication of The General Theory, Keynes not only remains adamant in his opposition to a free trade system, but even abandons the cause of multilateral monetary cooperation, as note his conversion to bilateralism.

As indicated many times in this thesis, the shaping of Keynes' thinking respecting international economic policy was largely determined by the internal requirements of the home economy, and the home economy was, of course, Britain. Keynes' advocacy of planned trade through barter agreements and the control of capital movements was, in effect, simply another attempt to meet the internal needs of his country. The conscious linking of imports and exports through bilateral agreements would obviate the disinvestment attending Great Britain's foreign trade. And the regulation of capital transfers to abroad would permit the Treasury to undertake a loan expenditure program, which was designed to fill the void in home investment without fear of impairing its gold reserve position.

The above evidence, then, gives further demonstration of Keynes' abiding concern with the domestic welfare of Great Britain and, even more significantly, of his subordination of international economic policies to purely national considerations.

---

1. J. M. Keynes, "The Future of the Foreign Exchanges," Lloyd's Bank Monthly, Oct., 1935, op. cit., pp. 527-535.

PART IV

KEYNES OF THE WORLD WAR II ERA

Scope of Part IV

During the latter half of the 'thirties, Keynes devoted much less attention to monetary problems than he had at any time in the past and, as a result, his concern with international economics fell off appreciably. Keynes' interest in international trade and finance was expressed largely through the effects which they exerted on the domestic interest rate and on national monetary policy; hence, it was only natural that his de-emphasis of money should also cause him to accord less attention to international economics.

It was only well after the outbreak of World War II that Keynes returned once again to the monetary sphere and more particularly to the area of international economics. In this field he spent the last academic as well as physical efforts of his life.[1] Numbered among his contributions of this period are the Clearing Union plan, his deliberations at Bretton Woods and his efforts in behalf of the Anglo-American Financial Agreement - achievements which we shall have occasion to examine in the ensuing chapters of this section.

---

1. S. Harris, "International Economics: Introduction," The New Economics, op. cit., pp. 257-258.

CHAPTER XVIII

THE INTERNATIONAL CURRENCY PROPOSALS

During the autumn of 1941, Keynes, who was now in the service of the British Treasury, turned his attention to the international economic problems that would confront Great Britain in the post-war period. Of particular concern to him was the tremendous balance of trade difficulties that would be inherited by her at the conclusion of hostilities. Keynes understood well the need for Britain to retain in the post-war period the system of international trade which it had developed during the emergency - a system characterized by tight controls, blocked accounts and bilateral bargains.[1] But however expedient such arrangements might have been, Great Britain could not resort to them in the post-war world. For in accepting Lend-Lease assistance from the United States, at a time when such aid was vital to her, she committed herself to the elimination of discrimmation and the reduction of other trade obstacles.[2]

Keynes understood well the implications of Great Britain's pledge to pursue a non-discriminatory trade policy in the post-war world; hence, the only way out would be to devise measures which would help to solve Great Britain's post-war trade difficulties and

---

1. R. F. Harrod, The Life of John Maynard Keynes, op. cit., p. 525.
2. This "consideration" was ultimately written into Article VII of the Mutual Aid Agreement (Feb. 2, 1942.) It called for "the elimination of all forms of discriminatory treatment in international commerce and...the reduction of tariffs and other trade barriers." Incidentally, this clause was incorporated into the Agreement largely at the instigation of Mr. Cordell Hull who was U. S. Secretary of State at the time.

at the same time be acceptable to the United States. Therefore, it was out of this attempt to meet the American point of view[1] that was born Keynes' plan for greater international monetary cooperation - the Clearing Union. In these proposals, Keynes set forth the minimum terms on which the British could find it possible to set aside their authority and participate in a movement for greater freedom of international trade.[2]

---

1. Apart from the fact that Great Britain would have to accept the State Department doctrine, if it expected to receive favorable American treatment after the war, Professor R. F. Harrod feels that Keynes moved towards greater international cooperation at this time for still another reason. According to Professor Harrod, Keynes could not subscribe to a policy of international cooperation during the pre-war period, because most nations of the world had not as yet been won over to his system of economics. But during the early 'forties, it seemed that the world was becoming more amenable to his point of view, and so it might now be possible to apply Keynesian economics on an international as well as on a national level.

    Professor Harrod states his argument in the following terms. "He, like the Americans, disliked reverting to the law of the jungle. His instincts were for international cooperation. If these instincts had been dormant in the years before the war,* that was because such cooperation seemed impracticable; the internationalists tended to be those who had not accepted Keynesian economics, and to hand international arrangements over to them would, in his judgment, be fatal. Until the world should be converted to his views, one must aim at trying them out in Britain, even if this meant some insulation. But was the world changing now?.... Perhaps the time was almost ripe to attempt to apply Keynesian thought on a world scale; that would be much better than doing so on a national scale only."

    * The fact that Keynes' "instincts for international cooperation" had been "dormant" during the pre-war period implies Harrod's admission that during the 'thirties, at least, Keynes could not be counted among the ranks of the free traders. (Vide R. F. Harrod, The Life of John Maynard Keynes, op. cit., pp. 525-526.)

2. R. F. Harrod, The Life of John Maynard Keynes, op. cit., p. 526.

In formulating his scheme for an International Clearing Union, Keynes obviously had to abandon the bilateralist approach which he had espoused prior to the outbreak of World War II. However, this change of attitude did not cause him to contradict his basic position respecting the priority of domestic over international considerations. For, in advocating greater international monetary cooperation, both in his own scheme and later at Bretton Woods, Keynes made this priority of domestic considerations the sine qua non for such cooperation. He was absolutely emphatic in demanding that this greater monetary cooperation among nations should in no way circumscribe their authority in the determination of domestic policies. Thus, in setting forth his own plan and in later subscribing to the tenets of the International Monetary Fund, Keynes did not in any way contradict the principle of national monetary independence[1] which he had fought so zealously for from the early 'twenties to the mid-'thirties.

In subscribing to greater international cooperation, it should be understood that Keynes did so only in the field of money. His attitude on commercial policy did not, insofar as may be determined from the Clearing Union proposals, undergo any radical change at this time. Although he approved of greater international cooperation in the monetary sphere, he did not, by reason of this, endorse a similar policy of multilateralism and free dealing on the side of commercial policy. This may be clearly evidenced from the following statement

---

1. S. Harris, "International Economics: Introduction," *The New Economics, op. cit.*, p. 253.

made by Professor Harrod.[1]

> Now that Keynes' enthusiasm was harnessed to his own scheme, (The Clearing Union) his ambivalence on the main issue of an internationalist as against a Schactian policy in the field of money and foreign exchange faded out. His own natural internationalism came to the surface. There had been a consistent thread running through all his work on public policy from the Tract to the Means to Prosperity, advocating an international handling of the monetary problem as the correct solution for our troubles. It must be recorded, however, that he continued to have grave doubts until a very late stage of the feasibility of a return to an open-non-discriminatory system in commercial policy.[2]

Although it be true that Keynes did not, by virtue of his support of greater monetary cooperation among nations, sanction a return to an open free trade system, it should not be concluded that, therefore, he must have been a confirmed protectionist at this time. However, the fact of the matter is that, because of his enduring adherence to the thesis that external economic considerations should not interfere with the maintenance of domestic full employment and the pursuance of other purely domestic policies, he was still obliged to favor some restriction of international trade,

---

1. Additional proof that Keynes was still skeptical of the virtues of free trade as of 1941 may be demonstrated from his reaction to a memorandum prepared on the free trade question by Mr. Leo Pasvolsky, assistant to Mr. Cordell Hull, at this time. In his note, Mr. Pasvolsky observed that it would be a fatal mistake for Great Britain to divorce herself from her traditional policy of free trade. In retort, Keynes dubbed our State Department official "a Rip Van Winkle, who knew nought of the stresses and strains to which trade had been subjected in the 'thirties or of modern diagnoses of those maladies." (Vide R. F. Harrod, The Life of John Maynard Keynes, op. cit., p. 528.)
2. R. F. Harrod, The Life of John Maynard Keynes, op. cit., p. 531.

as he had during the pre-war period.

In formulating the Clearing Union proposals and in later supporting the International Monetary Fund, Keynes continued to uphold his pre-war conviction that each nation should be free to advance domestic policies autonomously, and more specifically, that the necessity for maintaining external equilibrium should not introduce an element of instability into home employment. But to enjoy such autonomy, a nation would have to retain control over its balance of payments, and this it could do only by exercising control over its international transactions.

To prove our contention that Keynes of the early 'forties, notwithstanding his advocacy of greater international monetary cooperation, was still in favor of some restriction of foreign trade, we must first demonstrate that, in drawing up his Clearing Union proposals and in subsequently accepting the Bretton Woods Agreement, he remained faithful to the principle of national autonomy, which he had fought so tenaciously for during the inter-war period; and then explain why such national autonomy presupposes the need for at least some degree of restriction over international trade. But before we undertake this task, it would be well to give a brief account of the Clearing Union and Bretton Woods proposals.

The Proposals for an International Clearing Union

Keynes fully recognized that there were many facets to the post-war problem of international trade and finance; however, he believed that the mechanism of currency and exchange in international trade should be given first consideration. For, unless this matter was first resolved, it would be difficult to make any progress towards the other important questions of commercial policy, investment assistance to under-developed areas and a stabilization of primary commodity markets.[1]

The main purpose of Keynes' Clearing Union Plan[2] was to assist the nations of the world to enjoy more fully the advantages of mutual trade.[3] This it hoped to accomplish by restoring a multilateral clearing of international payments.[4] Clearly, the advantages of international trade cannot be secured unless each country is first assured of facilities for spending in one country what it earns in another. However, each nation must be accorded not only the opportunity to spend its receipts in any part of the world, but it must also be assured of a sizable quantity of monetary reserves.[5] Specifically, it was this lack of adequate reserves which was largely responsible for the emergence of exchange controls and bilateral agreements during the inter-war period.

It is apparent, therefore, that, if Keynes' plan was to succeed in restoring a multilateral trading system, it would first have to

---

1. "Proposals for an International Clearing Union," reprinted in The New Economics, S. Harris, ed., op. cit., p. 324. (All ensuing quotations of this work will be taken from this source.)
2. Although the Clearing Union scheme embodied the efforts of a number of British Treasury experts, most of the credit for the plan must go to Keynes.
3. D. H. Robertson, "The Post-War Monetary Plans," The Economic Journal, LIII, 210-211, Dec., 1943, p. 353.
4. J. M. Keynes, "The International Clearing Union," (Speech delivered from the House of Lords, London, May 18, 1943), reprinted in The New Economics, S. Harris, ed., op. cit., p. 360. (All subsequent quotations of this work will be taken from this source.)
5. Ibid., pp. 360-361.

relieve the pressure on each nation's monetary reserves.[1] To accomplish this Keynes suggested that the reserves of every participating country be supplemented by according it the right to borrow from an International Clearing Union up to an assigned amount.[2] This additional purchasing power would be made available not in terms of national currencies, but in the form of bancor - an international bank-money.[3] This international currency could be created by any member of the Union in one of two ways - either by making an overdraft, i.e. by borrowing funds from the Union, or by selling gold to it.[4]

Under the Keynes Plan the value of bancor would be defined by the Governing Board in terms of gold; however, it would be subject to change from time to time. Although bancor could not be redeemed in gold, it would be accepted as the equivalent of gold by all the members of the Union in settling their international accounts.[5] Given the gold value of bancor, the member States would then determine among themselves the initial values of their own currencies in terms of bancor.[6] Once established, however, these values could not be altered, except in special circumstances, without the consent of

---

1. R. G. Hawtrey, Bretton Woods for Better or Worse, London, Longmans, Green and Co., 1946, p. 26.
2. Ibid.
3. D. H. Robertson, "The Post-War Monetary Plans," op. cit., p. 357.
4. J. Robinson, "The International Currency Proposals," The Economic Journal, LIII, 209-210, June-September, 1943, reprinted in The New Economics, S. Harris, ed., op. cit., p. 344. (All subsequent quotations of this article will be taken from the latter source.)
5. A. W. Crawford, World Currency Stabilization Proposals, Finance Department, Chamber of Commerce of the United States, June, 1944, p. 10.
6. "Proposals for an International Clearing Union," op. cit., p. 327.

the Governing Board.[1] The reason why Keynes applied this stricture is that he hoped to achieve thereby some degree of exchange stability in the short run.[2] This, it will be recalled, was an objective pursued by him from the time of his writing *A Tract on Monetary Reform*.

Under Keynes' scheme no provision was made for a fund of stated assets at the time of its organization. Instead, overdraft facilities were to be made available to each participating nation.[3] Each country would have assigned to it a quota which would determine how much credit, stated in terms of bancor, it might receive from the Clearing Union.[4] In exchange for this line of credit each member country would accept the obligation to accumulate credit balances to the same extent to which the debtor nations would utilize their over-draft privileges at the Clearing Union.[5]

In reference to the size of the quotas, Keynes suggests that they should be proportioned to the volume of foreign trade conducted by each country.[6] Accordingly, he recommends that the quota for

---

1. *Ibid.*
2. In the period following their abandonment of the gold standard, Great Britain, the United States, France and the other major powers attempted to iron out seasonal and other short-term fluctuations in the external value of their currencies through the mechanism of exchange equalization funds. These national funds tried to stabilize their currencies by selling their own money when it appeared to be appreciating inordinately and by buying it when it seemed to be depreciating excessively. (Vide S. Enke and V. Salera, *International Economics*, second edition, New York, Prentice-Hall, Inc., 1951, pp. 109-111.)
3. A. W. Crawford, *op. cit.*, p. 8.
4. R. G. Hawtrey, *The Balance of Payments and the Standard of Living*, London, The Royal Institute of International Affairs, Oxford University Press, 1950, p. 91.
5. G. N. Halm, "The International Monetary Fund," *The Review of Economic Statistics*, XXVI, 4, Nov. 1944, p. 172.
6. J. M. Keynes, "The International Clearing Union," *op. cit.*, p. 360.

each member should initially be equal to 75 per cent of its total annual exports and imports averaged over the last three years prior to the war.[1] On the basis of this formula, the total world quota would amount to circa 35 billion dollars.[2] This figure would not remain fixed for all time. For after the transitional period, each participating country's quota would be recalculated every year on the basis of a five year moving average of its total exports and imports.[3] Consequently, these quotas would rise or fall automatically with a change in the aggregate value of international trade, and so would be pretty much geared to the needs of commerce.[4]

---

1. J. H. Williams, "International Monetary Plans," *Foreign Affairs*, XXIII, 1, Oct. 1944, p. 43.
2. F. A. Lutz, "International Monetary Mechanisms - The Keynes and White Proposals," *Essays in International Finance #1*, Princeton, N.J., International Finance Section, Princeton University, July, 1943, p. 4.
3. "Proposals for an International Clearing Union," op. cit., p. 328.
4. This feature of the Keynes Plan was deemed inflationary by the creditor countries, the argument being that an increase in world prices would lead to an increase in the size of the quotas and the additional purchasing power forthcoming from the enhanced quotas, would, in turn, induce a further rise in prices. In effect, quotas and inflation would feed upon each other. (Vide F. A. Lutz, "International Monetary Mechanism - the Keynes and White Proposals," op. cit., p. 8.)

    In retort to this allegation it might be pointed out that the inflationary bias of the Bancor Plan is really not so great as might at first appear. For the full effect on quotas of a price increase in any one year would be spread over a period of five years. For example, if the world price level increased by 20 per cent in a particular year, the quotas at the next annual revision would be increased by only 4 per cent. Despite this slight increase in its quotas, each member nation might still have to resort to deflation as a means of bringing back its money flow and price level into due relation with its monetary reserves and quotas. (Vide R. G. Hawtrey, *Bretton Woods for Better or Worse*, op. cit., p. 27.)

In practice, the Clearing Union would operate in the following manner. A country incurring an unfavorable trade balance may, through its Treasury or Central Bank, draw upon its overdraft facilities which it has available in the Clearing Union.[1] The Union will thereupon make the following entries in its books: on the assets side it will record the value of the loan in terms of bancor which it has granted to the country drawing the check and, on the liabilities side, it will enter the same amount to the account of the member which receives and deposits this check with it.[2] The Union would create financial resources only as determined by the needs of its members. As deficits occur in the international accounts of certain member States, those countries experiencing export surpluses would be called upon to extend the requisite credit to them.[3] Considered from the overall point of view, this simply means that the creditor nations as a group extend credits to the debtor nations as a group. Whereas countries with favorable balances of payments would develop credit balances, countries experiencing unfavorable balances would incur debit balances in the Clearing Union.[4]

The idea underlying Keynes' proposal is quite simple. Fundamentally, it is based on the same principle which supports a closed banking system, namely, the necessary equality of credits and

---

1. J. Robinson, "The International Currency Proposals," op. cit., p. 344.
2. F. R. Lutz, op. cit., pp. 4-5.
3. A. H. Hansen, *International Monetary and Financial Programs*, New York, Council on Foreign Relations, 1944, p. 13.
4. A. W. Crawford, op. cit., p. 13.

debits.[1] If the credits earned cannot be removed outside the Clearing system, but can only be transferred within it, the Union can never run the risk of being unable to honor checks drawn against it. It can make any advances it wishes to the participating countries, because it is absolutely certain that these moneys will be returned to it via the clearing accounts of other members.[2] In short, the Union creates its own funds through the debiting and crediting process and, so long as member countries with export surpluses are willing to extend credit to those with import balances, it need never run short[3] of funds.[4]

Under the Bancor Plan, each participating country looks upon its quota in the Union as a reserve of international currency similar to the gold reserve which it held under the gold standard.[5] Instead of surrendering gold to satisfy the claims against it, a country, under the Clearing Union mechanism, would simply draw on its overdraft facilities. This using up of its quota would correspond to a nation's losing gold reserves under the international gold standard. Similarly, an increase in a member's credit balance at the Union would correspond to an accretion of its gold reserve under the gold standard system.[6] The accumulation of such a credit balance

---

1. "Proposals for an International Clearing Union," op. cit., p. 327.
2. Ibid.
3. G. N. Halm, op. cit., p. 172.
4. So long as a creditor nation promises in advance to accumulate an unlimited amount of bancor credits, it follows that no currency may become scarce. This is the reason, therefore, why the Keynes Plan failed to deal with any scarce currency clause as does the International Monetary Fund.
5. F. A. Lutz, op. cit., p. 7.
6. Ibid.

with the Clearing Union may be further likened to the importation of gold in that the country holding it is voluntarily abstaining from the immediate use of purchasing power.[1] However, the analogy between the Clearing Union and the international gold standard ceases at this point. For, unlike the importation of gold, an improvement in a member's credit balance would not involve any withdrawal of purchasing power from circulation nor the application of deflationary pressures on the community of nations.[2] Thus, under the Keynes Plan, the creditor countries do not withdraw from use that which they do not choose to employ for the time being. Instead, they provide the Clearing Union with the resources for extending loans to those countries which need them. In this manner, their accumulation of bancor credit does not in any way restrict the world's capacity either to consume or to produce.[3]

These properties of Keynes' Clearing Union make the analogy between it and a closed banking system complete. A person who deposits a part of his income in a commercial bank does not cause any inconvenience to others, because the balances which he keeps idle are used to finance their business.[4] Whereas, if that individual were to hoard a part of his income in the form of gold coins in his pockets or in his safe, this would exert a serious deflationary effect on the economic system.[5] Thus, the development of national

---

1. "Proposals for an International Clearing Union," op. cit., p. 331.
2. Ibid., pp. 331-332.
3. Ibid., p. 332.
4. Ibid.
5. J. M. Keynes, "The International Clearing Union," op. cit., p. 363.

319

banking systems, by enabling individuals as well as business enterprises to hoard in the form of bank deposits rather than in the form of coin, has provided the facilities for offsetting a sizable portion of the community's hoarding.[1] By extending this same banking principle to the international sector through the agency of his Clearing Union, Keynes hoped "to offset the contractionist pressure which might otherwise overwhelm in social disorder and disappointment the good hopes of our modern world."[2]

Although the Clearing Union can never run into financial difficulty, Keynes recognizes that measures are necessary for preventing the piling up of credit and debit balances without limit. For, unless the clearing system possesses "sufficient capacity for self-equilibrium"[3] to achieve this objective in the long run, the plan would be doomed to failure.[4] In considering measures for dealing with large-scale disequilibrium, the Keynes Plan gives attention to both the problems of the chronic debtor and the chronic creditor nations.

Consider first the position of a chronic debtor country. Under Keynes' scheme, each country has an initial reserve which is a once-for-all endowment. Therefore, there is a risk that the clearing mechanism will break down because some improvident country has exhausted its quota and has no means left with which to meet its

---

1. Ibid.
2. "Proposals for an International Clearing Union," op. cit., p. 332.
3. Ibid., p. 327.
4. Ibid.

obligations.[1] To deal with such situations is a very delicate matter, for it may appear to involve interference with a country's internal policies – a prospect very much abhorred by Keynes.[2] Nonetheless, some provision must be made for deterring nations from constantly living beyond their means.

Accordingly, the Bancor Plan stipulates that a member nation may run an overdraft up to a quarter of its quota without sanction; however, should it incur an average debit balance in excess of this amount, it would have to pay a penalty of 1 per cent per annum on it.[3] Should a country's average overdraft be greater than one-half of its quota, it would have to pay a penalty of 2 per cent per annum on this excess.[4] However, before it would be granted permission to increase its debit balance to this amount, the participating country might be requested to satisfy all or any of the following requirements. In the first place, it might be ordered to reduce the exchange value of its currency by a stated percentage.[5] Secondly, it might be requested to impose controls on outward capital transactions. Thirdly, it might be asked to surrender outright to the Union a suitable proportion of its gold or other liquid reserves in its possession. Lastly, the Governing Board of the Union might

---

1. J. M. Keynes, "The International Clearing Union," op. cit., pp. 361-362.
2. "Proposals for an International Clearing Union," op. cit., p. 324.
3. F. A. Lutz, op. cit., p. 11.
4. J. Robinson, "The International Currency Proposals," op. cit., p. 352.
5. A country whose debit balance exceeds one-fourth of its quota may, on its own initiative, depreciate the external value of its currency by an amount up to 5 per cent. However, any subsequent devaluation would require the approval of the Governing Board of the Clearing Union.

recommend to the member State whatever internal measures it might deem appropriate for the restoration of equilibrium in its international balance.[1] But while a member country might be permitted to increase its debit balance to a figure in excess of one-half of its quota, this balance may not under any circumstances exceed its quota.[2] In fact, should a participating country's average debit balance over the course of a year exceed three-quarters of its quota, that country may be declared in default by the Union and denied additional facilities.[3]

Keynes by no means places all of the responsibility for the world's trading difficulties on the improvidence of debtor countries. Turning his attention to the creditor countries, he points out that they, too, must be held accountable for the world's trading problems. For by withdrawing international money from circulation and hoarding it, instead of returning it to the international spending stream either through the purchase of goods for home consumption or through foreign investment, these creditor nations can exercise a strong deflationary pressure on all other countries.[4] It is only in recent times, avers Keynes, that we have come to realize more fully that employment and income can only be maintained through the expenditure of income previously earned on goods and services.[5] This is just as

---

1. "Proposals for an International Clearing Union," op. cit., p. 328.
2. Ibid., p. 330.
3. J. Robinson, "The International Currency Proposals," op. cit., p. 352.
4. J. M. Keynes, "The International Clearing Union," op. cit., p. 362.
5. Ibid.

true in the foreign as it is in the domestic sector. Foreign countries can, by hoarding reserves beyond their reasonable needs, generate world-wide deflation and unemployment. Thus, because of the implications which the accumulation of large credit balances may have for world prosperity, Keynes feels that his plan should address itself to this problem. This, though, is not an easy task, for a creditor country is likely to be even more averse to outside interference and advice than is a debtor country.[1]

Under the Keynes scheme, there is no limit set on the size of credit balances as there is on debit balances.[2] The only limitation on the size of a particular country's credit balance is imposed on it from the debtor side.[3] This may be illustrated in the following way. On the supposition that all nations joined the Clearing Union, the total value of quotas would amount to 36 billion dollars.[4] Assuming that the United States were the only creditor nation in the world, the size of its credit balance could not possibly exceed circa 24 billion dollars. For with the United States debit quota fixed at 3 billion dollars, this would mean that the debit quotas of all other countries would amount to 33 billion dollars. But since these other countries could avail themselves of only three-fourths of this amount, it follows that their debit balances or, too, the United States credit balance could not exceed much more than 24

---

1. Ibid.
2. "Proposals for an International Clearing Union," op. cit., p. 330.
3. J. Robinson, "The International Currency Proposals," op. cit., p. 346.
4. The average annual value of world imports and exports for the 3 years prior to the war was 48 billion dollars and 75 per cent of this figure would clearly be equal to 36 billion dollars.

billion[1] dollars.[2] Thus, under the Keynes Plan almost the entire value of all overdraft privileges could, theoretically, become the credit balance of a single country.[3]

Although it is entirely conceivable that a nation's credit balance might equal the sum of the overdraft quotas assigned to all other countries, this cannot happen in practice, for, as we have already noted, there are many strictures applied on debtor countries which would preclude such a possibility. Moreover, the Clearing Union also provides measures for dealing with an excessive credit balance. In the first place, a creditor country must pay a penalty of 1 per cent on that part of its credit balance in excess of one-quarter of its quota and an additional 1 per cent on that part of its balance in excess of one-half of its[4] quota.[5] In the second place, the Governing Board would discuss with a member, whose credit balance has exceeded one-half of its quota, appropriate measures it might pursue to restore equilibrium in its international account. These measures would include domestic credit expansion, exchange appreciation, reduction of trade barriers and the extension

---

1. J. Robinson, "The International Currency Proposals," op. cit., p. 346.
2. Although the United States credit balance was in fact limited under the Clearing Union, American officials who studied the proposal insisted that for all practical purposes it constituted an "unlimited liability." (Vide R. F. Harrod, The Life of John Maynard Keynes, op. cit., p. 542.)
3. G. N. Halm, op. cit., p. 172.
4. J. Robinson, "The International Currency Proposals," op. cit., p. 346.
5. Professor F. A. Lutz claims that this proposal to tax the balances of creditor countries is a feeble attempt to implement Silvio Gesell's idea of taxing cash balances in the field of international finance. (Vide F. A. Lutz, "International Monetary Mechanism - the Keynes and White Proposals," op. cit., p. 11.)

of international development loans. But though the Clearing Union authorities might recommend these and other courses of action to it, the creditor country would retain the right to accept or reject them.[1]

This imposition of at least some measure of responsibility on creditor nations for assisting debtor countries in the restoration of equilibrium constitutes a novel approach to the solution of international economic problems. Keynes' inclusion of this provision in the Clearing Union proposals was, no doubt, largely motivated by his strong dislike of deflation.[2] For he was convinced that it would be far more damaging to the debtor nations to have them pursue deflationary policies, in an attempt to achieve equilibrium, than it would be to the creditor countries to have them expand their foreign investments and purchases of imports.[3]

One of the more surprising features of Keynes' Clearing Union scheme is its connection with gold. But there are a number of important reasons why Keynes did well to incorporate gold into his plan.

For one thing, gold still possessed tremendous psychological value; hence, there remained a strong desire on the part of nations to set aside gold reserves for unforeseen contingencies.[4] Also, by making some provision for gold in his plan, Keynes was more certain

---

1. "Proposals for an International Clearing Union," op. cit., p. 329.
2. It should be noted that Keynes had consistently advocated expansive policies for the solution of economic problems from the time of his writing A Tract on Monetary Reform in the early 'twenties. (Vide Part I of this thesis.)
3. A. Smithies, op. cit., p. 592.
4. "Proposals for an International Clearing Union," op. cit., pp. 334-335.

of receiving the support of the gold interests and the conservatives.[1] And most important of all, it would be completely futile to ask the United States and the British Empire to demonitize their gold stocks."[2] Keynes understood well the strong position enjoyed by the precious metal in these countries and he recognized even more clearly that no international currency proposal would have much of a chance of being accepted unless it made some provision for the monetary use of gold.[3]

Although Keynes did make some provision for gold under his scheme, the yellow metal would not perform the same function that it did under the traditional international gold standard. For, although gold might be exchanged for bancor, there was no provision in the plan for the free convertibility of bancor into gold. Were this the case, gold reserves would have to be maintained against bancor balances, with the result that the Clearing Union scheme would be made synonymous with the international gold standard. However, there is nothing in the exchange of bancor for gold which would admit of such a possibility. The Clearing Union scheme would simply provide for "a one-way convertibility"[4] and in this way would supplant gold as a governing factor,[5] although it would not dispossess it completely from its traditional use. By such means Keynes hoped to avoid "the many obvious difficulties and disadvantages of proposing that the

---

1. G. N. Halm, op. cit., p. 170.
2. J. H. Williams, op. cit., p. 43.
3. F. A. Lutz, op. cit., p. 8.
4. J. M. Keynes, "The International Clearing Union," op. cit., p. 361.
5. A. W. Crawford, op. cit., p. 10.

old money, gold, should be demonitized."[1]

In view of the fact that the Clearing Union is concerned with current trade transactions, it is not within its province to deal with capital movements. Nonetheless, it is Keynes' opinion that each country should, according to its own needs, establish some measure of control over both inward and outward capital movements.[2] This control should be exercised not only over hot money flows which arise out of exchange speculation or which are attributable to political considerations, but also over the aggregate of new long-term investments which private citizens and business are free to make overseas. Control over the latter type of capital outflow is especially important in Keynes' estimate, for, unless the volume of new foreign investment forthcoming is limited to an amount no greater than the size of the favorable trade balance, the monetary authority will lose control over the domestic rate of interest.[3] Thus, if the monetary authority wishes to retain control over the all important domestic rate of interest, it is absolutely essential that capital movements be controlled.

Although Keynes strongly favored control over capital movements, this should not be interpreted to mean that he was completely opposed to international investment. His purpose was simply to discourage the extension of those loans and credits which would serve to create

---

1. J. M. Keynes, "The International Clearing Union," op. cit., p. 361.
2. "Proposals for an International Clearing Union," op. cit., p. 335.
3. J. M. Keynes, "The International Clearing Union," op. cit., pp. 353-354.

an imbalance in a nation's external accounts. This, Keynes thought, could be accomplished by setting up some sort of capital control authority in each country.[1] The main responsibilities of such an agency would be to distinguish the legitimate long-term loans of creditor nations from those loans of debtor nations which serve to engender international disequilibrium and to control all types of short-term speculative movements.[2] But, however essential the institution of this capital control machinery may have been in the post-war economic environment, Keynes did not regard it as a responsibility of the Clearing Union. For he felt that the method and degree of control over capital movements should be left to the discretion of each member country.[3]

In addition to the clearing function, Keynes thought that the Union might also perform other valuable international services. In fact, it might eventually serve as the nucleus of an economic government of the world. More proximately, however, he thought that it could assist international bodies charged with post-war relief, rehabilitation and reconstruction by serving as their fiscal agent.[4] The Clearing Union organization could also be used to promote price stability and to control the trade cycle. This it could do in concert with other international organizations, v.g. an International Economic Board, by exercising contractionist or expansionist

---

1. "Proposals for an International Clearing Union," op. cit., pp. 336-337.
2. Ibid.
3. Ibid., p. 336.
4. Ibid., p. 338.

influence on the system as a whole or on particular countries in the system.[1] However, these suggestions do not raise any important issues affecting the fundamental constitution of the proposed Union. These are cited simply to complete the picture of the wider purposes which the Clearing Union structure might have served had it been accepted at Bretton Woods.

The International Monetary Fund

Although Keynes' Clearing Union proposal had great merit, his plan was turned down in favor of that presented by the American Treasury expert, Harry Dexter[2] White.[3]

The basic difference between the Keynes and White proposals rests in their treatment of reserves. Whereas Keynes had suggested that monetary reserves be supplanted by the drawing of advances in the form of bancor from the Clearing Union, Harry White recommended that an International Fund be created to which each member country should contribute a quota of its own currency plus gold. Unlike the Clearing Union scheme, these quotas would be paid into the Fund in

---

1. Ibid., p. 339.
2. For a point by point comparison of the Keynes and White proposals vide J. Robinson, "The International Currency Proposals," reprinted in The New Economics, op. cit., pp. 342-358.
3. Keynes' proposal was largely turned down for two reasons. First, it was believed by the Americans that under the terms of the Bancor Plan the liability of the United States might become grossly excessive. Second, the notion of an international institution creating international credit and lending it on overdraft to the Central Banks of those countries experiencing balance of payment difficulties was entirely too novel to most of the conferees. (Vide J. H. Williams, "International Monetary Plans," op. cit., p. 43. Also Cf. "The Joint Currency Scheme," The London Economist, CXLVI, 5253, April 29, 1944, pp. 560-561.)

advance.[1] Thus, should a "credit balance" country accumulate claims on other members of the system, these claims would be exercised against monetary assets actually on deposit in the Fund.[2] And in the case of "debit balance" countries, they would draw upon this reserve of foreign currencies by exchanging their money (within limits) for whatever foreign exchange they might require.[3]

Under the White Plan each country's quota was determined by an index representing its gold stocks, its level of national income and the fluctuations of its balance of trade.[4] On the basis of these calculations, the total value of all quotas contributed to the Fund would be equal to $8,800 millions. Of this amount, $2,750 millions would be subscribed to by the United States. The United Kingdom and the Soviet Union would be alloted quotas of $1,300 millions and $1,200 millions respectively. And seven other nations would account for $2,400 millions, leaving a balance of $1,150 millions to be subscribed to by the remaining 35 member States. These quotas would be satisfied by a deposit of national currencies and gold. The gold portion would be equal either to 25 per cent of the prospective member country's quota or to 10 per cent of its net official holdings of gold and United States dollars, whichever is less.[5]

---

1. R. G. Hawtrey, Bretton Woods for Better or Worse, op. cit., p. 34.
2. A. H. Hansen, International Monetary and Financial Problems, op. cit., p. 14.
3. R. G. Hawtrey, Bretton Woods for Better or Worse, op. cit., p. 34.
4. J. Robinson, "The International Currency Proposals," op. cit., p. 345.
5. R. G. Hawtrey, Bretton Woods for Better or Worse, op. cit., p. 34.

330

Another very significant difference between the Clearing Union and the International Monetary Fund scheme which was adopted at Bretton Woods is that whereas the former could create its own resources through the expansion of debit and credit balances, the latter can not. For its resources are restricted to a pool of national currencies made available to it by the participating countries. Thus, because the Clearing Union did not have to depend upon any prior contribution from its members, but could create, instead, its own international bank money (bancor) through the extension of credit to deficit countries, it was potentially far more expansive than the International Monetary Fund.

A final difference between the Keynes Plan and the International Monetary Fund is to be found in their manner of dealing with debtor and creditor countries. The Clearing Union was less uniform than the Fund in its treatment of deficit and surplus countries.[1] Under the provisions of Keynes' proposal, deficit countries were permitted to draw bancor checks only up to 75 per cent of their respective quotas, while no direct limitation was placed on the obligation of surplus countries to accept these checks. There was, however, some indirect check placed on the accumulation of credit balances, for, as limitations are imposed on the increase of debit balances, these will also serve to limit the size of the credit balances accruing to surplus countries.

Under the terms of the International Monetary Fund, limitations

---

1. G. N. Halm, *Monetary Theory* (Second Edition), Philadelphia, The Blakiston Company, 1946, p. 271.

331

are placed on both debtor and creditor nations in a more uniform way. Consider first the case of the debtor countries. According to the provisions of the Bretton Woods Agreement, each member of the Fund is entitled to purchase foreign exchange from it by depositing with it a like sum of its own national currency.[1] However, a member is not entitled to buy the currency of another member from the Fund without limitation. In the first place, a participating country may not be entitled to buy a national currency which has been declared to be in short supply by the Fund.[2] Furthermore, the proposed exchange of a particular country's currency for that of another country would have to be such as not to cause the Fund's holdings of the purchasing member's currency to increase by more than 25 per cent of its quota during the twelve months preceding the date of purchase. This restriction would apply only if the proposed purchase of the member's currency would cause the Fund's holdings of that currency to exceed 75 per cent of its quota. But at no time could the Fund's supply of a particular national currency exceed 200 per cent of its[3] quota.[4]

---

1. It should be noted that a member purchases currency from the Fund. It does not borrow the required foreign exchange, for the Fund is not a lending organization as the Clearing Union would have been. Thus, instead of paying off a "loan" of foreign currency, the member nation, to delete its obligation with the Fund, simply repurchases its own currency with other currencies or gold when it is able. (Vide A. G. Hart, Money, Debt and Economic Activity, New York, Prentice Hall, Inc., 1948, p. 405.)
2. U. S. Department of State, Articles of Agreement of the International Monetary Fund, Washington, D.C., U. S. Government Printing Office, 1945, p. 6.
3. Ibid., pp. 7-8.
4. These provisions refer only to the purchase of foreign exchange with paper currencies. They do not apply to an exchange of foreign currencies for gold.

In addition to these strictures on the purchase of foreign currencies, the Fund tries to discourage deficit countries from availing themselves too freely of its facilities by imposing certain charges on them. Any member country which procures the currency of another country from the Fund must pay a service charge of 1/2 to 1 per cent on the amount purchased.[1] In addition to this service charge, a member which has on deposit with the Fund an average daily balance of its own currency in excess of its quota, is subject to the following charges. On amounts not exceeding 25 per cent of its quota, a member State is not required to pay anything for the first 3 months; however, it is obliged to pay 1/2 per cent per annum for the next nine months and thereafter it must pay an additional 1/2 per cent for each subsequent year. On amounts greater than 25 per cent, but less than 50 per cent of its quota, a member is required to pay an additional 1/2 per cent for the first year and an additional 1/2 per cent for each subsequent year. And on each additional bracket of 25 per cent in excess of its quota, the deficit country is constrained to pay an additional 1/2 per cent for the first year and an additional 1/2 per cent for each subsequent year.[2] This means that a country which has purchased foreign exchange over a three year period, at an annual rate of 25 per cent of its quota, would, at the expiration of that third year, have to pay an interest charge of 1 1/2 per cent per annum on the balances of its currency held by the Fund over and above its regular quota.

---

1. U. S. Department of State, *Articles of Agreement of the International Monetary Fund*, op. cit., p. 8.
2. *Ibid.*, pp. 8-9.

Whenever the Fund's supply of a member's currency reaches a point where the interest charge which applies to any of the above brackets for any period is equal to 4 per cent, the Fund and the member in question shall consider means whereby the Fund's holdings of its currency can be reduced.[1] Although the Fund Agreement does not specify what "means" are to be urged upon the deficit member, the possibilities are well known. Fundamentally, the deficit country will either have to increase its exports or decrease its imports. This it may attempt to do through deflation, depreciation of its currency, import restrictions, subsidies to exports and exchange control.[2]

Although there is nothing in the Bretton Woods Agreement explicitly debarring a member from resorting to deflation, it is not likely that the Fund authorities would rely too heavily upon it,[3] for one of the purposes of the organization is to provide members with an opportunity "to correct maladjustments in their balance of payments without resorting to measures destructive of national or international prosperity."[4] It is far more likely that the Fund authorities would urge exchange depreciation upon the deficit country,[5] provided, of course, that they are convinced that the disequilibrium is fundamental and that it can be cured by a

---

1. Ibid., p. 9.
2. G. N. Halm, Monetary Theory, op. cit., p. 276.
3. R. G. Hawtrey, Bretton Woods for Better or Worse, op. cit., p. 36.
4. U. S. Department of State, Articles of Agreement of the International Monetary Fund, op. cit., p. 1.
5. G. N. Halm, Monetary Theory, op. cit., p. 277.

devaluation of the currency.[1] The Fund authorities might also suggest exchange control for the deficit country if they feel that the cause of the disequilibrium is to be found in a long and continued outflow of capital.[2] Under these circumstances, member countries may exercise such controls as are necessary to regulate international capital transfers.[3] However, the Fund Agreement cautions that no member may ordinarily employ these control instruments to restrict payments for current transactions or to delay unduly transfers of funds in

---

1. Under the clauses of Article IV, Section 5, the Fund Agreement provides that a member can propose a change in the par value of its currency only on condition that such an alteration is expected to correct a fundamental disequilibrium. If the proposed change, together with all previous changes, does not exceed 10 per cent of the original par value, a member may alter the value of its currency without incurring any objection from the Fund. Should the suggested change be equal to more than 10 but less than 20 per cent of the initial par value, the Fund may either concur or object, but must make its position known within three days if the member so requests. If the desired change is equal to 20 per cent or more, the Fund may concur or object, but will be entitled to a longer period in which to render its decision. However, should the Fund be convinced that such a change is required to correct a condition of fundamental disequilibrium it will agree to the proposed change. Provided that this condition is satisfied, the Fund cannot reject the request of the member country to alter the value of its currency on any other grounds, v.g. opposition to a suggested change "because of the domestic, social or political policies of the member proposing the change." (Vide U. S. Department of State, Articles of Agreement of the International Monetary Fund, op. cit., Article IV, Section 5, pp. 4-5.)
2. G. N. Halm, Monetary Theory, op. cit., p. 276.
3. With respect to this question of international capital transfers, it should be indicated that, like the Clearing Union, the International Monetary Fund is opposed to the use of its resources for the financing of such capital movements. Accordingly, the Fund Agreement stipulates that members should exercise whatever controls are necessary to prevent such employment of its funds. Should a nation fail to abide by this regulation, it may have its privileges in the Fund revoked. (Vide U. S. Department of State, Articles of Agreement of the International Monetary Fund, op. cit., p. 9.)

settlement of previous commitments.[1]

Let us now consider the fashion in which the Fund deals with the surplus countries. A member becomes a surplus country when the Fund's holdings of its currency become less than the amount which was originally contributed[2] to it.[3] This "surplus" position becomes critical when "the demand for a member's currency seriously threatens the Fund's ability to supply that currency."[4] When the Fund finds that a general scarcity of a particular country's currency is taking place, it may issue a report citing the causes of the scarcity as well as suggested measures for overcoming that scarcity. However, the Fund Agreement, unlike the Clearing Union plan, does not disclose what these measures shall be.

To replenish the Fund's supply of a "scarce" currency, the authorities may ask the country in question to exchange its currency for gold or, too, they may propose that it extend a loan of its currency to the Fund on terms and conditions mutually agreeable.[5] The fact that the Fund Agreement does provide for such a limitation constitutes a basic difference between it and the Clearing Union. The latter, it will be recalled, did not impose any rigid restriction upon the size of a surplus nation's credit balances in the Fund.[6]

---

1. Ibid., p. 10.
2. The supply of a surplus country's currency is reduced, because the deficit countries are exchanging their currencies for it. In effect, the Fund accumulates the currencies of deficit countries and loses those of surplus countries.
3. G. N. Halm, Monetary Theory, op. cit., p. 277.
4. U. S. Department of State, Articles of Agreement of the International Monetary Fund, op. cit., p. 11.
5. Ibid., p. 10.
6. "Proposals for an International Clearing Union," op. cit., p. 330.

336

If, despite its efforts to increase its supply of a particular currency, the Fund should fail, it may thereupon "declare such currency scarce and shall thenceforth apportion its existing and accruing supply of the scarce currency with due regard to the relative needs of members, the general international economic situation and any other pertinent considerations."[1] The Fund may also authorize its members, after consultation with it, to place limitations on the freedom of exchange operations in the scarce currency.[2] The members would have complete freedom in selecting the type of exchange control to be used. However, it must be understood that this exchange control machinery is not to be of a permanent nature, nor is to be more restrictive than is necessary to balance the demand for the scarce currency with its supply.[3]

These are but some of the more pointed differences between the Clearing Union Plan and the International Monetary Fund. But despite these and other less consequential differences, it should not be

---

1. U. S. Department of State, Articles of Agreement of the International Monetary Fund, op. cit., p. 11.
2. The scarce currency clause of the Bretton Woods Agreement carries a serious implication for the surplus country. For should that member's currency be declared "scarce", it will have to consent to exchange control by the Fund and its other members, which means, of course, that its goods will be subject to discrimination in foreign markets.

    This prospect of having its exports discriminated against constitutes a good inducement for creditor countries to assist debtor nations in achieving equilibrium in their foreign accounts. In effect, the scarce currency clause serves to place a large measure of responsibility on the surplus countries for the maintenance of general international equilibrium. (Vide A. E. Robinson, "John M. Keynes," The Economic Journal, op. cit., p. 54.)
3. U. S. Department of State, Articles of Agreement of the International Monetary Fund, op. cit., p. 11.

supposed that the two plans were completely antithetical to one another. For, albeit they differed in structure, their objectives were the same. Just as the main purpose of the Clearing Union was to promote a multilateral clearing system devoid of exchange restrictions, so, too, it was the objective of the Fund to promote "orderly exchange arrangements" and "to assist in the establishment of a multilateral system of payments in respect of current transactions between members and in the elimination of foreign exchange restrictions which hamper the growth of world trade."[1] In fact, it was precisely because the principles underlying the Fund were so much in accordance with his own views that Keynes was able to lend his support to it without fear of contradicting his former position.

Having completed our summary of the principal features of the Clearing Union and Bretton Woods proposals, we are now prepared to indicate how Keynes, in supporting these plans, sustained the principle of national autonomy. Specifically, our objective in the next chapter will be to show how many of the provisions contained in these proposals are completely in conformity with his nationalistic thinking of the 'twenties and 'thirties. And that as a result, Keynes did, in subscribing to the Clearing Union scheme and the Bretton Woods Agreement, continue to adhere to the principle evolved by him from the *Tract* to the *General Theory*, namely, that a nation should be free to gear its international economic policy to the particular needs of the domestic economy, e.g. a high level of home

---

1. *Ibid.*, p. 1.

employment, stability of prices, etc., and not the other way round. Following this, we shall then attempt to explain why at least some restriction over the channels of international trade is absolutely required for the realization of national autonomy and the promotion of purely internal objectives.

CHAPTER XVIX

KEYNES' FORMULATION OF THE CLEARING UNION AND HIS SUBSEQUENT ENDORSEMENT OF THE INTERNATIONAL MONETARY FUND AGREEMENT DID NOT CAUSE HIM TO RESCIND THE HIGH PRIORITY WHICH HE HAD ATTACHED TO NATIONAL ECONOMIC CONSIDERATIONS DURING THE INTER-WAR PERIOD, BECAUSE BOTH SCHEMES UPHOLD THE RIGHT OF EACH MEMBER STATE TO DETERMINE ITS OWN POLICIES.

Although it is true that Keynes of the Clearing Union and Bretton Woods era became more conscious of the need for international monetary cooperation, this should not be construed to mean that he therefore reduced the high priority which he had assigned to purely national economic considerations during the 'twenties and 'thirties.[1]

---

1. Neither should it be supposed that Keynes of this period was less British than the Keynes of the inter-war years. For much of his international monetary thinking of this time seems to have been inspired by a consideration of Great Britain's post-war economic needs. The large credit accommodation which he sought for prospective debtor nations is a good case in point. Keynes was quite aware that Great Britain would require large imports of foodstuffs and raw materials in the post-war period; however, he also recognized that she would not possess the necessary means with which to pay for these goods. The only way out of this dilemma would be, therefore, for other countries, principally the United States, to extend to Great Britain a sufficiently large volume of credit. This Keynes hoped to obtain through the large bancor quotas provided by his Clearing Union. (Cf. A. W. Crawford, op. cit., pp. 2-3.)

Another property of the Clearing Union which leads one to suspect that Keynes was gearing his thinking to Great Britain's post-war needs is the responsibility placed by his plan on creditor nations to assist debtor countries in achieving equilibrium in their foreign accounts.* Did the fact that Great Britain would be a debtor nation in the post-war era influence Keynes in inserting this completely novel principle into his international currency scheme? This is, indeed, a moot question; however, one cannot help but suspect that this was in fact a primary consideration.

(* The Fund Agreement sustains the Keynesian principle that "pressure should be applied on creditor as well as on debtor countries to restore equilibrium" through the "scarce currency clause.")

For in advancing his own Clearing Union plan and in later subscribing to the tenets of the International Monetary Fund, he remained steadfast to the principle that each country should be free to pursue its own domestic economic policies without fear of interference from forces of an international character.

As a matter of fact, Keynes' thinking of this period was largely based on the theoretical foundations established by him[1] in the years from 1923 to 1933.[2] As noted in the early chapters of this thesis, there is to be found running throughout all his works of this period, e.g. the *Tract* and the *Treatise*, the principle of national autonomy – the right of each nation to promote policies designed to achieve the domestic welfare without interference from the external sector. And because the Clearing Union proposals and the International Monetary Fund both reaffirm this right of national independence, our contention that, Keynes did not, in favoring greater international monetary cooperation, thereby alter his nationalistic sentiments of the 'twenties and 'thirties, is entirely justified.[3]

---

1. S. Harris, "International Economics: Introduction," *The New Economics*, op. cit., pp. 251-259.
2. In fact, one has but to review Keynes' *Treatise on Money* or his *Means to Prosperity* to find outlined herein proposals for an international monetary agency not unlike the one he advocated in his Clearing Union proposals. (Vide J. M. Keynes, *A Treatise on Money*, op. cit., vol. II, book VII; and J. M. Keynes, *The Means to Prosperity*, op. cit., pp. 28-34.)
3. Professor S. Harris lends support to this point of view as note his following comment. "Above all, he now said and reiterated that Great Britain would not subject its economy to controls from without; that a country pursuing prudent policies at home must not be embarrassed by strains originating abroad; (and) that domestic policies of each country are the primary concern." S. Harris, "International Economics: Introduction," *The New Economics*, op. cit., p. 259.

Whether one refers to the Clearing Union proposals or to the Bretton Woods Agreement to which Keynes later subscribed, one will find that in neither case did he sacrifice any important national prerogatives or authority for the sake of greater international monetary cooperation.

In fact, he expressly stipulates that the retention of this national autonomy must be one of the primary prerequisites for a workable international economic system. In the opening pages of the Clearing Union proposals, Keynes asserts unequivocally that each country should be at liberty to pursue whatever domestic policies it deems desirable for the promotion of its national welfare without fear of being subjected to interference or pressure from the external sector.[1] Moreover, he specifies that the plan should work not only to the general advantage, but to the particular advantage of each member state and that no participant must be requested to do or offer to do anything that would be counter to its own long-term interest.[2]

The International Monetary Fund also upholds this principle of national autonomy. Specifically, this guarantee of non-interference with domestic policies is contained in Article IV, Section 5 of the

---

1. Keynes' desire to insulate the domestic economy from external pressures was, no doubt, an instrumental factor in his advocating the large national quotas that he did in his Clearing Union plan. The larger a nation's quota, the less imminent is the need for it to transmit the effects of an external imbalance to the domestic economy and the longer it is able, therefore, to pursue policies designed to advance purely domestic objectives. (Vide G. N. Halm, Monetary Theory, op. cit., p. 270.)
2. "Proposals for an International Clearing Union," op. cit., pp. 324-325.

Fund Agreement.¹ This clause provides that the Fund shall not object to a proposed change in a member's exchange rate because of the "domestic social or political policies" being pursued by it.² In effect, this Article, by permitting variations in a participating country's exchange rate and by insuring its freedom to pursue whatever domestic policies it deems vital for its own welfare, lends strong support to Keynes' own position on foreign trade, namely - that a nation's external affairs should be made to conform to its internal requirements instead of the other way round.³ Thus, Keynes firmly believed that, in accepting the "manifold and substantial benefits" of the International Monetary Fund, Great Britain would not have to surrender anything which was vital for the ordering of her own domestic affairs as she saw fit.⁴ For "sovereignty was retained in the one matter where it was absolutely necessary - the right to follow an internal economic policy consistent with full employment."⁵

Nowhere did Keynes' quest for national autonomy assert itself

---

1. This principle of non-interference with domestic policies is considered to be the major concession won by the British at Bretton Woods. (Vide G. N. Halm, "The International Monetary Fund," op. cit., p. 171.)
2. U. S. Department of State, Articles of Agreement of the International Monetary Fund, op. cit., p. 5.
3. Under the international gold standard system, a nation would have to order its internal economic affairs to correspond with its external affairs. This gearing of domestic policies to a nation's external requirements was one of the basic reasons, it will be recalled, for Keynes' abhorrence of the traditional gold standard. (Vide Chapters 2-4 of this thesis.)
4. J. M. Keynes, "The International Monetary Fund," (Speech delivered before the House of Lords, May 23, 1944), reprinted in The New Economics, op. cit., p. 374. (All subsequent quotations of this address will be taken from the latter source.)
5. A. E. Robinson, op. cit., p. 55.

with greater force than in the sphere of money. The dominant theme of his monetary theory and policy was the insulation of the home economy from external forces.[1] To enable countries to undertake economic programs calculated to maximize their domestic welfare,[2] and at the same time to maintain balance in their external accounts, he recommended at one time or another in the inter-war period the following monetary policies: a flexible instead of a rigid exchange rate, an autonomous instead of an internationally determined interest rate, control over capital movements, devaluation, avoidance of deflation from abroad, widening of the gold points, greater utilization of gold reserves for meeting trade deficits, forward exchange dealings and the abandonment of the orthodox gold standard itself.[3]

It was largely as the result of his attempt to achieve national autonomy through these monetary devices, it will be recalled, that we labelled Keynes of the inter-war years an economic nationalist. And it is precisely because he tried to safeguard in the monetary plans of the 'forties the internal equilibrium of each member State through many of these same devices, that we are forced to conclude

---

1. S. Harris, "International Economics: Introduction," The New Economics, op. cit., p. 251.
2. Keynes spelled domestic welfare largely in terms of high levels of employment, output and income and stable prices.
3. Keynes also urged policies of a non-monetary character for the realization of national autonomy. One of the most outstanding of all his suggestions was the revenue tariff of 1931. Keynes hoped that, by protecting the foreign balance, the imposition of such a measure would permit the undertaking of an expansionist policy at home. For unless the international balance were so protected, such an expansive policy would induce an increase in imports and a decrease in exports, thereby causing imbalance in Great Britain's foreign account.

that he was just as much concerned with promoting the national welfare during this phase of his career as during the 'thirties.

One of the most important of all monetary policies advocated by Keynes during the period from the *Tract on Monetary Reform* to *The General Theory* for the realization of national autonomy was his advocacy of flexible over rigid exchange rates. As already noted in an earlier phase of this paper, a nation must, if it wishes to maintain the parity of its exchange, keep its efficiency-wages and other costs of production in conformity with those of other countries.[1] Consequently, it is not completely free to pursue whatever domestic policies it desires, for some of these may have a disequilibrating effect on its cost and price structure.[2] Under a flexible exchange rate system, however, there is no need for a nation to gear its internal costs and prices to those of other countries, because the external value of its currency is made to conform to its internal value, as determined by these costs and prices, instead of the other way round.[3] In effect, should there occur any variation in a nation's cost and price levels, due to the particular economic policies being pursued by it, these costs and prices would be allowed to seek their own levels and the necessary adjustment would be effected, instead, by an alteration in the external value of its currency. Thus, by freeing each member State from the necessity of keeping its cost and

---

1. J. M. Keynes, "The International Clearing Union," op. cit., p. 363.
2. J. A. Estey, *Business Cycles*, New York, Prentice Hall Inc., 1950, p. 369.
3. J. M. Keynes, "The International Monetary Fund," op. cit., p. 374.

price levels in step with those of other countries, as a means of preserving its par of exchange, a flexible exchange rate system would enable it to pursue independently whatever internal monetary and fiscal policies it deemed essential for the promotion of the domestic welfare.

The importance of a flexible exchange rate to national autonomy was fully recognized by both the Clearing Union proposals and the International Monetary Fund. Insofar as the former is concerned, we have Keynes' personal assurance that "the British proposals nowhere envisage exchange rigidity."[1] For under the terms of the Clearing Union, a member State may, subject to the approval of the Governing Board of the Union,[2] alter the value of its exchange by more than a certain amount by demonstrating that such a change is required by the actual state of its foreign trade.[3] And insofar as the latter

---

1. J. M. Keynes, "The International Clearing Union," op. cit., p. 364.
2. The reason why the Clearing Union scheme specified that changes, when made, be made by agreement and not by unilateral action is that exchange rate variations necessarily affect two parties equally. Moreover, should each member feel completely free to alter its exchange rate at random, this would frustrate one of the primary objectives of the Bancor Plan, namely, short term exchange stability.*

    (* Like the Tract on Monetary Reform, the Clearing Union sought to find the middle road between exchange fixity and the other extreme of leaving the exchanges completely subject to short-term market forces and the political and financial policies of individual countries. Ideally, the Clearing Union sought long term flexibility and short term stability of exchange rates. The latter would be especially important to a financial center such as London. Vide A. E. Robinson, op. cit., p. 54 and A. Smithies, op. cit., p. 592.)
3. J. M. Keynes, "The International Clearing Union," op. cit., p. 364.

346

is concerned, ample provision is made in Article IV of the Bretton Woods Agreement for the alteration of a member's exchange rate,[1] so that it may "conform to whatever de facto internal value results from domestic policies, which themselves shall be immune from criticism by the Fund."[2]

In view of the fact that the Clearing Union proposals and the Bretton Woods Agreement both contain provisions for the variation of exchange rates, so that they may conform to whatever internal policies a member nation may wish to pursue, it is apparent that, from this standpoint at least, they support the principle of national autonomy. This is but another reason, therefore, for arguing that, in formulating the Clearing Union plan and in later endorsing the Fund Agreement, Keynes did not contradict in any way his pre-war position on the paramountcy of domestic considerations. As during the inter-war period, Keynes did in the 'forties remain steadfast to the conviction that each nation should be free to pursue whatever domestic policies it deemed necessary for the attainment of high levels of activity without hindrance or interference from the external sector.

A principle long sought by Keynes during the inter-war period for insuring a nation's right to determine its own economic destiny was the retention of control by it over the domestic rate of interest.[3]

---

1. U.S. Department of State, Articles of Agreement of the International Monetary Fund, op. cit., pp. 3-6. Also vide the preceding chapter for a fuller consideration of this clause.
2. J. M. Keynes, "The International Monetary Fund," op. cit., p. 376.
3. Writing in 1935, Keynes asserted that, "it is essential that they (the interest rate and the volume of credit) should be employed in future with exclusive regard to internal conditions and, in particular, the state of employment." (Vide J. M. Keynes, "The

However, it would be impossible for the monetary authority to fix the interest rate to conform with internal requirements and at the same time manipulate it to cope with external gold and capital movements. Clearly, the Central Bank could utilize the interest rate instrument for satisfying domestic requirements, e.g. full employment, only on condition that it be freed from the responsibility of employing the same tool for dealing with external capital movements. To accomplish this, Keynes urged, on a number of occasions during the inter-war period, the establishment of a national capital control board with authority to scrutinize and pass upon all such capital transfers.

Keynes was just as convinced of this need for regulating capital movements, as a means of insuring control over the domestic interest rate,[1] during the Bretton Woods era as he had been prior to it. For in addressing the House of Lords in May, 1944, he averred, "We intend to retain control of our domestic rate of interest, so that we can keep it as low as suits our own purposes,[2] without interference

---

3. Future of the Foreign Exchanges," Lloyd's Bank Monthly, Oct. 1935, op. cit., p. 531.)
1. To retain control over the domestic rate of interest, the monetary authority, according to Keynes, must make certain that the overall volume of new investments which individuals are free to make overseas must not exceed the size of the favorable balance of trade. (Vide J. M. Keynes, "The International Clearing Union," op. cit., pp. 364-365.)
2. It would appear that Keynes was even more opposed to the dictation of the domestic rate of interest from external factors after 1935. For one of the main policy recommendations in his General Theory was the maintenance of a low interest rate by the monetary authority in order to stimulate the level of investment. But the interest rate cannot be so pegged, if it is to be left open to fluctuations in the volume of international trade and to "the ebb and flow of international capital movements or flights of hot money"; hence, the reason for the increased importance of freeing the domestic rate of interest

348

from the ebb and flow of international capital movements or flights of hot money."[1]

Needless to say, the Clearing Union and the International Monetary Fund both acknowledged this right of their member States to determine autonomously their own domestic interest rates, by according them the prerogative to control international capital movements. The Clearing Union, as noted in the previous chapter, advocated the setting up of control machinery to distinguish between "long-term loans of creditor countries, which help to maintain equilibrium and develop the world's resources, from movements of funds out of debtor countries which lack the means to finance them; and of controlling short-term speculative movements or flights of capital."[2] And similar provision is made by the Fund Agreement in Article VI, Section 3 which states that "members may exercise such controls as are necessary to regulate international capital movements."[3] That this clause adequately insures control over capital movements and thereby permits the realization of an autonomous interest rate policy is ably supported by Keynes in the following terms.

> Let me take first...our power to control the domestic rate of interest so as to secure cheap money. Not merely as a feature of the transition, but as a permanent arrangement, the plan accords to every member government the explicit right to control all capital

---

2. from outside forces after 1935.
1. J. M. Keynes, "The International Monetary Fund," op. cit., p. 374.
2. "Proposals for an International Clearing Union," op. cit., p. 337.
3. U. S. Department of State, Articles of Agreement of the International Monetary Fund, op. cit., p. 10.

> movements. What used to be a heresy is
> now endorsed as orthodox. In my own
> judgment, countries which avail themselves
> of this right may find it necessary to
> scrutinize all transactions, so as to
> prevent evasion of capital regulations.
> Provided that the innocent current trans-
> actions are let through, there is nothing
> in the plan to prevent this. In fact, it
> is encouraged. It follows that our right
> to control the domestic capital market is
> secured on firmer foundations than ever
> before, and is formally accepted as a
> proper part of agreed international
> arrangements.[1]

Thus, the fact that both the Clearing Union proposals and the International Monetary Fund contain provisions for the regulation of capital transfers between nations, as a means of assuring each member State the right to determine its own interest rate, gives further evidence that Keynes' thinking of the Bretton Woods era did not contravene his nationalistic thinking of the inter-war period, viz. that foreign considerations should not be permitted to interfere with the promotion and maintenance of domestic well-being.

Another important point of agreement between Keynes' thinking of the inter-war period and the international monetary proposals is that deflation, which is brought about by a raising of the bank rate and a contraction of credit, is to be shunned as a means of restoring equilibrium in a member country's balance of payments. Both monetary plans recognize, of course, the necessity for correcting external maladjustments. However, they try to effect this correction not by applying pressure on debtor countries to deflate, but by applying

---

1. J. M. Keynes, "The International Monetary Fund," op. cit., p. 375.

pressure on creditor countries to inflate. In effect, the plans shift some of the responsibility on creditor nations for the attainment of equilibrium in the foreign accounts of debtor nations. This is, indeed, a novel principle.

The Bancor Plan tried to enlist the support of creditor nations in assisting debtor countries to achieve external equilibrium by exacting a penalty on their excessive credit balances in the Union.[1] The levying of such a fine on these credit balances, Keynes thought, would force creditor countries to expand their foreign investments and purchases of imports, thereby assisting debtor nations to achieve equilibrium in their balances of payments[2] without having to resort to[3]

---

1. J. Robinson, "The International Currency Proposals," op. cit., p. 346.
2. Keynes was antipathetic towards creditor nations because he felt that their behavior was largely responsible for Great Britain's difficulties in the 'twenties. Keynes was especially irked by the policies of the United States and France during this period. Instead of utilizing their favorable trade balances to increase their imports or extend foreign loans, they demanded gold from the deficit countries. And it was this loss of the precious metal which caused Great Britain and other debtor nations to institute deflationary policies.
3. Prof. Thomas Balogh believes that Keynes hoped, through this provision, to insulate "the world economic system from the consequences of a slump in any one country by forcing that country to undertake readjustments." It is reasoned by Balogh that a country experiencing a recession would, as a consequence of its lower price level, enjoy an increase in its volume of exports. However, these increased sales to abroad would be made at the expense of foreign producers, with the result that activity, employment and income in those countries would be adversely affected. Such a transmission of economic fluctuations can be mitigated, avers Balogh, through the placing of responsibility on surplus nations to divest themselves of their credit balances. Some of the means suggested by him whereby these balances might be reduced are an appreciation of the exchange, reduction of high tariffs and an increase of money wages. (Vide T. Balogh,

deflation.¹

Insofar as the International Monetary Fund is concerned, it too tries to obviate the need for deflation on the part of debtor nations by encouraging creditor nations to pursue expansive policies. This it attempts to do through the instrumentality of its "scarce currency clause." By the terms of this article, the Fund may, if it finds it difficult to supply a particular currency, declare that currency "scarce" and thereafter ration whatever supply it may have of it. Such a declaration by the Fund serves as an authorization to any member State, after consultation with it, "temporarily to impose limitations on the freedom of exchange operations in the scarce currency."² The imposition of such exchange controls would, in effect, permit all other members to discriminate against the goods of the creditor country whose currency had been declared scarce.³

Such a stricture cannot be taken lightly by the creditor country. According to Keynes, the scarce currency clause "puts the creditor country on the spot so acutely that in the view of us all,

---

3. "The International Aspects of Full Employment," *The Economics of Full Employment*, Oxford, Basil Blackwell, 1945, p. 163.)
1. Prof. A. E. Robinson claims that the responsibility thus placed on creditor nations to assist debtors was an essential property of the Clearing Union plan, as note his following assertion. "It was an essential part of the Keynes plan that the responsibility of relative adjustment, where the existing exchange and price relations did not provide a basis for equilibrium, should be laid on creditors as well as debtors so that the pressure on the debtor to deflate and contract activity and incomes should be mitigated." (Vide A. E. Robinson, *op. cit.*, pp. 54-55.)
2. U. S. Department of State, *Articles of Agreement of the International Monetary Fund*, *op. cit.*, p. 11.
3. It should be understood that under the Fund set-up a nation whose currency on deposit in the Fund is scarce is a creditor and a member whose currency is in abundant supply is a debtor.

the creditor country simply cannot afford to let such a situation arise."[1] Therefore, rather than run the risk of suffering a reduction in the volume of its exports, a creditor country would, in all likelihood, take appropriate measures to prevent its currency from ever becoming scarce.[2] This it could do by encouraging long-term loans to abroad, stimulating purchasing power at home or increasing its volume of imports. But in pursuing these policies, a creditor country would assist debtor nations to achieve equilibrium in their foreign accounts without having to resort to deflation.

Keynes attributed the highest importance to this "scarce currency clause," for it sustained his principle that responsibility for achieving external equilibrium rests with both creditor and debtor nations.[3] The placing of such responsibility on creditor nations, he argued, would eliminate one of the main causes of the type deflation that took place in the inter-war period, namely "the draining of reserves out of the rest of the world to pay a country which was obstinately lending and exporting on a scale immensely greater than it was lending and importing."[4] For under the terms of the scarce currency clause, "a country engages itself, in effect, to prevent such a situation from arising again, by promising, should it fail, to release other countries from any obligation to take its exports, or if taken, to pay for them."[5] Such a

---

1. R. F. Harrod, *The Life of John Maynard Keynes*, op. cit., p. 571.
2. *Ibid.*, p. 544.
3. T. Balogh, *Dollar Crisis - Causes and Cure*, Oxford, Basil Blackwell, 1949, p. 207.
4. J. M. Keynes, "The International Monetary Fund," op. cit., p. 373.
5. *Ibid.*

sanction, continues Keynes, would never be allowed to come into effect, for, "if by no other means than lending," a creditor country will always seek some way of squaring its account on the "imperative grounds of its own self-interest."[1]

From the foregoing, it may be established that both the Clearing Union and Bretton Woods plans did conform to the Keynesian principle that a nation should not accept deflation as a means of forcing its domestic economy into balance with external factors. Thus, in advancing his own Clearing Union proposals and in subsequently lending his support to the International Monetary Fund, Keynes remained faithful to the thesis that a nation should be entirely free to pursue its own internal policies without embarrassment from outside forces.

Closely connected with Keynes' fight to safeguard the domestic equilibrium from disruptive external forces during the inter-war period was his repudiation of the traditional gold standard. As a proponent of national autonomy, he had no alternative but to oppose such a standard, for national monetary independence and the gold standard are antithetical. If, therefore, it can be demonstrated that the international monetary plans did not constitute a return to the international gold standard system, as was alleged in certain quarters,[2] this should further substantiate the view that Keynes did in the

---

1. Ibid.
2. In view of the facility with which one may prove the proposition that the monetary plans do not involve a reversion to the orthodox gold standard, it is difficult to understand why this misconception was entertained in high places both in the United States and Great Britain. Even the London Economist fell victim to this error. (Vide "Keynes on Gold and Sterling," The London Economist, July 15, 1944, p. 89.)

'forties remain steadfast to his pre-war conviction that each nation should enjoy a high degree of autonomy, so that it might promote the domestic equilibrium without being unduly hampered by external considerations.

Keynes' endorsement of the Bretton Woods proposals cannot be construed as a desire on his part to return to the orthodox gold standard.[1] For, although the Fund does make provision for defining national currencies in terms of gold, this of itself cannot justify its identification with the gold standard. The essence of the gold standard rests in something altogether different, as witness Keynes' contention.

> If I have any authority to pronounce on what is and what is not the essence and meaning of a gold standard, I should say that this plan is the exact opposite of it.... The gold standard, as I understand it, means a system under which the external value of a national currency is rigidly tied to a fixed quantity of gold which can only honorably be broken under force majeure; and it involves a financial policy which compels the internal value of the domestic currency to conform to this external value as fixed in terms of gold. On the other hand, the use of gold merely as a convenient common denominator[2] by means of

---

1. We have already established in the preceding chapter the fact that the Clearing Union proposals did not spell a return to the gold standard, as such; hence, our main effort in this chapter will be to show that the International Monetary Fund similarly does not involve a return to such a monetary standard.
2. As in the case of the Clearing Union, one of the more compelling reasons for introducing gold into the Fund scheme was the fact that it would be extremely imprudent for a sponsor of an international monetary plan to propose a departure from "the gold link" and at the same time hope to receive the cooperation of the powerful gold-holding countries, e.g. the United States, Great Britain and Russia. It was principally in deference to these countries that Keynes was prepared to make some allowance

> which the relative values of national currencies - these being free to change - are expressed from time to time, is obviously quite another matter.¹

As already noted in connection with our consideration of flexible exchange rates in this chapter, the International Monetary Fund nowhere stipulates that a nation's currency be tied rigidly to a fixed amount of gold or that it pursue monetary policies which will force the internal value of its currency to conform to its external value as fixed in terms of gold. In fact, the Fund recommends and makes provision for just the opposite policies. For instead of specifying that the internal value of a member's currency be made to conform to its external value, it provides that its external value be made to correspond to whatever internal value results from its domestic policies, which themselves are not to be questioned by it.²

Thus, because of the flexible nature of the monetary standard proposed by the Fund, we are forced to concur with Keynes that it is the exact opposite of the orthodox gold standard. Moreover, because it acknowledges the priority of domestic policies over the maintenance of a rigid exchange rate, we are obliged to conclude that the Fund, like the Clearing Union plan, is entirely in keeping with Keynes' desire to attain a high degree of autonomy for each nation

---

2. for gold as a common monetary denominator. In this respect, Keynes asserts, "no one in his senses would want to make gold resources of the world useless or throw the gold miners of the world out of employment." (Vide "Bretton Woods," The London Economist, August 12, 1944, p. 215.)
1. J. M. Keynes, "The International Monetary Fund," op. cit., pp. 375-376.
3. Ibid., p. 376.

356

in the pursuance of its domestic policies. The fact that both the
Clearing Union and International Monetary Fund sustain this principle gives further substance to the claim, therefore, that Keynes
did not, in supporting the monetary proposals of the 'forties,
alter his pre-war conviction that international economic considerations should be made subservient to those of a purely internal
character.

Summary

On the basis of the foregoing evidence, we may conclude that
Keynes' formulation of the Clearing Union plan and his subsequent
support of the International Monetary Fund did not cause him to
contradict in any way his position of the pre-war period, viz. that
each nation should enjoy the right to order its internal affairs
without interference from external forces. For both the Clearing
Union and the International Monetary Fund, though they sought to
promote greater international monetary cooperation, recognized
this principle of national self-determination.

This they did by incorporating into their structures various
mechanisms which would permit member States to continue their own
policies, v.g. a cheap money policy for attaining full employment,
without fear of external interference. Among the more important
principles written into the plans to insure such national autonomy
were flexible exchange rates, the right to pursue an autonomous
interest rate policy and insulation from foreign-induced deflation.

In fact, these are the very instruments which Keynes had
fought so stubbornly to establish during the inter-war period as

the means for guaranteeing to each nation the right to promote autonomously policies designed to restore or safeguard internal equilibrium. On these grounds, therefore, Keynes did not, in approving greater international monetary cooperation, impair in any way the high priority which he had assigned to purely national economic considerations in the period between the two wars.

That Keynes remained faithful to this principle of national autonomy in endorsing the currency proposals may be further corroborated by his declaration to this effect.

> Have those responsible for the monetary proposals been sufficiently careful to preserve these principles from the possibility of interference? I hope your Lordships will trust me not to have turned my back on all I have fought for. To establish those three principles[1] which I have just stated has been my main task for the last twenty years. Sometimes almost alone, in popular articles in the press, in pamphlets, in dozens of letters to The Times, in text books, in enormous and obscure treatises I have spent my strength to persuade my countrymen and the world at large to change their traditional doctrines and, by taking better thought, to remove the curse of unemployment. Was it not I, when many of today's iconoclasts were still worshippers of the Calf, who wrote that 'Gold is a barbarous relic?' Am I so faithless, so forgetful, so senile that, at the very moment of the triumph of these ideas when, with gathering momentum, governments, parliaments, banks, the press, the public, and even economists, have at last accepted the new doctrines, I go off to help forge new chains to hold us fast in the old dungeon? I trust, my Lords, that you will not believe it.[2]

Having thus established the fact that Keynes did sustain the

---

1. The three principles referred to by Keynes are a flexible exchange rate, an autonomous interest rate policy and freedom from foreign-induced deflation.
2. J. M. Keynes, "The International Monetary Fund," op. cit., pp. 374-375.

principle that each nation should be free to determine its own economic destiny, in his international monetary thinking of this period, our task in the next section of this chapter is to infer from this the proposition that each nation can enjoy such autonomy only on condition that it be accorded the prerogative to pursue a restrictive trade policy; and that, therefore, Keynes of the Bretton Woods era was still inclined towards some restriction of trade.

The Pursuance of Autonomous National Policies in Economic Matters Requires at Least Some Degree of Restriction Over International Trade.

A nation's right to pursue autonomous economic policies, especially with respect to full employment, has far-reaching consequences for international trade and commercial policy.[1] Each country is linked with all other countries through its international trade; consequently, foreign developments may, by upsetting its balance of payments, impair the execution of its specific programs. Similarly, because a nation's economic policies influence the volume of its merchandise trade and the movement of capital funds, any adverse effect on the balance of payments will interfere with its promotion of purely domestic policies.[2] In effect, foreign economic relations circumscribe a country's freedom to promote autonomous economic programs, for in order to protect its balance of payments, it may have to refrain from advancing those policies which, however essential to domestic well-being, are disruptive of external equilibrium.

---

1. N. S. Buchanan and F. A. Lutz, Rebuilding the World Economy, op. cit., p. 279.
2. Ibid., pp. 279-280.

Such a prospect would definitely be ruled out by Keynes for, as noted in the previous section of this chapter, he was quite adamant in his demand that the currency proposals[1] recognize the right of each nation to promote domestic policies without interference or pressure from outside forces. But if the carrying out of purely domestic policies, v.g. full employment, is to have priority over international considerations, as Keynes insists, then it is absolutely essential that each nation retain some degree of control over its balance of payments. This clearly implies some form of trade restriction, for to exercise such control over its foreign account a nation must regulate its imports and exports as well as the flow of capital funds into and out of its borders. Perhaps the following exposition will show more distinctly why such control over foreign trade is required to insure the success of national economic policies such as

---

1. That the Bretton Woods Agreements upheld this principle of national autonomy may further be established from the following excerpts taken from p. 280 of *Rebuilding the World Economy* by N. S. Buchanan and F. A. Lutz. "The Bretton Woods Agreements and the American *Proposals for Expansion of World Trade and Employment* (to be examined in the next chapter) explicitly recognize that the new rules for international trade must leave governments free to follow an autonomous economic policy....

   The Monetary Fund Agreement stipulates, in effect, that if a nation's full employment policy conflicts with the maintenance of stable exchange rates, the stability of the exchange rates may be sacrificed.... Similarly, a country may control capital movements if they disturb the domestic economy. Foreign exchange control on current account is permissible for a 'scarce' currency.... Many other provisions could be cited. But the important point is that both the Bretton Woods Agreements and the trade proposals attempt to prescribe standards of conduct that, while acknowledging the priority of national full employment policies, still try to minimize their adverse effects on international trade."

full employment.

As indicated above, the continuance of a nation's purely domestic policies may be threatened by an upsetting of her balance of payments, which may be caused by either external factors, v.g. an economic slump originating abroad, or by internal forces, v.g. a cheap money policy. In view of the fact that many of the effects of disequilibrium which result from internal and external causes are much the same, we can combine both of them in a single analysis.

Suppose that a depression occurs in Country A, a major industrial power. As a result of this downturn of activity, the exports of Country B and all other countries to it will be reduced. Obviously, this causes a loss of employment and income in the export industries of Country B and, unless this decline is checked in time, it is likely to lead via the multiplier mechanism to a general and cumulative depression in the home market as well.[1] Internationally, of course, Country B is confronted with a balance of payments deficit due to the reduction of its exports.[2] What measures can Country B take to cope with these problems?

In terms of the Keynesian analysis, she must try to sustain the level of aggregate demand by increasing her domestic expenditures to the same extent that foreign expenditures for her exports have been

---

1. R. Nurkse, Conditions of International Monetary Equilibrium, Princeton, International Finance Section, Princeton University, 1945, p. 11.
2. In time, the depression at home, if allowed to run its course, would bring about a reduction of imports large enough to balance the loss of exports and thus restore equilibrium in the balance of payments. Such an adjustment through deflationary means is, however, completely ruled out by Keynes.

reduced.[1] This she may attempt to do through the institution of a public works program and/or a cheap money policy. But while this may help to solve the domestic problem, it will further complicate the balance of payments difficulty. For the promotion of an expansionist monetary policy, by stimulating the level of home investment, will generate an increase in the level of employment and income. And this enhanced volume of national output and income will, in turn, cause an increase in the demand for imports of raw materials, foodstuffs and finished[2] goods.[3] But while this increase in production, prices and income in Country B stimulates a greater demand for imports, it leads to a further reduction in her volume of exports, because of the higher domestic price level which results from the expansive monetary policy being pursued in that country.[4] Thus, given this increased volume of imports and a further reduced level of exports, it is apparent that Country B is faced with an even more serious deficit in her balance of payments than if she had not undertaken an

---

1. R. Nurkse, Conditions of International Monetary Equilibrium, op. cit., p. 11.
2. A part of the increase in the aggregate income which accompanies the expansion of investment will be spent directly on increased imports of finished products; however, a much larger part is likely to be spent on domestic goods produced in part out of imported primary products. (Vide A. H. Hansen, "Economic Stability in the Postwar World," Readings in Business Cycles and National Income, A. H. Hansen and R. V. Clemence (editors), New York, W. W. Norton and Co., 1953, p. 393.)
3. J. E. Meade, Public Works in their International Aspect, London, The New Fabian Research Bureau, May, 1933, pp. 17-20. Cf. E. Staley, World Economic Development - Effects on Advanced Industrial Countries, Montreal, International Labour Office, 1944, pp. 127-134.
4. N. S. Buchanan, International Investment and Domestic Welfare, op. cit., p. 234.

expansive program.¹ Moreover, this disequilibrium in the balance of payments, caused by the imbalance between exports and imports, may be further aggravated by the fact that the prevalence of a lower interest rate at home will induce an efflux of both short-term and long-term capital funds to international financial centers paying a higher rate of return.²

It is quite conceivable from the foregoing that such a deficit in Country B's international balance of payments might be more than she could finance out of her gold reserves and foreign balances. Consequently, in order to restore equilibrium in the foreign sector, she would have to initiate opposite policies.³ By pursuing a tight money policy and a balanced budget, Country B would be better able to reverse the movement of capital funds and, by reducing incomes and prices, discourage imports and encourage exports. But in carrying out these policies, she would be pinned on the other horn

---

1. A country undertaking a policy of domestic expansion in an effort to reduce unemployment would be able to avoid such complications in its balance of payments only on condition that other countries followed suit.* In this way, domestic incomes in the various nations would move pretty much in consonance with one another, with the result that no country would have to fear a deficit in its balance of payments greater than could be serviced by its gold and other international reserves.

   * We assume, of course, that no inordinate capital movements are taking place. (Vide N. S. Buchanan and F. A. Lutz, Rebuilding the World Economy, op. cit., pp. 234-235.)

2. J. E. Meade, An Introduction to Economic Analysis and Policy, London, Oxford University Press, 1937, p. 327.
3. If the expanding nation owned a large volume of international reserves or, too, could easily borrow such reserves, it would not have to view with too great alarm the deterioration of its balance of payments position and could, therefore, continue its autonomous policies. This is the very reason, as a matter of fact, why Keynes proposed such large "bancor" balances in his International Clearing Union scheme.

of the dilemma, for she would now have to leave unsolved the pressing problem of domestic unemployment.[1] How, then, could Country B escape both horns of this dilemma? The answer to this quite simply is that she would have to "resort to restrictive measures which allow it to follow an expansionist policy without having to cope with disequilibrium in its balance of payments."[2] In effect, she would have to be in a position to restrict imports and to exercise control over foreign capital movements. This she could do by introducing the following restrictive devices: exchange rate variation,[3] exchange

---

1. B. Ohlin, The Problem of Employment Stabilization, New York, Columbia University Press, 1949, p. 45.
2. N. S. Buchanan and F. A. Lutz, Rebuilding the World Economy, op. cit., p. 234.
3. It is believed in certain quarters that, if a nation had a completely flexible exchange rate, this would automatically restore equilibrium in its balance of payments. For when a nation pursues an expansive policy, the increased demand for imports would cause its currency to depreciate "to the point where the higher prices of imports and exports (in the depreciated domestic currency) have sufficiently discouraged imports and encouraged exports to make them equal to each other again." (Vide A. Lerner, "Economic Liberalism in the Postwar World," Postwar Economic Problems, S. Harris (editor), New York, McGraw Hill Book Co., Inc., 1943, pp. 133-134. Also Cf. C. Whittlesey, International Monetary Issues, op. cit., p. 117.)

    This, though, is a simplification of the problem, for it fails to take into consideration such factors as demand, supply and income elasticities. Also, it fails to take into account the possibility that speculative capital movements would be induced by every expected change in the exchange rate and thus introduce another element of instability into the balance of payments. (Vide G. Haberler, "Some Factors Affecting the Future of International Trade and International Economic Policy," Economic Reconstruction, S. Harris (editor), New York, McGraw Hill Book Co., Inc., 1945, pp. 331-333.) To be effective, exchange variation must be combined with the control of capital movements, as suggested by the Bretton Woods Agreement. When these two instruments are so joined together, they are hardly less efficient than foreign exchange control and decidedly

control and import restriction by tariffs, quotas,[1] etc.[2] And to pursue an autonomous interest rate policy, she would have to be accorded special measures for regulating short-term as well as long-term capital[3] transfers.[4] Thus, in order for a nation to enjoy autonomy in the execution of its domestic policies, it is imperative that she utilize such restrictive devices. Should she fail to do so, then she will be constrained to gear her internal economic policies to external requirements and thus forfeit her right of self-

---

3. more effective than quotas or tariffs. (Vide N. S. Buchanan and F. A. Lutz, Rebuilding the World Economy, op. cit., p. 241.)
1. These measures would not only help to correct the foreign balance, but would also contribute on their own account towards neutralizing the fall in expenditure and employment which accompanies the decline in exports. Those restrictions which curtail imports divert the flow of expenditure from foreign goods to the home market; and those which encourage exports tend to increase or restore employment and income in the export industries. Thus, though intended to correct the balance of payments, these instruments can also exert a favorable effect on the aggregate level of home employment and income. (Vide R. Nurkse, "Domestic and International Equilibrium," op. cit., p. 278.)
2. G. Haberler, "Some Factors Affecting the Future of International Trade and International Economic Policy," op. cit., p. 330.
3. J. H. G. Pierson, Full Employment, op. cit., pp. 185-189.
4. A nation which is pursuing an expansionist policy is justified in employing these restrictive measures as a means of protecting its balance of payments. The imposition of such controls over its foreign account cannot be construed as a "beggar-my-neighbor" policy, for there is no attempt on the part of the expanding country to "export unemployment." Rather, all it tries to do is prevent any "spilling over" of its expansion program into other countries, which are not promoting such expansive policies, via an increased volume of imports. Its objective is not to reduce the exports of other countries, but to keep them from upsetting its balance of payments. Otherwise, it will be unable to continue its internal expansion program.

determination.[1]

Having thus substantiated the proposition that national autonomy requires some degree of restriction over the channels of international commerce,[2] because of the disequilibrium which would otherwise attend the balance of payments; and having established earlier the premise that Keynes was a staunch advocate of national independence in economic matters, we are thus justified in concluding that Keynes of the Bretton Woods era was still inclined towards some degree of restriction over foreign trade and finance. This conclusion may be further supported by the fact that, in advancing his own Clearing Union scheme and in later endorsing the Bretton Woods plan, Keynes made certain that adequate provisions were incorporated into these plans, whereby member States could exercise control over their international transactions, v.g. exchange control over "scarce" currencies, exchange variation and control of capital transfers.[3] And yet,

---

1. T. Balogh, "The International Aspects of Full Employment," op. cit., p. 130.
2. This is particularly important when a nation undertakes an expansive program in a depressed world environment.
3. It should not be supposed that, because the International Monetary Fund fails to consider commercial policy in the traditional sense, i.e. tariffs and commercial treaties, it does not, therefore, deal with restrictive trade measures at all. As a matter of fact, a number of its devices, v.g. currency devaluation and exchange control, are far more restrictive and at times more objectionable than tariffs. Moreover, many of the monetary instruments provided by the Fund are considered by most authorities to be part and parcel of commercial policy. Nowadays, it is quite common to include all restrictive devices, commercial or otherwise, v.g. tariffs, quotas, devaluation, marks of origin, exchange control, etc., under this heading of commercial policy. L. W. Towle, for example, defines this term as "all measures regulating the external relations of a country - measures adopted by a government to assist or hinder the export or

notwithstanding his desire to accord nations the right to impose trade restrictions as a means of safeguarding their autonomy, it would be erroneous to categorize Keynes of this period as a consummate protectionist. This, however, is a matter which will have to be considered in the next chapter.

---

3. import of goods and services." (Vide L. W. Towle, _International Trade and Commercial Policy_, New York, Harper and Bros., 1947, p. 215. Also Cf. Advisory Committe on Economics, "World Trade and Employment," _Studies in World Trade and Employment_, New York, The Committee on International Economic Policy, 1947, p. 8.)

CHAPTER XX

THE ANGLO-AMERICAN FINANCIAL ARRANGEMENTS

The end of hostilities in Europe brought no change in Keynes' status at the Treasury, for shortly thereafter he was invited by Dr. Hugh Dalton, the new Chancellor of the Exchequer, to stay on as his Financial Adviser.[1] Throughout most of the war, Keynes had been largely preoccupied with Great Britain's post-war problems; hence, when American Lend-Lease Assistance was abruptly terminated shortly after V-J Day, there were few persons in Britain better qualified than he to deal with this crisis.

Inspired by his previous successes in dealing with the Americans, v.g. Bretton Woods, Keynes suggested to his superiors that it would be entirely possible to receive from Washington ₤ 1,500 million as a free gift or, at least, as an interest free loan.[2] In setting forth his plan to the Labour Cabinet, he warned, however, that some concessions would have to be made in consideration of this grant, for the U. S. State Department was still adamant in its demand that the British implement the provisions of Article VII of the Mutual Aid Agreement.[3] Keynes had no illusions on this matter, for he knew quite well that "strings" would be attached to the assistance, "including a British commitment on open commercial policy."[4] But this was no time to worry about fundamental principles! Keynes'

---

1. A. E. Robinson, op. cit., p. 61.
2. R. F. Harrod, The Life of John Maynard Keynes, op. cit., p. 596.
3. Ibid., p. 597.
4. R. F. Harrod, The Life of John Maynard Keynes, op. cit., p. 597.

rhetoric, if not his plan, convinced the British Ministers that some effort should be made along these lines. Accordingly, they sent him to Washington at the head of a delegation to determine what credit arrangements could be made to cope with the emergency.[1]

The negotiations[2] opened on September 11, 1945 and lasted until early December of that year. In the course of these protracted discussions, the two Governments reached an understanding not only on Britain's future external financial needs, but also on a final settlement of all obligations under Lend-Lease and Reciprocal Aid.[3] The agreement was published in December, 1945[4] and was approved by Parliament within the month. Congress, however, did not ratify the agreement until July, 1946.

The principal feature of the agreement was, of course, the American loan[5] to the United Kingdom, which was designed to assist the latter in overcoming its post-war transitional difficulties.[6]

---

1. A. E. Robinson, op. cit., p. 61.
2. The loan negotiations were conducted on four separate levels: one on financial matters, one on commercial policy, one on Lend-Lease, and one on surplus property disposal.
3. Britain and World Trade, London, Political and Economic Planning, 1947, p. 68.
4. British White Paper, Cmd. 6708, Financial Agreement Between the Governments of the United States and the United Kingdom, Dated 6th December, 1945, together with a Joint Statement Regarding Settlement for Lend-Lease, Reciprocal Aid, Surplus War Property, and Claims.
5. The British also succeeded in obtaining a similar loan from Canada. The amount involved was Can. $1,136 million.
6. More specifically, Article 2 of the agreement states that, "The purpose of the line of credit is to facilitate purchases by the United Kingdom of goods and services in the United States, to assist the United Kingdom to meet transitional post-war deficits in its current balance of payments, to help the United Kingdom to maintain adequate reserves of gold and dollars and to assist the government of the United

This loan amounted to "a line of credit of $3,750,000,000" which was to be drawn upon at any time between July, 1946 and the end of 1951.[1] With respect to the amortization schedule and interest terms, the Agreement stipulated that the amount of the credit drawn by Dec. 31, 1951 should be repaid in 50 annual installments beginning on that date.[2] The interest rate on the loan was 2 per cent per annum with the interest to be computed on the amount of the obligation outstanding as of the first of January of each year. However, this interest payment could be waived in any year if the income of the United Kingdom from exports plus net income from invisible current transactions was on the average of the five preceding calendar years insufficient to finance a volume of imports equivalent to the 1936-1938 level.[3] The United Kingdom might also request to be released from this obligation if it found that such a waiver was made necessary by "the present and prospective conditions of international exchange and the level of its gold and exchange reserves."[4] To obtain this waiver of interest, though, the United Kingdom would in the year that it received this consideration have to reduce its payments or

---

6. Kingdom to assume the obligations of multilateral trade, as defined in this and other agreements." (Vide British White Paper, Cmd. 6708, Financial Agreement Between the Governments of the United States and the United Kingdom, reproduced in Appendix 2 of Rebuilding the World Economy by N. S. Buchanan and F. A. Lutz, op. cit., p. 390. All subsequent quotations of the "Agreement" will be taken from this source.)
1. Financial Agreement Between the Governments of the United States and the United Kingdom, op. cit., p. 390.
2. Ibid.
3. Britain and World Trade, op. cit., p. 69.
4. Financial Agreement Between the Governments of the United States and the United Kingdom, op. cit., p. 391.

releases of foreign-owned sterling balances proportionately.[1]

In consideration of this loan, Great Britain did, as Keynes had anticipated, have to subscribe to a number of conditions. From the standpoint of the United States, the loan was designed to accomplish a great deal more than simply assist the British in making the transition to peace. One of the primary objectives sought by the Americans through this extension of credit was the early establishment of a multilateral system of trade and exchange - a system in which nations could trade with one another in relative freedom, in which preferential treatment for the imports of certain countries would be banned, and in which international commerce would be permitted to make its maximum contribution to world prosperity.[2] But before such a system could be instituted, it was imperative that the following conditions be satisfied: the dissolution of the Sterling Area "dollar pool," the removal of exchange restrictions, the eradication of discrimination in the use of quantitative import restrictions and the settlement of the accumulated sterling balances;[3] hence, this is the reason why the United States made the granting of the loan contingent upon the United Kingdom's acceptance of these provisions. In effect, these terms which are expressly set forth in Articles 7 through 10 of the agreement constitute the so-called "strings"[4] alluded to by Keynes prior to his departure from London.

---

1. Ibid., pp. 391-392.
2. Britain and World Trade, op. cit., p. 69. Also Cf. Financial Agreement Between the Governments of the United States and the United Kingdom, op. cit., p. 394.
3. Britain and World Trade, op. cit., p. 69.
4. According to Professor Harrod, these "strings" were not novel, for they "consisted in nothing more than the reaffirmation and

During the war, exchange transactions between members of the Sterling Area[1] were subject to little restriction. However, commercial relations with countries outside of the Sterling Bloc were rigidly regulated, so as to conserve valuable dollar and gold resources. Agreements were also in force whereby all dollar and gold earnings realized by the countries within the group were pooled and allocated according to their needs for prosecuting the war.[2]

Such an arrangement was very much needed during the emergency, but to carry it over into peace-time would clearly contravene the principle of world-wide multilateralism which the Americans were presently trying to implement. Therefore, to assist them in the realization of this objective, the loan agreement stipulated that the Government of the United Kingdom complete arrangements within one year after the effective date of its approval by Congress, unless in exceptional cases a later date be set by mutual consent, for the dissolution of the Sterling Area[3] "dollar pool."[4] After the completion of such arrangements, all dollar and sterling receipts

---

4. application of the policy to which Britain had pledged herself by the signature of Article VII of the Mutual Aid Agreement." (Vide R. F. Harrod, *The Life of John Maynard Keynes*, op. cit., p. 605.)
1. The Sterling Area at the end of 1946 comprised most of the British Empire (Canada and Newfoundland excepted), Egypt, the Anglo-Egyptian Sudan, Iraq, Iceland and the Faroe Islands.
2. *Britain and World Trade*, op. cit., p. 70.
3. *Financial Agreement Between the Governments of the United States and the United Kingdom*, op. cit., p. 392.
4. Under the terms of the agreement, only the "dollar pool" was to be dissolved. The Sterling Area, as such, was entirely free to revert to its pre-war form. (Vide "Towards an Expanding World Economy," *The Banker*, London, January, 1946, p. 7.)

realized by the Sterling Area countries from their current transactions would be freely convertible into any other currency, with the consequence that any discrimination arising from the so-called sterling area "dollar pool" would be "entirely removed."[1]

Insofar as the dissolution of the Sterling Area "dollar pool" is concerned, Great Britain did not surrender so much to the Americans as might at first be supposed. For, in Keynes' estimate, there was little hope that the stronger nations of the Sterling Area would care to continue their membership in such a system beyond July, 1947.[2] Certainly, countries such as India and South Africa which enjoyed a dollar or gold surplus would prefer to make their own arrangements. However, once these surplus countries severed their relations with the "dollar pool," argued Keynes, it would be better to dissolve the whole system, for, otherwise, Great Britain would have to assume responsibility not only for her own dollar deficit, but for that of all the other members as well.[3]

Moreover, Keynes pointed out that should the British refuse to comply with the American request to dissolve the "dollar pool," and

---

1. *Financial Agreement Between the Governments of the United States and the United Kingdom*, op. cit., p. 392.
2. J. M. Keynes, "The Anglo-American Financial Arrangements," (Speech delivered before the House of Lords December 18, 1945), reprinted in *The New Economics*, S. Harris (editor), op. cit., p. 390. (All subsequent quotations of this address will be taken from this source.)
3. Keynes' desire to promote first the economic interests of Great Britain may be further evidenced in the following comment. "This arrangement (the "dollar pool") is only of secondary use to us, save in the exceptional wartime conditions when those countries were, very abnormally, in a position to lend to us." (J. M. Keynes, "The Anglo-American Financial Arrangements," op. cit., p. 390.)

thus forfeit the loan, they would be compelled to ask the owners of sterling balances not only to postpone liquidation, but also to borrow additional sums from them.[1] To prefer this alternative to the loans offered by the United States and Canada[2] would, in Keynes' estimate, constitute an act of insanity, as note his following remark.

> It seems to me a crazy idea that we can go on living after 1947 by borrowing on completely vague terms from India and the Crown Colonies. They will be wanting us to repay them. Two-thirds of what we owe to the sterling area is owed to India, Palestine, Egypt and Eire. Is it really wise to base our financial policy on the loyalty and good will of those countries to lend us money and leave out of our arrangements Canada and the United States?[3]

Should it be so decided to reject this financial assistance from Canada and the United States, then, continues Keynes, in a rather sarcastic vein,

> The alternative is to build up a separate economic bloc which excludes Canada and consists of countries to which we already owe more than we can pay, on the basis of their agreeing to lend us money they have not got and buy only from us and one another goods we are unable to supply.[4]

In the light of these considerations, the British did not, in consenting to break up the Sterling Area "dollar pool," give up so much as the proponents of such an arrangement contended, for had

---

1. Britain and World Trade, op. cit., p. 74.
2. Canada was even more adamant than the United States in demanding that Britain liberate the current earnings of the Sterling Area. (Vide J. M. Keynes, "The Anglo-American Financial Agreements," op. cit., p. 391.)
3. J. M. Keynes, "The Anglo-American Financial Agreements," op. cit., pp. 390-391.
4. Ibid., p. 392.

Britain rejected the loan, it is highly doubtful that she could have fallen back on the type of pooling arrangement that existed during and immediately following the war. But even apart from this question of alternatives, Keynes felt that it was to the best interests of the British to accede to American wishes in making sterling freely convertible.[1] For if London was to retain her position in the international banking community, it was absolutely essential that sterling be made freely convertible.[2] Keynes clearly recognized that Britain, with her dependence on invisible income and her extreme sensitivity to international capital movements, could not prosper unless sterling were convertible.[3] Moreover, only by restoring sterling to its pre-war status, he argued, could the Sterling Area be saved for Great Britain. "The way to destroy the sterling area," he said, "is to exploit it and try to live on it; the way to retain it is to restore its privileges and opportunities as soon as possible to what they were before the war."[4]

A further condition imposed by the loan agreement on the United Kingdom was that she would have to terminate exchange controls on all

---

1. The one feature of sterling convertibility that Keynes was opposed to was the early date at which it was to become effective. And it was largely as the result of his strong opposition that the Americans consented to insert a clause in Article VII of the Financial Agreement making possible the postponement of such convertibility after consultation between the two countries. (Vide R. F. Harrod, The Life of John Maynard Keynes, op. cit., pp. 605-606. And Cf. Financial Agreement Between the Governments of the United States and the United Kingdom, op. cit., p. 392.)
2. J. M. Keynes, "The Anglo-American Financial Arrangements," op. cit., p. 392.
3. R. F. Harrod, The Life of John Maynard Keynes, op. cit., p. 594.
4. J. M. Keynes, "The Anglo-American Financial Arrangements," op. cit., p. 392.

current transactions with the United States after July, 1946.[1] Hereafter, she could reintroduce foreign exchange controls on dollar payments only during such periods as the dollar was declared "scarce" by the International Monetary Fund.[2] Under the terms of this same Article (VIII), the United Kingdom also agreed to eliminate exchange restrictions on payments and transfers arising out of current transactions with all other countries by July, 1947.[3] In assuming this obligation, the United Kingdom was forced to waive her right to invoke Article XIV, Section 2 of the Bretton Woods Agreement. For under the provisions of this clause the British could have maintained during the post-war transitional period whatever exchange restrictions on current international transactions they may have deemed necessary for protecting their balance of payments.[4] In thus agreeing to make sterling freely convertible in current transactions at a time when most other countries were permitted to retain restrictions on their exchange dealings, the British did, indeed, make a major concession to the American point of view.[5]

Although the British made a sizable concession in agreeing to the removal of exchange controls, this was largely counterbalanced by the provisions contained in the agreement with respect to import restrictions. To insure that the British would not squander the

---

1. N. S. Buchanan and F. A. Lutz, Rebuilding the World Economy, op. cit., p. 123.
2. Financial Agreement Between the Governments of the United States and the United Kingdom, op. cit., p. 392.
3. Ibid., p. 393.
4. U. S. Department of State, "Articles of Agreement of the International Monetary Fund," op. cit., p. 22.
5. Britain and World Trade, op. cit., p. 70.

loan "in an orgy of reckless importing," Article IX of the agreement provided that the United Kingdom could retain its system of import licensing.[1] The only condition required for the continuance of such quantitative import restrictions was that they be administered on a non-discriminatory basis.[2] In effect, by so regulating the transactions which give rise to foreign exchange dealings, instead of controlling the exchange dealings themselves, the British could achieve the same results of foreign exchange control without having to resort to it.[3] Thus, although the British did forego the use of foreign exchange restrictions, their loss of authority over the balance of payments was not so great as might at first appear.

Lastly, the loan agreement established certain principles for the settlement of sterling balances accumulated by the Sterling Area and other countries up to the time of this understanding.[4] First, the agreement obliged the United Kingdom to make arrangements with the countries holding these balances whereby a part of these accounts would be released at once, another part "by installments over a period of years beginning in 1951" and a third part would be cancelled.[5] Secondly, it stipulated that the United Kingdom should not use any part of the proceeds forthcoming from the loan to repay its short-term

---

1. Ibid.
2. Financial Agreement Between the Governments of the United States and the United Kingdom, op. cit., p. 393.
3. N. S. Buchanan and F. A. Lutz, Rebuilding the World Economy, op. cit., p. 125.
4. As of June 30, 1945, these balances were equal to ₤ 3355 million. (Vide R. F. Harrod, The Life of John Maynard Keynes, op. cit., p. 606.)
5. Financial Agreement Between the Governments of the United States and the United Kingdom, op. cit., p. 393.

debts to other countries. And lastly, it directed that any sterling balances released or otherwise available for current payment should within one year after the effective date of this agreement, unless a later date was agreed upon both both parties, "be freely available for current transactions in any currency area without discrimination."[1]

In addition to their acceptance of the Financial Agreement, which we have briefly outlined above, the British were constrained to satisfy a number of other prerequisites before being awarded the loan. In matters of international exchange and investment, the United Kingdom was required to subscribe to both the International Monetary Fund and the International Bank for Reconstruction and Development. And in the sphere of commercial policy,[2] it was asked to accept the principles of the proposed International Trade Organization.

Having completed our consideration of the financial as well as the other clauses attending the American Loan, our next task is to discern from this agreement Keynes' attitude on the question of international economic policy as of this time. But before doing so, it should be emphasized that the Washington Agreement does not completely represent either Keynes' position or that of the British.

---

1. *Financial Agreement Between the Governments of the United States and the United Kingdom*, op. cit., p. 394.
2. The commercial proposals agreed to by Britain were published at the same time as the text of the Anglo-U.S. Financial Agreement (December, 1945) under the title of *Proposals for Consideration by an International Conference on Trade and Employment*.

   Although these proposals were accepted by the United Kingdom as a condition for obtaining the loan, Keynes had nothing to do with their formulation. In the commercial policy negotiations, Great Britain was represented by Sir Percivale Liesching and Professor Lionel Robbins.

For in the course of these negotiations, the British did not enjoy equal bargaining power with the Americans who were intent on using the loan as a wedge for instituting a non-discriminatory, multilateral trade system. The British came to Washington in desperate need of financial assistance; hence, they had to make concessions which they otherwise might not have made. Keynes and his fellow-negotiators could not afford to worry too much about principles, for they had to concentrate upon the more pressing question of what it was prudent to do here and now and in the immediate days ahead.[1] Moreover, Keynes and his associates were not permitted by the Americans to forget, as the British public was wont,[2] that by Article VII of the Mutual Aid Agreement, the United Kingdom had already obliged itself, at a time when American assistance was desperately needed, to eliminate all forms of discriminatory treatment in international commerce and to reduce tariffs and other trade barriers.[3] With these qualifications in mind, let us now turn to an appraisal of the financial and commercial clauses contained in the Washington Agreement.

Compared with the Bretton Woods plan, there is no question but that the financial clauses greatly accelerated Great Britain's movement towards a multilateral trade system.[4] And yet, there is nothing contained in the Financial Agreement which would contradict Keynes' basic position on the question of foreign trade policy,

---

1. R. F. Harrod, The Life of John Maynard Keynes, op. cit., p. 605.
2. Ibid., p. 612.
3. A. E. Robinson, op. cit., p. 56.
4. Britain and World Trade, op. cit., pp. 72-73.

namely, that a nation's international trade considerations should be made subservient to its purely domestic requirements. Although it be true that Great Britain relinquished an important instrument of control over her balance of payments when she consented to the removal of exchange restrictions by mid-1947, the fact of the matter is that she lost little, if any, authority over her external economic affairs. For she was still permitted to retain quantitative import restrictions as a means of safeguarding equilibrium in her international accounts. Then, too, she could still have recourse to many of the instruments available in the International Monetary Fund Agreement, v.g. variation of her exchange rate and employment of discriminatory measures against countries whose currencies become "scarce", for maintaining control over the balance of payments and thereby insuring her autonomy. Thus, though Keynes may have made certain concessions to the Americans, v.g. the handling of sterling balances, the time element on the convertibility question, etc., in concluding the Financial Agreement, there is nothing contained in the clauses of this compact which would indicate any fundamental change in his attitude on foreign trade policy.

If any modification did occur at this time in Keynes' position on international economic policy, this change should be found expressed in his attitude towards the currency and commercial policy clauses attached to the loan.[1] Although there can be no denying

---

1. In view of the fact that we have already established Keynes' attitude towards the currency proposals in the preceding chapters of this section, we shall devote most of our present attention to an appraisal of the commercial policy clauses.

that the proposed International Trade Organization, in keeping with
the objectives of the Atlantic Charter and Section VII of the Mutual
Aid Agreement,[1] did constitute another step towards the removal of
trade barriers and discriminations which impede the expansion of
multilateral trade, the fact that Keynes endorsed it does not necessarily
mean that he sacrificed his former position. For according
to his own testimony before the House of Lords, neither the acceptance
of the currency nor the commercial policy proposals by Britain
would interfere in any way with her pursuance of purely domestic
objectives,[2] nor with her power to exercise control over her international
commerce.[3] Because of the pivotal importance of this
statement to our position in this thesis, it is well to quote Keynes
specifically on this point.

> In working out the Commercial Policy Paper,...
> I believe that your representatives have been
> successful in maintaining the principles and

---

1. The Trade Proposals reaffirm the principles of Article VII of
the Mutual Aid Agreement in the following terms. "In the light
of the principles set forth in Article VII of the Mutual Aid
Agreement, members should enter into arrangements for the substantial
reduction of tariffs and for the elimination of tariff
preferences, action for the elimination of tariff preferences
being taken in conjunction with adequate measures for the substantial
reduction of barriers to world trade, as part of the
mutually advantageous arrangements contemplated in this document."
(Vide U. S. Department of State, Proposals for
Consideration by an International Conference on Trade and
Employment, Washington, D.C., U. S. Government Printing Office,
December, 1945, Chapter III, Section B. These proposals are
also reproduced in the following source: N. S. Buchanan and
F. A. Lutz, Rebuilding the World Economy, op. cit., Appendix
III, pp. 397-414. All subsequent quotations of the Trade
Proposals will be taken from this text.)
2. S. Harris, "International Economics: Introduction," The New
Economics, op. cit., p. 262.
3. J. M. Keynes, "The Anglo-American Financial Arrangements,"
op. cit., pp. 392-393.

objects which are best suited to the predicaments of this country. The plans do not wander from the international terrain and they are consistent with widely different conceptions of domestic policy.... It is not true, for example, to say that state trading and bulk purchasing are interfered with. Nor is it true to say that the planning of the volume of our exports and imports, so as to preserve equilibrium in the international balance of payments, is prejudiced. Exactly the contrary is the case. Both the currency and the commercial proposals are devised to favor the maintenance of equilibrium by expressly permitting various protective devices when they are required to maintain equilibrium and by forbidding them[1] when they are not so required.[2]

That the proposed International Trade Organization recognizes the need for leaving governments free to pursue autonomous economic policies may be further evidenced by the high priority it attaches to the promotion of domestic full employment and by the authority it permits nations to exercise over their balance of payments. With respect to the question of employment, the proposals assert that the maintenance of high and stable levels of employment is a necessary condition for the expansion of international trade[3] and for the full

---

1. A country pursuing an expansionist policy is justified in utilizing these devices when its objective is to close a deficit or maintain equilibrium in its balance of payments. It is not justified in using them, however, when its purpose is to create a surplus in the balance of payments or to increase a surplus already existing. (Vide R. Nurkse, "Domestic and International Equilibrium," op. cit., p. 274.)
2. J. M. Keynes, "The Anglo-American Financial Arrangements," op. cit., p. 393.
3. N. B. how this pronouncement conforms with Keynes' view, as established in the General Theory, that the comparative cost principle and the free trade argument are efficacious only when there obtains full utilization of manpower and resources in the trading countries.

realization of the objectives of all liberal international agreements in the fields of commercial policy, monetary stabilization and investment.[1] To insure the realization of high levels of employment throughout the world, the proposals direct each of the signatory nations to "take action designed to achieve and maintain full employment within its own jurisdiction, through measures appropriate to its political and economic institutions."[2] But if each nation is charged with the responsibility of achieving and maintaining full employment, then it must be permitted to advance autonomous policies and this means, of course, that it must be relieved of any anxieties that might arise in consequence of its balance of payments position. To insure such autonomy, the Trade Proposals provide that "members confronted with an adverse balance of payments should be entitled to impose quantitative import restrictions as an aid to the restoration of equilibrium in the balance of payments."[3] Thus protected from a loss of reserves, each member State can continue to promote its domestic full employment policy without hindrance from external factors.[4]

---

1. Proposals for Consideration by an International Conference on Trade and Employment, op. cit., pp. 396-397.
2. Ibid., p. 397.
3. Ibid., p. 401.
4. By being accorded the prerogative to impose import restrictions at such times as the equilibrium of its balance of payments is disturbed, a nation may, anomolous as it may seem, actually further rather than hinder the expansion of international trade. For, as indicated by the Trade Proposals themselves, free multilateral trade can flourish only in an environment of world-wide full employment. (Vide Proposals for Consideration by an International Conference on Trade and Employment, op. cit., pp. 396-397. Also Cf. A. H. Hansen, America's Role in the World Economy, op. cit., pp. 179-180; W. Beveridge, Full Employment in a Free Society, op. cit., p. 33; and W. A. Salant, "Foreign

From the foregoing, then, it is quite apparent that Keynes did not, in subscribing to the currency and commercial clauses attached to the loan, have to change his attitude on the preeminence of national autonomy. Neither was he constrained to alter his position on the need for restrictive trade measures as a means of insuring that autonomy.[1] Notwithstanding the fact that he was a staunch advocate of national autonomy and therefore compelled to favor some degree of restriction over foreign trade, it would be erroneous, on the basis of this, to conclude that Keynes of the World War II period was an absolute protectionist.

Theoretically, if nations could learn to maintain high and stable levels of employment, it would be entirely possible for Keynes to revert to free trade, since, under these conditions, the need to employ restrictive trade measures would be greatly attenuated.

---

4. Trade Policy in the Business Cycle," op. cit., p. 226.)
1. In reality, there is no reason why Keynes should have changed his position on either question, since both the currency* and commercial proposals constitute a reflection of the type of international system which he had hoped to implement during the inter-war years. The main features of this Keynesian system are, as we have noted in the pages of this dissertation, the existence of high levels of employment, especially in the major industrial countries, freedom from a rigid international monetary standard such as gold, flexible exchange rates, the right of each nation to pursue an autonomous monetary policy, freedom from external fluctuations and the right to exercise control over the balance of payments through the regulation of capital movements and the flow of imports and exports - the very principles acknowledged by both the Bretton Woods Agreement and the Trade Proposals.

(* With specific reference to the currency proposals, Keynes said, "They lay down by international agreement the essence of the new doctrine, far removed from the old orthodoxy." Vide J. M. Keynes, "The International Monetary Fund," op. cit., p. 376.)

Paradoxical as it may seem, the more successful nations, as a whole, are in achieving high and sustained levels of activity through the promotion of autonomous full employment policies, as advocated by Keynes, the less need will they have of resorting to those protective devices which are required to safeguard their freedom in the execution of those policies. For if they can learn to promote full employment policies simultaneously, the pressure on each country's foreign balance, which results from its increased expenditures, will cancel out; hence, the necessity of employing restrictive trade devices as a means of safeguarding external equilibrium is appreciably reduced.[1] Also, the more widespread full employment is throughout the world, the less often will nations, attempting to preserve their own internal stability, have to impose trade restrictions as a means of insulating their economies from an external slump.

In addition to the fact that the attainment of full employment

---

1. Keynes emphasized the need for simultaneity in the execution of national full employment policies as early as 1933 and again in 1936. Writing in the *Means to Prosperity*, he said, "We should attach great importance to the simultaneity of the movement towards increased expenditure. For the pressure on its foreign balance which each country fears as the result of increasing its own loan-expenditure, will cancel out if other countries are pursuing the same policy at the same time." (J. M. Keynes, *The Means to Prosperity*, op. cit., p. 24.) And writing in the *General Theory*, he noted, "And it is the simultaneous pursuit of these policies by all countries together which is capable of restoring economic health and strength internationally, whether we measure it by the level of domestic employment or by the volume of international trade." (J. M. Keynes, *The General Theory*, op. cit., p. 349.) (An acknowledgement is due to Professor R. Nurkse who brought this point to our attention in his article, "Domestic and International Equilibrium," op. cit., pp. 281-285.)

on a world-wide basis would lessen the need for protection, by relieving the pressure on each country's foreign balance, there is another reason for supposing that the realization of this objective would further reduce the need for restrictionist policies and thus make Keynes more amenable to a policy of freer trade. If nations can maintain high levels of employment through their central controls, then they need no longer resort to the practice of excluding imports in the hope that they might thereby create additional employment opportunities for the home industries.[1] For given a condition of high and sustained internal activity, their concern is no longer one of maximizing domestic production, but of maximizing national productivity[2] - an objective which can best be attained by extending the division of labor to the international sector and by adhering to a policy of free trade. That the existence of widespread full employment throughout the world eliminates the need for protection and

---

1. Commenting on this point in the "Proposals for an International Clearing Union," Keynes said, "There is great force in the contention that, if active employment and ample purchasing power can be sustained in the main centres of the world trade, the problem of surpluses and unwanted exports will largely disappear, even though, under the most prosperous conditions, there may remain some disturbances of trade and unforeseen situations requiring special remedies." ("Proposals for an International Clearing Union," op. cit., p. 334.)
2. Whereas the primary objective to be realized by a "full employment" economy is the maximization of productivity through the optimum allocation of scarce factors among alternate and competing uses, the primary concern of a "less than full employment" economy is to find the means first of employing its idle resources and manpower, let along worrying about their efficient utilization. (Cf. Chapter 14 of this thesis for a more exhaustive treatment of this difference in the nature of the problems confronting a full and "less than full employment" economy.)

that he himself would under these circumstances fully endorse a
policy of free trade may be conclusively established from the
following assertion made by Keynes in the General Theory.

> If nations can learn to provide themselves with
> full employment by their domestic policy, there
> need be no important economic forces calculated
> to set the interest of one country against that
> of its neighbours. There would still be room
> for the international division of labour and for
> international lending in appropriate conditions.
> But there would no longer be a pressing motive
> why one country need force its wares on another
> or rebuke the offerings of its neighbour, not
> because this was necessary to enable it to pay
> for what it wished to purchase, but with the
> express object of upsetting the equilibrium of
> payments so as to develop a balance of trade in
> its own favour. International trade would cease
> to be what is, namely, a desperate expedient to
> maintain employment at home by forcing sales on
> foreign markets and restricting purchases, which,
> if successful, will merely shift the problem of
> unemployment to the neighbour which is worsted
> in the struggle, but a willing and unimpeded
> exchange of goods and services in conditions of
> mutual advantage.[1]

In effect, the more successful nations are in promoting autonomous full employment policies and in averting foreign-induced deflation, the less frequently will they have to resort to restrictive trade measures as a means of preserving their internal and external equilibrium, and the more often, therefore, can the "classical medicine" be made "to do its work." In fact, it is precisely because the currency and commercial plans recognized the prior right of each nation to safeguard autonomously its own equilibrium, that Keynes held out such high hope for their success in leading the world to a

---

1. J. M. Keynes, The General Theory, op. cit., pp. 382-383.

system of more liberal trade. This may be evidenced from the following remarks made by him in defence of these proposals.

> The outstanding characteristic of the plans is that they represent the first elaborate and comprehensive attempt to combine the advantages of a freedom of commerce with safeguards against the disastrous consequences of a laissez-faire system which pays no direct regard to the preservation of equilibrium and merely relies on the eventual working out of blind forces.
>
> Here is an attempt to use what we have learnt from modern experience and modern analysis, not to defeat, but to implement, the wisdom of Adam Smith....[1]
>
> We have here sincere and thorough-going proposals,[2] advanced on behalf of the United States, expressly directed towards creating a system which allows the classical medicine to do its work.[3]

That Keynes was convinced of the efficacy of free trade, when made to operate in the proper setting, may be established even more conclusively from the following observation made by him in his last article which appeared posthumously in the Economic Journal.

> I find myself moved, not for the first time, to remind contemporary economists that the classical teaching embodied some permanent truths of great significance, which we are liable today to overlook because we associate them with other doctrines which we cannot now accept without much qualification. There are in these matters deep undercurrents at work, natural forces, one can call them, or even the invisible hand, which are operating towards equilibrium. If it were not so,

---

1. J. M. Keynes, "The Anglo-American Financial Arrangements," op. cit., p. 393.
2. Keynes is referring here to the Proposals for Consideration by an International Conference on Trade and Employment.
3. J. M. Keynes, "The Balance of Payments of the United States," The Economic Journal, LVI, 222, June, 1946, p. 186.

> we could not have got on even so well as we
> have for many decades past.[1]

On the basis of the above evidence, then, our contention that Keynes of World War II could not be categorically classified as a protectionist, is adequately sustained. Yet it would be a mistake to assume that Keynes of this period was reverting to the free trade views which he had espoused prior to the depression of the 'thirties.[2] There could be no such return for him to the ranks of the doctrinaire Free Traders.[3] For even if nations could achieve reasonably high levels of employment and income, he would still be constrained to favor some protection. The volume of employment has an inherent tendency to stabilize at a point below full employment; therefore, the task of maintaining it at a reasonably high level is a continuous one. Conscious control is required at all times. And if each nation is to succeed in realizing a condition of enduring full employment within its own confines, it must, as noted in the foregoing chapter, be at liberty to impose restrictions over its international transactions, in order to safeguard its autonomy in the execution of policies designed to achieve this objective. Thus, because of the peculiar nature of the employment problem, Keynes could not divorce himself completely from a protectionist policy. That this, basically, was his ultimate position on the question of foreign trade policy may be substantially confirmed by reference to his last pronouncement on this matter.

---

1. J. M. Keynes, "The Balance of Payments of the United States," op. cit., p. 185.
2. R. Hinshaw, op. cit., p. 322.
3. Ibid.

I must not be misunderstood. I do not suppose
that the classical medicine will work by itself
or that we can depend on it. We need quicker
and less painful aids of which exchange variation and overall import control are the most
important. But in the long run these expedients
will work better and we shall need them less,
if the classical medicine is also at work. And
if we reject the medicine from our systems altogether, we may just drift from expedient to
expedient and never get really fit again. The
great virtue of the Bretton Woods and Washington
proposals, taken in conjunction, is that they
marry the use of the necessary expedients to the
wholesome long-run doctrine. It is for this
reason that, speaking in the House of Lords, I
claimed that 'Here is an attempt to use what we
have learnt from modern experience and modern
analysis, not to defeat, but to implement the
wisdom of Adam Smith.'[1]

Summary

Thus, we must conclude that at the close of his life Keynes could not be categorically classified as either a protectionist or a free trader. Essentially, he was forced to this position because of his involvement with the domestic welfare and more specifically with the level of home employment.

By Keynes' own admission, there was nothing fundamentally wrong with classical theory, including the doctrine of free trade. Taken apart from the assumption of full employment, Keynes would find it difficult to take exception with the classical approach to interna-tional trade. For many of the problems it deals with, v.g. comparative cost structures, the play of relative prices, the shifts required between production for the home and for foreign markets,

---

1. J. M. Keynes, "The Balance of Payments of the United States," op. cit., p. 186.

the forces of international competition, etc. are completely valid subjects of theoretical investigation and practical concern.[1]

Basically, classical foreign trade theory deals with the optimum division of labor between differently endowed countries; consequently, it must rely quite extensively upon the opportunity cost analysis. Such an approach, however, has complete validity only under conditions of full employment, for only in this type environment is there any possibility of engaging the productive factors in one fashion rather than another. Given a condition of less than full employment, the alternative to employing manpower and resources counter to the principle of comparative advantage may be not to employ them at all. In these circumstances, a country may enjoy a higher national product, notwithstanding a reduction in its level of productivity, by adhering to a restrictionist instead of a free trade policy. Although the productivity factor is somewhat lessened by a protectionist trade program, the increase that it generates in the level of domestic employment may be more than enough to offset this loss of efficiency and, as a consequence, may make possible an increase in home output. Thus, although it has much to commend it, classical international trade theory, like classical theory in general, has limited applicability. For though there can be no faulting it when combined with a condition of full utilization of manpower and resources, it leaves much to be desired when made to operate in an environment of less than full employment.

Not only does classical trade theory become inappropriate under

---

1. R. G. Nurkse, "Domestic and International Equilibrium," op. cit., p. 279.

conditions of widespread labor and capital displacement, because of its reliance on the opportunity cost approach, but also because it tends to discourage the restoration of internal equilibrium, by engendering imbalance in a nation's foreign account. If a nation, which is attempting to restore its level of employment through an increase in domestic expenditures, continues to adhere to a free trade policy, it will leave itself open to a disequilibrium in its balance of payments, due to the increase in imports, decrease in exports and efflux of capital funds, which its expansive policy is likely to induce. To protect itself from such an imbalance which, if sufficiently protracted, will threaten its internal expansion, a country must necessarily take measures to restrict imports and the outflow of funds to foreign centers offering a higher rate of return. Thus assured of control over its balance of payments, the expanding nation may continue to pursue its recovery program free of interference from outside forces.

In view of the fact that Keynes was primarily concerned with the level of employment, it is only natural that, in conditions of widespread unemployment, he should be biased towards the imposition of restrictive trade measures. But this is not to deny that he would welcome a policy of freer trade under conditions of full utilization of manpower and resources. Ideally, Keynes wished to combine the advantages of both free trade and protection in a single system. This he thought could be best accomplished by allowing the free trade doctrine to function over the long run, provided that a restrictive policy could be employed, whenever expedient, to protect the home economy from short run disruptions which usually characterize an open free trade system.[1] The advantages of such a synthesis, according to Keynes, is that it will permit fundamental forces[2] to restore, in the long run, any disturbed equilibrium and at the same time provide immediate protection against short run disequilibrium, which a free trade policy is unable to deal with effectively. The fact that the American currency and commercial proposals attempted to combine the long term advantages of free trade with the short term advantages of protectionism was, no doubt, one of the most important considerations in Keynes' acceptance of these proposals. For, as he indicated, "The great virtue of the Bretton Woods and Washington proposals, taken in conjunction, is that they marry the use of the necessary expedients (restrictive devices) to the wholesome long-run (classical) doctrine."[3]

---

1. The writer finds it difficult to understand just how Keynes intended to combine the virtues of free trade and protection. For if a restrictive trade policy is to be allowed to operate whenever necessary, this would seem to interfere with the operation of the free trade forces which he was relying upon to help restore equilibrium in the long run. Perhaps, there is some truth after all in the *Economist's* allegation that at this juncture, "Keynes the statesman took charge of Keynes the economist." (Vide "John M. Keynes," *The Economist*, CLV, 5492, April 27, 1946, p. 658.)
2. The fact that the United States is becoming a high-living, high-cost country is a good illustration of these "fundamental forces." It is Keynes' contention that, because the United States is becoming such "a high-living, high-cost country," it "will discover ways of life which, compared with the ways of the less fortunate regions of the world, must tend towards, and not away from, external equilibrium." (Vide J. M. Keynes, "The Balance of Payments of the United States," *op. cit.*, p. 185.)
3. J. M. Keynes, "The Balance of Payments of the United States," *op. cit.*, p. 186.

CHAPTER XXI

CONCLUSION

In setting forth our conclusions on Keynes' position on foreign trade theory and policy, we find that it is impossible to assay properly his views on these questions unless reference be made to specific dates. For his thinking on international economics underwent constant change from the earliest right down to the very last days of his illustrious career. However, insofar as the particular task of this thesis is concerned, viz. the determination of his ultimate position on foreign trade policy, we can assert with complete confidence that at the close of his life Keynes could not be classified as a free trader. Although he did in the mid-'forties modify considerably his protectionist sentiments of the 'thirties, it was impossible for him to revert unequivocally to the principles of doctrinaire free trade which he had endorsed in the early 'twenties.

Fundamentally, he could not return to the free trade school, because of the precedence which he accorded to internal over external economic requirements. From the very outset of his career Keynes had been primarily interested in advancing the internal welfare of each country, particularly that of Great Britain, in terms of high levels of employment and stable prices. The one dominant theme running through all of his writings of the inter-war period was his desire to achieve domestic equilibrium and, once attained, to safeguard it from the disturbances of the outer world. Specifically, it was this concern with internal equilibrium and with the promotion of those policies which were best suited for its realization that caused him first to part company with the traditional international gold standard and then to abandon the doctrine of free trade itself.

Keynes was opposed to the traditional gold standard for two reasons: it often achieved external balance at the expense of internal equilibrium, and it did not permit each nation to pursue an autonomous monetary policy attuned to its own domestic requirements. More precisely, he was opposed to the pre-1914 gold standard, because, by permitting gold coin to remain in the pockets of the public, it reduced the size of the gold reserve which the monetary authority might otherwise have available. Were these gold stocks concentrated in the Central Bank, the monetary authority would be better able to withstand the pressures against its balance of payments and could, therefore, postpone their transmission to the internal economy for a longer period of time.

Another reason for Keynes' hostility towards the pre-war gold standard was that each nation in the system had to gear its price level to that of all other members. Consequently, if nations got out of step with one another in the movement of their relative prices, due to differences in their efficiency wages and other costs, the latter would have to be forced back into line with those prevailing elsewhere. This, though, might only be accomplished by creating a condition of widespread deflation and unemployment. To obviate such a prospect, Keynes suggested that national wage and cost structures be left to seek their own levels and that the required adjustment be effected in the external sector via an alteration of the exchange rate.

Keynes was further opposed to the traditional gold standard, because it did not permit a nation to follow an independent monetary policy. An autonomous national monetary policy was ruled out under the gold standard, because each Central Bank had to formulate its policy in a way to forestall any disequilibrating capital and gold movements and to insure that its price level corresponded to the average world price level. Each nation, in order to preserve its external equilibrium, was compelled to keep its monetary policies in step with those of all other countries. But economic conditions and problems are not the same throughout the world; therefore, contended Keynes, adherence to a common monetary policy, such as is required by membership in the gold standard system, cannot be relied upon to give satisfactory solutions in all cases. "If the force of gravity was materially different in different countries," he observed, "the same might apply to the standard of weight."[1]

Keynes gave further indication of his desire to accord priority to internal over external considerations by his advocacy of a managed gold standard. The prime objectives of this monetary scheme, in contradistinction to the traditional gold standard, were the attainment of external equilibrium with a minimum of internal disruption and the realization of national monetary autonomy. Keynes hoped to realize the first of these objectives by relying upon the following devices: variation of the Central Bank's gold buying and selling

---

1. J. M. Keynes, A Treatise on Money, op. cit., vol. II, p. 332.

prices, centralization of gold reserves, divorce of the gold reserve from the note issue, forward exchange dealings, a widening of the spread between the gold points and control of long-term capital transfers. The employment of these instruments would not only help a nation to achieve external equilibrium with a minimum of internal disturbance, but would also enable it to pursue an autonomous monetary policy. For if these devices could succeed in attaining and preserving equilibrium in the foreign account, there would no longer be any need to utilize the bank rate for this purpose; hence, it could then be used exclusively for the promotion of stable internal prices and for the encouragement of domestic investment, employment and income.

Keynes' opposition to the traditional gold standard, by helping to establish the premise that he was primarily interested in having each nation promote its own internal equilibrium with a minimum of external interference, gives an important clue to the determination of his ultimate position on the question of foreign trade policy. For when in later years he began to realize that participation in an open free trade system would, like membership in the gold standard system, seriously interfere with a nation's attainment of internal equilibrium, it was this same concern for the domestic welfare that caused him to question the efficacy of the classical free trade arguments.

In the early phase of his career and for some time following World War I, Keynes was entirely orthodox in his thinking on the question of commercial policy. But as Great Britain found it increasingly difficult to achieve internal equilibrium after her return to the gold standard in 1925, he became more and more skeptical that she could resolve her basic economic problems by continuing to adhere to a free trade policy.

Keynes first gave indication of this change of attitude in the pages of his *Treatise on Money* - a work which he largely thought out in the depressed British environment of the late 'twenties. In this tract, Keynes expressed considerable concern over the disparity between the volume of foreign lending and the size of the foreign trade balance. The latter was not keeping pace with the former, because of the higher British production costs and the existence of tariff barriers abroad. To rectify such a condition of external disequilibrium, Keynes suggested that it might be well to increase the size of the foreign trade surplus by "applying usefully some method of establishing differential prices for home and foreign goods."[1]

Although Keynes' support of a tariff in the *Treatise* was couched in rather "elaborate theoretical language," his subsequent defense of protection before the Macmillan Committee in 1930 was far less cryptic. To cope with Great Britain's economic slump, he suggested that the government undertake a widespread expansion program. But the promotion of a cheap money policy by Britain in a depressed world environment would engender a condition of external disequilibrium, for on the one hand it would increase the volume of lending abroad and on the other it would reduce the size of the trade surplus. Should this imbalance be sufficiently prolonged, it would bring the domestic

---

1. J. M. Keynes, *A Treatise on Money*, op. cit., vol. II, p. 189.

monetary expansion to an end, thereby frustrating the attainment of internal equilibrium. To eliminate such a prospect, Keynes urged in the special appendix to the Macmillan Report that the British foreign balance be protected through the imposition of tariffs on imports and the granting of bounties to exports. In effect, Keynes' position was that, if any adjustment had to be made to preserve balance in the foreign account, the incidence of that correction should be made to fall on the external and not on the internal sector. Thus, as in the gold standard issue, Keynes, in his deliberations on the question of commercial policy, was prompted chiefly by considerations of what would best further the domestic welfare.

In the spring of 1931, Keynes came out even more strongly for protection by urging a revenue tariff for Great Britain. His reasons for sponsoring such a measure were that it would bolster business confidence, relieve the pressure on the Budget, increase the surplus on the foreign trade balance, and reduce the level of domestic unemployment. But within a week after Great Britain's abandonment of the gold standard (September 21, 1931), he asked that consideration of his tariff proposal be postponed. And well he might, for Britain stood to gain far more from the devaluation of the pound which attended her divorce from gold than from a revenue tariff. Keynes' volte face on the tariff issue is but another example of the high priority which he assigned to national and particularly to British considerations.

After Great Britain went off the gold standard, Keynes had little else to say respecting the question of foreign trade policy. And it was only after the collapse of the World Economic Conference in the summer of 1933 that he made it definitely known that he was still to be identified with the protectionists. Convinced by the demise of the London Conference that the world was not yet prepared to undertake any of his policies for achieving full employment, he suggested that they be implemented on a national level. To insure the success of these experiments, he urged a restriction of foreign commerce and finance. He also recommended a greater degree of national self-sufficiency on grounds that the advantages associated with free trade no longer obtained. The economic climate of the twentieth century, he argued, was unlike that of the nineteenth. Moreover, he felt that a policy of national autarky would, by eliminating many international economic entanglements, be more promotive of world peace than the existing order.

In The General Theory of Employment, Interest and Money, Keynes confined himself chiefly to domestic economic problems. Nevertheless, there are a number of implications for international trade theory and policy to be found in this work. The most important of these is that the orthodox doctrine of free trade, like other aspects of classical economic theory, can be valid only under conditions of full employment. Given an environment of less than full utilization of manpower and resources, the free trade doctrine which is predicated upon the opportunity cost analysis becomes open to question. In these circumstances, the comparative cost principle is not too meaningful, for the alternative to employing manpower and resources at less than optimum efficiency, as would be the case under a protectionist policy, is not to employ them at all. In effect, there would be little point to economize in the use of labor only to have it go to waste in mass unemployment. Notwithstanding the fact that a protective trade policy would reduce productivity, it might, by expanding employment opportunities in the import-competing industries, make possible a higher level of national product and income than would a free trade policy in such a state of depressed activity. Therefore, because protectionism is more likely to increase the level of home employment and income, especially in a nation which has a large import surplus, the advantages of adhering to a free trade policy in conditions of widespread labor and capital displacement are seriously challenged.

Considered from the standpoint of a single country experiencing under-employment equilibrium, a protective trade policy would be an effective means of increasing the level of home employment. The improvement of the foreign trade surplus which such a policy makes possible is synonymous with an increase in investment. And since investment activity in the Keynesian system is the primary determinant of the level of employment, it follows that an increase in the foreign trade surplus, when coupled with the multiplier, should have a highly stimulating effect on that nation's level of employment and income.

In the years following the publication of The General Theory, Keynes gave far more substantial evidence respecting his outlook on foreign trade policy than he did in that work. During this period, he moved so far from the doctrine of free trade as to abandon all hope of monetary let alone commercial cooperation between nations. In an important letter written to the London Times in the fall of 1938, he suggested that the proper solution of Great Britain's international economic problems rested in bilateral trade. This, in effect, represented the culmination of his movement towards planned trade - an objective which he had first sought to achieve in the period following the breakdown of the London Conference.

The outbreak of World War II did not cause Keynes to alter appreciably his point of view on the need for planned trade in the post-war world. However, towards the end of 1941 some change did start to take place in his thinking on the question of post-war international monetary cooperation. This modification was caused in no small measure by the generous Lend-Lease assistance provided by the Americans to Great Britain and by their intention to promote in the post-war era a multilateral trade system. But though Keynes altered his outlook on the need for greater international monetary cooperation, he remained steadfast to his convictions respecting the commercial policy aspects of foreign trade.

In formulating his Clearing Union proposals and in later supporting the International Monetary Fund, Keynes continued to adhere to the notion that a nation's external activity should not frustrate the attainment of full employment and other purely domestic objectives. The reason why Keynes could favor greater monetary cooperation among nations and at the same time not contradict his view that external economic considerations should remain subservient to those of a purely national character is that both of these plans were completely in consonance with this principle.

As a result of the high priority which he accorded to internal requirements, even while advocating greater international monetary cooperation, Keynes could not possibly re-subscribe to the tenets of classical free trade. The promotion of programs designed to achieve full employment and membership in an open free trade system are often times incompatible. And because Keynes gave top priority to the solution of internal problems, one may rightfully infer that he could no more sanction a policy of doctrinaire free trade in the 'forties than he could during the 'thirties.

Fundamentally, the reason why Keynes could not revert to his free trade position of the early 'twenties was rooted in his assumption that the economy tends to equilibrate at a level of less than full employment. Given a condition of widespread labor displacement and the need to implement full employment policies which cannot always be effectively executed in an open free trade system, Keynes was constrained to reject free trade for all levels of employment. Thus, just as his postulate of less than full employment caused him to part company with the classicists in the field of general economic theory, so, too, it was this hypothesis which caused him to take specific exception with their endorsement of free trade for any and all levels of internal equilibrium.

Although Keynes could not completely subscribe to the tenets of doctrinaire free trade during the 'forties, neither could he fully agree with the precepts of protectionism. For by his own admission, there was much to commend the free trade dogma in an environment of full employment. Ideally, therefore, he sought to combine the advantages of free trade and protection in a single system. Such a fusion of the two policies, he believed, would permit fundamental free trade forces to restore any disturbed equilibrium in the long run and the necessary expedients, v.g. import control, to provide immediate protection against short run disequilibria which a policy of free trade is unable to deal with effectively. Whether such a scheme would actually work out in practice is entirely problematic. However, the one thing that we may be completely certain of is that over the course of his life Keynes fought consistently and with notable success in liberating the domestic economy from depressing external forces. Truly, he reduced his foreign trade thinking to a function of the national prosperity.

BIBLIOGRAPHY

I. BOOKS AND PAMPHLETS BY JOHN M. KEYNES

Keynes, J. M.: Indian Currency and Finance, London, Macmillan and Co., Ltd., 1913.

_____: The Economic Consequences of the Peace, New York, Harcourt, Brace and Howe, 1920.

_____: Monetary Reform, New York, Harcourt, Brace and Co., 1924. (The English edition is entitled A Tract on Monetary Reform.)

_____: The Economic Consequences of Sterling Parity, New York, Harcourt, Brace and Co., 1925. (The English edition is entitled The Economic Consequences of Mr. Churchill.)

Keynes, J. M. and Henderson, H. D.: Can Lloyd George Do It? An Examination of the Liberal Pledge, London, The Nation and Athenaeum, 1929.

Keynes, J. M.: A Treatise on Money, 2 vols., London, Macmillan and Co., Ltd., 1930. Vol. I The Pure Theory of Money, Vol. II The Applied Theory of Money.

_____: Essays in Persuasion, New York, Harcourt, Brace and Co., 1932.

_____: Essays in Biography, London, Macmillan and Co., Ltd., 1933.

_____: The Means to Prosperity, New York, Harcourt, Brace and Co., 1933.

_____: The General Theory of Employment, Interest and Money, New York, Harcourt, Brace and Co., 1936.

_____: How to Pay for the War, New York, Harcourt, Brace and Co., 1940.

II. PERIODICAL ARTICLES BY JOHN M. KEYNES

Keynes, J. M.: "Recent Economic Events in India," The Economic Journal, March, 1909, (XIX, 73), 51-67.

_____: "Report upon the Operations of the Paper Currency Department of the Government of India during the Year 1910-11," The Economic Journal, March, 1912, (XXII, 85), 145-147.

_____: "Currency in 1912," The Economic Journal, March, 1914, (XXIV, 93), 152-157.

_____: "War and the Financial System, August, 1914," The Economic Journal, (XXIV, 95), December, 1914, 460-486.

_____: "The City of London and the Bank of England, August, 1914," The Quarterly Journal of Economics, November, 1914, (XXIX, 1), 48-71.

_____: "The Prospects of Money, November, 1914," The Economic Journal, December, 1914, (XXIV, 95), 610-634.

_____: "The Stabilization of the European Exchanges - I," The Manchester Guardian Commercial, Reconstruction in Europe, April 20, 1922, (I), 3-5.

_____: "The Theory of the Exchanges and Purchasing Power Parity," The Manchester Guardian Commercial, Reconstruction in Europe, April 20, 1922, (I), 6-8.

_____: "The Forward Market in Foreign Exchanges," The Manchester Guardian Commercial, Reconstruction in Europe, April 20, 1922, (I), 11-15.

_____: "The Reconstruction of Europe: A General Introduction," The Manchester Guardian Commercial, Reconstruction in Europe, May 18, 1922 (II), 66-67.

_____: "The Genoa Conference," The Manchester Guardian Commercial, Reconstruction in Europe, June 15, 1922, (III), 132-133.

_____: "Inflation as a Method of Taxation," The Manchester Guardian Commercial, Reconstruction in Europe, July 27, 1922, (V), 268-269.

_____: "The Consequences to Society of Changes in the Value of Money," The Manchester Guardian Commercial, Reconstruction in Europe, July 27, 1922, (V), 321-328.

_____: "Is a Settlement of the Reparation Question Possible Now?" The Manchester Guardian Commercial, Reconstruction in Europe, Sept. 28, 1922, (VIII), 462-464.

_____: "Speculation in the Mark and Germany's Balances Abroad," The Manchester Guardian Commercial, Reconstruction in Europe, Sept. 28, 1922, (VIII), 480-482.

_____: "The Stabilization of the European Exchanges - II," The Manchester Guardian Commercial, Reconstruction in Europe, Dec. 7, 1922, (XI), 658-661.

_____: "The Underlying Principles," The Manchester Guardian Commercial, Reconstruction in Europe, Jan. 4, 1923, (XII), 717-718.

_____: "Professor Jevons on the Indian Exchange," The Economic Journal, March, 1923, (XXXIII, 129), 60-65.

_____: "Is Credit Abundant?" The Nation and the Athenaeum, July 7, 1923, (XXXIII, 14), 470.

_____: "Bank Rate at Four Per Cent," The Nation and the Athenaeum, July 14, 1923, (XXXIII, 15), 502.

_____: "Bank Rate and Stability of Prices - A Reply to Critics," The Nation and the Athenaeum, July 21, 1923, (XXXIII, 16), 530.

_____: "The Measure of Deflation," The Nation and the Athenaeum, July 28, 1923, (XXXIII, 17), 558.

_____: "Mr. Baldwin's Task," The New Republic, August 1, 1923, (XXXV, 452), 252-253.

_____: "The American Debt," The Nation and the Athenaeum, August 4, 1923, (XXXIII, 18), 566-567.

_____: "Currency Policy and Unemployment," The Nation and the Athenaeum, (XXXIII, 19), August 11, 1923, 611-612.

_____: "Free Trade," The Nation and the Athenaeum, Nov. 24, 1923, (XXXIV, 8), 302-303.

_____: "Free Trade and Unemployment," The Nation and the Athenaeum, Dec. 1, 1923, (XXXIV, 9), 335-336.

_____: "Free Trade for England," The New Republic, Dec. 19, 1923, (XXXVII, 472), 86-87.

_____: "A Reply to Sir William Beveridge," The Economic Journal, Dec., 1923, (XXXIII, 131), 476-486.

_____: "Gold in 1923," The Nation and the Athenaeum, Feb. 2, 1924, (XXXIV, 18), 623-624.

_____: "The Prospects of Gold," The Nation and the Athenaeum, Feb. 16, 1924, (XXXIV, 20), 692-693.

_____: "Gold in 1923," The New Republic, Feb. 27, 1924, (XXXVIII, 482), 10-11.

_____: "The Prospects of Gold," The New Republic, March 12, 1924, (XXVIII, 484), 66-67.

_____: "The Franc," The Nation and the Athenaeum, March 15, 1924, (XXXIV, 24), 823-824.

_____: "The Franc," The New Republic, March 26, 1924, (XXXVIII, 486), 120-121.

_____: "Does Unemployment Need a Drastic Remedy?" The Nation and the Athenaeum, May 24, 1924, (XXXV, 8), 235-236.

_____: "A Drastic Remedy for Unemployment," The Nation and the Athenaeum, June 7, 1924 (XXXV, 10), 311-312.

_____: "Public and Private Enterprise," The Nation and the Athenaeum, June 21, 1924 (XXXV, 12), 374-375.

_____: "The Policy of the Bank of England," The Nation and the Athenaeum, July 19, 1924, (XXXV, 16), 500-501.

_____: "Foreign Investment and National Advantage - An Address to the Liberal Summer School at Oxford," The Nation and the Athenaeum, August 2, 1924, (XXXV, 19), 584-587.

_____: "The Return Towards Gold," The Nation and the Athenaeum, Feb. 21, 1925, (XXXVI, 21), 707-709.

_____: "The Bank Rate," The Nation and the Athenaeum, March 7, 1925, (XXXVI, 23), 790-792.

_____: "The Return Towards Gold," The New Republic, March 18, 1925, (XLII, 537), 92-94.

_____: "The Problem of the Gold Standard," The Nation and the Athenaeum, March 21, 1925, (XXXVI, 25), 866-870.

_____: "Is Sterling Overvalued?" The Nation and the Athenaeum, April 4, 1925, (XXXVII, 1), 28-30.

_____: "Is Sterling Overvalued - II?" The Nation and the Athenaeum, April 18, 1925, (XXXVII, 3), 86.

_____: "The Gold Standard," The Nation and the Athenaeum, May 2, 1925, (XXXVII, 5), 129-130.

_____: "Is the Pound Overvalued?" The New Republic, May 6, 1925, (XLII, 544), 286-287.

_____: "The Gold Standard - A Correction," The Nation and the Athenaeum, May 9, 1925, (XXXVII, 6), 169-170.

_____: "England's Gold Standard," The New Republic, May 20, 1925, (XLII, 546), 339-340.

_____: "The Arithmetic of the Sterling Exchange," The Nation and the Athenaeum, June 13, 1925, (XXXVII, 11), 338.

_____: "The Committee on the Currency," The Economic Journal, June, 1925, (XXXV, 138), 299-304.

_____: "The Gold Standard Act, 1925," The Economic Journal, June, 1925, (XXXV, 138), 312-313.

_____: "Am I a Liberal - I?" The Nation and the Athenaeum, Aug. 8, 1925, (XXXVII, 19), 563-564.

_____: "Am I a Liberal - II?" The Nation and the Athenaeum, Aug. 15, 1925, (XXXVII, 20), 587-588.

_____: "Great Britain's 'Cross of Gold'," The New Republic, Sept. 16, 1925, (XLIV, 563), 88-90.

_____: "The French Franc," The Nation and the Athenaeum, Jan. 9, 1926, (XXXVIII, 15), 515-517.

_____: "The French Franc - A Reply," The Nation and the Athenaeum, Jan. 16, 1926, (XXXVIII, 16), 544-545.

_____: "Some Facts and Last Reflections about the Franc," The Nation and the Athenaeum, Jan. 30, 1926, (XXXVIII, 18), 603-604.

_____: "Coal: A Suggestion," The Nation and the Athenaeum, April 24, 1926, (XXXIX, 4), 91-92.

_____: "Back to the Coal Problem," The Nation and the Athenaeum, May 15, 1926, (XXXIX, 16), 159.

_____: "The First Fruits of the British Gold Standard," The New Republic, June 2, 1926, (XLVII, 600), 54-55.

_____: "The First Fruits of the Gold Standard," The Nation and the Athenaeum, June 26, 1926, (XXXIX, 12), 344-345.

_____: "The Franc Once More," <u>The Nation and the Athenaeum</u>, July 17, 1926, (XXXIX, 15), 435-436.

_____: "The Future of the Franc," <u>The New Republic</u>, Aug. 11, 1926, (XLVII, 610), 328-329.

_____: "The End of Laissez-Faire - I," <u>The New Republic</u>, Aug. 25, 1926, (XLVIII, 612), 13-15.

_____: "The End of Laissez-Faire - II," <u>The New Republic</u>, Sept. 1, 1926, (XLVIII, 613), 37-41.

_____: "The Autumn Prospects for Sterling," <u>The Nation and the Athenaeum</u>, Oct. 23, 1926, (XL, 3), 104-105.

_____: "The Position of the Lancashire Cotton Trade," <u>The Nation and the Athenaeum</u>, Nov. 13, 1926, (XL, 6), 209-210.

_____: "Will England Restrict Foreign Investments?" <u>The New Republic</u>, Dec. 1, 1926, (XLIX, 626), 34-36.

_____: "Mr. McKenna on Monetary Policy," <u>The Nation and the Athenaeum</u>, Feb. 12, 1927, (XL, 19), 651-653.

_____: "The Colwyn Report on National Debt and Taxation," <u>The Economic Journal</u>, June, 1927, (XXXVII, 146), 198-212.

_____: "The British Balance of Trade, 1925-1927," <u>The Economic Journal</u>, Dec., 1927, (XXXVII, 148), 551-565.

_____: "Note on the British Balance of Trade," <u>The Economic Journal</u>, March, 1928, (XXXVIII, 149), 146-147.

_____: "The Stabilization of the Franc," <u>The Nation and the Athenaeum</u>, June 30, 1928, (XLIII, 13), 416-417.

_____: "The Amalgamation of the British Note Issues," <u>The Economic Journal</u>, June, 1928, (XXXVIII, 150), 321-328.

_____: "Is there Enough Gold?" <u>The Nation and the Athenaeum</u>, Jan. 19, 1929, (XLIV, 16), 545-546.

_____: "The Bank Rate - Five and a Half Per Cent," <u>The Nation and the Athenaeum</u>, Feb. 16, 1929, (XLIV, 20), 679-680.

_____: "The German Transfer Problem," <u>The Economic Journal</u>, March, 1929, (XXXIX, 153), 1-7.

_____: "The Treasury Contribution to the White Paper," <u>The Nation and the Athenaeum</u>, May 18, 1929, (XLV, 7), 227-228.

_____: "The Question of High Wages," <u>Political Quarterly</u>, Jan., 1930, (I,1), 110-124.

_____: "British Industry, Unemployment and High Wages," Barron's - The National Financial Weekly, March 24, 1930, (X, 12), 22-23.

_____: "The Industrial Crisis," The Nation and the Athenaeum, May 10, 1930, (XLVII, 6), 163-164.

_____: "Economic Possibilities for Our Grandchildren - I," The Nation and the Athenaeum, Oct. 11, 1930, (XLVIII, 2), 36-37.

_____: "Economic Possibilities for Our Grandchildren - II," The Nation and the Athenaeum, Oct. 18, 1930, (XLVIII, 3), 96-98.

_____: "The Great Slump of 1930 - I," The Nation and the Athenaeum, Dec. 20, 1930, (XLVIII, 12), 402.

_____: "The Great Slump of 1930 - II," The Nation and the Athenaeum, Dec. 27, 1930, (XLVIII, 13), 427-428.

_____: "Proposals for a Revenue Tariff," The New Statesman and Nation, March 7, 1931, (I, N.S. 2), 53-54.

_____: "Further Reflections on a Revenue Tariff," The New Statesman and Nation, March 21, 1931, (I, N.S. 4), 142-143.

_____: "Economic Notes on Free Trade - The Export Industries," The New Statesman and Nation, March 28, 1931, (I, N.S. 5), 175-176.

_____: "Economic Notes on Free Trade - A Revenue Tariff and the Cost of Living," The New Statesman and Nation, April 4, 1931, (I, N.S. 6), 211.

_____: "Revenue Tariff for Great Britain," The New Republic, April 8, 1931 (LXVI, 853), 196-197.

_____: "Economic Notes on Free Trade - The Reaction of Imports on Exports," The New Statesman and Nation, April 11, 1931, (I, N.S. 7), 242-243.

_____: "Some Consequences of the Economy Report," The New Statesman and Nation, Aug. 15, 1931, (II, N.S. 25), 189-190.

_____: "A Gold Conference," The New Statesman and Nation, Sept. 12, 1931, (II, N.S. 29), 300-301.

_____: "The Budget," The New Statesman and Nation, Sept. 19, 1931, (II, N.S. 30), 329.

_____: "Mr. Keynes' Theory of Money: A Rejoinder," The Economic Journal, Sept., 1931, (XLI, 163), 412-423.

_____: "A Reply to Dr. Hayek: The Pure Theory of Money," *Economica*, Nov., 1931, (XI, 34), 387-397.

_____: "The Prospects of the Sterling Exchanges," *The Yale Review*, March, 1932, (XXI, 3), 433-447.

_____: "Reflections on the Sterling Exchange," *Lloyds Bank Monthly Review*, April, 1932, (III, N.S. 26), 143-160.

_____: "The World's Economic Outlook," *The Atlantic Monthly*, May, 1932, (CXLIX, 5), 521-526.

_____: "The Monetary Policy of the Labour Government - I," *The New Statesman and Nation*, Sept. 17, 1932, (IV, N.S. 82), 306-307.

_____: "The Monetary Policy of the Labour Government - II," *The New Statesman and Nation*, Sept. 24, 1932, (IV, N.S. 83), 338-339.

_____: "A Note on the Long-Term Rate of Interest in Relation to the Conversion Scheme," *The Economic Journal*, Sept., 1932, (XLII, 167), 415-423.

_____: "The World Economic Conference, 1933," *The New Statesman and Nation*, Dec. 24, 1932, (IV, N.S. 96), 825-826.

_____: "A Programme for Unemployment," *The New Statesman and Nation*, Feb. 4, 1933, (V, N.S. 102), 121-122.

_____: "The Multiplier," *The New Statesman and Nation*, April 1, 1933, (V, N.S. 110), 405-407.

_____: "National Self-Sufficiency," *The Yale Review*, June, 1933, (XXII, 4), 755-769.

_____: "National Self-Sufficiency - I," *The New Statesman and Nation*, July 8, 1933, (VI, N.S. 124), 36-37.

_____: "National Self-Sufficiency - II," *The New Statesman and Nation*, July 15, 1933, (VI, N.S. 125), 65-67.

_____: "Mr. Keynes' Control Scheme," *American Economic Review*, Dec., 1933, (XXIII, 4), 675.

_____: "President Roosevelt's Gold Policy," *The New Statesman and Nation*, Jan. 20, 1934, (VII, N.S. 152), 76-77.

_____: "A Self-Adjusting Economic System?" *The New Republic*, Feb. 20, 1935, (LXXXII, 1054), 35-37.

_____: "The Report of the Bank for International Settlements, 1934-1935," The Economic Journal, Sept., 1935, (XLV, 179), 594-597.

_____: "The Future of the Foreign Exchanges," Lloyd's Bank Monthly Review, Oct., 1935, (VI, N.S. 68), 527-535.

_____: "The Supply of Gold," The Economic Journal, Sept., 1936, (XLVI, 183), 412-418.

_____: "The General Theory of Employment," The Quarterly Journal of Economics, Feb., 1937, (LI, 2), 209-223.

_____: "Alternative Theories of the Rate of Interest," The Economic Journal, June, 1937, (XLVII, 186), 240-252.

_____: "The 'Ex Ante' Theory of the Rate of Interest," The Economic Journal, Dec., 1937, (XLVII, 188), 663-669.

_____: "Mr. Keynes' Consumption Function: Reply," The Quarterly Journal of Economics, Aug., 1938, (LII, 4), 709-712.

_____: "The Policy of Government Storage of Foodstuffs and Raw Materials," The Economic Journal, Sept., 1938, (XLVIII, 191), 449-460.

_____: "Relative Movements of Real Wages and Output," The Economic Journal, March, 1939, (XLIX, 193), 34-51.

_____: "The Concept of National Income," The Economic Journal, March, 1940, (L, 197), 60-65.

_____: "The Objective of International Price Stability," The Economic Journal, June - Sept., 1943, (LIII, 210-211), 185-187.

_____: "The Balance of Payments of the United States," The Economic Journal, June, 1946, (LVI, 222), 172-187.

III. NEWSPAPER ARTICLES, LECTURES AND SPEECHES BY JOHN M. KEYNES

Keynes, J. M.: "Monetary Policy - Relation of Price Levels," The London Times, Sept. 4, 1925, 20.

_____: "The Issues for Free Traders," (Letter to the Editor), The London Times, March 21, 1931, 8.

_____: "Mr. J. M. Keynes' Rejoinder," (Letter to the Editor), The London Times, March 27, 1931, 10.

_____: "Revenue Tariffs - Effects on Home Production," (Letter to the Editor), The London Times, April 2, 1931, 6.

_____: "The Tariff Question," (Letter to the Editor), The London Times, Sept. 29, 1931, 15.

_____: "An Economic Analysis of Unemployment," Unemployment as a World Problem, (ed. Q. Wright), Chicago, University of Chicago Press, 1931, 3-42.

_____: "Halley-Stewart Lecture (1931)," The World's Economic Crisis and the Way of Escape, New York, The Century Company, 1932, 55-75.

_____: "Mr. Keynes' Programme," (Letter to the Editor), The Economist, March 25, 1933, (CXVI, 4674), 642.

_____: "Public Works," (Letter to the Editor), The London Times, July 28, 1933, 10.

_____: "Mr. Roosevelt's Experiments," The London Times, Jan. 2, 1934, 11-12.

_____: "From Keynes to Roosevelt: Our Recovery Plan Assayed," The New York Times, Dec. 31, 1934, p. 2, sec. VIII.

_____: "How to Avoid a Slump - I: The Problem of the Steady Level," The London Times, Jan. 12, 1937, 13-14.

_____: "How to Avoid a Slump - II: Dear Money," The London Times, Jan. 13, 1937, 13-14.

_____: "How to Avoid a Slump - III: Opportunities of Policy," The London Times, Jan. 14, 1937, 13-14.

_____: "The Boom and the Budget," (Letter to the Editor), The Economist, Jan. 30, 1937, (CXXVI, 4875), 240.

_____: "Bankers, Boom and Budget," (Letter to the Editor), The Economist, Feb. 13, 1937, (CXXVI, 4877), 359.

_____: "The Gold Problem," (Letter to the Editor), The London Times, June 10, 1937, 17.

_____: "Public Works - Improvisation or Planning?" (Letter to the Editor), The London Times, Jan. 3, 1938, 13.

_____: "Interest Rates and the Treasury," (Letter to the Editor), The Economist, March 5, 1938, (CXXX, 4932), 499-500.

_____: "Foreign Trade - The Barter Aspect," (Letter to the Editor), The London Times, Oct. 7, 1938, 10.

_____: "Crisis Finance - I: Employment and the Budget," The London Times, April 17, 1939, 13-14.

_____: "Crisis Finance - II: The Supply of Savings," The London Times, April 18, 1939, 15-16.

_____: "Borrowing by the State - I: High Interest and Low," The London Times, July 24, 1939, 13-14.

_____: "Borrowing by the State - II: A Programme of Method," The London Times, July 25, 1939, 13-14.

_____: "The International Clearing Union," (Speech delivered before the House of Lords, May 18, 1943), The New Economics, (ed. S. Harris), New York, Alfred A. Knopf, 1947, 359-368.

_____: "The International Monetary Fund," (Speech delivered before the House of Lords, May 23, 1944), The New Economics, (ed. S. Harris), New York, Alfred A. Knopf, 1947, 369-379.

_____: "Bretton Woods," (Letter to the Editor), The Economist, Aug. 12, 1944, (CXLVII, 5268), 215.

_____: "The Anglo-American Financial Arrangements," (Speech delivered before the House of Lords, December 18, 1945), The New Economics, (ed. S. Harris), New York, Alfred A. Knopf, 1947, 380-395.

IV. GENERAL PERIODICAL ARTICLES

Ackerman, Clement: "The Economic Consequences of the Peace," Pacific Review, I (1920), 93-108.

Adarkar, B. P. and Gosh, D.: "Mr. Keynes' Theory of Interest," The Indian Journal of Commerce, XXI (1941), 285-300.

Adler, Hans J.: "U. S. Import Demand During the Interwar Period," American Economic Review, XXXV (1945), 418-427.

Anderson, Karl L.: "Protection and the Historical Situation: Australia," The Quarterly Journal of Economics, LIII (1938), 86-104.

Balogh, T.: "Some Theoretical Aspects of the Gold Problem," Economica, IV N.S. (1937), 274-294.

_____: "League of Nations on Post-War Foreign Trade," The Economic Journal, LIV (1944), 256-261.

_____: "The American Loan," The Economist, CL (1946), 12.

Balogh, T.: "The Balance of Payments and Domestic Economic Policy," Bulletin of the Oxford University Institute of Statistics, XIII (1951), 55-64.

_____ and Streeten, P. P.: "The Inappropriateness of Simple 'Elasticity' Concepts in the Analysis of International Trade," The Bulletin of the Oxford University Institute of Statistics, XIII (1951), 65-77.

_____: "International Equilibrium and U. S. Private Investment," Bulletin of the Oxford University Institute of Statistics, XIII (1951), 247-255.

The Banker: "Death of a Genius," The Banker, LXXVIII, (1946), 74-80.

Benham, F.: "The Terms of Trade," Economica, VII (1940), 360-376.

_____: "The Muddle of the Thirties," Economica, XII (1945), 1-9.

Beveridge, W. H.: "The Case for Free Trade," The London Times, London, March 26, 1931, 10.

_____: "An Analysis of Unemployment," Economica, III (1936), 357-386.

Burns, A. F.: "Keynesian Economics Once Again," The Review of Economic Statistics, XXIX (1947), 256-267.

Burrows, H. R.: "J. M. Keynes - Part I - His Life and Thought," The South African Journal of Economics, XX (1952), 149-164.

_____: "J. M. Keynes - Part II - His Theory," The South African Journal of Economics, II (1952), 242-260.

Bloomfield, A. I.: "Postwar Control of International Capital Movements," American Economic Review, XXXVI (1946), 687-709.

Champernowne, D. G.: "Unemployment, Basic and Monetary: The Classical Analysis and the Keynesian," The Review of Economic Studies, III (1936), 201-216.

Chang, T.C.: "The British Demand for Imports in the Inter-War Period," The Economic Journal, LVI (1946), 188-207.

Clark, C.: "Determination of the Multiplier from National Income Statistics," The Economic Journal, XLVIII (1938), 435-448.

Condliffe, J. B.: "The Value of International Trade," Economica, V (1938), 123-137.

_____: "Exchange Stabilization and International Trade," The Review of Economic Statistics, XXVI (1944), 166-169.

Curtis, M.: "Foreign Trade and Employment," The Economist, CXLVIII (1945), 76.

De Vegh, J.: "Imports and Income in the U. S. and Canada," Review of Economics and Statistics, XXIII (1941), 130-146.

Day, Clive: "Keynes' Economic Consequences of the Peace," American Economic Review, X (1920), 299-312.

Dillard, D.: "Keynes and Proudhon," The Journal of Economic History, II (1942), 63-76.

The Economist: "Protection and Britain's Future," The Economist, Aug. 16, 1930, (CXI, 4538), 307-308.

_____: "Second Thoughts on Protection," The Economist, Feb. 7, 1931, (CXII, 4563), 279.

_____: "The Inconsequences of Mr. Keynes," The Economist, March 14, 1931, (CXII, 4568), 549-550.

_____: "Mr. Keynes and the Tariff," The Economist, April 4, 1931, (CXII, 4571), 722.

_____: "Tariffs, Wages and Exports," The Economist, April 11, 1931, (CXII, 4572), 771-772.

_____: "The Election and Fiscal Policy," The Economist, Oct. 10, 1931, (CXIII, 4597), 645-646.

_____: "Sanity versus Tariffs," The Economist, Oct. 17, 1931, (CXIII, 4599), 696-697.

_____: "Stark and Unashamed," The Economist, Feb. 6, 1932, (CXIV, 4615), 293-294.

_____: "Mr. Keynes' Programme," The Economist, March 18, 1933, (CXVI, 4673), 568-569.

_____: "World Economic Conference," The Economist, June 10, 1933, (CXVI, 4685), 1-11.

_____: "The Gospel of Self-Sufficiency," The Economist, July 22, 1933, (CXVII, 4691), 171-172.

_____: "Mr. Keynes and Exchange Stabilisation," The Economist, Oct. 12, 1935, (CXXI, 4807), 700.

_____: "Mr. Keynes on Money," The Economist, Feb. 29, 1936, (CXXII, 4827), 471-472.

_____: "Full Employment," The Economist, April 4, 1936, (CXXIII, 4832), 5-6.

The Economist: "Five Years off Gold," The Economist, Sept. 19, 1936, (CXXIV, 4856), 503-504.

_____: "A Chance for Statesmanship," The Economist, Oct. 10, 1936, (CXXV, 4859), 49-50.

_____: "Mr. Keynes on British Policy," The Economist, Jan. 16, 1937, (CXXVI, 4873), 108.

_____: "An Anti-Tariff Move," The Economist, Feb. 6, 1937, (CXXVI, 4876), 285-286.

_____: "Is it Inflation?" The Economist, March 13, 1937, (CXXVI, 4881), 578-579.

_____: "The Terms of Trade," The Economist, Feb. 5, 1938, (CXXX, 4928), 310-311.

_____: "The Freedom to Trade," The Economist, Aug. 23, 1941, (CXLI, 5113), 220-222.

_____: "The Principles of Trade," The Economist, Nov. 8, 1941, (CXLI, 5124), 553-554.

_____: "The Problem of Stabilisation," The Economist, Sept. 11, 1943, (CXLV, 5220), 374.

_____: "The Principles of Trade," The Economist, Jan. 1, 1944, (CXLVI, 5236), 4-5.

_____: "Balance of Payments," The Economist, Jan. 8, 1944, (CXLVI, 5237), 32-34.

_____: "Trade and Employment," The Economist, Jan. 15, 1944, (CXLVI, 5238), 64-65.

_____: "The Multilateral Approach," The Economist, Jan. 22, 1944, (CXLVI, 5239), 94-96.

_____: "Planned Expansion," The Economist, Jan. 29, 1944, (CXLVI, 5240), 136-137.

_____: "The Regional Solution," The Economist, Feb. 5, 1944, (CXLVI, 5241), 169-170.

_____: "Prices and Markets," The Economist, Feb. 12, 1944, (CXLVI, 5242), 204-205.

_____: "The New Liberalism," The Economist, Feb. 19, 1944, (CXLVI, 5243), 232-233.

_____: "The Joint Currency Scheme," The Economist, April 29, 1944, (CXLVI, 5253), 560-561.

The Economist: "Trade and Employment," The Economist, May 27, 1944, (CXLVI, 5257), 701-702.

_____: "Keynes on Gold and Sterling," The Economist, July 15, 1944, (CXLVII, 5264), 89.

_____: "John Maynard Keynes," The Economist, April 27, 1946, (CL, 5357), 657-658.

_____: "The Law and the Prophet," The Economist, Nov. 27, 1948, (CLV, 5492), 879.

Egle, W.: "The Spreading of the Gold Points as a Means of Controlling the Movement of Foreign Short Term Balances," The Journal of Political Economy, XLVII (1939), 857-866.

Elliott, G. A.: "The Significance of the General Theory of Employment, Interest and Money," The Canadian Journal of Economics and Political Science, XIII (1947), 372-378.

Einaudi, Luigi: "Il Mio Piano Non E'Quello di Keynes," La Riforma Sociale, XLIV (1933), 129-142.

Einzig, P.: "Gold Points and Central Banks," The Economic Journal, XXXIX (1929), 379-387.

_____: "Some New Features of Gold Movements," The Economic Journal, XL (1930), 56-63.

_____: "International Monetary Fund - Is it a Gold Standard?" The Banker, LXXI (1944), 112-117.

_____: "Economic Peace in our Time?" The Banker, LXXVII (1946), 13-17.

_____: "Lord Keynes - An Appreciation," The Banker, LXXVIII (1946), 80-81.

Ellis, H. S.: "Notes on Recent Business Cycle Literature," The Review of Economic Statistics, XX (1938), 111-119.

Fellner, W. and Somers, H.: "Alternative Monetary Approaches to Interest Theory," The Review of Economic Statistics, XXIII (1941), 43-48.

Gilbert, J.C.: "The Present Position of the Theory of International Trade," The Review of Economic Studies, III (1935), 18-34.

Grether, E. T.: "The Means to Prosperity - A Review," American Economic Review, XXIII (1933), 347-349.

Haberler, G.: "Currency Depreciation and the International Monetary Fund," The Review of Economic Statistics, XXVI (1944), 178-181.

_____: "The Choice of Exchange Rates after the War," American Economic Review, XXXV (1945), 308-318.

_____: "The Relevance of the Classical Theory under Modern Conditions," American Economic Review, XLIX (1954), 543-551.

Halm, G. N.: "The International Monetary Fund," The Review of Economic Statistics, XXVI (1944), 170-174.

Hansen, A. H.: "Mr. Keynes on Underemployment Equilibrium," The Journal of Political Economy, XLIV (1936), 667-686.

_____: "A Brief Note on Fundamental Disequilibrium," The Review of Economic Statistics, XXVI (1944), 182-184.

_____: "Dr. Burns on Keynesian Economics," The Review of Economic Statistics, XXIX (1947), 247-251.

Harris, S. E.: "The Contributions of Bretton Woods and some Unsolved Problems," The Review of Economic Statistics, XXVI (1944), 175-177.

Hawtrey, R. G.: "Review of a Tract on Monetary Reform," The Economic Journal, XXXIV (1924), 227-235.

Henderson, H. D.: "The Case Against Returning to Gold," Lloyd's Bank Limited Monthly Review, VI (1935), 338-345.

Hicks, J. R.: "Mr. Keynes' Theory of Employment," The Economic Journal, XLVI (1936), 238-253.

Hinshaw, R.: "American Prosperity and the British Balance of Payments Problem," The Review of Economic Statistics, XXVII (1945), 1-9.

_____: "Foreign Investment and American Employment," American Economic Review, XXXVI (1946), 661-671.

Hirschman, A. O.: "Devaluation and the Trade Balance," Review of Economics and Statistics, XXXI (1949), 50-53.

Hobson, J. A.: "A World Economy," The New Statesman and Nation, I (1931), 274-275.

Holden, G. R.: "Mr. Keynes' Consumption Function and the Time Preference Postulate," The Quarterly Journal of Economics, LII (1938), 281-296.

_____: "Mr. Keynes' Consumption Function: Rejoinder," The Quarterly Journal of Economics, LII (1938), 708.

Hoover, C.: "Keynes and the Economic System," *The Journal of Political Economy*, LVI (1948), 392-402.

Jastram, R. W. and Shaw, E. S.: "Mr. Clark's Statistical Determination of the Multiplier," *The Economic Journal*, XLIX (1939), 358-365.

Johnson, A.: "Keynes on Monetary Reform," *The New Republic*, XXXVII (1924), 288.

Jones, Homer: "The Optimum Rate of Investment, the Savings Institutions and the Banks," *American Economic Review*, XXXVIII (1948), 321-339.

Kahn, R. F.: "The Relation of Home Investment to Unemployment," *The Economic Journal*, XLI (1931), 173-198.

Kaldor, N.: "Stability and Full Employment," *The Economic Journal*, XLVIII (1938), 642-658.

Kalecki, M.: "Multilateralism and Full Employment," *The Canadian Journal of Economics and Political Science*, XII (1946), 322-327.

Klein, L. R.: "Theories of Effective Demand and Employment," *The Journal of Political Economy*, LV (1947), 108-131.

Knight, F. H.: "Unemployment: And Mr. Keynes' Revolution in Economic Theory," *The Canadian Journal of Economics and Political Science*, III (1937), 100-123.

Kurihara, K.: "Foreign Investment and Full Employment," *The Journal of Political Economy*, LV (1947), 459-464.

Lachmann, L. M.: "Notes on the Proposals for International Currency Stabilization," *The Review of Economic Statistics*, XXVI (1944), 184-191.

Lary, H. L.: "The Domestic Effects of Foreign Investment," *American Economic Review*, XXXVI (1946), 672-686.

Leontief, W.: "The Fundamental Assumption of Mr. Keynes' Monetary Theory," *The Quarterly Journal of Economics*, LI (1936), 192-197.

Lerner, A.: "Saving Equals Investment," *The Quarterly Journal of Economics*, LII (1938), 297-309.

_____: "Alternative Formulations of the Theory of Interest," *The Economic Journal*, XLVIII (1938), 211-230.

Lovasy, G.: "International Trade under Imperfect Competition," *The Quarterly Journal of Economics*, LV (1941), 667-683.

Lutz, F.: "The Outcome of the Saving-Investment Discussion," The Quarterly Journal of Economics, LV (1938), 588-614.

———: "Saving and Investment: Final Comment," The Quarterly Journal of Economics, LIII (1939), 627-631.

Machlup, F.: "The Theory of Foreign Exchanges," Economica, VI (1939), 375-397. Also VII (1940), 23-49.

———: "Period Analysis and Multiplier Theory," The Quarterly Journal of Economics, LIV (1939), 1-27.

Mackintosh, W. A.: "Keynes as a Public Servant," The Canadian Journal of Economics and Political Science, XIII (1947), 379-383.

Maffry, A.: "Foreign Trade in the Post-War Economy," The Survey of Current Business, November (1944), 5-14.

Marsh, D. B.: "The Scope of the Theory of International Trade under Monopolistic Competition," The Quarterly Journal of Economics, LVI (1942), 475-486.

Meek, Ronald L.: "The Place of Keynes in the History of Economic Thought," The Modern Quarterly, VI (1950-1951), 34-51.

Metzler, L.: "Underemployment Equilibrium in International Trade," Econometrica, X (1942), 97-112.

The Midland Bank: "The Pound and the Dollar," Monthly Review, Dec. (1938), January (1939), 1-3.

Mikesell, R. F.: "The Role of the International Monetary Agreements in a World of Planned Economies," The Journal of Political Economy, LV (1947), 497-512.

Mitchell, A. A.: "A Retrospect of Free Trade Doctrine: A Comment," The Economic Journal, XXXV (1925), 214-220.

Neisser, H.: "Secondary Employment: Some Comments on R. F. Kahn's Formula," The Review of Economic Statistics, XVIII (1936), 24-30.

The New Republic: "Laissez-Faire vs. Nation Building," The New Republic, XXXVII (1923), 84-85.

The New Statesman and Nation: "A Revenue Tariff - Correspondence," The New Statesman and Nation, I (1943), 103-105.

Nicholson, J. S.: "The Report on Indian Finance and Currency in Relation to the Gold Exchange Standard," The Economic Journal, XXIV (1914), 236-247.

O'Neil, H. C.: "Men of Today," *Today and Tomorrow*, I (1931), 130-135.

Paish, F. W.: "The British Exchange Equalisation Fund," *Economica*, III (1936), 78-83.

_____: "Banking Policy and the Balance of International Payments," *Economica*, III (1936), 404-422.

Pigou, A. C.: "Mr. J. M. Keynes' General Theory of Employment, Interest and Money," *Economica*, III (1936), 115-132.

Plumptre, A. F. W.: "The Distribution of Outlay and the 'Multiplier' in the British Dominions," *Canadian Journal of Economics and Political Science*, V (1939), 363-372.

_____: "Keynes in Cambridge," *The Canadian Journal of Economics and Political Science*, XIII (1947), 366-371.

Polak, J. J.: "Exchange Depreciation and International Monetary Stability," *The Review of Economic Statistics*, XXIX (1947), 173-182.

Reddaway, W. B.: "The General Theory of Employment, Interest and Money," *The Economic Record*, XII (1936), 28-36.

_____: "Special Obstacles to Full Employment in a Wealthy Community," *The Economic Journal*, XLVII (1937), 297-307.

Rist, C.: "Keynes: The Means to Prosperity," *The Economic Journal*, XLIII (1933), 269-271.

Robertson, D. H.: "Keynes: Economic Consequences of the Peace," *The Economic Journal*, XXX (1920), 77-84.

_____: "Mr. Keynes' Theory of Money," *The Economic Journal*, XLI (1931), 395-411.

_____: "Some Notes on Mr. Keynes' General Theory of Employment," *The Quarterly Journal of Economics*, LI (1936), 168-191.

_____: "The Future of International Trade," *The Economic Journal*, XLVIII (1938), 1-14.

_____: "Changes in International Demand and the Terms of Trade," *The Quarterly Journal of Economics*, LII (1938), 539-540.

_____: "Mr. Keynes and Finance," *The Economic Journal*, XLVIII (1938), 314-320.

_____: "Mr. Clark and the Foreign Trade Multiplier," *The Economic Journal*, XLIX (1939), 354-356.

Robertson, D. H.: "The Post-War Monetary Plans," *The Economic Journal*, LIII (1943), 352-360.

Robinson, Austin: "John M. Keynes," *The Economic Journal*, LVII (1947), 1-68.

Robinson, J.: "The Theory of Money and the Analysis of Output," *The Review of Economic Studies*, I (1933), 22-26.

_____: "Official Papers: The U. S. in the World Economy," *The Economic Journal*, LIV (1944), 430-437.

Robbins, L.: "A Reply to Mr. Keynes," *The New Statesman and Nation*, I (1931), 98-100.

_____: "The Problem of Stabilization," *Lloyd's Bank Limited Monthly Review*, VI (1935), 207-218.

Roos, Charles F.: "The Demand for Investment Goods," *American Economic Review*, XXXVIII (1948), 311-320.

Rueff, J.: "The Fallacies of Lord Keynes' General Theory," *Quarterly Journal of Economics*, LXI (1947), 343-367.

Salant, W. S.: "The Domestic Effects of Capital Export under the Point IV Program," *American Economic Review*, XL (1950), 495-510.

Samuel, A. M.: "Has Foreign Investment Paid?" *The Economic Journal*, XL (1930), 64-68.

Samuelson, P. A.: "Interactions between the Multiplier Analysis and the Principle of Acceleration," *The Review of Economic Statistics*, XXI (1939), 75-78.

Schumpeter, J. A.: "Keynes: Essays in Biography," (Review) *The Economic Journal*, XLIII (1933), 652-657.

Shaw, E. S.: "A Note on the Multiplier," *The Review of Economic Studies*, III (1936), 60-64.

Singer, Kurt: "Recollections of Keynes," *The Australian Quarterly*, XXI (1949), 49-59.

Smith, J. C.: "Economic Nationalism and International Trade," *The Economic Journal*, XLV (1935), 619-649.

Smithies, A.: "Full Employment in a Free Society," *American Economic Review*, XXXV (1945), 355-367.

_____: "The Multiplier," *American Economic Review*, XXXVIII (1948), 299-305.

Smithies, A.: "Reflections on the Work and Influence of John M. Keynes," The Quarterly Journal of Economics, LXV (1951), 578-601.

Somers, H. M.: "Monetary Policy and the Theory of Interest," The Quarterly Journal of Economics, LV (1941), 488-507.

Soule, C.: "Mr. Keynes' Recipe for Stabilization," The Week, LXVI (1931), 360-361.

Stamp, J.: "The Report of the Macmillan Committee," The Economic Journal, XLI (1931), 424-435.

_____: "Mr. Keynes' Treatise on Money," The Economic Journal, XLI (1931), 241-249.

Swan, T. W.: "Economic Interpretation of J. M. Keynes," The Australian Quarterly, XI (1939), 62-70.

Tarshis, L.: "An Exposition of Keynesian Economics," American Economic Review, XXXVIII (1948), 261-290.

Taussig, F. W.: "Great Britain's Trade Terms After 1900," The Economic Journal, XXXV (1925), 1-10.

_____: "Employment and the National Dividend," The Quarterly Journal of Economics, LI (1936), 198-203.

Timlin, M.: "John M. Keynes," The Canadian Journal of Economics and Political Science, XIII (1947), 363-365.

Viner, J.: "Mr. Keynes on the Causes of Unemployment - A Review," The Quarterly Journal of Economics, LI (1936), 147-167.

_____: "International Finance in the Postwar World," The Journal of Political Economy, LV (1947), 97-107.

Von Hayek, F. A.: "Reflections on the Pure Theory of Money," Economica, XI (1931), 270-295.

_____: "The Pure Theory of Money: Rejoinder," Economica, XI (1931), 398-403.

_____: "Reflections on the Pure Theory of Money of Mr. John M. Keynes - Part II," Economica, XII (1932), 22-44.

Warming, J.: "International Difficulties Arising out of the Financing of Public Works during Depression," The Economic Journal, XLII (1932), 211-224.

The Week: "On Keynes' Revenue Tariff," The Week, LXVI (1931), 190-191.

Whale, P. B.: "International Trade in the Absence of an International Standard," *Economica*, III (1936), 24-38.

Williams, J. H.: "International Monetary Plans," *Foreign Affairs*, XXIII (1944), 38-56.

_____ : "An Appraisal of Keynesian Economics," *American Economic Review*, XXXVIII, 273-290.

Winston, R. P.: "Does Trade 'Follow the Dollar'," *American Economic Review*, XVII (1927), 458-477.

Wright, D. M.: "The Future of Keynesian Economics," *American Economic Review*, XXXV (1945), 284-307.

V. GENERAL WORKS

Abbati, Alfred H.: *Lord Keynes' Central Thesis and the Concept of Unclaimed Wealth*, Cardiff, William Lewis, 1947.

American Economic Association: *Readings in the Theory of International Trade*, (ed. H. S. Ellis and W. Metzler), Philadelphia, The Blakiston Co., 1949.

Angell, J. W.: *Theory of International Prices*, Cambridge, Harvard University Press, 1926.

_____ : *Investment and Business Cycles*, New York, McGraw-Hill Book Co., Inc., New York, 1941.

Balogh, T.: "The International Aspects of Full Employment," *The Economics of Full Employment - Six Studies in Applied Economics*, Oxford, Basil Blackwell, 1945.

_____ : *Studies in Financial Organization*, Cambridge, Cambridge University Press, 1947.

_____ : *Dollar Crisis, Causes and Cure*, Oxford, Basil Blackwell, 1949.

Banerji, B.: *A Guide to the Study of Keynesian Economics*, Calcutta, N. N. Dey, 1951.

Bell, J. F.: *A History of Economic Thought*, New York, Ronald Press Co., 1953.

Beveridge, W. H.: *Causes and Cures of Unemployment*, London, Longmans, Green and Co., 1931.

Beveridge, W. H. and Others: *Tariffs: The Case Examined*, London, Longmans, Green and Co., 1932.

Beveridge, W. H.: *Full Employment in a Free Society*, London, George Allen and Unwin, Ltd., 1944.

Bidwell, Percy W.: *A Commercial Policy for the United Nations*, New York, The Committee on International Economic Policy, 1945.

Bloomfield, A. I.: "Foreign Exchange Rate Theory and Policy," *The New Economics*, (ed. S. Harris), New York, A. A. Knopf, 1947, 293-314.

Brenier, Henri: *The Revision of the Treaty of Versailles*, Marseilles, Comite' de Relations Internationales, 1922.

British Treasury: *Proposals for an International Clearing Union*, Cmd. 6437, London, H. M. Stationery Office, 1943. (Reprinted in *The New Economics*, (ed. S. Harris), New York, A. A. Knopf, 1947, 342-358.

Buchanan, N. S.: *International Investment and Domestic Welfare*, New York, Henry Holt and Co., 1945.

Buchanan, N. S. and Lutz, F. A.: *Rebuilding the World Economy*, New York, The Twentieth Century Fund, 1947.

Burns, Emile: *Mr. Keynes Answered*, London, Lawrence and Wishart, Ltd., 1940.

Butlin, S. J.: *John M. Keynes*, Sydney, The Economic Society of Australia and New Zealand, 1946.

Cassel, G.: *Money and Foreign Exchange after 1914*, London, Constable and Co., Ltd., 1922.

_____: *Postwar Monetary Stabilization*, New York, Columbia University Press, 1928.

_____: *The Crisis in the World's Monetary System*, (second edition), London, Oxford University Press, 1932.

_____: *The Downfall of the Gold Standard*, London, Oxford University Press, 1936.

Chang, Tse Chun: *Cyclical Movements in the Balance of Payments*, Cambridge, Cambridge University Press, 1951.

Clark, C. and Crawford, J. G.: *The National Income of Australia*, London, Angus and Robertson, Ltd., 1938.

Clark, C.: *The Control of Investment*, London, The New Fabian Research Bureau, 1933.

_____: *National Income and Outlay*, London, Macmillan and Co., Ltd., 1937.

Clark, C.: *Conditions of Economic Progress*, London, Macmillan and Co., Ltd., 1940.

_____: "Principles of Public Finance and Taxation," (The Third Arthur C. Moore Research Lecture), Brisbane, Federal Institute of Accountants, 1950.

Committee on Finance and Industry (Macmillan): *Report of the Committee on Finance and Industry*, Cmd. 3897, London, H. M. Stationery Office, June, 1931.

Committee on International Economic Policy: *World Trade and Employment*, New York, The Committee on International Economic Policy, 1944.

Committee on International Policy of the National Planning Association: *The Stakes of Bretton Woods*, Washington, D.C., National Planning Association, 1945.

Condliffe, J. B.: *The Foreign Economic Policy of the U. S.*, (Memorandum No. 11), New Haven, Yale Institute of International Studies, 1944.

_____: *Exchange Stabilization*, New York, The Committee on International Economic Policy, 1945.

Corbett, P. E.: *The Dumbarton Oaks Plan*, (Memorandum No. 13), New Haven, Yale Institute of International Studies, 1944.

Cortney, Philip: *The Economic Munich*, New York, Philosophical Library, 1949.

Crawford, F. W.: *Proposed United Nations Bank for Reconstruction and Development*, Washington, D.C., Finance Dept., Chamber of Commerce of the U. S., 1944.

_____: *International Monetary Developments between the First and Second World Wars*, Washington, D.C., Finance Dept., Chamber of Commerce of the U. S., 1944.

_____: *World Currency Stabilization Proposals*, Washington, D. C., Finance Dept., Chamber of Commerce of the U. S., 1944.

_____: *The Bretton Woods Proposals*, Washington, D.C., Finance Dept., Chamber of Commerce of the U. S., 1945.

_____: *Financial Agreement with the U. S.*, Washington, D.C., Finance Dept., Chamber of Commerce of the U. S., 1946.

Crossland, C. A. R.: *Britain's Economic Problem*, London, Jonathon Cape, 1953.

Currie, L.: "Some Theoretical and Practical Implications of J. M. Keynes' General Theory," *The Economic Doctrines of John M. Keynes*, New York, National Industrial Conference Board, 1938, 15-27.

Daniels, G. W. and Campion, H.: "The Relative Importance of British Export Trade," (Special Memorandum No. 41), The Executive Committee of the London and Cambridge Economic Service, August, 1935.

Dillard, D.: *The Economics of John Maynard Keynes*, New York, Prentice-Hall, 1948.

Eaton, John: *Marx Against Keynes*, London, Lawrence and Wishart Ltd., 1951.

Edie, L. S.: "The Future of the Gold Standard," *Gold and Monetary Stabilization*, (Harris Foundation Lectures), Chicago, University of Chicago Press, 1932.

_____: "The Practical Importance of Keynes' Doctrine," *The Economic Doctrines of John M. Keynes*, New York, National Industrial Conference Board, 1938, 73-78.

Einzig, P.: *The Tragedy of the Pound*, London, Kegan Paul, French, Trubner and Co., Ltd., 1932.

_____: *The Comedy of the Pound*, London, Kegan Paul, French, Trubner and Co., Ltd., 1933.

_____: *The Future of Gold*, London, Macmillan and Co., Ltd., 1934.

Ellis, H. S.: "Bilateralism and the Future of International Trade," *Essays in International Finance #5*, Princeton, International Finance Section, Princeton University, 1945.

_____: *A Survey of Contemporary Economics*, Philadelphia, Blakiston Co., 1948.

Ellsworth, P. T.: *International Economics*, New York, Macmillan and Co., 1938.

_____: *The International Economy*, New York, Macmillan and Co., 1950.

Enke, S. and Salera, V.: *International Economics*, (second edition), New York, Prentice-Hall, Inc., 1951.

Federal Reserve Board: *Prices, Wages and Employment*, (Postwar Studies No. 4), Washington, D.C., United States Federal Reserve Board, 1945.

Feis, H.: *The Changing Pattern of International Economic Affairs*, New York, Harper Bros., 1940.

Findlay, R. M.: *Britain Under Protection*, London, George Allen and Unwin, Ltd., 1934.

Gayer, A. D.: *Public Works in Prosperity and Depression*, New York, N. B. E. R., 1935.

_____: *Monetary Policy and Economic Stabilization*, London, A. and C. Black, Ltd., 1935.

_____: *The Lessons of Monetary Experience*, New York, Farrar and Rinehart, 1937.

Giuffre', A.: *Studi Keynesiani*, Milano, Instituto di Economica e Finanza della Facotta' Giuridica di Roma, 1953.

Graham, F. D.: "Fundamentals of International Monetary Policy," *Essays in International Finance* #2, International Finance Section, Princeton, Princeton University, Autumn, 1943.

Greidanus, Tjardus: *The Development of Keynes' Economic Theories*, London, P. S. King and Son, Ltd., 1939.

Gulick, R. L.: *Imports - The Gain from Trade*, New York, The Committee on International Economic Policy, 1946.

Haberler, G.: "Money and the Business Cycle," *Gold and Monetary Stabilization*, (Harris Foundation Lectures), Chicago, University of Chicago Press, 1932.

_____: *Theory of International Trade*, London, William Hodge and Co., Ltd., 1936.

_____: *Prosperity and Depression* (third edition), Geneva, League of Nations, 1941.

_____: *Quantitative Trade Controls - Their Causes and Nature*, Geneva, League of Nations, 1943.

Hajela, Prayag Das: *Keynes' General Theory and Theories of Trade Cycle and Foreign Exchange*, Allahabad, Pothishala, Ltd., 1952.

Halm, G. N.: *Monetary Theory*, (second edition), Philadelphia, Blakiston Co., 1946.

Hansen, A. H. and Clemence, R. V.: *Readings in Business Cycles and National Income*, New York, W. W. Norton and Co., 1953.

Hansen, A. H.: *Full Recovery or Stagnation?* New York, W. W. Norton and Co., 1938.

Hansen, A. H.: *After the War – Full Employment*, Washington, D.C., National Resources Planning Board, 1942.

_____: *International Monetary and Financial Programs*, New York, Council on Foreign Relations, 1944.

_____: *America's Role in the World Economy*, New York, W. W. Norton and Co., Inc., 1945.

_____: *Economic Policy and Full Employment*, New York, McGraw-Hill Book Co., Inc., 1947.

_____: *A Guide to Keynes*, New York, McGraw-Hill Book Co., Inc., 1953.

Harris, S. E.: *Monetary Problems of the British Empire*, New York, Macmillan Co., 1931.

_____: *Postwar Economic Problems*, New York, McGraw-Hill Book Co., Inc., 1943.

_____: *Economic Reconstruction*, New York, McGraw-Hill Book Co., Inc., 1945.

_____: "International Economics: Introduction," *The New Economics*, (ed. S. Harris), New York, A. A. Knopf, 1947, 245-263.

_____: (editor), *The New Economics*, New York, A. A. Knopf, 1947.

_____: *John M. Keynes, Economist and Policy Maker*, New York, Charles Scribner's Sons, 1955.

Harrod, R. F.: *The Trade Cycle*, Oxford, Oxford University Press, 1936.

_____: *International Economics*, (second edition), London, Cambridge University Press, 1939.

_____: *Towards a Dynamic Economics*, London, Macmillan and Co., Ltd., 1949.

_____: *The Life of John Maynard Keynes*, London, Macmillan and Co., Ltd., 1951.

_____: *Economic Essays*, London, Macmillan and Co., Ltd., 1952.

Hart, A. G.: *Money, Debt and Economic Activity*, (second edition), New York, Prentice-Hall, 1953.

Hawtrey, R. G.: *Monetary Reconstruction*, New York, Longmans, Green and Co., 1923.

_____: *Art of Central Banking*, London, Longmans, Green and Co., 1932.

_____: *Capital and Employment*, London, Longmans, Green and Co., 1937.

_____: *The Gold Standard in Theory and Practice*, London, Longmans, Green and Co., 1939.

_____: *Bretton Woods for Better or Worse*, London, Longmans, Green and Co., 1946.

_____: *Currency and Credit*, London, (fourth edition), Longmans, Green and Co., 1950.

_____: *The Balance of Payments and the Standard of Living*, London, Royal Institute of International Affairs, Oxford University Press, 1950.

Heilperin, M. A.: *International Monetary Economics*, London, Longmans, Green and Co., 1939.

_____: *International Monetary Organization*, Geneva, International Institute of Intellectual Cooperation, League of Nations, 1939.

_____: *International Monetary Reconstruction: The Bretton Woods Agreements*, New York, American Enterprise Association, 1945.

_____: *The Trade of Nations*, (second edition), New York, Alfred A. Knopf, 1952.

Hinshaw, R.: "Keynesian Commercial Policy," *The New Economics*, (ed. S. Harris), New York, A. A. Knopf, 1947, 315-522.

Hobson, J. A.: *International Trade*, London, Methuen and Co., 1904.

_____: *The Economics of Unemployment*, London, George Allen and Unwin, Ltd., 1922.

Hoover, C. B.: *International Trade and Domestic Employment*, New York, McGraw-Hill Book Co., Inc., 1945.

Hoselitz, B. F.: *British Trade Policy and the U. S.*, (Memorandum No. 5), New Haven, Yale University Institute of International Studies, Oct., 1943.

Hutt, W. H.: The Theory of Idle Resources, London, Jonathon Cape, 1939.

Institute of Statistics, Oxford University: The Economics of Full Employment - Six Studies in Applied Economics, Oxford, Basil Blackwell, 1945.

International Monetary Fund: Balance of Payments Manual, Washington, D. C., International Monetary Fund, Jan., 1950.

_____: International Financial News Survey, Washington, D. C., V, Nos. 1-50, July 1952 - June, 1953; VI, Nos. 1-50, July, 1953 - June, 1954.

Irving Trust Co.: International Financial Stabilization - A Symposium, New York, Irving Trust Company, 1944.

James, Cyril F.: "Some Practical Effects of the Doctrines Suggested by Mr. John M. Keynes Prior to 1930," The Economic Doctrines of John M. Keynes, New York, National Industrial Conference Board, 1938, 1-11.

Jenks, L. H.: The Migration of British Capital to 1875, New York, A. A. Knopf, 1927.

Kahn, Alfred E.: Great Britain in the World Economy, New York, Columbia University Press, 1946.

Kindleberger, C.: International Economics, Homeward, Richard D. Irwin, Inc., 1953.

Klein, L. R.: The Keynesian Revolution, New York, Macmillan Co., 1947.

Kriz, M. A.: "Postwar International Lending," Essays in International Finance #8, Princeton, International Finance Section, Princeton University, Spring, 1947.

Lehmann, Fritz: "The Role of the Multiplier and the Interest Rate in Keynes' General Theory," The Economic Doctrines of John M. Keynes, New York, National Industrial Conference Board, 1938, 52-72.

Loftus, P. C.: A Main Cause of Unemployment, London, Sir Isaac Pitman and Sons, Ltd., 1932.

_____: Money and National Reconstruction, London, Economic Reform Club and Institute, 1941.

Lutz, F.: "International Monetary Mechanisms - The Keynes and White Proposals," Essays in International Finance #1, Princeton, International Finance Section, Princeton University, July, 1943.

Machlup, F.: International Trade and the Foreign Trade Multiplier, Philadelphia, Blakiston Co., 1943.

Macmillan, H.: *The Next Step*, London, E. T. Heron and Co., Ltd., 1933.

_____: *Reconstruction*, London, Macmillan and Co., Ltd., 1933.

Mandelbaum, K.: "An Experiment in Full Employment Controls in the German Economy, 1933-1938," *The Economics of Full Employment - Six Studies in Applied Economics*, Oxford, Basil Blackwell, 1945.

Mantoux, Paul: *The Carthaginian Peace*, New York, Charles Scribner's Sons, 1952.

Martin, P. W.: *An International Monetary Agreement*, London, The New Fabian Research Bureau, 1933.

Meade, J. E.: *Public Works in their International Aspect*, London, The New Fabian Research Bureau, 1933.

_____: *An Introduction to Economic Analysis and Policy*, (second edition), London, Oxford University Press, 1937.

_____: *A Geometry of International Trade*, London, George Allen and Unwin, Ltd., 1951.

Metzler, L. A.: "The Theory of International Trade," *A Survey of Contemporary Economics*, (ed. H. S. Ellis), Philadelphia, Blakiston Co., 1948, 210-254.

Metzler, L. and Others: *Income, Employment and Public Policy*, New York, W. W. Norton and Co., Inc., 1948.

Metzler, L., Triffin, R. and Haberler, G.: *International Monetary Policies* (Postwar Economic Studies #7), Washington, D. C., Board of Governors, Federal Reserve System, 1947.

Mikesell, R. F.: *Foreign Exchange in the Postwar World*, New York, The Twentieth Century Fund, 1954.

Miller, David H.: "The Economic Consequences of the Peace," (An Address delivered to the League of Nations Association), New York, 1920.

Mosak, J. L.: *General Equilibrium Theory in International Trade*, Bloomington, Cowles Commission for Research in Economics, 1944.

Musgrave, R. A.: "Fiscal Policy, Stability and Full Employment," *Public Finance and Full Employment*, (Postwar Economic Studies #3), Washington, D. C., 1945, 1-21.

National Planning Association: *Britain's Trade in the Postwar World*, Washington, D. C., National Planning Association, 1941.

Neisser, H.: *Some International Aspects of the Business Cycle*, Philadelphia, University of Pennsylvania Press, 1936.

Nicol, Finlay: *Prosperity by all Means*, Edinburgh, The Scots Free Press, 1933.

Nurkse, R.: "Conditions of International Monetary Equilibrium," *Essays in International Finance #4*, Princeton, International Finance Section, Princeton University, Spring, 1945.

_____: "Domestic and International Equilibrium," *The New Economics*, (ed. S. Harris), New York, A. A. Knopf, 1947, 264-292.

Ohlin, B.: *Interregional and International Trade*, Cambridge, Harvard University Press, 1933.

_____: *The Problem of Employment Stabilization*, New York, Columbia University Press, 1949.

Pierson, J. H. G.: *Full Employment*, New Haven, Yale University Press, 1941.

_____: *Full Employment and Free Enterprise*, Washington, D. C., Public Affairs Press, 1947.

Pigou, A. C.: *Economic Science in Relation to Practice*, London, Macmillan and Co., Ltd., 1908.

_____: *Memorials of Alfred Marshall*, London, Macmillan and Co., Ltd., 1925.

_____: *Economics in Practice*, London, Macmillan and Co., Ltd., 1935.

_____: *Employment and Equilibrium*, London, Macmillan and Co., Ltd., 1949.

Pigou, A. C. and Clark, C.: "The Economic Position of Great Britain," (Special Memorandum No. 43), London, London and Cambridge Economic Service, April, 1936.

Polanyi, Michael: *Full Employment and Free Trade*, (second edition), Cambridge, Cambridge University Press, 1948.

Political and Economic Planning: *Britain and World Trade*, London, Political and Economic Planning, 1947.

Research Committee of the C. E. D.: *The Bretton Woods Proposals*, New York, Committee for Economic Development, 1944.

Research Committee of the C. E. D.: *International Trade, Foreign Investment and Domestic Employment*, New York, Committee for Economic Development, 1945.

Robertson, D. H.: *Essays in Monetary Theory*, Westminster, P. S. King and Son, Ltd., 1940.

Robinson, J.: *Essays in the Theory of Employment*, London, Macmillan and Co., Ltd., 1937.

_____: *Introduction to the Theory of Employment*, London, Macmillan and Co., Ltd., 1937.

_____: "Proposals for an International Clearing Union," *The New Economics*, (ed. S. Harris), New York, A. A. Knopf, 1947, 343-358.

Rostow, N. W.: "Explanations of the Great Depression," *British Economy of the Nineteenth Century*, London, Oxford University Press, 1948, 145-160.

Rowse, Alfred L.: *Mr. Keynes and the Labour Movement*, London, Macmillan and Co., Ltd., 1936.

Salant, W. A.: "Foreign Trade Policy in the Business Cycle," *Public Policy*, (vol. II), Cambridge, Harvard University Press, 1941.

Salter, A.: "Foreign Investment," *Essays in International Finance #12*, Princeton, International Finance Section, Princeton University, Feb., 1951.

Saulnier, Raymond J.: *Contemporary Monetary Theory*, New York, Columbia University Press, 1938.

Schumpeter, J. A.: *Ten Great Economists from Marx to Keynes*, New York, Oxford University Press, 1951.

Shackle, G. L. S.: *Expectations, Investment and Income*, London, Oxford University Press, 1938.

Siegfried, A.: *England's Crisis*, London, Jonathon Cape, 1933.

Staley, E.: *World Economic Development - Effects on Advanced Industrial Countries*, Montreal, International Labour Office, 1944.

Stevens, R.: *The New Economics and World Peace*, Philadelphia, The Pacifist Research Bureau, 1944.

Swanson, E. S. and Schmidt, E. P.: *Economic Stagnation or Progress*, New York, McGraw-Hill Book Co., Inc., 1946.

Taussig, F. W.: *Selected Readings in International Trade and Tariff Problems*, New York, Ginn and Co., 1921.

_____: *International Trade*, New York, Macmillan and Co., Ltd., 1927.

Taylor, A. E.: *The 'Ten Per Cent' Fallacy*, New York, The Committee on International Economic Policy, 1945.

Terborgh, G.: *The Bogey of Economic Maturity*, Chicago, Machinery and Allied Products Institute, 1945.

Timlin, M. F.: *Keynesian Economics*, Toronto, University of Toronto Press, 1942.

Tucker, R. S.: "Mr. Keynes' Theories Considered in the Light of Experience," *The Economic Doctrines of John M. Keynes*, New York, National Industrial Conference Board, 1938, 28-51.

_____: "Mr. Keynes' Theories Considered in the Light of Experience," *The Economic Doctrines of John M. Keynes*, New York, National Industrial Conference Board, 1938.

U. S. Department of State: *Proposals for Expansion of World Trade and Employment*, Washington, D.C., U. S. Government Printing Office, 1945.

_____: *Articles of Agreement of the International Monetary Fund*, Washington, D.C., U. S. Government Printing Office, 1946.

U. S. Department of the Treasury: *Financial Agreement Between the Government of the United States and the United Kingdom*, Washington, D. C., U. S. Government Printing Office, 1946.

Viner, J.: "International Aspects of the Gold Standard," *Gold and Monetary Stabilization*, (Harris Foundation Lectures), Chicago, University of Chicago Press, 1932.

_____: *Studies in the Theory of International Trade*, New York, Harper and Brothers, 1937.

_____: *Trade Relations Between Free-Market and Controlled Economies*, Geneva, League of Nations, 1943.

_____: *Two Plans for International Monetary Stabilization*, (Memorandum No. 2), New Haven, Yale Institute of International Studies, 1943.

_____: *International Economics*, Glencoe, The Free Press, 1951.

Von Hayek, F. A.: *Monetary Theory and the Trade Cycle*, London, Jonathon Cape, 1933.

──────────── : *Monetary Nationalism and International Stability*, London, Longmans, Green and Co., 1937.

Whale, P. B.: *International Trade*, London, Thornton Butterworth, Ltd., 1952.

Whidden, Howard P.: *Preferences and Discriminations in International Trade*, New York, The Committee on International Economic Policy, 1945.

Whittlesey, C. R.: *International Monetary Issues*, New York, McGraw-Hill Book Co., Inc., 1937,

Williams, J. H.: "Monetary Stability and the Gold Standard," *Gold and Monetary Stabilization*, (Harris Foundation Lectures), Chicago, University of Chicago Press, 1932.

──────────── : *Postwar Monetary Plans*, Oxford, Basil Blackwell, 1949.

Wilson, J. S. G.: *Lord Keynes and the Development of Modern Economic Theory*, Sydney, The Economic Society of Australia and New Zealand, 1946.

Wright, Q.: *Unemployment as a World Problem*, Chicago, University of Chicago Press, 1931.

For Product Safety Concerns and Information please contact our EU
representative GPSR@taylorandfrancis.com
Taylor & Francis Verlag GmbH, Kaufingerstraße 24, 80331 München, Germany

www.ingramcontent.com/pod-product-compliance
Lightning Source LLC
Chambersburg PA
CBHW071235300426
44116CB00008B/1043